JOURNEYS:

The Parallel Journeys of the Israelites, Each Christian, and the True Church

Susan Pryor

Journeys: The Parallel Journeys of the Israelites, Each Christian, and the True Church
By Susan Pryor

ISBN-13:978-0692185902

Copyright © 2018 Susan Pryor

All rights reserved by Susan Pryor.
Please email the author at susanpryor777@gmail.com for permission to republish or reprint any portion of this book.

Interior design: Aydin Tasdeler
Cover design: Aydin Tasdeler
Editor: Megan Tasdeler

Published by: Psalm 45 Publishing

>To God who calls us out
>To Jesus who journeys with us
>To Holy Spirit who lights our way

All scriptures are quoted from the *New American Standard Bible* unless otherwise noted.

To William

His earthly journey done;
his heavenly journey begun.

To William

His earthly journey done,
his heavenly journey begun

TABLE OF CONTENTS

BOOK 1: FREEDOM FROM BONDAGE

INTRODUCTION   12

PART I: PREPARATION FOR SALVATION

Chapter 1 The Israelites' Preparation For The Exodus From Egypt	38
Chapter 2 Each Saint's Preparation For The Exodus From Sin	46
Chapter 3 The Church's Preparation For The Exodus From The False Church System	52

PART II: THE EXODUS

Chapter 4 The Israelites' Salvation From Egypt	68
Chapter 5 Each Saint's Salvation From Sin	74
Chapter 6 The Church's Salvation From The False Church System	88

PART III: THE RED SEA

Chapter 7 The Israelites' Deliverance From Egypt	100
Chapter 8 Each Saint's Deliverance From Sin	108
Chapter 9 The Church's Deliverance From The False Church System	118

BOOK 2: THE DESERT

PART IV: THE DESERT

Chapter 10 The Israelites' Sanctification Of A Nation	134
Chapter 11 Each Saint's Personal Sanctification	164
Chapter 12 The Church's Sanctification	214

PART V: INTERLUDE

Chapter 13 The Israelites' Time To Remember   284
Chapter 14 Each Saint's Time To Remember   296
Chapter 15 The Church's Time To Remember   312

BOOK 3: THE PROMISED LAND

PART VI: CROSSING THE JORDAN

Chapter 16 The Israelites Entering Into The Promised Land 332
Chapter 17 Each Saint Entering Into God's Promises   336
Chapter 18 The Church Entering Into God's Promises   342

PART VII: THE PROMISED LAND

Chapter 19 The Israelites' Union With The LORD   352
Chapter 20 Each Saint's Intimacy With Jesus   370
Chapter 21 The Church's Communion With God And
            With Each Other   392

PART VIII: JOURNEY'S END

Chapter 22 The City Of God   430

BOOK 1:

FREEDOM FROM BONDAGE

INTRODUCTION:

THE ISRAELITES', EACH SAINT'S, AND THE CHURCH'S JOURNEYS

THE ISRAELITES' JOURNEY

In a court of law, there is a process known as "cause of action." By it, a plaintiff presents his (or her) case, outlining the reasons that have prompted him to initiate a lawsuit or a legal proceeding. In his cause of action, he must state his case in detail, support his case with facts, and ask for action or resolution. While not in any way promoting the idea that the Church of God should involve itself in legalism, there is still good reason to urge it to action. In this book, the Church's case, freedom and maturity in order to worship and serve God (Exodus 8:1), will be stated in some detail. Its case will be supported by facts, and its action will be a wider awareness of and a deepening maturity into the heart of true God. To gain this end, the book begins with a detailed account of early biblical history in order to understand the reasons why an action, in this case, a journey, is in order.

To Establish His People

Long ago God formed a man and a woman placed them in the Garden of Eden to live. This man and woman, named Adam and Eve, were given the highest honor that was bestowed upon all of creation. Their natures were innocent and their characters were pure because they were created in the image of God. In time, Adam and Eve disobeyed their Creator God and sinned. One consequence of this rebellion was their ejection from the garden where they had walked and talked in personal, intimate communion with God. Therefore, their (and thus mankind's) first journey was to find their way back into the grace and presence of God.

A second consequence of Adam and Eve's disobedience was the loss of their godly nature; because of their sin they were no longer innocent and pure. This change in their beings didn't catastrophically affect just their own lives; rather, it affected the lives of all of their descendants or the whole of the human race. When Adam fathered children, his offspring were born in his, not God's, image. Therefore, these descendants were not holy and innocent; instead, they too had a fallen, sinful nature.

Adam was an ancestor of Noah (Genesis 5). In turn, Noah was the father of three sons. The oldest was Shem (Genesis 10:21), the next was Japheth, and the youngest was Ham (Genesis 9:24).

In spite of their fallen natures, God intended that children should honor their parents. One of His later commandments was: *"Honor your father and your mother"* (Exodus 20:12). The promised result of disobedience to this command was fearsome: *"Cursed is he who dishonors his father or mother"* (Deuteronomy 27:16).

Unfortunately, Ham did not honor his father. After surviving the flood that drowned all of mankind except Noah and his family (Genesis 6-8), Noah planted a vineyard and drank of its wine. Becoming drunk, he uncovered himself in his tent. Seeing this, Ham did nothing about it. He made no move to correct the situation. Instead, he perpetuated it. While Noah had uncovered himself physically, Ham exposed him in a worse way. He scorned and shamed his father, revealing his sin and weakness through gossip (Genesis 9:20-22).

Upon hearing Ham's news concerning their father, Shem and Japheth acted with a different heart. With eyes averted, they covered Noah – both his body and his honor. The result of the incident was not judgment on Noah; God did not punish him for drunkenness. Yet God was exceedingly wroth with Ham. When Noah awoke, he discovered what his youngest son had done to him. Since Noah's son, Ham, had humiliated and scorned his father, Ham's son, Canaan, would be dishonored. Noah issued a curse:

> *"Cursed be Canaan; a servant of servants he shall be to his brothers ... Blessed be the LORD, the God of Shem; and let Canaan be his servant. May God enlarge Japheth, and let him dwell in the tents of Shem; and let Canaan be his servant."* (Genesis 9:25-27)

By such pronouncement, God was teaching the principle that transgression would separate the sons of righteousness from the sons of evil, that it would divide those acting in honor from those abiding in dishonor. From the earliest days, it was made clear that God would recognize and deal with right behavior through blessing and wrong behavior through cursing. Established by God, this principle still exists today.

As time passed, Ham's cursed son, Canaan, became the ancestor of iniquity. His descendants include Nimrod (whose kingdom was Babel), the Philistines, the Sidonians, the Jebusites, the Amorites, the Girgashites, and the Hivites, all of whom became sworn enemies of the descendants of Abram (Genesis 10:6-20).

In complete contrast, Shem, a son of honor, became the ancestor of Nahor, Terah, and Abram, a man mightily blessed of God and the father of the children of faith (Genesis 11:10-27). With Abram's birth and life came a remarkable series of events that have affected and afflicted the world, its lands, and its peoples to this very hour.

This man, Abram, is unique. Abram met with God's approval; he also met with God. God spoke to him, appeared to him, and cut covenant with him.

To Establish His Land

To establish a land for those chosen to be His people, another journey was required. God told Abram to leave his country, his relatives, and even his father's house and to go to a different land where God would make him a great nation (Genesis 12:1-2). In obedient response, Abram set out for the land of Canaan with his wife, Sarai, his nephew, Lot, and his possessions (Genesis 12:5).

In Canaan, the LORD appeared to Abram and made a promise: *"To your descendants I will give this land"* (Genesis 12:7). God Himself was going to give Abram, the descendant of Shem, the son of honor, the land in which he was sojourning. Later, after Lot had seemingly chosen the better portion of the land for himself and he and Abram had separated, the LORD spoke once again to Abram: *"Now lift up your eyes and look from the place where you are, northward and southward and eastward and westward; for all the land which you see, I will give it to you and to your descendants forever"* (Genesis 13:14-15). By His words, the LORD again declared that a particular land, Canaan, was to belong to a particular people, Abram's descendants.

Some time later, after his victory in the War of the Kings and his meeting with Melchizedek, king of Salem and priest of God Most High, Abram once again heard God speak: *"I am the LORD who brought you out of Ur of the Chaldeans, to give you this land to possess it"* (Genesis 15:7). To make what He was saying more emphatic and sacred, God made a covenant with Abram (Genesis 15:12-21).

To Establish His People In His Land

Having established ownership of the land, God began to disclose the people who were to possess it and to dwell in it. Declaring His will, God told Abram that he would have a son and heir (Genesis 15:4). Not only would he be the father of a son, but also his descendants would be as countless as the stars (Genesis 15:5). God then warned Abram that perilous times were ahead for his descendants and told him that they would be strangers in a land that would enslave and oppress his offspring for hundreds of years (Genesis 15:13-14). Then, to encourage him, God assured Abram that his descendants would return to Canaan (Genesis 15:16).

However, as time went on and the promised son did not arrive, Abram and Sarai took matters into their own hands. Prompted by his wife to do so, Abram fathered a son by Sarai's maid, Hagar (Genesis 16:1-4). This was not the promised son, but the offspring of flesh. Of him, the Angel of the LORD said,

> *"....you shall call his name Ishmael because the LORD has given heed to your affliction. He shall be a wild donkey of a man; his hand will be against everyone, and everyone's hand will be against him; and he will live in defiance of all his brethren."* (Genesis 16:11-12)

Even in those days, man's plan was not God's plan, and Abram and Sarai's attempt to bring about the word of God in their own way and time was not acceptable to God. To emphasize His will in the matter and to show that God distinguishes between the fruit of spirit and the fruit of flesh, God promised that Sarah, Abraham's wife, and not Hagar, Sarah's slave, would birth the son of God's favor (Genesis 18:10; 21:12). So important to God was the birth of this son, Isaac, so unmistakably did God want to stress the difference between His will and the will of man, and so perfectly did He want it to be clear for whom His land was set aside that He proclaimed:

> *"Sarah your wife will bear you a son, and you shall call his name*

Isaac; and I will establish My covenant with him for an everlasting covenant for his descendants after him. And as for Ishmael, I have heard you; behold, I will bless him, and will make him fruitful, and will multiply him exceedingly. He shall become the father of twelve princes, and I will make him a great nation. But My covenant I will establish with Isaac...." (Genesis 17:19-21)

God sealed His word with another covenant. This covenant was to be an everlasting covenant even as the land was to be an everlasting possession and His people an everlasting people. This covenant was not made with the blood sacrifice of animals as the earlier covenant concerning the land had been; instead, this one required a bloody incision, the identifying mark of circumcision, on Abraham and all his male heirs (Genesis 17:10-12).

Gloriously, God's word came to pass just as He had spoken. Sarah conceived and bore a son, Isaac, to Abraham in his old age (Genesis 21:2). Sadly, as the actions of flesh intruded in people's lives before, they did so again. When Hagar began to despise Sarai (Genesis 16:4) and Ishmael began to scoff and laugh at Isaac (Genesis 21:9), God separated the sons physically as well as spiritually. God commanded Abraham to drive out Hagar and her son. Specifically so that the older son of flesh would not be heir with the younger son of promise, Ishmael was sent away.

As the firstborn son, Ishmael would normally have inherited a double portion of his father's lands and possessions as well as the position of head of the family. However, because he was neither the son of Abraham's wife, Sarai, nor the son of God's promise, he would not know those joys or blessings. By command of God, Isaac was to be heir; by promise of God, Isaac was to inherit the land; by declaration of God, Isaac was the one with whom God would continue the covenant and through whom Abraham's descendants would be named (Genesis 21:12). God promised to bless Ishmael, but His covenant and birthright went to Isaac.

Great blessings are sometimes followed by great tests. After longing for a son, after receiving the promise that he would have a son, after waiting so long for the birth of his son, God tested Abraham concerning his son. As He had done with Adam and Eve, God sent Abraham on a journey, one that would threaten the life of his son. Incredibly, with no biblical note of hesitation, Abraham did as he was told to do. He took wood, a fire, and his son to the land of Moriah. He built an altar, bound his son, and had the knife in his hand to slay him when God called out, *"Do not stretch out your hand against the lad and do nothing to him; for now I know that you fear God, since you have not withheld your son, your only son, from Me"* (Genesis 22:12).

Years later, after the death of Abraham, God did as He said He would do. He renewed His covenant with Isaac.

> *The LORD appeared to him [Isaac] and said, "Do not go down to Egypt; stay in the land of which I shall tell you. Sojourn in this land and I will be with you and bless you, for to you and to your descendants I will give all these lands, and I will establish the oath which I swore to your father Abraham. I will multiply your descendants as the stars of heaven, and will give your descendants all these lands; and by your descendants all the nations of the earth shall be blessed; because Abraham obeyed Me and kept My charge, My commandments, My statutes and My laws."* (Genesis 26:2-5)

As years passed, Isaac too had sons born to him: Esau and Jacob. Although Isaac loved Esau (Genesis 25:28), Esau despised and sold his birthright (Genesis 25:29-34). Later, through Jacob's deception, Esau also lost his blessing (Genesis 27:30-35). Once again, God, in fulfilling His will, had not allowed the natural course of events to take place. Once again, He interrupted and redirected the human choices or will and established the younger son as His heir.

Shortly after these events, Jacob was sent away in order to save his life from the murderously angry Esau. Having received Isaac's direction (Genesis 28:2) and blessing (Genesis 28:2-4), Jacob, like his forefathers, experienced the supernatural intervention and visitation of God in his life. While on his journey to his mother's people, he met the LORD.

> *Then Jacob departed from Beersheba and went toward Haran. He came to a certain place and spent the night there, because the sun had set; and he took one of the stones of the place and put it under his head, and lay down in that place. He had a dream, and behold, a ladder was set on the earth with its top reaching to heaven; and behold, the angels of God were ascending and descending on it. And behold, the LORD stood above it and said, "I am the LORD, the God of your father Abraham and the God of Isaac; the land on which you lie, I will give it you and to your descendants. Your descendants shall also be like the dust of the earth, and you shall spread out to the west and to the east and to the north and to the south; and in you and*

in your descendants shall all the families of the earth be blessed. Behold, I am with you, and will keep you wherever you go, and will bring you back to this land; for I will not leave you until I have done what I have promised you." (Genesis 28:10-15)

So arrested and awestruck was Jacob by this dream that upon awakening, he set up the stone he had been sleeping on as a pillar to God, poured oil on it, and made a vow to God:

"If God will be with me and will keep me on this journey that I take, and will give me food to eat and garments to wear and I return to my father's house in safety, then the LORD will be my God. This stone, which I have set up as a pillar, will be God's house; and of all that You give me I will surely give a tenth to You." (Genesis 28:20-22)

Having heard and having made a promise, Jacob spent the next twenty years in exile. He served his mother's brother, Laban, in Paddan-aram as a keeper of the flocks. While there, he married Leah and Rachel and became the father of a large family. After Joseph, the eleventh son, was born, Jacob asked Laban to release him from service (Genesis 30:25). In his heart, he knew it was time to return to the promised land.

After first putting it in his heart to go, God then directly commanded Jacob: *"Return to the land of your fathers and to your relatives, and I will be with you"* (Genesis 31:3), and *"I am the God of Bethel, where you anointed a pillar, where you made a vow to Me; now arise, leave this land, and return to the land of your birth"* (Genesis 31:13). In other words, Jacob, like his ancestors, was asked to go on a journey.

He quickly did so. He gathered his wives, family, livestock, and property and journeyed back toward Canaan (Genesis 31:18). Though being pursued by Laban, he was protected by God. When fearful of his reunion with his estranged brother, Esau, Jacob addressed a prayer to God that reminded Him of His promise:

"O God of my father Abraham and God of my father Isaac, O LORD, who said to me, 'Return to your country and to your relatives, and I will prosper you,' I am unworthy of all the lovingkindness and of all the faithfulness which You have shown to Your servant; for with my staff only I crossed this Jordan, and now I have become two companies. Deliver me, I pray, from the hand of my brother, from the hand of Esau; for I fear him, that he will come and attack me and the mothers with the children. For

> You said, 'I will surely prosper you and make your descendants as the sand of the sea, which is too great to be numbered.'" (Genesis 32:9-12)

Jacob then sent a gift before him to his brother and secured the safety of his wives and children by sending them away. When Jacob was left alone, a man wrestled with him until daybreak. When this man saw that he had not prevailed against Jacob, he touched socket of Jacob's thigh, causing that that thigh to be dislocated (Genesis 32:24-25).

In his desire for a blessing and in his willingness to struggle or wrestle as long as necessary to receive it, Jacob truly met God. Since he persisted until he prevailed, even to the point of incurring a horrendous physical injury, God mightily blessed him. As He had done in blessing Abram, God changed a name. Jacob was no longer to be known as Jacob, the deceiver or supplanter; now he was to be Israel, he who strives with God. Thus, the covenant, the land, and the people belonged to Israel (Genesis 32:26-28).

Although God sustained Jacob wherever he went, although He watched over him as he journeyed back to the land of his birth, and although the meeting with his brother Esau had gone well, problems arose when Israel did not keep his promise to God by completing his journey. He had vowed to return to Bethel, but he did not do so. When he returned to Canaan, he stopped short of the promised destination. As a result, at Shechem, his daughter was disgraced. The ensuing actions of his sons, Simeon and Levi, added to the disaster through treachery and murder.

At this point, God told Israel to continue on his journey to Bethel. When he arrived there, God appeared to him, blessed him, and extended His covenant through him.

> "I am God Almighty; be fruitful and multiply; a nation and a company of nations shall come from you, and kings shall come forth from you. The land which I gave to Abraham and Isaac, I will give it to you. And I will give the land to your descendants after you." (Genesis 35:11-12)

Journeying on, Israel lost Rachel, his wife, while she gave birth to his twelfth son, Benjamin. At last, he came back to his father Isaac in Hebron (Genesis 35:27).

Yet, God didn't stop there. Though the promises were given, the covenant concerning land and people was not yet outworked. His plan for mankind was only beginning to unfold.

To the human mind, it might have seemed impossible to sort out who was who or who was to inherit what among all of Israel's twelve sons. No such problem existed with God! He knew exactly which son had been chosen to carry out His will. The next standard bearer for God was the eleventh son of Israel, Joseph.

Joseph was both loved and hated. He was the best loved of his father, a son of Israel's beloved wife Rachel, and born in Israel's old age (Genesis 37:3). That he was favored by his human father is shown by the bright, many-colored tunic that Israel gave him (Genesis 37:4). That he was favored by his spiritual Father is shown by the dreams, visions, and blessings that God gave him.

On the other hand, Joseph was hated by his brothers. They detested him because of their father's greater love for him (Genesis 37:4). Just as they envied Israel's favoritism, they scorned, rejected, and despised God's anointing on Joseph. As their jealousy mounted, their hatred outstripped their honor. They conspired against Joseph and sold him into slavery.

In so doing, in abusing God's anointed, a new chapter in history opened. Now Joseph would go on an unplanned, unwelcome journey. In a land and to a people already marked by deception, manipulation, and rebellion, it was again time for a test.

From the God of power had come the promise of eternal possession of Canaan. From the God of miracles had come forth a special, chosen people who were to inherit and inhabit that land. From the God of love had poured forth blessing, goodness, and a Father's pride in His son, Israel.

Now God wanted to see if His heirs would walk in His covenant or just use and abuse their privilege. Now God wanted to test those He had chosen to see if they would choose Him. He had forewarned Abraham that his people would be tested and oppressed in a foreign land (Genesis 15:13), and now the time of difficulty was upon them. With Joseph's cruel, treacherous displacement into Egypt, the drama began.

After seizing him, Joseph's brothers planned to kill him (Genesis 37:18). However, since God's eye was upon him, he was instead captured and thrown in a pit (Genesis 37:23-24). While there, a new idea for dishonor presented itself to his brothers. A caravan of Ishmaelites was traveling from Gilboa to the south. In spite of the fact that God had markedly separated Isaac and Ishmael, in spite of the fact that God made a clear division between His chosen sons of promise and the sons of flesh, the lure of material gain won the day. The brothers sold Joseph to the ungodly group of Ishmaelites for twenty shekels of silver (Genesis 37:28), and the Ishmaelites then convoyed him to Egypt.

At the time that his journey and testing began, Joseph was only seventeen years old (Genesis 37:2). Though seemingly so young and perhaps immature, God had definite reasons for allowing these things to happen to him. First, though not apparent at the time, Joseph was sent ahead of his people to prepare their way. As Psalm 105:17 declares: *"He [God] sent a man before them, Joseph, who was sold as a slave."*

Second, God needed to test Joseph, and once he had been strengthened by tempering, God raised him up. *"They afflicted his feet with fetters, he himself was laid in irons; until the time that his word came to pass, the word of the LORD tested him. The king sent and released him, the ruler of peoples, and set him free"* (Psalm 105:18-20).

The circumstances of Joseph's trial seem very harsh. In reality they were God's blessings and mercy on a chosen people in order to bring them unto Him. Thus, it was a part of God's plan, protection, and care that when Joseph arrived in Egypt, he was resold as a slave to Potiphar, an Egyptian officer of Pharaoh and captain of his body guard (Genesis 39:1). The Lord prospered Joseph in his duties to this man. Joseph found favor in his master's sight and was raised to a position of prominence as the overseer of his master's house and all his possessions (Genesis 39:5).

Just as things were looking up, treachery again raised its serpentine head. Joseph was handsome, and Potiphar's wife began to lust after him (Genesis 39:6-12). When he rejected her, she became furious and wrongfully accused him of abusing her.

Again a garment got him into trouble. As his multi-colored tunic had raised the ire of his brothers and had been used by the brothers to falsely testify of Joseph's death (Genesis 37:31-33), so now a garment, stripped from him when he fled from evil, was used by Potiphar's wife to falsely testify against him (Genesis 39:12-18). As a result of her lie, Joseph was immediately sent to jail.

Even in jail, God blessed Joseph. Able by God's grace to interpret dreams, he was eventually brought before Pharaoh. Since he was able to give the meaning of Pharaoh's dream concerning the coming years of abundance and famine and since he had wisely counseled Pharaoh to store produce from the land during the years of abundance in order to save the land and people during the prophesied famine, Joseph was promoted to the position of overseer (Genesis 41:14-44). He was set over all the land of Egypt to carry out the plan. Again Joseph performed his task well, preparing for the upcoming disaster. By his actions, he proved that he, the one who had been sent ahead by God, had been a good choice.

Then, changing the story from concern over one man, the Bible once again expands the story to include a whole family and then a whole race. Famine did indeed strike. Its effects were felt first in Egypt and then in all lands, growing and expanding until it covered the face of the earth (Genesis 41:54-57). Included among those suffering was Joseph's family in Canaan.

To get grain for food, Jacob sent his sons to Egypt. There they came face to face with Joseph. The dream Joseph had had which showed his brothers as sheaves bowing down to him (Genesis 37:7) proved to be true.

On a return visit, Joseph revealed himself and provided for those who had treated him so miserably. He then invited his whole family to live with him in Egypt and to share his prosperity. By moving to Egypt, that family of seventy people (Genesis 46:27) began a journey in history that is unparalleled in majesty, drama, and power.

As the years passed, *"the children of Israel were fruitful and increased greatly, and multiplied, and became exceedingly mighty...."* (Exodus 1:7). After Joseph died and a new leader arose in Egypt who did not know him, trouble began. Growing concerned that the Israelites outnumbered and outpowered his own people and fearful that they might rise up to fight against the Egyptians, he set taskmasters over the Israelites and reduced them to slavery.

After being held for four hundred years in captivity, bondage, and slavery, the people of Israel embarked on a journey out of Egypt. Through a God-planned, God-initiated, miraculous escape known as the Exodus, the Hebrew children were released from their tormentors. Placing the blood of slain lambs on their doorposts and lintels so the death angel would pass over them, they left Egypt, passed through the Red Sea, traveled through the desert, crossed the Jordan River on dry ground, and finally journeyed back to Canaan as God had long ago promised.

At this point, many observations can be made. Although having only reviewed highlights from the first book and a half of the sixty-six books in the Bible, there is much to learn from all this activity. Just a few nuggets of golden truth are:

- God will intervene in human affairs to ensure that His will is done. He will do anything necessary to keep His word or to fulfill what He has promised.

- All people are accountable for holy living. In exactly the same circumstances, different people do different things. Yet, no matter the situation or the choice made, God holds each of us accountable for our behavior. (Ham, Joseph)

- God makes a clear distinction between righteousness and unrighteousness, honor and dishonor, godliness and ungodliness. He marks this by blessing what is true. (Shem)

- God demanded a separation between holy and unholy and between flesh and spirit. He still does. (Ishmael, Isaac)

- God does not tempt His children, but He can and does test them. (Abraham)

- God is sovereign. He can choose a land and a people by His authority and power. He can give gifts and blessings to some and yet reserve His birthright and covenant for others. He is accountable to no one for His choice for grace.

- Obedience brings blessings. Greater obedience leads to greater blessings and to the presence of God. (Abraham, Jacob)

- God blesses prevailing prayer. He does not appreciate those who follow the "theology" of ask once and forget it, of demand, of command, of presume, or of "Gimme, or else, God!" Instead, He favors those who pray through. (Jacob)

- God meets people on journeys. He met Abram going to Canaan, Isaac going to Mount Moriah, Jacob going to and coming from Paddam-aram, and Joseph going to Egypt.

Why does God engage His people in seemingly endless journeys? One reason is so they can enjoy coming home again.

In the natural sense, God created mankind, and from all of mankind He chose a particular people (the Hebrews). God also created the earth, and from all of the earth He gave His people a particular land. Yet He sent them on an extended journey out of and then back to their land. In the spiritual sense, God created mankind, and from all of mankind He chose a particular people (all who would come to Him). God also created a garden for His people in which to live and enjoy His presence. He sent fallen mankind on an extended journey out of the garden. Now He is calling us back. Are we ready for the journey?

EACH SAINT'S JOURNEY

We left God's people in a strange land. Just so, we often find ourselves in an alien place, a place that is not right for us, a place we can never call home, a place that is not God's choosing for us.

The Israelites had to decide whether to stay where they were or to press on. We too are faced with that choice. We must choose to put up with present adverse and ungodly circumstances or to follow God to a new and better land.

Examine yourself. Are you willing to leave familiar faces and places in order to search for God, His land, and His people?

What is your choice? If you choose to remain stationary, to set up your tent, and to stay where you are, then we must say goodbye. However, if you choose to press on to find God and to seek the place He has for you, then you must follow two instructions: gird up your loins and pick up your walking stick.

THE CHURCH'S JOURNEY

As each of us who calls ourselves by Christ's name (i.e. Christian) has had to make an individual journey from sin to salvation and then to maturity and rest in Him, so each of us will find ourselves repeating that journey as part of a corporate body. After our rebirth into the kingdom of God, we find that we are referred to as saints. We are also called living stones. As such, we are being built up as a spiritual house of God for His holy priesthood (1 Peter 2:5). Each living stone and the sum of the living stones comprise this spiritual house, called the Church. It is with this corporate body that we find ourselves once more on a journey.

The Church, or the universal fellowship of believers whose sins are forgiven through the blood of Jesus Christ, began two thousand years ago. Its Author and Founder is God. In the first century, echoing endlessly across the corridors of time, the prophetic trumpet of God sounded forth: *"and upon this rock I will build **My** church; and the gates of Hades will not overpower it"* [emphasis added] (Matthew 16:18).

The rock or the foundation upon which the Church was to be established is Jesus Christ (1 Corinthians 3:11). The purpose of the Church is to preach the gospel of the kingdom and to carry out the works that Jesus began while He was here on earth.

Jesus's specific commands to His faithful were:

"Go, therefore and make disciples of all the nations, baptizing them in the name of the Father and the Son and the Holy Spirit, teaching them to observe all that I commanded you; and lo, I am with you always, even to the end of the age." (Matthew 28:19-20)

Further, He promised them:

"These signs will accompany those who have believed: in My name they will cast out demons, they will speak with new tongues; they will pick up serpents, and if they drink any deadly poison, it will not hurt them; they will lay hands on the sick, and they will recover." (Mark 16:17-18)

Most poignantly, He also asked them to care for those who would follow Him: *"Tend My lambs ... Shepherd My sheep ... Tend My sheep"* (John 21:15-17).

Both the raising up and empowerment of His Church were to be special. They came at a great price.

First, to raise up a separated body that would do as He asked of them, God the Father sent Jesus, His Son, to redeem and reconcile fallen mankind to God. Jesus was anxious to do so for He knew that those redeemed would be His bride. Just as when you truly love someone, you are willing to sacrifice your life for his/hers, so Jesus willingly surrendered Himself even unto death so His beloved would be delivered from her bondage and would be free to marry Him.

At the set time, Jesus allowed all the sins of the world to be placed on Him. He suffered and died the cruel, horrible death for all those sins, paying the penalty for them in full by His blood and His death. Then, by the power of the Holy Spirit, He rose again, making salvation available to all who would call on His name and who would ask Him to be their Savior.

Then, to empower the Church, after His death, resurrection, and ascension, 120 men and women, all faithful followers of Jesus Christ, gathered in an upper room in Jerusalem. Knowing that powerless people could not carry out His commission by their own power, and must not carry it out by an evil power, God equipped the Church with a special blessing: His Holy Spirit. *"Gathering them together, He commanded them not to leave Jerusalem, but to wait for what the Father had promised ... you will be baptized with the Holy Spirit not many days from now"* (Acts 1:4-5).

While on earth, Jesus had revealed this coming blessing. *"I will ask the Father, and He will give you another Helper that He may be with you forever"* (John 14:16). He identified this Helper as the Holy Spirit *"....whom the Father will send in My name, [and] He will teach you all things, and bring to your remembrance all that I said to you"* (John 14:26). He also declared how the Spirit would come. *"But I tell you the truth, it is to your advantage that I go away; for if I do not go away, the Helper will not come to you; but if I go, I will send Him to you"* (John 16:7). In other words, Jesus' physical presence would be replaced by God's spiritual presence.

The miracle happened to those disciples who were obedient to the call to separate, to come away, and to wait on Him.

> *When the day of Pentecost had come, they were all together in one place. And suddenly there came from heaven a noise like a violent rushing wind, and it filled the whole house where they sitting. And there appeared to them tongues as of fire distributing themselves, and they rested on each one of them. And they were all filled with the Holy Spirit and began to speak with other tongues, as the Spirit was giving them utterance.* (Acts 2:1-4)

The Holy Spirit descended on the faithful, immersing them into the presence and power of Jesus. The result was a total transformation of the disciples from fearful to fearless, from powerless to powerful. It was also a final nail in the coffins of the old religious systems. This event marked the beginning of the new way; it was the inauguration of the Church.

This new Church manifested and still manifests the presence and power of God. It had and still has only one standard bearer – Jesus. Since He is the Son of God as well as the Son of Man, He commands, is preeminent over, and is Head of the Church. Jesus' first appearance in the world birthed the Church; His second coming will see her fulfillment.

As Jesus is the only Head of the Church (Colossians 1:18), He was, is, and always will be the authority over every living stone who comprises the Church. As Jesus is the only begotten Son of God, He receives the privilege of birthright and blessing accorded to the firstborn in Jewish families. As Jesus is the true and good One, He was, is, and always will be the one true standard by which every expression of faith, grace, mercy, gift, or fruit is measured.

As the Church arose, numbers were added to it daily. The preaching of the Word was followed by supernatural demonstrations of holy power that overwhelmed sinners and blessed saints. As commanded, the Church spread the good news of the kingdom of God, healed the sick, delivered the demon-possessed, cared for its own, and worshipped the one true God. Through the active, able ministry of its leaders and saints, it turned the world upside down.

To a world that was either Jew or Gentile, all these references to a Church must have been confusing. To the Jews, steeped in the religious ritual of Temple worship, the Church sounded blasphemous; to the Gentiles who idolized wisdom and who worshipped a plethora of false gods in manmade temples, the Church seemed unnecessary. Both viewed it as a challenge and a threat. Both were right in being concerned.

The birth and growth of the Church set the old orders, the religious systems of both Jew and Gentile on notice. Concerning the Jews, by offering Himself as the perfect sacrifice for sin, Jesus made obsolete or ended for all time the need to offer animal sacrifice as a means of atonement for sin. Further, since there was no need of sacrifice, the Levitical priesthood which offered the sacrifices also became passé. This was clearly signaled by God when the curtain in the Temple was supernaturally torn in two from top to bottom just after Jesus' death (Matthew 27:51). Such a demonstration of power opened the way for common men and women to worship a most uncommon God in His very presence and without officiating religious leaders.

The coming of Jesus and His perfect sacrifice on behalf of all mankind also announced to the Gentile world that its religious practices did not serve the true and living God. For Gentiles too, the only way to God was through Jesus' atonement for sin. When Jesus announced that God was spirit and that those who wished to do so must worship Him in spirit and truth (John 4:23), He was declaring that mental "worship" did not serve Him; He was stating that human reason, intellect, and flights of knowledge were only prideful puffery. While they may have satisfied the requirements of worship for other gods, they were not acceptable as service or worship to Him. God also burst the Gentile bubble of arrogance by declaring that all their temples and the gods and goddesses honored in them were an abomination. He directly challenged idolatry by teaching saints that He, and He only, was the one true God and that they, as individuals and as His corporate Church, were His temple (1 Corinthians 3:16; 2 Corinthians 6:16).

The religious leaders among Jews and Gentiles tried to keep these truths from becoming evident, but they did not succeed. They also tried to enforce traditional ways of worship, those which God had declared outmoded and abominable, to keep their religious systems going, but again, they did not succeed.

Holy truth cannot long be hidden. People could do nothing to keep God's light from shining. Hearts hungry for relationship with the living God could not be filled by ritual and formality. Souls athirst for the presence and power of God could not be satisfied by the brackish waters of idolatry.

Out of the ranks of the hungry and searching, a small group began to break off from the main body of religion. First a trickle and then a torrent of the frustrated and the enslaved broke away from the centuries-old practices of ritual and religion to follow the living God, the Breath of Life, the Living Water. As they did so, they joined a called out, separated assembly. They became God's Church. *"There is neither Jew nor Gentile, neither slave nor free, nor is there male and female; for you are all one in Christ Jesus"* (Galatians 3:28 NIV).

It was this body of which the Word now testifies: *"But you are A CHOSEN RACE, a royal PRIESTHOOD, A HOLY NATION, A PEOPLE FOR God's OWN POSSESSION, so that you may proclaim the excellencies of Him who has called you out of darkness into His marvelous light"* (1 Peter 2:9).

Anything mushrooming into prominence as quickly as did the early Church was bound to raise the suspicions and the ire not only of religious bodies but of the civil government as well. Imperial Rome felt threatened by this new attention and worship to God. When Christians absolutely refused to acknowledge or honor the Roman emperors as God, persecution broke out.

As a result of this evil, the Church scattered all over the known world. This was good news in that it aided in the spreading of the gospel. Yet it was bad news in that it weakened the effectiveness of legitimate, godly authority. With Christians spread far and wide, heresies crept into the true gospel and people began to grab for power and position. What had begun as a marvelous burst of blessing fell on hard times.

As we have learned, God has a habit of testing His own. While He already knows all about us, He examines us: 1) to ensure that we understand the depth (or lack of it) of our faith in and our relationship to Him; and 2) to see if, when hard times come, we will stand or fall away. Tests that seem so harsh are really God's blessing and mercy on us, His chosen ones, in order to bring us to Him. The tests He allows are specifically designed to send us into the valley of decision in order to force us to choose between Him or another god, Him or another way.

As He had once tested Abraham concerning his son and has tested the individual members of the Church (and each of us) concerning His Son, so now God was testing His new Church as a body.

Around 400 AD, the Roman emperor Constantine is said to have converted to Christianity. However, rather than giving up his false gods and the pagan rites by which they were worshipped, he compromised the Church with them. The Church then became a curious amalgamation of Christianity and pagan religion. It claimed to honor Christ at the same time it celebrated pagan holidays, kept pagan religious rituals, and worshipped false gods.

What at first had seemed to be a great blessing became a disaster of immeasurable proportions. What had appeared to be the bringing of the pagan world into the Christian fold was total deception. In fact, the hybrid religion did exactly the opposite; it brought all but a tiny remnant of the Church into the pagan camp. The ultimate result of allowing false gods to steal God's honor was bondage. The Church, once free to worship God, had surrendered her freedom. She had fallen into a satanic snare and found herself bound in religious slavery.

Time went on. Roman religion assumed more and more command of life. It grew in dominance and control and ultimately became the state religion, the single most powerful force of the age. It survived the fall of the Roman Empire and became the official religion of the nation-states that sprang up in the empire's place. Through the blessing and mercy of God alone, the dimmest flicker of the candle of the light of faith showed through the devastating horror now known as the Dark Ages. By the Middle Ages, the treachery and excesses of the Roman church system had become obvious to even the most jaded and hardened of heart.

Through all of these trying centuries, God was yet faithful. He remembered His promise of a Church, a beautiful, spotless bride for His Son. He reached out, not to those prospering in the false religious system, but to those who truly desired to find God. God raised up men like Luther, Wycliffe, Calvin, and Huss to bring about a great religious change. Despite persecution and martyrdom, great groups of people broke away from Roman religion and began to truly serve God. Protesting the abuses in the church system and calling for change, the Protestant Reformation was born.

Soon, problems broke out once again. As the newness of religious freedom wore off, intolerance of one another grew within the ranks of the Protestants. Schisms formed as each group declared it had found the only way to God. Since each group believed it had the only valid interpretation of Scripture, any who challenged them must be wrong.

The fruit of this division was sectarianism. God had said He would build His Church (singular), not churches (plural). Yet denomination after denomination sprang up, pushing their own beliefs and ways while mocking and condemning those of others. Each claimed to have the truth and each promised freedom to worship – as long as its rules were followed. At the beginning of the Reformation the Church had won a great battle, but as time passed the victors turned on themselves and engaged in religious war with each other.

As denominations became more and more locked into tradition, insistence on manmade rules rather than on the Spirit to govern the Church and doing things the "proper" or traditional way rather than through God's Spirit prevailed. As a result, death settled in.

Even yet, God reached out. Occasionally, He sent holy fires of revival. Evangelical and Pentecostal bodies broke away from the Protestant groups and declared themselves to be the true Church. Sadly, they too fell into argument and division. Due to people's unwillingness to submit fully to the One True God, the promise of one true Church remained unfulfilled.

What had started as one Church had grown into a bulging balloon of humanism, sectarianism, and evil. When pricked with the needle of truth, that balloon had blown apart, scattering bits and pieces of debris all over. What God had announced as Church had become, at the hands of mankind and the enemy, many church systems. They had also become shams, pretenses, and counterfeits of the real thing. Even today, these systems do not honor God. For the most part they enjoy neither the presence nor the power of God; in no way do they fulfill the promise of Christ to build His Church.

Joshua once spoke to his people: *"If it is disagreeable in your sight to serve the LORD, choose for yourselves today whom you will serve ... but as for me and my house, we will serve the LORD"* (Joshua 24:15). It seems that the true Church must make that same choice.

Hopefully, after our individual entry into the kingdom of God, we were rightly told that we had become part of God's family and members of His Church. There are no independent Christians. If we are saints, we are His Church. The two are inseparable.

Yet which Church did we become a part of – the true Church of Jesus Christ or the church system of man? Did we find His true house of worship or did we unknowingly surrender our freedom to worship God to the illegal, corrupt, counterfeit church? Did we wait on God and have Him place us in His family or did we just join a particular group, denomination, or "church" because we were told to do so or because it tickled our fancies? Did we find the true Church or are we still wandering around as lost sheep?

As God called us out of sin as individuals, so now He calls us out as His whole Church. He is asking His true bride to prepare herself. He is asking those who truly seek only Him to lay aside all encumbrances and to set out in search of Him and the place He has for us. As long as we fail to do so, His promise concerning His Church will remain unfulfilled.

On the other hand, if the true Church obeys Him and agrees to go on a journey, she will find herself traveling some familiar roads. If she is careful to observe, she will see a well-marked, well-traveled path. Like the ancient Hebrews and each individual saint had to do, she will also start in Egypt, pass through the Red Sea, wander in the desert, cross the Jordan River, and finally arrive in Canaan. Wandering the difficult highways and byways, she will have the distinct impression that others have passed this way before and experienced the same hardships. Yet, in traveling from Egypt to Canaan, she will become the people of God.

Christians, let us examine ourselves! Are we willing to leave the old and familiar to search for the new and true? In spite of the persecution of those saying we are in ignorance and arrogance, are we willing to come out of the church system and to find our collective way to God? Do we see ourselves as one body, one bride, one Church? Do we serve Him in joy or in slavery? Do we see the true Church of God freely worshipping Him in ways of His choosing or do we see a religious church system somehow perpetuating itself in its own dead rituals?

The Israelites could not leave Egypt without hardship and pain. Each saint could not leave the world system without fear and trembling. The Protestants could not leave the Roman system without inquisitions and wars. Those in the church system will come against those who have rejected their false values and who want to leave. They will try to shut down what they perceive as heresy and rebellion.

Those who are seeking to emerge from bondage and to be free to worship God must not succumb to intimidation or threats. What is your decision, brothers and sisters? If you are in the church system and desire to stay there, then we must part. However, if you desire with all your heart to seek and serve God and if you want a place and a part in His true Church, then a journey is in order.

****

The Israelites went on a physical pilgrimage whereby natural men and women undertook a physical journey traversing a physical land in order to arrive at God's chosen destination. However, today things are different. We now find ourselves on a spiritual pilgrimage whereby spiritual men and women must undertake a spiritual journey traversing a spiritual land in order to arrive at God's chosen destination. This expedition will take them, as it did the Hebrew children, out of the mud pits of Egypt, through the Red Sea, into the desert, across the Jordan River, and into Canaan or the kingdom of God. Only when the journey is complete with no parts left out or too quickly skipped over, with no detours or premature stops made, will anyone reach the place of rest and inheritance that God has planned for them. The areas His chosen people physically walked in and the events they participated in and grew from are the sign posts that God's spiritual children, His sons and daughters by adoption, must look for along their own way.

Scripture supports this premise. For example, 1 Corinthians 15:46 points out *"....the spiritual is not first, but the natural; then the spiritual."*

Further, there is another portion of Scripture that amasses the evidence that God's children of today must spiritually follow the leaders of yesterday:

> *For I do not want you to be unaware, brethren, that our fathers were all under the cloud and all passed through the sea; and all*

were baptized into Moses in the cloud and in the sea; and all ate the same spiritual food; and all drank the same spiritual drink, for they were drinking from a spiritual rock which followed them; and the rock was Christ. Nevertheless, with most of them God was not well-pleased; for they were laid low in the wilderness. Now these things happened as examples for us, so that we would not crave evil things as they also craved ... Now these things happened to them as an example, and they were written for our instruction, upon whom the ends of the ages have come. (1 Corinthians 10:1-6,11)

The purpose of this book is to declare that all people everywhere must go on a journey if they wish to find God. As a fallen man and woman had to leave Eden and thus leave the presence of God, so after salvation, redeemed men and women must journey back into the presence of God. As Abram had to leave his family and his familiar land and had to journey to strangers in an unfamiliar land in order to walk in right relationship and in renewed covenant with God, each saint must do so as well. As Jacob's and Moses' journeys were to bring God's people back to the promised land, so the Church's journey is to present the kingdom of God in action, to restore the blessings lost in the fall, and to usher in the worldwide worship of the one true God.

Are we ready?

The journey begins!

PART I:

PREPARATION FOR SALVATION

PART II

PREPARATION FOR SALVATION

Chapter 1

EGYPT:

THE ISRAELITES' PREPARATION FOR THE EXODUS FROM EGYPT

God spoke this promise to the patriarch Israel: *"I am God, the God of your father; do not be afraid to go down to Egypt, for I will make you a great nation there. I will go down with you to Egypt, and I will also surely bring you up again"* (Genesis 46:3-4). Israel believed God's word and acted on it; he and his family moved to Egypt. Leaving Canaan and the dreadful famine that was ravaging both land and people and arriving in the midst of the abundance of Egypt must have been an amazing experience for the Hebrews. Leaving home and arriving in the court of Pharaoh where one of their own was second in command must have produced gasps of awe and admiration. Being reunited as a family, forgiven and blessed, must have set hearts at rest. The move to Egypt must have appeared to be the answer to all of the Israelites' needs and dreams.

Yet things often are not what they outwardly appear to be. When the Israelites first arrived, admiration for their relative, Joseph, caused the Egyptians to welcome and shelter the refugees from Canaan. However, not long afterwards the descendants of Israel found themselves in difficulty. They had become official residents in an alien land. Having many gods of its own, Egypt was hostile to the one true God of Israel. Called the land of Ham (Psalm 105:23) after Noah's cursed son, it was a hard land. In addition, the Word provides another description of Egypt that summarizes the situation. In Deuteronomy 4:20 Moses refers to Egypt as an iron furnace.

So it proved to be!

CAUSES OF THE ISRAELITES' BONDAGE AND SLAVERY

By a decision of their free wills, the descendants of Israel had traveled to and entered Egypt. Once there, Joseph told them to claim that they were shepherds. Since this occupation was an abomination to the Egyptians (Genesis 46:34), Pharaoh instructed them to go to Goshen to settle and work (Genesis 47:6a). In Goshen, the pastureland of Egypt, God kept them safe, and they thrived in their new jobs as overseers of Pharaoh's livestock (Genesis 47:6b). As a separated and yet whole people, the Israelites prospered in the best of the land of Egypt. They acquired possessions, were fruitful, and greatly multiplied in number (Genesis 47:27).

In time, Israel, their patriarch, died (Genesis 49:33). After more years, Joseph, his brothers, and their whole generation died (Exodus 1:6). Then, *"a new king arose over Egypt, who did not know Joseph"* (Exodus 1:8). He grew afraid of the descendants of Israel living in the midst of his nation because they were greater in both numbers and might than the Egyptians (Exodus 1:9; Psalm 105:24).

Fearful that the Israelites might join with Egypt's enemies in overthrowing him and afraid that the Israelites would leave but more afraid that they would stay, Pharaoh set about to remedy the situation. Claiming to be wise, he instead acted treacherously and harshly with the people of God's covenant (Exodus 1:10-11).

Pharaoh's Treachery

Pharaoh determined in his evil heart to reduce the number of those he now perceived as enemies. He formulated a plan meant to cause the eventual extinction of the Israelites. At first, in order to force the Israelites to do his wicked work for him or to destroy themselves, he ordered the Hebrew midwives to kill all male newborns (Exodus 1:15-16).

Much to Pharaoh's disappointment, the plan backfired. The midwives refused to cooperate in such iniquity or to be a part of genocide. Choosing instead to obey God and not Pharaoh, they let their children live (Exodus 1:17). As a result of this obedience, the descendants of Israel grew even more numerous.

Yet Pharaoh was not done with his wickedness. When thwarted in this attempt to manipulate and control Hebrew women to destroy their children, he began an open campaign of murder, a systematic extermination of the descendants of Israel, this time using his own people as the vessels of treachery. He ordered the Egyptians to cast all the male babies of the Israelites into the Nile (Exodus 1:22).

Pharaoh's Harshness

Even as Pharaoh was trying to extinguish a new generation of Israelites by slaughtering the male babies, he was also actively at work overseeing the destruction of the old generation. He set taskmasters over the Israelites and reduced them to utter slavery (Exodus 1:11). In the dreadful living conditions that such bondage brings, they were compelled to build Pharaoh's kingdom with hard labor.

> *So they appointed taskmasters over them to afflict them with hard labor. And they built for Pharaoh storage cities, Pithom and Raamses ... The Egyptians compelled the Israelites to labor rigorously; and they made their lives bitter with hard labor in mortar and bricks and at all kinds of labor in the field, all their labors which they rigorously imposed on them.* (Exodus 1:11,13-14)

As the Israelites became more and more afflicted with hard labor, they began to cry out for deliverance. With no kindness shown to them by people, they called out to the God of Abraham, Isaac, and Jacob. God, in faithfulness and mercy, heard their groaning and remembered His promise to them (Exodus 2:23-24).

GOD'S PRESENCE WITH MOSES

In response to the Israelites' anguish, God set in motion the plan for their freedom. He raised up a man called Moses, one of their own from the tribe of Levi, to be the human vessel through whom God's power of salvation would flow.

As God had worked on the people to temper them in the hot furnace so they would call out to Him and would accept His will for them, so now He had to work with the man chosen as leader of this people. He blessed Moses with His presence, His promise, and His power.

God had birthed Moses and had miraculously saved him from the death edict ordered for the male Israelite babies. He had raised Moses in Pharaoh's court so he would be educated in the language and customs of Egypt. Then, after Moses killed an Egyptian, He sent Moses to the desert to learn the ways of God.

While Moses was in the desert, God commissioned him to be the leader of His people (Exodus 3:10). Capturing Moses' attention by appearing in the midst of a bush that burned but was not consumed by the flames, God introduced Himself to Moses and told him that He was the God of his forefathers (Exodus 3:2-6). When pressed to reveal His name, God responded, *"I AM WHO I AM"* (Exodus 3:14). Further, God told Moses to identify Him to the people as the LORD, the strong, powerful God of salvation and deliverance, the One who would fulfill His covenant to bring His people back to the land of Canaan.

Moses also understood the symbolism of the burning bush – the bush that burned with fire but was not destroyed because of God's presence in the midst of it represented the Israelites, who, although they were being burned in Pharaoh's iron furnace, would not be annihilated because of God's presence in their midst. Moses truly came to know that the power guarding and maintaining his people was God. He also realized that he was standing in the presence of that awesome God.

GOD'S PROMISE TO MOSES

To grant His promise, God told Moses that He was the LORD, the God of the Hebrews (Exodus 3:18). He wanted it clearly understood that He was *the* LORD, their only God. Further, in proclaiming this title, God was differentiating Himself from other so-called gods. He was setting Himself apart from and in authority over the numerous gods of Egypt.

Once God had done that, He made a promise that only He could keep:

> *"So I said, I will bring you up out of the affliction of Egypt to the land of the Canaanite and the Hittite and the Amorite and the Perizzite and the Hivite and the Jebusite, to a land flowing with milk and honey ... So I will stretch out My hand, and strike Egypt with all My miracles which I shall do in the midst of it; and after that he [Pharaoh] will let you go."* (Exodus 3:17,20)

GOD'S POWER GIVEN TO MOSES

Finally, to show Moses that He intended to work through him, God granted Moses miraculous power. To bolster Moses' unbelief, God commanded him to perform miracles concerning blood, a serpent, and a disease, all prophetic of things to come. To further allay his fears, God sent Aaron, Moses' brother, to work with him.

With these preliminaries completed, God then sent Moses back to Egypt. There, Moses met with the elders of the Hebrews, spoke God's words to them, and performed His signs. By these, the people believed, and they recognized him as their leader. Their immediate response was to bow down and worship God (Exodus 4:31).

The Israelites now had a God, a promise, and a leader. God now had a people. Though the path had been long and arduous, He finally had His people where they needed to be: calling out to Him for help (instead of relying on themselves or on some unknown god), believing His promise, submitting to His chosen authority, and worshipping Him.

As a result of seeing their affliction and hearing their cry, God would move on their behalf. All the pieces were set in place. All the participants in a drama unparalleled in mercy, power, and majesty were ready.

PASSOVER

Even with God's promise of freedom sounding a clarion call, life did not immediately get better for the descendants of Israel. In fact, it became decidedly worse. Thinking his puny, satanically-inspired power was a match for God's holy power, Pharaoh challenged Him. Pharaoh flatly refused to comply when God commanded him to let His people go so they would be free to worship Him. Then, in open defiance of Mighty God, Pharaoh increased the hardship of the people of God's own heart. He escalated and extended their labor and misery, exacting a frightful toll in suffering and sorrow. Calling the Israelites lazy, he multiplied the workload of a people already dying of slavery.

> "You are no longer to give the people straw to make brick as previously; let them go and gather straw for themselves. But the quota of bricks which they were making previously, you impose on them; you are not to reduce any of it. Because they are lazy, therefore they cry out, 'Let us go and sacrifice to our God.' Let the labor be heavier on the men, and let them work at it that they will pay no attention to false words." (Exodus 5:7-9)

Since this requirement was too much for the people to bear, they were not able to make their quotas. Pharaoh's taskmasters then beat the foremen of the Israelites and demanded, *"Why have you not completed your required amount either yesterday or today in making brick as previously?"* (Exodus 5:14).

Pharaoh thought that if he heightened his demands, created new hardships, and increased the misery that was specifically designed to keep God's people endlessly performing works of flesh in order to satisfy his tyrannical demands, the Israelites would have no time or energy to do as God wanted – to worship Him.

Pharaoh was wrong. In this darkest of hours, God once again spoke.

> *"But I will harden Pharaoh's heart that I may multiply My signs and My wonders in the land of Egypt. When Pharaoh does not listen to you, then I will lay My hand on Egypt and bring out My hosts, My people the Israelites, from the land of Egypt by great judgments. The Egyptians shall know that I am the LORD, when I stretch out My hand on Egypt and bring out the sons of Israel from their midst."* (Exodus 7:3-5)

The time had come. The people were prepared. God was now ready to move to save His people from Egypt.

And so He did. By the might of His great power, by unimaginable miracles, by power wrought through the hand of Moses, God moved. Through plagues, He brought judgment on the gods of Egypt (Exodus 12:12), judgment on Pharaoh (Exodus 12:29), and judgment on the land and people of Egypt for being so hostile to God's chosen ones.

During a night now known as Passover, God instructed those desiring freedom from slavery to mark the doorposts and lintels of their homes with the blood of a slain lamb (Exodus 12:7,22). The LORD then passed through the land. Any home on which the LORD saw blood was passed over; He did not allow the destroyer to stop there. However, any household without the blood was judged, the sentence of death pronounced, and the sentence then carried out. The firstborn of every human and beast of Egypt was struck down. God, by the sign of the blood, separated His own people, broke the power of Pharaoh over their lives, and saved them from the hands of their oppressors and tormentors.

As a result of this mighty action, Pharaoh called Moses to him. He commanded that God's people rise up and go. He, in the face of awesome power and terrible tragedy, released God's people to go and worship their God. Pharaoh's power over them was broken. The bondage and slavery suffered in Egypt was over.

God had called Israel His son, His firstborn (Exodus 4:22). With compassion and great longing, He had looked on the plight of His beloved child. Seeing him in captivity, God had ransomed him with the firstborn of the sons of his captors. When His son was redeemed, he was released from his torment. He was free to go and worship his Father, God.

Chapter 2

EGYPT:

EACH SAINT'S PREPARATION FOR THE EXODUS FROM SIN

Years ago when people asked directions to a certain place, they might have heard the amusing and popular reply, "You can't get there from here." Such may once have seemed applicable to the Hebrews, entombed in Egypt, when they wondered how to get to the promised land. Yet by God's grace and sovereign acts of power, they were released from slavery in Egypt to start their journey.

The Bible is filled with types and shadows. One such type was the nation of Egypt. In Scripture, Egypt is a symbol of the world. Perhaps more accurately, it represents sin. To the Hebrews, the nation of Egypt was both a place of refuge and a place of oppression. It was a beautiful, enticing land, but one with an undercurrent of darkness, abuse, and evil. While it seemed religious in its practice of polytheism, it was wholly opposed to the one true God. Egypt was the location of the Hebrews' bondage and slavery to an evil master.

So too today, many people find themselves in Egypt. That is, although they are not living in the physical country of Egypt, they are yet living in the world of sin. Like the Egypt of thousands of years ago, this Egypt is a place of oppression where the unbelievers and the unsaved live in the company of those who are opposed to God and are surrounded by darkness, abuse, and evil. Those who live in this dark place are like the fallen Adam and Eve; they find themselves separated from the presence of God because of sin. They have not had a salvation experience through which their sins are forgiven and through which they regain relationship with God. They have not been reborn out of the kingdoms of this world and have not been welcomed into the kingdom of God.

In the midst of slavery to the systems that prevail in the world, the unsaved are being called to the promised land. From their point of view, the journey may seem insurmountable or even impossible, yet, to God, it is not. If you are one of these who is yet living in the world and separated from God, be assured that, as with the descendants of Israel, although Egypt or the world of sin is the starting point of a long journey, you **can** get to the promised land, the kingdom of God, from where you are.

CAUSES OF EACH SAINT'S BONDAGE AND SLAVERY

The first step on every individual's journey to freedom from sin and to reconciliation with God is to admit that he or she is in bondage. Many do not believe they are in Egypt. Many deny they are enslaved by sin. Whether they believe it or not is not the issue. Everyone living, every person reading this book, is now or has been in Egypt, the land of sin. It is Satan's express desire to keep them in bondage to sin so they will be his slaves and build his empire.

Why is that true? How did mankind get into the land of sin? The Bible gives two indisputable reasons. The first is because of our inheritance.

Our Inheritance Of Sin

As the whole generation of Hebrews at the time that God was preparing them for freedom had been born in Egypt, so too, all of mankind prior to the time of individual salvation from sin was born into the world and was (or is) living in sin.

Each member of the human race is a descendant of Adam and Eve. Adam and Eve were the culmination of God's creation. As the first human beings, and they were made in God's image (Genesis 1:26). God's plan was for them to be the ancestors, the forerunners, or the representatives of a whole race of men and women who would love Him, fellowship with Him, and worship Him forever.

Unfortunately, Adam and Eve did not hold relationship with God to be sacred. Oh, too soon, they fell. As a result of pride, covetousness, deception, and disobedience that revealed the rebellion in their hearts, they both sinned. By an act of will, they did exactly what they were warned not to do and ate the fruit God had forbidden to them. In so doing, they became sinners. The results of their unholy choices were twofold: first, they were sentenced to death (Genesis 3:19); second, they were driven from God's presence (Genesis 3:24).

The problem of sin did not stop with Adam and Eve. All children subsequently born to them found themselves victims of that terrible decision. These children were no longer born in the image of God but in the image of fallen man (Genesis 5:3).

As Adam and Eve's children inherited certain physical and mental characteristics from their parents, they also inherited the sin found in their natures. Thus, sin, in particular the sin of rebellion against God, became part of the nature of mankind. It became a part of each generation from Adam's son, Seth, to Noah to Abraham to Moses to David to Paul and to us. With only one exception, Jesus Christ, every single man and woman who has ever been born has a sin nature or is disposed to sin as part of his or her being. This includes Mary, the mother of Jesus who herself declared her own need of a Savior (Luke 1:46-47).

For that reason, each of us – every man, woman, and child, including you and I – was born in sin, a product of inherited evil. For that reason each of us needs a Savior, someone to free us from sin.

Alas, with our inherent sin natures, no one can live a perfect life. At some point in our lives each of us gives in to and acts out of this propensity to sin, and then each of us continues to sin over and over again. Thus, each of us by our decisions of will and our behavior, compounds the problem of sinfulness.

Our Own Sin

The second reason that each of us has sojourned (or continues to sojourn) in Egypt is that every one of us commits sin. Each of us can and does sin. In spite of all public protest to the contrary, in the private corners of our hearts, each of us knows that we sin and that we have repeatedly come up short of the mark. Each of us may be living up to our own self-established standards of goodness, changing them or bending them at will to suit our desires or the pressures of the ever-lowering standards of modern culture. However, we forget we aren't the ones who set the standard; God is. Since we are His people created for His purposes, He is in authority over us. He establishes the standard (in fact, as Jehovah-nissi, He *is* the standard), and we are required to meet it. If each of us follows our own rules, we are not obeying His. If we are not under His authority or doing His will, then we are in sin. For us too, the wages of sin is death (Romans 6:23).

In short, each of us adds to the account already held against us by God (because of our inheritance from Adam and Eve) by committing our own willful acts of sin, transgression, and wickedness. Each of us and all of us are like sheep who have rebelled and gone astray (Isaiah 53:6). Each of us has sinned and fallen short of God's glory (Romans 3:23).

Only one Man was born without sin, and that is because He was born the Son of God, not of a man. Therefore, only one Man could and did live a sinless life. His name is Jesus.

If we do not know Jesus as Savior, then both by birth and by behavior we are in the land of Egypt, the place of sin and death. We are as firmly ensconced in Egypt spiritually as our forefathers were physically. Each of us is as much a slave of sin, performing its dead works, as the Israelites were slaves to Pharaoh. Although loved by God, our birth in and our participation in sin separate us from God.

EACH SAINT'S PASSOVER

As the Israelites were persecuted by a nation that represented sin and were pursued by its God-hating overlord, so each person who has not been reborn spiritually must realize is that he (or she) is being tormented, abused, and tyrannized by the world of sin and hunted, hounded, and stalked by its leader, Satan. Even so, like Exodus 8:1, the cry of each bound heart must be *"Let me go that I may serve God."*

Needless to say, the taskmaster of each grieving heart does not want to hear this plea; he does not want to lose even one soul who is bound to his system of sin. Like before, his plan is to introduce him (or her) to new hardships or horrors; to increase his slave's distress, heartbreak, pain, and suffering; and to keep the unsaved one in such misery that he is unable to pursue freedom.

However, as Pharaoh miscalculated his ability to retain his slaves, so does Satan. As God miraculously moved to release a nation from bondage, so He will powerfully move to release each individual who asks Him for freedom from sin. Since all forgiveness from sin stems from the shed blood of Jesus Christ at the cross, any who wishes to be free needs to approach God, symbolically apply Jesus' blood to the lintel and doorposts of his (or her) heart, ask that his sins be forgiven through that blood, and, by faith, believe that those sins are forgiven. As soon as he does so, his slavery is over. He is set free. He is translated from the kingdom of darkness into God's marvelous light so that he may proclaim the praises of his Savior (1 Peter 2:9). In other words, he is now free to worship his God.

Chapter 3

EGYPT:

THE CHURCH'S PREPARATION FOR THE EXODUS FROM THE FALSE CHURCH SYSTEM

The true Church is the sum of those who have been reborn out of the kingdom of darkness and translated into God's kingdom of light. In towns and cities, believers in each community comprise their local Church. Around the world, all believers from all local Churches comprise the universal Church. According to *The New Strong's Exhaustive Concordance of the Bible*, the Greek word for church is *ekklesia*. It means the called out ones; a religious congregation; a Christian community of members on earth or saints in heaven, or both. In other words, God's true Church is that group of born-again believers who are purchased by Christ (Acts 20:28), sanctified by Christ (Ephesians 5:26-27), founded on Christ (Ephesians 2:19-20), and called out of the world system into the kingdom of God. Rather than reflect, mimic, act like, or accept the world's values, Christians are to present God's values to the world and to be His agents of change in the world. They are to present His kingdom to the world until *"the kingdom of this world has become the kingdom of our Lord and of His Christ"* (Revelation 11:15). Like the Christians in the first century, Christians today are to turn the world upside down (Acts 17:6).

However, as it once was in ancient Egypt with Pharaoh's religious leaders miring the people in the worship of false gods and as it was in first-century imperial Rome with its corrupt, self-serving religious leaders commanding the worship of a pantheon of false gods, so today in the false church, some of the religious leaders do not even know the Lord they claim to serve and so are leading their followers into the worship of false gods. As incredible as it may seem, some have labeled themselves Christians, have risen to places of highest authority in the Church, oversee multitudes, and affect the lives of many, *and yet they do not know God.* Further, some in the laity of the Church go through the motions, do as they are told, observe rite and ritual blindly, promote the religious system faithfully, *and yet they do not know God.* To all of these, God would cry out, "Come away! Come out of the false church system and come into the true Church."

The Church is in slavery for two reasons: 1) our ancestors In faith sinned; and 2) leaders and members of the Church sin. Whether from faulty spiritual heritage or the poor choices of the leadership and membership of the present Church, the Church reflects the sin, suffering, and bondage of its collective saints.

It may be a surprise to many that sin is in the Church, However, each saint is a member of the body of Christ. The Word says that what affects one part of the body affects the whole body (1 Corinthians 12:26). Therefore, to the degree that sin is tolerated or practice in individual lives, to the measure that any individual saint brings his or her own fleshly, carnal practices into the Church, the Church is unholy. When the sum of the unholiness of all of the believers is totaled up, the Church can only stagger under the burden of its lack of sanctification.

To some degree, the enslaved Church has become more of a church system than the true Church of God, one that has so accepted the political, religious, cultural, and humanist values of the world system that it is difficult to distinguish it from the world.

CAUSES OF THE CHURCH'S BONDAGE AND SLAVERY

Faulty Spiritual Heritage

Our early Church forefathers harmed God's true Church when they admitted foreign gods and rituals into its service of worship. Instead of throwing off the encroaching yoke of paganism, the Church compromised its foundational belief in the one true God by "Christianizing" pagan rituals, idols, and holy days. For example, December 25th was once the pagan Roman winter solstice festival honoring Saturn. False gods and idols were renamed, introduced into, and worshipped as "saints" by the weakened Church. Over time, the Church began to be governed by unholy leaders who led it into unholy ways. This led to generation after generation being born into the disgraced, surrendered "church" and to the unrepented sins of their forefathers becoming a part of their heritage (See Psalm 78:5-8). With compromise, rather than Jesus, as its cornerstone, the religious church system then proceeded to weaken God's Church further and to replace the God of the true Church with human tradition.

The Aggrandizement Of People

One of the primary hallmarks of the religious system is people's insistence on aggrandizing other people. If one man (or woman) is being raised above all others and saints have been taught to think of him and to treat him as God, that is a sign that the religious system, not the true Church, in operation. If all one man thinks or says has to be blindly and instantly obeyed with no call for discernment or prayer, the church is as enslaved to him as Israel was to Pharaoh.

True Christianity never promotes the rise of spiritual dictatorships. God has never given people the power to dominate or control other people's lives. If any man (or woman) enforces his rules on saints' lives or someone other than the Holy Spirit guides their way, they're in the false church system. They are being governed by a false leader and are being led by a false spirit.

The Israelites' Deliverer was the LORD. Every saint's Deliverer is Jesus Christ. Since the Church is the sum of the saints, the Church's Deliverer is also Jesus Christ. If He should choose to raise a saint as a channel of blessing, the presence of God will be with him (or her) and the power of God will be manifested through him too. Even so, a chosen vessel of God does not – must not – become God in the eyes or in the behavior of the saints.

On the other hand, if a man (or woman) has raised himself as a deliverer, the presence of man, not of God, rests on him. Therefore, the power a person utilizes to have his own way or to do his own thing is but flesh. The results of his labors are soulish. Yet, some who may have been served by him may feel pressured or commanded to follow him since "he" or "his" ministry saved them.

The Building Of A Human Kingdom

If the purpose of the Church is to respond to non-stop fundraising with moneys raised and then spent on building the kingdom of a leader or the dreams of the pastor, this is a mark of the false church system rather than of the true Church. If these financial schemes are nothing more than human-announced, human-enforced, endless works which keep saints too busy to worship God, that is a sign of the system. In contrast, Jesus provides for all He ordains without the struggle of flesh.

Inherited Or Human-Appointed Leadership

Those whose personal behavior or those whose ministries do not honor God are not honored by God. Those who refuse to repent and who fail to desist in wrongdoing are not His true body. Instead, they comprise, at both universal and local levels, a humanist religious system. This pretentious organization then opposes and oppresses the saints who serve in the true Church of God.

Long ago, a man named Eli was a priest, a minister in God's house during a dark time in Israel's history. This priest was so out of touch with God that he was unable to distinguish prayer from drunkenness (1 Samuel 1:12-13). Worse, he had two sons, Hophni and Phineas, who were worthless and corrupt. The Bible calls them sons of Belial, a term which applies to liars (1 Kings 21:10), the wicked (1 Samuel 30:22), the rebellious (1 Samuel 10:27), seducers (Deuteronomy 13:13), and fools (1 Samuel 25:25). The Bible further declares that Hophni and Phineas were priests of the Lord (1 Samuel 1:3), but they did not know God. *"Now the sons of Eli were worthless men; they did not know the LORD and the customs of the priests with the people"* (1 Samuel 2:12-13a).

In part, the same situation exists in the religious church system today. Some ministers (e.g. priests and pastors) serve in God's house but do not serve Him well. They know the rituals of their denominations, but they don't have a relationship with God. For example, some ministers preach the doctrine of works rather than faith for salvation. In so doing, they deny that salvation from sin can only come by a born-again experience through the blood of Jesus Christ. Such churches would be hard pressed to know or honor the God they claim to be professing. Or, similar to Eli's situation, some ministers have a problem with hereditary ministry. A father can begin a ministry as one truly called of God. Then, he (rather than God) calls his sons or other family members to carry on the work. Placed in office by man, they often end up despising God but are allowed (or forced) to serve anyway. Such ignorance and excess muddies the whole ministry and creates a stumbling block for people seeking to know Christ.

Then, even with problems obvious to all, instead of those in error repenting and giving up all outward ministry in order to allow God to minister to them inwardly, they deny there is a problem, attack those who question them, cover up, and carry on. Instead of honoring God, the sole purpose of the ministry becomes the perpetuation of the ministry.

Spiritual Abuse By Leadership

In His Word, God outlined His plan for leadership in His Church (Ephesians 4:11-13). Apostles, prophets, evangelists, pastors, and teachers were a gift to the Church *"for the equipping of the saints, for the work of service, to the building up of the body of Christ; until we all attain to the unity of the faith, and of the knowledge of the Son of God...."* (Ephesians 4:12-13). In recent centuries, God's plan for governing His true Church has been denied. Some of our forefathers, who were apostles and prophets, were to lay the foundation of the Church (Ephesians 2:20) and were to point the way for it to go. Rather than being respected and obeyed, they were viewed with contempt; their ministry voices were stifled; and their offices were openly condemned and declared obsolete. This freed people to build their own churches, allowing them to substitute self for God and to follow their own directions.

Adding to their sin, our ancestors watched as evangelists began to attract sinners into the substitute religious system of which they had become a part. In their orations, some didn't present the true word of salvation through Jesus Christ. Instead, they presented a lukewarm, watered down version of the gospel; left out essentials such as repentance and confession of sin; or distorted the good news into a series of sermons on what sinners could obtain from God. Often, these false evangelists were never corrected or disciplined as long as they attracted large numbers into the religious system.

Our predecessors in faith saw pastors brutalize saints at will. They knew there was little or no proper, loving care being administered to new lambs and sheep. They observed teachers teaching human reasoning, denominational doctrine, and faulty theology instead of pure biblical truth. They approved as the church system produced generations of those labeled "Christian" who fed on error and who fled in terror at the first sound of spiritual warfare. In allowing the development of a religious system that did not honor God, they became a part of the synagogue of Satan.

As our predecessors grieved God concerning leadership, so also some grieved Him concerning their personal lives. They were involved in such shameful deeds as to make those in the world blush. Some did abominable things in private and believed their sins would never be found out. Others blatantly immersed themselves in the very things that Jesus condemned. These false leaders declared themselves communicators of God's will when they didn't know His will, believers in His Word when they hadn't heard His Word, and followers of His way when they were not following His way.

Questionable Membership Practices

When the body of Christ obeys the apostle Paul's scriptural command to examine all things to see whether they are from God (1 John 4:1), it might ask if one of the primary goals of denominations or of local churches is to increase numbers. If the pressure is always there to add to the congregation in order to keep church hierarchy from complaining, that is a sign of the false church system. If the methods chosen to add to the numbers are suspect, such as raiding the flocks of other shepherds or dragging drunkards who, with no preliminaries such as repentance or confession of sin, are led to make besotted, verbal expressions of sainthood, that is a sign of the false church system. In God's true Church, numbers are added daily by the work of the Holy Spirit guiding holy men and women, not by acts of undisciplined flesh.

Lack Of Discernment

Worse, the Church is being assaulted by those who claim to be its deliverers but in reality who are demonic angels of light. They bring the presence of Satan into the false religious system.

Only discernment can speak the truth to the true Church. Only God's gift of grace to His people perceives truth from lies and speaks to inquiring hearts, confirming whether they are serving God or people – or Satan. Anything that does not serve God is a part of the false church system.

SIGNS OF THE CHURCH'S BONDAGE

To keep the true Church in captivity, Satan has utilized a plan. It is based on the same tactics that were unsuccessful for him in ancient Egypt. In a two-pronged effort, he: 1) is determined to wipe out a whole generation of children among whom the deliverers of the Church might arise; and 2) has decided to preserve and build his kingdom by forcing the members of the Church into religious slavery and killing them off by endless works.

Genocide

Concerning the first part of his plan, the extermination of the newborn, Satan is riding a tidal wave of evil that is inundating the whole globe. That wickedness is called abortion. In the most disgusting, abominable, horrifying ways, human babies are being ripped from the protecting wombs of rejecting mothers and then are being thrown out as trash or their body parts sold for cash.

To a large degree, women who declare that they have a right to control their own bodies don't admit that they didn't control them or they wouldn't be pregnant. Instead of dealing with the root of the problem, sin, they punish the fruit of the problem, innocent children, with death. In so doing, those who wanted control don't realize that they are being manipulated and controlled. They are playing into the hands of and acting as agents of Satan's sweep of death; they are Satan's vessels to eliminate and destroy any threat to his throne.

Is it unrealistic to believe that babies and children are a threat to evil forces? God told Jeremiah that He had consecrated him to be a prophet to the nations before he was born (Jeremiah 1:5). Samuel was dedicated to God before he was born and taken to serve God as soon as he was weaned (1 Samuel 1:11, 24-28). Josiah became king of Israel at age eight, and he did what was right in the sight of the Lord (2 Kings 22:1-2). By the age of twelve, Jesus was astonishing the religious community with His knowledge of and authority in Scripture (Luke 2:42-47). David was a youth when he was chosen and anointed as king (1 Samuel 16:11-13). All of these rose to deliver and serve God's people.

Scripture says that a child will be born to us whose name is Wonderful Counselor, Mighty God, Eternal Father, and Prince of Peace (Isaiah 9:6). The Bible also says a child shall lead them (Isaiah 11:6). As once before He sent a Child, so God wishes to send children now. Satan's only option is to destroy them, to slaughter the many in order to kill the few who might rise up and defeat him.

Enforced Slavery

Pertaining to the second part of his diabolical plan, Satan is forcing oppressed saints into slavery. Pharaoh, in days gone by, forced his slaves to build and perpetuate his kingdom. Today, saints in religious bondage are often forced to do those things that promote the religious church system rather than those things that magnify the kingdom of God on earth.

The basis of all bondage is enforced works. A chief characteristic of the religious system is its insistence on works. Even today the battle still rages concerning justification by works or by faith. Those ministries that openly preach salvation by works then try to ensure (to their way of thinking) that their followers will go to heaven by defining what those works should be. They set forth various and seemingly endless rules and regulations and declare that doing them guarantees the workers a place in the presence of God eternally.

Such is folly! These works lead to death, not life. They are service to the erroneous doctrines of people rather than obedience to the Word of God. In effect, they are dead works, evidences of trying to earn salvation rather than evidences of obedience to God after salvation (Ephesians 2:8-10).

Forced Attendance

One of the symptoms of slavery in the religious church system includes endless parades to a church building. Whenever the doors are open, all saints are expected to be in attendance. Once there, an endless beehive of activity awaits. On different nights there are prayer meetings, missionary gatherings, Bible studies, choir practice, board meetings, instruction classes, youth groups, or fellowship dinners. The list goes on. Absent saints are called or visited and "asked" why they were not in attendance. When this system rules, a desire for rest, a planned vacation, a clash of schedules, and even an illness are not acceptable as reasons for not being "in church." Guilt trips and veiled threats abound.

Division

Another mark of the religious system is division. One such division involves gender. Ignoring Galatians 3:28, which states that in God's house there is no spiritual differentiation between male and female, men and women are separated, assigned work, and told what they can or cannot do according to gender: men can preach and teach and fix balky plumbing or leaky roofs, while women can work on bazaars and bake sales and tend to the children. In addition to divisions in gender, there may be further separations concerning age, race, and culture.

Another such division is in the numerous denominations that exist. Each denomination believes that its interpretation of Scripture is the "correct" one and that other denominations are in error. The Church is supposed to be one body serving one God with one guidebook, the Bible. However, over the years the Church has become fractured into many bodies which often vie with each other for prominence on a national level, often steal sheep from each other's flocks on the local level, and often don't realize that unity is the key to overcoming the world.

Dictatorship

A fifth hallmark of a religious church system is dictatorship. God's true Church should have a multitude of leadership. His Word describes the character and the function of elders and deacons (1 Timothy 3) and of the apostles, prophets, evangelists, pastors, and teachers (Ephesians 4:11-13), all of whom are to be leaders in His New Testament Church.

However, bodies locked in the religious system often have one leader who, in effect, rules as a dictator. What he says goes. Even if there are people called elders, deacons, or department heads, they sometimes cannot function under an anointing of God because they are under the thumb of the despot instead.

As the modern version of Pharaoh ordering his slaves to make bricks in order to build his human kingdom but giving them no straw with which to do so, today's dictators order the saints to work, but they give the saints no authority by which to accomplish their demands. Authority, the key ingredient to make and hold God's work together, is concentrated in one person, usually the priest or pastor, and he or she will not willingly relinquish any of it to the minions. By whip cracking and tongue lashing, saints are punished for not doing what they are unable to do.

Death

Many people attend churches that have little or no life, and therefore they find themselves just going through religious motions. In some local churches or more widely known denominations, a dead or dying church is a sign of the false religious system. Those bodies that do not know God are not known by Him; those who do not honor Him are not honored by Him. He will not place His grace and mercy on those who don't preach about the sacrifice of His Son, explain the path to salvation, or walk in the power of the risen Christ. If a body is confused as to who is to be worshipped, who is to lead, and when and how to serve God, the breath of God is not there to keep it alive. Its ultimate fate is death.

THE CAPTIVITY OF THE CHURCH

Those currently hiding behind the false front of religion are fearful that if the number of true saints who discerns the truth grows, the true saints will overthrow these empires of flesh. False leaders are even more fearful to release the saints from their influence because these very saints are needed to finance and, through religious slavery, to preserve the system. Such a system reacts with hostility to true saints who might begin to make waves concerning the truth. Like Pharaoh of old, a false religious system will act quickly, treacherously, and harshly to quell the rumble for salvation and deliverance from evil by its members so its members may be free to go and serve the Lord.

As Israel was in bondage under Pharaoh and as each saint was in slavery to sin under the evil mastery of Satan, so now all must realize that the true Church suffers similar enslavement. Once again, Satan, former taskmaster of each living stone, has usurped and is yet trying to gain unauthorized control over the whole spiritual house of living stones, the true Church. Due to his deep fear and hatred of God, he has captured a large proportion of the Church, used it, exploited it, manipulated it, and held it in captivity. Satan has done so and continues to do so because he knows that if the whole true Church were to awaken from its present slumber, realize its strength in God, and cast off the shackles of bondage it could bind this strongman and could participate in God's victory over him. Satan, wanting to take down as many as possible, cannot allow that to happen.

THE CHURCH'S PASSOVER

The picture of the religious church system is not a pretty one. For years, Protestants have been pointing their fingers at the Roman Catholic Church and declaring all this dysfunction and evil to be its doing. Similarly, evangelicals and Pentecostals have blamed both Catholics and Protestants. Can we not see the truth that no one entity is to blame? Can we not see that **all** churches, denominations, ministries, and ministers who reduce Christianity to a system of slavery instead of amplifying it as a living relationship with God form the false church rather than God's true Church? Can we not see that this counterfeit religious organization is holding a large portion of God's true Church in bondage? Can we not see that in one way or another this evil has infected us all? Can we not admit before holy God that, at one time or another, all of us have been a part of this false church system? Can we not confess that because of ignorance and passivity in allowing it to be so we are all equally guilty of failing God?

If we can, even in the smallest measure, see the reality of this religious system in our community – or worse, if the local church that we are a part of fits the description of this evil system – then we must also see and admit that we, saints of God, are just as much abused and the true Church is just as much enslaved as were the Israelites in Egypt. To some degree, God's true Church is in bondage.

However, saints can abide only so much. It is time for the tide to turn and carry away all this evil. God is the only one who can truly help, and He can already hear the faint sounds of voices crying out for freedom. The petitions of the faithful are bypassing normal, human channels, where they are often stopped or disregarded within the religious church system and are being sent directly to His throne room. Many saints are joining the swelling chorus that is crying out to God for the salvation and deliverance of the true Church from the unholy bondage to religious slavery.

In yet extending His mercy to those of the generation that is being systematically smothered by the demands of religion, deliverance will come. To those of the generation being exploited by modern-day pharaohs, freedom to worship God will arrive.

In the Old Testament, Moses was a type of savior or deliverer. In the New Testament, Jesus is the fulfillment and the zenith of that type. As He saved each saint individually, so also He will save His Church corporately.

God's Word says, *"Truly, truly, I say to you, unless a grain of wheat falls into the earth and dies, it remains alone; but if it dies, it bears much fruit"* (John 12:24). As Jesus is the perfect Savior or Deliverer, so also He is that grain of wheat. After His crucifixion, He fell into the ground and died. While there was only one Seed, it is bearing much fruit.

The fruit is all who are believers, His true Church. In Jesus' name, an army of deliverers, the children of the Seed, saved from death, raised up, trained, and anointed, is going forth to save and deliver by His power. Even now, a vanguard of their number is walking through the land whispering truth to ears willing to hear. They will bring the true Church out from the counterfeit religious church system and bring in the harvest of the unsaved.

One person cannot do this job alone, and one person alone is not supposed to do it. Nor should one ministry or one denomination presume to try alone.

These warriors will manifest the presence, promise, and power of God. Like the burning bush, the true Church has been burning. It has burned through fiery trials, yet it has not been and will not be consumed. The presence of God is sustaining it. As God in former days first worked with His people by testing and tempering them through fire so they would call out to Him and then by raising up leaders for them, so now He is doing the same in the true Church. Like Moses, many of the chosen leaders have been raised within the counterfeit church system so they know it inside and out, have walked its corridors of power, have understood its language and customs, and then have chosen to reject its magnificent, enticing courts in favor of serving the true God in His true Church. Since they have chosen God over man, spirit over flesh, life over death, God will increasingly reveal His presence to them.

As God once displayed His might in releasing from Egypt all those He called His own, so also He is able to release from the world and from the false religious system the saints of His true Church, those who are His chosen generation, His royal priesthood, and His holy nation. He was Almighty God in Egypt, He was Almighty God in Rome, and He is Almighty God now. He is willing – eager – to employ His sovereign power on behalf of His beloved ones, His called out ones, His treasured ones.

With His presence, promise, and power, God's deliverers will appear among His chosen. Saints and the true Church will see and believe. They will loudly call out for help. The call for freedom and for the release of the saints won't immediately free the oppressed. In fact, it may first lead to an increase in harshness and cruelty by the oppressors. The Church body will be commanded to build with no straw for bricks; they will be told to deny the name, the blood, and the cross of Christ; they will be told to preach and teach the Word but not to tell the truth; they will be ordered to sing joyful songs to their captors.

In the midst of their torment, God will arise. He will give marching orders to His army. "Go to Pharaoh," He will say to them, "and command him, 'Let God's people go!'"

Feeling the safely of position and power, Satan and his religious system will defiantly scream back, "No!"

A showdown is both inevitable and shortly forthcoming.

At the very time when things look bleakest, God will move. With the power of His right hand, He will bring His judgment on the system that has so dishonored Him. He will judge its leaders and all who blindly follow their orders to be hostile to those He dearly loves. As 1 Peter 4:17 states, *"For it is time for judgment to begin with the household of God...."*

However He chooses to move, in a manifestation of the total victory won over Satan at the cross, Jesus will challenge every evil power and best it. He will break all satanic power over the Church, ransom and redeem the saint-slaves, and secure their release. Then the long-awaited call will ring out to deliverers and delivered alike: "Go! Go and serve your God!"

PART II:

THE EXODUS

PART II
THE EXODUS

Chapter 4

THE EXODUS:

THE ISRAELITES' SALVATION FROM EGYPT

To personalize the message of the Israelites' journey and to understand how to relate to it both as individuals and as the corporate Church, it must be remembered that biblical people, places, and circumstances are often symbols or types. They are shadows, events happening in other times and to other people that tell the same tale today.

To recall, Egypt equates with sin. The land of Egypt represents the land of sin, the vast world where iniquity reigns supreme. Egypt's king, Pharaoh, is a type of Satan. The Egyptian overseers or taskmasters are the demonic forces operating at his command which extend and govern his kingdom of darkness. Knowing they will feel the stings of the whips of satanic wrath on their own backs if they let any who are unsaved escape the bondage of darkness, demons are merciless in enforcing satanic dominion. Finally, in his role as the savior and deliverer of an oppressed people, Moses is a type of Jesus Christ.

MOSES WAS REJECTED AND SCORNED

It is easy to believe that a beleaguered people would instantly welcome and cooperate with the one whom God designated as their savior from slavery and their deliverer from bondage. Unfortunately, this was not the case.

When Moses approached Pharaoh requesting that he let the Hebrews go in order to worship their God, Pharaoh flatly refused. Further, he made life more miserable for the people by no longer furnishing straw to make bricks while at the same time demanding the Hebrews continue to produce the same quota of bricks (Exodus 5:3-8). This extra hardship caused the people to lose heart. They rejected Moses and accused him of causing their deaths (Exodus 5:21). Further, when Moses told the people about how God was going to deliver them from their captivity, they did not listen to him (Exodus 6:2-9).

Yet, Scripture says that weeping may last for the night but joy comes in the morning (Psalm 30:5). And so it was for the Hebrews. After a long, dark night of slavery and oppression, judgment fell on the Egyptians. Speaking to Moses, the Lord promised,

> "I have heard the groaning of the Israelites, because the Egyptians are holding them in bondage, and I have remembered My covenant. Say, therefore, to the Israelites, 'I am the LORD, and I will bring you out from under the burdens of the Egyptians, and I will deliver you from their bondage. I will also redeem you with an outstretched arm and with great judgments. Then I will take you for My people, and I will be your God; and you shall know that I am the LORD your God, who brought you out from under the burdens of the Egyptians. I will bring you to the land which I swore to give to Abraham, Isaac, and Jacob, and I will give it you for a possession. I am the LORD.'" (Exodus 6:5-8)

SALVATION

With faith in these promises, Moses undertook his role as deliverer of the Hebrews. Nine times he approached Pharaoh. Nine times he demanded that Pharaoh let God's people go or be released from Egypt in order to worship the one true God. Nine times Pharaoh refused. This unholy rebellion unleashed a ferocious series of plagues that devastated the land and people of Egypt.

Moses gave instructions to the Hebrews so they would be prepared for God's mighty display of power on their behalf. On the tenth day of the month of Nissan, each household was to obtain an unblemished lamb. On the fourteenth day of the month, at twilight, that lamb was to be slain. Some of the blood from the lamb was to be put on the doorposts and lintel of the house. Then the Israelites were to roast the lamb and eat it with unleavened bread and bitter herbs. Further, they were to do this with their loins girded, their sandals on their feet, and their staffs in their hands (Exodus 12:1-13).

After Moses once again approached Pharaoh with the demand

that he release the Hebrews so they could worship God and after Pharaoh once again refused, judgment fell. At midnight, the tenth and final plague began. The Lord sent an angel of death over the land. The angel of death passed over every house marked with the blood of the lamb on its doorposts and lintel. No death struck there. However, any house without the covering blood of the lamb was not passed over. Death struck the firstborn of man and beast throughout the land of Egypt. This began the Feast of Passover that the Israelites are commanded to commemorate to this very day.

When God had ordered the Israelites to eat the Passover meal with their loins girded, sandals on their feet, and staffs in hand, they knew exactly what that meant. These instructions were signs of a coming journey, a preparation for movement. God honored His order. Throughout the ensuing hours, the continual screams and wailing of the bereaved arose. Yet even as God was judging the Egyptians, He was blessing His people. As a result of this divine and supernatural action, Pharaoh summoned Moses and commanded that God's people rise up and go. In the face of awesome power and terrible tragedy, Pharaoh released the Israelites to go and worship their God. Pharaoh's power over them was broken. The bondage and slavery suffered in Egypt was over. While the Egyptians wept, the Israelites broke forth into joy. By morning, the people of Israel were on their way to freedom.

Fearful of what might happen next if the Israelites remained, the people of Egypt also urged the Israelites to depart without delay. Having been made ready, when the order came the Hebrews grabbed their bowls of unleavened dough; plundered Egypt of articles of silver, gold, and clothing (Exodus 12:36); and took their first steps toward freedom.

The journey the Israelites embarked upon is now known as the exodus. According to *Funk and Wagnalls Standard Dictionary*, an exodus is a going out from; it is a leave taking or a departure; it is a separation. It can involve a single person or a multitude. In this case, the Israelites' exodus was the departure of the whole nation of God from the land of Egypt. It was not only the physical separation of a people from the land of their torment, but it was also the spiritual separation or consecration. It was a setting aside of the chosen people of God from the world. It was a leave taking or exodus from slavery to freedom.

God's power had broken Pharaoh's (Satan's) power. God's plagues were judgments on the false gods of Egypt. Altogether, they destroyed the chains that bound the Hebrews to Egypt. The Hebrews, upon realizing that their release had been made available, acted. They quickly embarked on the path to liberty, putting as much distance as possible between themselves and their captors.

Leaving Rameses, they began their three-day journey. Six hundred thousand men along with women, children, flocks, herds, and livestock marched to Succoth (Exodus 12:37-38). It has been estimated by *The Interactive Bible* that in all, two to three million people were brought out of Egypt by the mighty hand of God.

The Feast Of Unleavened Bread

In the midst of the exodus, the Lord spoke to Moses. He told Moses that He was instituting a second part of the Feast of Passover, a celebration to be known as the Feast of Unleavened Bread. This was not to be a further commemoration of Passover, of God breaking the power of Pharaoh and his bondage over the Hebrews. Instead, it was to be the remembrance of the day God brought His children, the Israelites, out of Egypt. This feast, celebrating the exodus or the departure from slavery, was to be kept with unleavened bread as a reminder of the Hebrews' hurried leave taking from Egypt. Lasting one day in the midst of the seven days that mark the entire Feast of Passover, the Feast of Unleavened Bread was also to be observed throughout the generations (Exodus 12:14-20).

The Lord further declared to Moses that all the firstborn of the males of Israel, both children and livestock, were to be sanctified, or set apart unto God (Exodus 13:1-2). The sons could be redeemed with a lamb (Exodus 13:13). As the firstborn of man and beast in Egypt had paid the price of transgression among an evil people, so now God was claiming the firstborn of His chosen people. In no uncertain terms, they were to be His possession, not the people's.

The Presence Of God

Another awesome sight now met the eyes of a fleeing people. In grand display of His sovereignty, love, and power, the LORD Himself visibly joined His people on their march to freedom. Appearing as a pillar of cloud by day and a pillar of fire by night (Exodus 13:21-22), He joined the throng so His people might travel continuously. Wanting to deliver and separate those He had already saved, He led their way to the Red Sea.

Pursuit By The Enemy

Even as God's people hurried to the border of Egypt to be free of the land of oppression, God had some unfinished business with Pharaoh. God had freed and delivered His people so they would know He was LORD and would serve and worship Him (Exodus 12:31). In addition to the Israelites knowing that, God was determined that Egypt would know He was LORD too (Exodus 14:6).

Purposefully, the LORD led His people to a dangerous and vulnerable spot. After three days of marching, He brought them to Pi-hahiroth and had them camp by the Red Sea (Exodus 14:2). Viewing the Israelites as tattered, weakened, ignorant slaves who couldn't withstand him and believing their chance of escape was blocked by the sea, Pharaoh once again rose up against God's chosen. With renewed hardness in his heart, Pharaoh prepared to attack the Israelites with a vengeance. Motivated by the fact that he needed the slaves he had released (Exodus 14:5), by the desire for revenge for the death of his firstborn son, and by his sense of humiliation, he selected hundreds of chariots, horses, charioteers, and their officers (Exodus 14:7) and pursued the Israelites. Foaming with diabolic fury, Pharaoh once more charged after them, determined to annihilate them.

When the Israelites, who had been boldly departing Egypt, became aware of the situation, they grew afraid. With an army on one side and the sea on the other, their newfound boldness turned to terror. Quickly forgetting the glories of God in their immediate past, they faced an unknown present. As bad as things had been in Egypt, they now looked good when faced with what seemed like certain death. To a wavering people at the edge of freedom on the border of Egypt, giving up, surrendering, placating Pharaoh, and resubmitting to slavery seemed safer and preferable to trusting God and continuing. As long as the fear of man was more real and more pressing than the fear of God, the future looked hopeless.

So, the panicking people called out:

"Is it because there were no graves in Egypt that you have taken us away to die in the wilderness? Why have you dealt with us in this way, bringing us out of Egypt? Is this not the word that we spoke to you in Egypt, saying, 'Leave us alone that we may serve the Egyptians'? For it would have been better for us to serve the Egyptians than to die in the wilderness." (Exodus 14:11-12)

While the Hebrews had failed the test, God had not. Standing true to His people and His promise, He spoke through Moses: *"Do not fear! Stand by and see the salvation of the LORD which He will accomplish for you today; for the Egyptians whom you have seen today, you will never see them again forever. The LORD will fight for you while you keep silent"* (Exodus 14:13-14).

Earlier, in breaking Pharaoh's power, all the Israelites had to do was seek God. Now too, in separating from this evil by their exodus, the Israelites' only requirement was to seek God. If the Israelites would stop their fearful complaining and would rely on Him, He would do all that needed doing. If the Israelites would obey Him, He would free them. They would see the salvation that He, not they, would accomplish.

In the process, they would see death. It would not be the deaths of the oppressed Israelites as Pharaoh had planned; instead, it would be the death of the oppressors, the Egyptians. No matter how much satanic power Pharaoh mounted against the Israelites, he could not match or overcome God's power.

The exodus could not be stopped! The Hebrews were free!

Chapter 5

THE EXODUS:

EACH SAINT'S SALVATION FROM SIN

Anyone who has not had a personal born-again experience finds himself (or herself) in the same situation as did the Hebrews. Each is in utter bondage and slavery to sin; each knows in his heart that although some of the things he is doing are wrong and are against the heart, nature, character, and principles of God, he cannot seem to stop doing them. Further, since each is under the rule or authority of Satan, a merciless tyrant, each is separated from God. If anyone dies in this condition without passing over from sin to salvation, he will spend eternity in hell rather than in heaven in the presence of his Savior.

However, it was never God's plan to leave His beloved creatures in this desperate state. Before the foundation of the world, He had a plan of reconciliation. Hundreds of years after God visited His people with salvation and deliverance from the evil power that bound them in Egypt, He again looked on His people, the Israelites, and found them in bondage. This time the tyrant was not the Egyptian but the Roman Empire.

THE PRESENCE OF GOD

History was repeating itself. Fearful that the descendants of Israel might grow too numerous and rise up against her, imperial Rome, in an attempt to allay any perceived threat, reduced God's people to slavery. In so doing, the Israelites again became laborers, this time building Roman roads and palaces. Again a downtrodden people began to cry out to God. They knew from their Scriptures that a Messiah had been promised to them, and they earnestly began to call out to God to send Him.

Herod, the Roman-appointed king, also knew that a leader would be born to this people, a King who might rise up and release them from his sovereignty. In order to prevent that from happening, Herod, much like his satanic predecessor, Pharaoh ordered the slaughter of male children of Israel (Matthew 2:16).

As before, God's holy plan could not be thwarted by Satan's evil one. Jesus, the King of the Jews and the Ruler of all nations, was born in a manger in Bethlehem, which fulfilled the prophecy of Micah 5:2: *"But as for you, Bethlehem Ephrathah, too little to be among the clans of Judah, from you One will go forth for Me to be ruler in Israel."* Jesus' parents then took Him to Egypt, which was once again playing the role of a land of refuge for a few years. This fulfilled the prophetic word of Hosea 11:1: *"When Israel was a youth I loved him, and out of Egypt I called My son."*

Just as God had appeared in a burning bush to show Moses His presence, centuries later Jesus appeared among the vine that had come out of Egypt, the Jewish people (Psalm 80:8). He let the warmth, heat, and fire of His presence be manifested among His people. In various ways, He let them know He was God, the only God, and, in particular, their own God. Jesus, the exact representation of His nature (Hebrews 1:3), was God's presence among them; He was called Immanuel, God with us (Matthew 1:23).

Jesus was the fulfillment of the type of Moses, who was God's vessel of deliverance for the Hebrews in Egypt. However, Jesus had a two-fold problem: He was rejected as Messiah by the religious establishment and scorned as King by the civil government.

Jesus Was Rejected And Scorned

While the religious leaders professed to serve God, they did not recognize Jesus as their Messiah. Since only members of the tribe of Levi could be priests and since Jesus was from the tribe of Judah, they denied Him and defied Him. Further, when He challenged their authority, they tried to destroy Him (Matthew 12:14). They were so besotted with their power and enamored of their prestige (Matthew 23:5-7) that they had long since forgotten that they were to serve people in their approach to God rather than to serve themselves. Steeped in tradition and humanism, these religious leaders were looking for a strong political leader who would guide them out of their physical bondage to Rome.

Since Jesus did not meet their religious or political requirements and since He threatened their place, their prominence, and their self-gained glory, they wouldn't listen to Him, acknowledge Him, submit to Him, or worship Him. Instead, they plotted to kill him.

The civil community also challenged Him. Imperial Rome did not tolerate any threat to its authority. It enslaved its people in an evil system and forced them to travail in endless works of flesh in order to maintain its grip of power. Herod, its puppet ruler in Judea, was understandably troubled at the thought of a new King being born (Matthew 2:3). To prevent any challenge to his authority, he unsuccessfully attempted to kill the infant Jesus (Matthew 2:16). Once Jesus was grown and began His public ministry, one of His first acts was to introduce the kingdom of God (Matthew 3:2). Not understanding that this kingdom was not of this world (John 18:36-37), the Romans viewed it as a potential threat to their power. When Jesus was interrogated by Pilate and was identified as the King of the kingdom of God, Pilate had Jesus brutalized and crucified.

Bypassing the rejection of the religious system and the antagonism of civil leadership, Jesus appeared among the people. These people, in ever increasing agony, sought Him out, called on Him, and received Him. Allowing their suffering to continue only until they had learned that they had no one else to turn to but God, He, in faithfulness and mercy, answered their pleas.

The Promise And Power Of Jesus

As God had given the Israelites' ancestors a promise of freedom or of deliverance from their slavery, so now this first-century people received a promise that their salvation was at hand (Matthew 4:17). All who believed on the King of the kingdom would be saved (Romans 10:8-12). Previously, God had outworked His promise to the Israelites through His servant, Moses, but this time God was outworking His promise through Jesus, His Son and their Savior.

Along with God's presence and promise came God's power. His authority was in the word He spoke and in the signs, wonders, and miracles that accompanied and empowered that word. One of the ways God showed His authority over Pharaoh was to turn Moses' rod into a snake and then to have that snake swallow the snakes created by Pharaoh's court magicians. Hundreds of years later, God similarly displayed Jesus' authority over Satan when Jesus' rod of authority, His cross, swallowed him, the serpent. By that same cross, God showed that Jesus' blood would flow, and through the power of Jesus' blood His people would be given needed healing, refreshing, cleansing, and salvation.

In the face of religious and civil opposition, Jesus spoke His word and showed His wonders both to the people He had called and to the leaders He had raised up among those people. He revealed Himself to His own apostles and disciples. They looked on Him and believed (Mark 8:29).

As before, God moved on behalf of His people. In spite of those who challenged Him with their puny power, He brought deliverance to an enslaved people. On the very day that the religious system was legalistically celebrating the Feast of Passover by slaying innocent lambs as their offering for sin, Jesus, the sinless Lamb of God, became *the* sin sacrifice. On Him was laid all the sin of all mankind. The full sum of the transgression, the iniquity, and the wickedness of every man, woman, and child who had ever lived, was then living, or ever would live was placed on Him. As a result of the sin found on Him, He was sentenced to death (Romans 6:23). He was crucified under that appalling load of evil He had not committed but for which He lovingly paid the price.

In a court of law, when someone is found guilty of a crime, he (or she) must pay a penalty. When he receives a sentence, the requirements of that sentence must be fulfilled. In this case, although mankind had committed the crime (sinned) and was given a sentence for that crime (death), the penalty fell on Jesus. As mankind's Substitute, the sum or total of the punishment for all the crimes of the whole human race was required of and paid for by Him. Since the wages of sin is death, He suffered untold horrors and pain when He was crucified and anguish when He was separated from His beloved Father in order to serve mankind's sentence. Although we deserved it, Jesus died in our place.

However, death couldn't hold Him. Defeating the accumulated power, might, and hatred of Satan, Jesus came alive again by the power of the Holy Spirit, and He rose from the dead. Thus, in suffering, dying, and then living again, He had come against both the power of sin over men and women and the authority of the master of all sin, Satan, and defeated them resoundingly. Jesus vanquished the evil nature in mankind that induced us towards sin and conquered the one who compelled us to do it.

Jesus Defeated The Power Of Sin And Satan

In taking the sins of humanity on Himself and dealing with them for us, Jesus freed us from them. He purchased the salvation and deliverance of all mankind through His own blood. Through His sacrifice, He secured the release of His beloved people from their enforced slavery to sin in Satan's kingdom of darkness. In addition, since He fully paid our penalty for sin, He removed all accusation of guilt against us. Thus, Jesus made provision for the ransom and redemption of all who would call on His name. As a result of this magnificent victory, He broke the power of sin.

Like Pharaoh before him, Satan has a plan for the enslaved. The wisdom for this plan did not come from God above but is entirely demonic (James 3:15). Also, like Pharaoh before him, Satan desires the extinction of his subjects. His aim is to bring about peoples' deaths while they are in sin so they are eternally lost or everlastingly separated from God.

Satan treats his subjects cruelly, forcing them to do things they do not want to do. He uses them as channels of his evil while subjugating them to the basest position. He rules ruthlessly, commanding the harshest labor in order to increase his domain. In so doing, he locks all who are unsaved into the age-old battle of works versus faith: works that will perpetuate his slavery versus faith in God to free us from it.

Therefore, when Satan feels threatened, when he has a glimmer that one of his slaves desires freedom, when he realizes that God is about to free one of his slaves, he often increases the pressure, the suffering, and the misery of the tormented one. As Pharaoh did to the Israelites with the bricks and straw, he multiplies his demands even while ensuring that there is no way to fulfill them. The tormented one finds himself (or herself) a part of the performance of dead works by dead men and women to perpetuate a kingdom of darkness, a system of death.

While all of this may make seeking a way out of slavery to sin impossible, let it be known that two thousand years ago, Jesus conquered Satan at the cross. Satan is a defeated foe and Jesus can and does overcome all of his attempts to deny anyone salvation.

Jesus Has Authority Over Sin

Until Jesus' total defeat of him, Satan, a master sinner, had ruled the kingdom of darkness where men and women were enslaved to sin. In overcoming Satan, Jesus defeated him as the overlord of sinners and unbelievers. In so doing, Jesus allowed all who chose to do so to change both kingdoms and masters. With a born-again experience, they could escape their dark Egypt, enter the kingdom of light, and serve a different Lord.

The good news of the kingdom and of salvation through its King is both historical and biblical fact. Time after time we have heard these stories and pondered them. Perhaps in our meditation, God so moved in our hearts that we could see the truth: the Israelites were not alone in their trouble; the Israelites were not the only ones to find themselves in slavery to darkness and evil. Perhaps it is now our heart's cry to know if these objective facts about deliverance from sin for others could become subjective reality for us, to know if the story of salvation could apply to us personally, to know if we too can be free, to know if the journey from slavery in sin and Satan can be the beginning of our own journey to freedom and to God.

Psalm 106:7 declares the Israelites did not understand all of God's wonders or the things He did for them. Today, those who are spiritually enslaved in Egypt cannot know them either, for the things of God are foolishness to those who are perishing (1 Corinthians 1:18). Yet lack of comprehension should in no way lead to the underestimation of God. Pharaoh stretched to the limit of his power to prevent God from acting for His people. However, all that Pharaoh did was not even a challenge to God. God already knew what He was going to do, and no one and nothing could stop Him from doing it. From that, we can learn that as He did before, He can and will do today all that is necessary to free His beloved ones.

Any who are still held in bondage to sin in the world are those beloved (John 3:16). If you are one of them, as He prepared the Hebrew children in Egypt for their moment of departure, so also He has been preparing you. Gird up your loins, grab your staff, and get ready to go! And you can get there – saved, forgiven, and in right relationship with God – from here.

SALVATION

No one is born righteous. We are all born in sin. The way out of sin is not through a declaration of self-righteousness, such as "I'm a good person," but through the blood of the Lamb. Further, although we may attend the church that our family has attended for years or generations, our presence in a building or our participation in the rituals of a particular denomination doesn't count for anything as far as our salvation is concerned. In spite of family tradition or label, we are born sinners and we remain sinners until we call out to God for freedom.

One important question that everyone should ask themselves is: "Who is my pharaoh?" If you haven't asked Jesus to free you from sin, then Satan is your pharaoh. However, for those who have been reborn through the blood of Jesus but who are living less than victorious lives because someone or something is trying to control or enslave them, there may be another answer. Some possibilities to consider are: your spouse, parent, child, friend, past, job, unethical boss, illness, church denomination, or church leader.

For all who acknowledge their slavery to sin, who realize how far their hearts are from God, and who are longing for a closer relationship with God, the love of God is calling. As He once promised the Hebrews, so now He promises all who will come:

> "I am the LORD, and I will bring you out from under the burdens of the Egyptians, and I will deliver you from their bondage. I will also redeem you with an outstretched arm and with great judgments. I will take you for My people, and I will be your God, and you shall know that I am the LORD your God, who brought you out from under the burdens of the Egyptians. I will bring you to the land which I swore to give to Abraham, Isaac, and Jacob, and I will give it to you for a possession; I am the LORD."

(Exodus 6:6-8)

All who believe that Jesus is the Lord, that He will free them from the world, and that He will deliver them from the bondage of sin can be free of sin. All who choose to become God's son or daughter and who want Him to be their God can be redeemed by His great power even while the hand of judgment falls on the enemy of their souls. In order for any person to secure forgiveness from sin and release from the bondage of sin for his or her own personal Passover, there is a path to follow, a journey to take.

Each person who follows the path of salvation must realize that he (or she) can only follow that path for himself. He cannot save others. He can intercede for them, but he cannot force them to travel down the path or to be saved. All of his well-meaning works cannot save one spouse, parent, child, sibling, friend, neighbor, or co-worker. Each must individually realize his fallen position, individually call out to God, and individually respond to Him in faith.

Cry Out

For those who desire salvation, the first steps of the journey involve calling out to God like the Hebrews once did. Each individual must personally accept full responsibility for being where he (or she) is. Each must recognize and acknowledge that he is in a place he was not meant to be in and then must declare that he wants to be free. Each must tell God of the desire to be released from sin and the world system that promotes that sin. Further, each must declare, like Jacob once did, that he does not want to be buried in Egypt (Genesis 47:29). Without question, God will hear those cries.

One of the most diabolical lies of Satan says that we must be in a certain place or reach a certain degree of righteousness or holiness before God will deal with us. Without God there is no righteousness or holiness no matter what self-effort we engage in or what good works we involve ourselves in to try to achieve it. The truth is that God meets us just as we are and just where we are. His requirement for salvation is for us to call out, not to move about. God met the Israelites in the slime pits and fleshpots of Egypt. Can our condition be any worse? If He met them there, He will meet us there too.

Acknowledge Helplessness

Then, to be released from spiritual bondage, each must acknowledge the helplessness of his (or her) situation. He must see that he is in an awful plight and that he is totally unable to help himself. He must admit that he is in a situation from which no amount of self-effort or good works will release him. He must concede, as have all those who have walked in the way of the world, that Jesus is the Way out of the world (John 14:6).

Repent

While alive, the option to be forgiven of sin is presented to each human being. After death, there are no more opportunities to choose. For those who die in their sin, their journey has ended. They will be held in hell until the day of judgment and then will be cast into the lake of fire for all eternity (Revelation 20:15). Holding places, such as limbo or purgatory, which different denominations and religions claim to be way stations for the further sorting out of our eternal state, simply do not exist. Nowhere does the Bible mention such places. Death while unsaved and in sin is the eternal loss of being in the presence of Jesus in heaven; it is eternal residence in the lake of fire; it is a permanent, unalterable state, the result of one's own choice to stay in Egypt. There are no exceptions.

Due to the final nature of death, each person must repent while he (or she) has the opportunity. He does this by changing his mind about his behavior and then by determining to change the behavior itself. He must make an act of will to turn from the path of sin he's been following and to go another way.

Believe That Jesus Is The Lord Of Salvation

As part of the spiritual journey, each individual must agree that Jesus is his (or her) Savior (Matthew 1:21). He must believe that Jesus is the personal presence of God, that Jesus is near him in times of trouble, that Jesus is his only promise of salvation. He must believe that Jesus is God's power manifest and that His miracles on his behalf are his guideposts to freedom.

Prepare Your Heart

When all has been made ready for his (or her) deliverance, each seeker must spiritually anoint the doorposts and lintel of his heart with the blood of the Lamb by asking that the blood of Jesus cover him so the judgment of death will pass over him. He must acknowledge that, by God's provision, his own sins were placed on Jesus and that Jesus, as his substitutionary, sacrificial sin offering, shed His blood and personally died for him. He must believe that in Jesus both the power of sin and the mastery of Satan over his life can be broken.

Confess Sin

When all is ready, each confesses that he (or she) is a sinner to Jesus, the only One who can save him and deliver him from his sin. *Funk and Wagnalls Standard Dictionary* reveals that to confess is to acknowledge a fault; it is to admit or make known one's sins. Biblically, to confess is to agree with God that His mark has been missed and His standard has been compromised. Thus, when any person seeks salvation through forgiveness of sin and deliverance from the power of Satan, he must confess that his inherited sin and his personal sin have separated him from God. He must agree with God that sin has been committed.

Receive His Forgiveness

Then each needs to ask for, receive, and, in an act of faith, thank Him for His forgiveness. At this point, some people may not feel forgiven. They may think that nothing has happened. However, forgiveness is not a feeling. It is an incontrovertible fact once sin has been confessed and forgiveness has been asked for. Others may think they are not worthy to be forgiven. However, personal worthiness is not the question here. It is the worthiness of Jesus Christ, who appears before God the Father to declare that His blood has cleansed us from sin and who makes us worthy in Him, that counts.

Believe

The last step of the journey of salvation is that each must believe that no one and nothing can withstand the power of God. He (or she) must have faith that God will use His unmatchable power to bring him out of Egypt. As soon as a new saint calls, He will act. God will do all that needs doing to open the doors of His saint's freedom. He who planned the miracles that accomplished the release of a whole nation knows each person's personal needs, the forces that hold him, and how to break that power and secure his personal release.

Enjoy Your Passover And The Feast Of Unleavened Bread

Each saint is not required to slavishly perform the rituals associated with Old Testament worship. Yet, while he (or she) is free of the legal requirements of the law, he must yet honor and keep the principles of God.

As the Israelites were commanded to keep Passover, a celebration honoring God for breaking the power of Pharaoh, in every generation, so too, those who wish to be children of God must commemorate a spiritual Passover. Each must acknowledge and participate in the breaking of Satan's power over him (or her) and the ransoming and redeeming of his soul through the blood of the Lamb. He does so by being born again, by having spiritual rebirth.

Additionally, the Hebrews were commanded to keep the Feast of Unleavened Bread, a commemoration of God's ability to bring the Hebrews out of Egypt and to deliver them from the slavery of sin. So too, each new Christian is to acknowledge with a deeply grateful heart that God has brought him (or her) out of sin and released him from enforced slavery to sin.

IMMEDIATE RESULTS OF SALVATION

When someone receives salvation through the blood of Jesus, he (or she) is no longer a sinner but a saint. Therefore, he continues his spiritual journey as a saint.

Sanctification

When God broke the power of Pharaoh over the Israelites, it was not a singular act; rather, it was the first of many miracles by which He led His people into full freedom. As the Israelites' Passover was a type of salvation through the blood of the Lamb, so the Feast of Unleavened Bread is a type of separation from sin.

Immediately after their release from Pharaoh, God commanded the Hebrews to walk out of Egypt. They were to do so while carrying baskets of unleavened bread (Exodus 12:33-34). In the Old Covenant, leaven was equated with sin. Therefore, for the Israelites to walk with unleavened bread meant they were to walk without sin. As God's people begin their exodus from the land of their bondage, they were visibly accompanied by the presence of God.

Similarly, once free from the dominion of Satan, the presence of God indwells each saint, and he (or she) is called to depart from sin, as led by the Holy Spirit. He is not to delay or tarry but to move immediately into sanctification or consecration. No saint is saved and then allowed to camp in the world. God has no intention for any new saint to stay in or near the place of his (or her) worldly sorrows. He knows that certain people, places, things, habits, or attitudes that once ensnared the saint will do so again unless he is separated from them. In his weakened condition, having been freed from the power of slavery to sin but yet in too close proximity to it, he is in no position to attack, fight, or defeat such a deeply entrenched enemy. After salvation, there can be no pause. The new saint must continue on his journey away from the snare of sin.

God desires that each reborn saint leave his (or her) sinful past behind him and learn to walk without the sin that beset him before his salvation. Therefore, with no delay, regret, or looking back, each saint is called to put a distance between himself and sin. As the Israelites were commanded to leave Egypt, so each new saint is commanded to separate from his past, to depart from or to leave behind familiar, habitual sin. Not carrying the burden of sin with him, each is to march forth on his personal exodus, severing the ties that bind. Each must turn his back on sin and step out, leaving old ways behind. Boldly and confidently, each can walk away from his past and toward his future. This process of cleaning up his act is called sanctification. This is a gift that is both instantaneous and that lasts throughout his whole Christian walk.

Consecration Into The Priesthood

When free of Egypt and en route to the promised land, God also reminds each saint of His requirement concerning the consecration of the Israelites' firstborn sons (Exodus 13:2). Under the Old Covenant, the firstborn sons were to be God's. Later, He revealed that these sons were to be a kingdom of priests and a holy nation to Him (Exodus 19:6). From all the tribes of Israel, God claimed the tribe of Levi (Numbers 3:12). The Levites thus became the priestly tribe of the Old Covenant, serving Him in the tabernacle and temple.

Today, under the New Covenant, the Levitical priesthood has been done away with. God's Word declares that *all* the redeemed are His priesthood (1 Peter 2:9). It is not just one special race, tribe, people, denomination, or religious organization that is set apart for the service of God but all who have been born again. It is no longer just males who are sanctified but all saints. It is not just certain individuals who are to be consecrated unto Him but all those making the journey out of Egypt. In such a way, God is emphasizing that all His called and chosen ones have been ransomed and redeemed from sin, so all may worship Him. Through spiritual rebirth, each chosen one is His adopted son or daughter, each child of God is a saint, each saint is a priest, and each priest is a minister who offers the sacrifices of brokenness, thanksgiving, and worship unto Him.

The Indwelling Of The Holy Spirit

Even while each saint hurries away from the sin that held him (or her), God provides him with His presence. A saint's journey is never void of His presence or of the manifestation of His love and power. He accompanied the fleeing Hebrews by fire and by cloud in order to travel with them, to lead them, and to guide them. Both of these, fire and cloud, are symbols of God's Holy Spirit (Acts 2:3-4; Luke 9:34-35). When saints are reborn, God sends His Spirit to indwell them (Romans 8:11). As their Helper (John 14:16), the Spirit leads and guides them.

Pursuit By The Enemy

As the Israelites ended their Passover and celebrated the Feast of Unleavened Bread at the beginning of their three-day journey into the wilderness, a problem arose. Pharaoh had a change of heart and began to pursue them (Exodus 14:5-9). With this as a pattern, each new saint must realize that both before and after his salvation, he or (she) will be pursued by his past.

As the Hebrews' first days of freedom were exceptional in their walk with God, so too, the first few days after salvation are a critical time in a new saint's life. Often, his (or her) physical senses cannot ascertain God's spiritual victory, and he may doubt his deliverance. His mental faculties cannot understand or prove his salvation, so he is tempted into unbelief. When that happens, he is approaching a showdown with the enemy.

As surely as Pharaoh rose up and pursued the Israelites, so Satan pursues each new saint. Realizing he has lost a laborer for his kingdom, he doggedly charges after each one to draw him (or her) back under his control. Breathing fire, Satan attacks a new saint in the areas he is most vulnerable, tempting him to reenter familiar areas of sin. Satan tries to convince a new saint to have one more drink for old times' sake, one last indulgence in drugs, or one more fling with unholy sex. He sends family members to mock and accuse the saint of "becoming religious." He sends old friends to judge and condemn the saint's walk if it is no longer the same as theirs. Satan does all he can to pull the saint, either by deceit or by threat, back into his stinking pit. If the evil one can succeed in his enticements and can goad a newborn saint to return voluntarily to sin, he can reestablish his now illegal influence over him once again.

While Satan is taunting a new saint, God is testing him (or her). When a saint was born again, he had to learn that he could not save himself but had to cry out to God for forgiveness. Now, a newborn saint must also realize that he cannot separate himself from sin or make himself holy. Instead of walking in his own strength, he again must call out to God for help. When God responds and begins to lead him, he must follow. He must trust God to arrange and do whatever is necessary in order to destroy the enemy. Instead of fearing or fleeing the test or giving in to the enemy, the saint must let God be God.

Coming To The Place Of Decision

As the Israelites seemed trapped on the shores of the Red Sea while the troops of Pharaoh were closing in on them, so it will be that, soon after salvation, each saint will come to a hard place. Seemingly trapped with the enemy in hot pursuit, each may begin to waver. Each may find himself (or herself) disgusted with the past but afraid of the present and future. To some, as bad as the past was, it may seem preferable to the unknown or to the apparently insurmountable changes required.

When all seems utterly hopeless, when all appears lost, when it seems that disaster is imminent, when no human aid can extricate the saint from the situation he (or she) faces, when he has escaped the power of sin but is being furiously pursued by the hosts of Satan, he has reached the place of decision. He is right where God wants him; he is at the very place to which God has led him.

Although the enemy's power is broken, he will do all he can to make a new saint doubt that. He will throw all he has at him (or her), pressuring him in every way, harassing, deceiving, manipulating, and intimidating him to make him think he is still under the power of the evil one.

In spite of all of this, no matter how things look or feel, every Christian must believe God and call out to Him for help. He (or she) must know that Satan is a defeated foe who can no longer rule or enslave them. He must believe in God, and when He says "Go!" he must step out, leaving sin and Satan behind him. Pharaoh and his troops could not stop the Israelites. Similarly, Satan and his demonic hordes cannot stop the saints of God. As long as they trust in God, their exodus will lead them to safety and separation.

Chapter 6

THE EXODUS:

THE CHURCH'S SALVATION FROM THE FALSE CHURCH SYSTEM

As the Israelites were corporately saved by the blood of the lamb and commanded to flee from Egypt and as each saint is individually saved by the blood of the Lamb and told to separate from the world, so too God's Church has been corporately saved by the blood of the Lamb and is corporately being called to separate or make an exodus from the false religious system in order to worship and serve the one true God.

Sin is found in the world. The secular, humanist, liberal kingdom of the world, the sanctuary of the false religious system, neither accepts nor acknowledges that God created it and all the people and the things in it. Therefore, it denies His right to reign. As a consequence, the Godless world remains in darkness and sin. It should come as no surprise that the Church is commanded to separate from the world.

Two thousand years ago a large portion of the world had been Romanized. That is, it had been forced to come under Roman law, to accept Roman gods, and to practice Roman ways. Although the Church was birthed into this society, it was clear that the followers of Jesus were to follow a different way and to live a different lifestyle. They were to obey His word, to honor Him as the one true God, to follow His ways, and to accept any into its company who would renounce Roman tyranny and its false religious system and would accept Jesus as their leader. In other words, the early Church was not to be drawn into Roman culture but was to overcome that kingdom by demonstrating to it the values, principles, culture, and nature of the kingdom of God.

THE CHURCH SCORNED BY AND IN BONDAGE TO THE RELIGIOUS ESTABLISHMENT

So too today. A large portion of the true Church has come under the influence of a world religious system. Many in the true Church have not discerned that this system has laws contrary to the standard set by the Bible, is under the influence of gods who demand the worship due to the one true God, and follows the ways of the world. Rather than separating from the world, this religious system has accepted its methods, copied its practices, and adopted its culture until it has grown increasingly difficult to distinguish the world from the compromised church. Further, its false ministries and false teachings have decreased rather than increased the Church's dedication to God. Since much of this sin has not been recognized or acknowledged by the true Church, the true Church has not dealt with it. In spite of this, God's body of believers is still charged to overcome the religious system of this world. Once again, it is called to come out, to separate from the world, to live up to its name as a separated body, and to worship the one true God.

Like individual saints, it is entirely possible for the body of Christ to have been saved and delivered and yet still find itself in bondage. While it has escaped from the captivity of sin, it finds that it has been ensnared or is being held by something just as perverse: slavery to unholy religion. Some of the body of Christ has joined rather than separated from the counterfeit religious system that deceptively labels itself the Church.

Finding themselves in bondage serving the false religious system may surprise some saints. They never dreamed they would need to separate from this bondage, as it has so cleverly and deviously kept God's children from full freedom in Him.

Attacked at a vulnerable time when they had not yet learned the ways of God and could not yet spot deception, many saints, in their joy of new freedom and eagerness to please, did whatever they were told to do. They followed wherever they were led. In effect, they substituted one form of slavery for another.

To put it in more modern terms, these saints have gone out the frying pan into the fire. They were delivered out of sin by God, but instead of being led into the true Church under the mentoring or guidance of a man or woman who is truly anointed of God to lead, they were led into the religious church system under the authority of an individual, organization, or cult. Freed of personal sin, these saints are yet in the midst of corporate sin and are unable to freely worship God.

As the power of Satan was broken over individual saints and the command came forth for them to separate from sin, so also today the command is issuing forth for the sum of those saints, the true Church of God, to separate from both the world of sin and the false church system. There must be a division of true and false, of godly and ungodly. For the Church to stay in or even near that which has held it in bondage would only invite the same problems to reoccur. The Church must depart from all unholy ties that bind it. It must leave that which is evil and make a journey, an exodus, to freedom.

As God sent a deliverer to the Israelites and to each saint, He has sent One to His Church. His name is Jesus. As He commanded the Israelites to be ready to move, so He now instructs His Church. As He led the Israelites in an exodus from evil, so now He is separating His Church from the false religious system.

In long years of struggle and frustration, God has been preparing the hearts of the faithful for this journey. The Church has been allowed to suffer the oppression of the system so it will call out to Jesus. It has endured trauma, threats, embarrassments, slander, name calling, put downs, punishment, and forced labor while waiting for God to lead them out. In all of this, nothing has stopped the swelling tide of saints that is calling out for separation.

The Church has held firm, even grown stronger, in its determination to be released in order to worship God. Now, as the moment of crisis has come upon it, the true Church is girding up its loins, tying on its sandals, and waiting on God with walking stick in hand. It has heard His call to leave the false church, and it is already on the move.

It may not be apparent to many, but the exodus of the true Church from the false religious system has already begun; it is a work in progress. Outraged, ungodly religious authorities are watching while the true Church rejects and then separates from the system that bound them. They are observing while the true children of God flee. They are looking on as eager saints refuse denominationalism, legalism, heresies, faulty theology, slave labor, and all else that makes up the religious system. They are beholding as the Church approaches the borders of its religious bondage and prepares to cross over into religious freedom.

As before in ancient Egypt, now that the order to leave has come and the true Church is on the move, there will be repercussions for the false religious system. The Lord Jesus is mightier than any human taskmaster, such as Pharaoh. The Lord Jesus is stronger than any created being, such as Satan. The Lord Jesus is the Separator and

Sanctifier. With the true Church on the move to freedom, the false religious system will be stripped of its most valuable asset, the body of Christ. It will be stripped of and forced to release its treasure, the bride of Christ. That bride will, at long last, be free to join her Bridegroom and to worship her God.

Now the true Church is turning its back on religious bondage and is going forth. It is repenting that it has allowed human and satanic slavery to keep it from its Bridegroom. Changing its mind about whom it will serve and following that decision of will with a change of direction, it is drawing near to God. It is moving out to freedom.

The Feast Of Unleavened Bread

En route to the boundaries of freedom, the Church will spiritually celebrate the Feast of Unleavened Bread. It will acknowledge Jesus as the Bread of life (John 6:35). Then, since it wants to be fed and nourished by only Him, it will walk with no leaven or sin in relationship with Him. It will throw out the leaven of false teaching and faulty preaching. It will leave behind all theology that conflicts with or is placed above the pure Word. It will no longer endure the deceptions which mankind has engendered, allowing only the pure bread of life, the unadulterated Word of God, to strengthen its heart.

The Presence Of God

As the true Church walks its spiritual path, it will be visited by, inundated with, and led by the Holy Spirit, the visible presence and manifestation of God. Jesus told His disciples that He would be with them always (Matthew 28:20), and this would be made possible by His sending the Spirit to them (John 16:13). After Jesus' ascension, His disciples were filled with the Holy Spirit (Acts 2:2). The Spirit remained with them and guided them (Acts 11:1-18; 16:9-10). Through this outpouring the Spirit worked through the disciples, which resulted in the gospel being preached all over the world and the Church being built (Acts 2:14-42; see also the rest of Acts).

The Church today should expect no less from her mighty God. When a saint becomes a Christian he (or she) is indwelt with the abiding presence of the Holy Spirit, making the true Church or the corporate body of Christ a gathering of those in personal communion with God. Rather than following denominational dogma, the true Church follows His will. Rather than relying on programs, it relies on God to continue building His Church. It seeks to be with God simply because it loves God rather than having an ulterior motive to get something from God. Through good times and bad it rests in the knowledge that God is with it because He has promised He would never forsake it (Hebrews 13:5). In all things the Church enjoys the great blessing of the Lord's continual presence.

Pursuit By The Enemy

The Church will need to know that holy presence and power, because as soon as it is launched on its journey, it will find itself being followed. It will be pursued by the very religious system from which it is escaping. Not content with defeat, the religious system will once again lift its hand against the true Church – to its utter destruction.

As Pharaoh chased the Israelites, so the counterfeit religious system will pursue the true Church. This will not be done in order to apologize or repent for its abuse. Rather, it will be because the false religious system realizes that it has lost its laborers. Knowing it will be difficult to continue without them, it needs to get its former slaves back under its control.

Further, the system knows that the true Church, once freed, will, by the Spirit, spread around the globe, totally surpassing any fleshly or satanic network built by New Age slaves. The Church will work to defeat the age-old attempt to enthrone men and women by spreading the gospel of the kingdom, which enthrones God. Then it will back up the Word of God by holy, miraculous manifestations of the power of God that will set the stage for the greatest harvest of souls the world has ever seen. The humanist system can't let that happen.

The configuration of the pursuing army may shock the Church. The persecuting system's army will not be comprised of just those still in the world's systems but also of those in the counterfeit church system. First, the shallow or immature converts and much of the money raised for wrong reasons will be channeled into the effort to coerce the true Church to rejoin the system. Second, those who once called themselves brethren will attack the true Church by calling true saints blasphemers and heretics.

Even worse, false shepherds will lead the pursuing army. Like perfectly trained hounds in a hunting party, they, with hue and cry, will track down and try to destroy the true Church. The story found in 1 Samuel 21 and 22 is a warning to the Church. Doeg, the chief of King

Saul's shepherds (1 Samuel 21:7), told Saul evil stories and made accusations against David and the priests of God. Saul, a type of tyrannical leader like Pharaoh, was so angered at Doeg's report that he ordered the slaughter of God's priests in spite of all protests of innocence. When Saul's servants were unwilling to slay the Lord's anointed, Doeg, the shepherd, turned on and killed the holy men (1 Samuel 22:18).

Similar situations are happening now. While God's ministers and priests serve Him, the shepherds of the false religious system will endanger them. They will accuse them, slander them, turn on them, and even kill them in an effort to ingratiate themselves to the religious system.

As before, the persecution will be a test for the true Church. Once again God's people will be made to know their own natures better, to see if they will follow God at any cost. They will have to choose past or present; tradition or being led by the Spirit; slavery or service; man, Satan, or Christ. They must learn to stand in the face of evil and to trust God.

As Satan, his demonic hoards, and his human flunkies try to deceive, harass, threaten, pressure, and destroy the true Church, it should become apparent that the dominant spirit behind all this evil is witchcraft. Satan is attempting to impose his will on God's Church. The Church must stand firm in the knowledge that Satan has been defeated, and, in spite of all his bluster and threats, he no longer has any authority over the true Church.

God loves His Church and will never leave it or forsake it. One of His many attributes is omnipresence, His ability to be in all places at all times. He rules over all, for *"Heaven is My throne and the earth is My footstool"* (Isaiah 66:1). In addition, His Son Jesus *"will reign over the house of Jacob forever, and His kingdom will have no end"* (Luke 1:33). He will always be there for the Church through any hardship or persecution.

In the end, just as God kept His promise to the Israelites that He would fight for them, so He will fight for His Church. If His people will seek Him, He will respond. If they obey Him, He will free them and deliver them. And those who planned the destruction of the Church will instead find themselves being destroyed by the Church's Protector and Deliverer.

Apostasy Or Exodus?

Even now God is freeing and delivering His true Church from the false religious system. Believers are leaving their slavery to false gods and to people behind and are stepping out in faith to follow God.

One of the chief weapons used against the departing saints is the tongue. Gossip and slander will mount. Name-calling and accusation may reach such heights that even the most determined saint may waver. Therefore, it is important for the Church to know that there is a major difference between apostasy and the exodus.

Contrary to popular but false teaching within the Church, apostasy is not a severance from a particular denomination nor an abandonment of participation in a specific local church. Further, it is not disloyalty to a certain church leader or ministry. Apostasy is falling away **from** God. It is a desertion of faith **in** God. It is a personal decision to turn one's back **on** God. In other words, apostasy has nothing to do with the renunciation of a person and his or her created, godless works. Instead, true apostasy is backsliding from God.

On the other hand, an exodus is not a falling away but a commanded, purposeful leave taking. It is not synonymous with apostasy but is, is fact, the opposite – while apostasy is falling away from God and reentering sin, an exodus is leaving sin and moving toward God.

Holiness has always set apart the people of God. The word Church means called out ones or separated ones. Therefore, it should be no surprise that when the true Church hears God calling, it is wholly willing to separate from that which is not of Him. Those who are following the highway of holiness in a purposeful departure from the sin of the world and the unholy excesses of the religious system should not be discredited but commended. For false religious system leaders to accuse the innocent of apostasy when they are actually participating in a godly exodus is a horrible evil, one which will bring down the judgment of God on the accusers.

As difficult as things may seem for the true Church, the saints who comprise the true Church must understand that the grim life in the false religious system, the harassment that accompanies any attempt to change things within that system, and the difficult decision to leave that system are gifts from God. They are His love and mercy in action.

God promised to shake up His Church (1 Peter 4:17). All of its present difficulties are forcing His true Church to get down to business with Him. They are forcing His true Church to ask itself some difficult questions and then to decide how to respond to God's answers. Some of these queries may be:

1. Will any of us give up a church that our family founded or that we have been a part of for many years if that church has degenerated into a religious caricature of the true Church?

2. Will any of us be willing to give up all offices, positions, ministries, and titles in the false church system, and then, unencumbered with superficial importance, still choose to worship Him in His true Church?

3. Will any of us fight through deception until we arrive at God's truth?

4. As the Israelites did at the Red Sea, will any of us stand with our backs against the wall and, with all hope gone, face our enemy, and refuse his demands?

5. Will any of us agree to leave the unholy and walk with eagerness toward the holy?

PART III:

THE RED SEA

PART III:
THE RED SEA

Chapter 7

THE RED SEA:

THE ISRAELITES' DELIVERANCE FROM EGYPT

So it was that the Israelites came to the Red Sea.

The Hebrews had called out to God, waited on Him, obeyed His instructions about putting the Passover blood on the doorposts and lintels of their houses, prepared for a journey, and then followed Him as He led them in the exodus from Egypt.

PURSUIT BY THE ENEMY

The Hebrews' triumph was not welcome in Egypt. After the plagues, the people's homes, animals, and their means of making a living lay in tatters. The land was destroyed. Thwarted and enraged, Pharaoh regretted that he had let his slaves go and determined to follow them. He and his army pursued the Hebrews and overtook them near the banks of the Red Sea. Suddenly the once-freed children of God discovered that they had the sea before them and an enemy army behind them. Trapped between the two, they faced what seemed like certain disaster and death rather than freedom and new life. They were a new nation truly in need of deliverance.

The exodus was not going as planned. That is, although it was not going according to man's plan, it was right on schedule with God's. This new difficulty, facing enemies of the past, was a test.

Fear And Terror

The Israelites did not desire any more upheaval. They were not willing to submit to more trauma. When faced with the terrible sight of a vengeful enemy bearing down on them, fear took a mightier hold on them than it ever had before. Soon this fear turned to resentment at having to face more hardship and then to outright anger at those they held responsible for their predicament.

Rejection

Screaming their frustrations, they blasted God's servant, Moses (and therefore God Himself), with accusations of irresponsibility:

> *"Is it because there were no graves in Egypt that you have taken us away to die in the wilderness? Why have you dealt with us in this way, bringing us out of Egypt? Is this not the word that we spoke to you in Egypt, saying, 'Leave us alone that we may serve the Egyptians?'"* (Exodus 14:11-12a)

Scourging Moses with cruel and untrue words, the Israelites cast him off as their leader. They charged that his purpose among them was to bring death rather than life. Rather than recognizing their own powerlessness, they charged him with weakness. Rather than acknowledging that they had been miserable in Egypt and had therefore eagerly sought the exodus, they denied they were willing participants in their removal from Egypt. Finally, they spoke the thoughts of their hearts: *"For it would have been better for us to serve the Egyptians than to die in the wilderness"* (Exodus 14:12b).

These screams of defiance were not what God wanted to hear. These words, this implication that the Hebrews preferred to return to Egypt must have pierced into the deepest chamber of His heart. He knew that only by a complete separation of the old ways, kingdoms, and gods could there ever be the installation of the new. This new challenge was a test of their resolve and of their faith in Him.

God foreknew that His children would waver and that their fear would lead to defiance. To calm these fears, He had already made His will known about their going back to Egypt: *"Now when Pharaoh had let the people go, God did not lead them by the way of the land of the Philistines, even though it was near; for God said, 'The people might change their minds when they see war, and return to Egypt'"* (Exodus 13:17).

A later word made His desire on the subject even more emphatic: *"[T]he LORD has said to you, **'You shall never again return that way'*** [emphasis added] (Deuteronomy 17:16).

To those familiar with the geography of Egypt, it must have been apparent that the escaping masses were not embarked on the shortest or most direct path to freedom. Yet, since they were under the pillar of cloud or fire, it was equally obvious that God was leading them exactly where He chose. Therefore, any disagreement with His chosen way was also a disagreement with His will.

The children of Israel should have trusted God and known He had a good reason for leading them as He did. Instead, they rebelled. *"Our fathers in Egypt did not understand Your wonders; they did not remember Your abundant kindnesses, but rebelled by the sea, at the Red Sea"* (Psalm 106:7).

Unhappily, this was not an isolated incident. This rebellion at the Red Sea set an example that would mar and delay the journey to the promised land. It was the first but surely not the last of many episodes of rebellion which were all caused by forgetting who God was and what He could do.

In spite of the people's obstinacy, what happened next is a sublime example of the grace of God. It is a breathtaking manifestation of His mercy. Instead of raising His hand against this rebellious lot, He raised His hand for them.

Moses, too, rose to the occasion. In spite of the savage attack and the rejection aimed at him, he yet moved in love for his people. Proving that he had been a wise choice as leader, he exhorted them:

> *"Do not fear! Stand by and see the salvation of the LORD which He will accomplish for you today; for the Egyptians whom you have seen today, you will never see them again forever. The LORD will fight for you while you keep silent"* (Exodus 14:13-14)

Moses' constancy, devotion, loyalty, and trust must have thrilled God. One among many yet believed God would keep His word and lead His people out of Egypt. One among millions raised his voice for God rather than against Him. And the moment he did so, God trumpeted forth His answer: *"Then the LORD said to Moses, 'Why are you crying out to Me? Tell the sons of Israel to go forward'"* (Exodus 14:15).

WATER BAPTISM

Reversing the people's order to go back came the higher order to go forward. To enable the Israelites to do so, God sent Moses both a direction and a promise. *"As for you, lift up your staff and stretch out your hand over the sea and divide it, and the sons of Israel shall go through the midst of the sea on dry land"* (Exodus 14:16).

Announcing that Egypt would now know He was LORD, God quite literally moved for His people. The pillar of cloud that had been going before Israel to lead the way now moved behind them (Exodus 14:19-20). In its new position, it not only gave the Israelites light, but, resting between the two camps, it became a barrier for the Egyptians and a protection for the Israelites.

Acting as instructed, Moses stretched forth his hand over the sea. The LORD, exercising His authority over nature, caused a strong east wind to blow all night. The waters of the Red Sea parted and the exposed seabed became dry land. Wasting no time, with the wind in their faces, the Israelites plunged into the gap left by the parted waters and marched, unfettered, through the corridor of freedom out of the land of Egypt (Exodus 14:22).

While it has become fashionable of late to belittle this miracle of God, a pause to reflect on the truth will highlight its grandeur. Some say that the Red Sea was but a shallow puddle that the Israelites skipped and splashed through on the way to freedom. Others declare that the Israelites walked on sand bars, through the swampy, shallow end of the sea, or through water at low tide.

The Bible refutes such statements. It clearly states that the Hebrews crossed via a dry path into and through the sea. On either side of that path were towering walls of foaming water. Psalm 78:13 refers to the waters as standing up in heaps. The Word further declares: *"At the blast of Your nostrils the waters were piled up, the flowing waters stood up like a heap; the deeps were congealed in the heart of the sea"* (Exodus 15:8). In addition, when later referring to the LORD'S victory over Pharaoh's soldiers in the sea, the Word states: *"The deeps cover them; they went down into the depths like a stone"* (Exodus 15:5).

The Israelites wouldn't have been tested by sand bars; their enemies couldn't have been destroyed by puddles. The Israelites may have gulped once or twice before entering the Red Sea, but when they did so, they walked between walls of water.

To further magnify this miracle, the path through the sea could not have been a narrow one. It had to be wide enough for two to three million people, their possessions, and their animals to pass through to safety in the time frame of one night.

Soon after the Hebrews entered the sea, the Egyptians once more moved against them. Taking up their pursuit, they followed them into the sea. As God had blessed the Israelites in the sea, He now used the same arena to bring judgment on their enemy.

What a sight it must have been! Strong horses against weak men. Able, hate-filled soldiers against women and children. Chariots and weaponry against the unarmed. The noise and shouts of the predators sure of victory. The cries of the pursued fearful of defeat. One army fleeing, one charging after it. One advancing, one retreating. Or was it really two armies advancing, one to freedom and one to death?

Suddenly entering the fray, God struck the enemy with confusion (Exodus 14:24). Then He made the chariot wheels swerve and drive with difficulty, thus removing them as an effective weapon (Exodus 14:25a). He also sent fear among the Egyptians until they cried out: *"Let us flee from Israel, for the LORD is fighting for them against the Egyptians"* (Exodus 14:25b).

Then disaster fell upon the Egyptians. God commanded Moses, who had now passed through the sea and stood on the shore on the other side, to once again stretch out his hand. As he did so, the water returned to its normal place. Even as the Egyptians were still engaged in murderous pursuit of the Israelites, the walls of water turned on them, rolled over them, covered them, and totally inundated them.

Ironically, the arm that God used to save His chosen people was the same arm He used to destroy their enemy. So complete was God's work that not one of the enemy forces survived (Exodus 14:28). The Israelites were able to see their tormentors' dead bodies wash up on shore (Exodus 14:30). By night the Israelites were saved (Exodus 14:21); at daybreak the Egyptians were destroyed (Exodus 14:27). Once again, weeping lasted for a night but joy came in the morning (Psalm 30:5).

THE FEAST OF FIRST FRUITS

As a grand climax of God's intervention, miraculous power, love, and mercy, the Israelites were finally severed from the Egyptians. This wondrous day of the Israelites' journey had truly been spectacular. This special day, in the midst of the on-going Feast of Unleavened Bread, celebrated the total destruction of the enemy and the freedom and rising to new life of God's chosen people. It later became known as the Feast of First Fruits, the third and final part of the Passover celebration.

First Fruits, as described in Leviticus 23:9-14 and Deuteronomy 26:3-10, was to be commemorated as soon as the Israelites reaped the first harvest in the promised land. At this time the Israelites were to bring a sheaf of the first fruit of the yearly harvest to the house of the LORD where the priest would wave it before the LORD so that the people might be accepted by Him. This statute was to be obeyed perpetually.

However, for now, the Israelites had finally come to the end of what had seemed like a three-day death march and burial. They had followed God through Egypt to the Red Sea. After facing what seemed like certain death, they had walked through the sea and triumphantly arrived on the other side. God's chosen people had emerged not only in a new land but also to a new life. Delivered from the Egyptians and Pharaoh, they were God's first fruit. After a long night of death, a new day had dawned. After four hundred and thirty years of slavery, the Israelites exhilarated in a new breath of freedom.

The immediate results of all this activity were glorious:

First, the fear of people was replaced by the fear of God. When the Israelites saw God's power, they feared Him (Exodus 14:31). Further, knowing that God's power was with this people, other nations feared them (Exodus 15:14-16).

Next, the Hebrews believed in the LORD.

Further, the Hebrews believed in His chosen servant, Moses.

In addition, the Hebrews saw that God had done as He said He would do. He had given Egypt as a ransom for His people (Isaiah 43:3). He had redeemed them from slavery in the iron furnace (Deuteronomy 4:20). He had led them out of Egypt. The object of all these miracles was to release a beloved people so that they could worship their God. Wonderfully, so moved were they by all these happenings, they did just that. Led by Moses, a song of joy and worship rang out over the desert (Exodus 15:1-18).

Finally, the God who had saved the Israelites had now delivered them too. God showed His people that saving them from Egypt and delivering them from the power of Pharaoh who had kept them in bondage was a two-step process, and He had blessed them with both.

Chapter 8

THE RED SEA:

EACH SAINT'S DELIVERANCE FROM SIN

The Israelites' natural journey did not end with returning to Egypt or with disaster at the Red Sea. Neither does any saint's personal walk. As the Israelites continued with God, plunging into and through the Red Sea in order to emerge to new life in a new land, so each saint must journey on through the waters of God's love until death has yielded to life and the old has become new.

Like the Israelites, as each saint reaches his (or her) spiritual Red Sea in the flight from Egypt, the problems facing him must be realized, evaluated, and addressed. First among them is the immediate attack of the enemy.

PURSUIT BY THE ENEMY

Each saint's flight to freedom from the world of sin sends satanic hordes flying after him (or her). Immediately after any saint has accepted Jesus as Savior and has decided to separate from the world of sin and darkness, Satan, like Pharaoh, begins to pursue that new saint with the intention of drawing him back under his control. For those who are unprepared for such a test, the instant reaction to such hatred and violence is fear or terror.

Fear And Terror

Without question, the salvation of a new saint can sometimes become a stressful time. If the pressure is particularly intense and he (or she) has not yet learned to trust God in his new situation, then fear and terror may begin to surface, manifesting themselves in resentment and anger at both God and the Christians God had chosen to guide him out of Egypt.

These reactions of fear and terror to Satan's aggressive assault to recapture or harm his victim sometimes lead to confrontations between the victim and those trying to help the victim escape. Shouts of, "I trusted you and look where it got me!" or "Leave me alone!" fill the air, proving that he (or she) who is hurting is once more rejecting those who are helping him.

As each saint flees out of the world of sin and finds himself (or herself) trapped near the Red Sea, each has a brief moment to think about and answer some questions. In comparing the bedeviling of Satan with the conviction of the Lord, which manifests grace? Which is mercy unveiled? Which is God's expression of love for each sinner? Which allows every person to spend eternity in heaven? To which should a sinner yield? If each is honest with his answers, he will know and admit the truth that he was not better off before he was saved from his sins and that he should never go back into the world.

Rejection

An additional problem found at the Red Sea is the desire to reject the new way of life and to return to the old. Defiant cries of, "Nobody bothered me before. Nobody was trying to hurt me when I was in sin. I was better off as I was. I've had enough! I'm going back!" are now heard.

Sadly, these desperate declarations are filled with error, for Satan was, in fact, bothering the new saint before his (or her) salvation. Since his purpose is to steal, kill, and destroy (John 10:10), Satan was keeping the new saint under his mastery, was fettering him in slavery to sin, and was trying to harm him. The new saint was not better off before his salvation; his only future was in hell rather than in heaven in the presence of God.

While Satan was badgering each new Christian before his (or her) salvation, someone else was troubling him too. In His great love for His child, God was also disturbing him. God the Father, Son, and Holy Spirit made it their business to intervene in his unholy life.

The Bible makes it clear that no one can come to Jesus for

salvation without the drawing power of God, Father, Son, and Holy Spirit. Jesus said, *"No one can come to Me unless the Father who sent Me draws him"* (John 6:44). Further, Jesus said, *"And I, if I am lifted up from the earth, will draw all men to Myself"* (John 12:32). Finally, the Holy Spirit draws people by convicting each person of his (or her) sin (John 16:8), wooing him to the Savior, and teaching him about the Father and Son. In so doing, He gives each person good reason to leave the old life and to move on with God.

Doubt

Or, perhaps the new Christian's defiance is less an outward expression of rejection than an inward expression of doubt. Perhaps he (or she) is led to believe that he is being tempted beyond his ability to cope. With Satan's evil forces breathing down his neck, he sees a war breaking out over his soul and spirit. Believing it to be something he has caused, he believes it is something he must stop. Therefore, he comes to the conclusion that for his own good or for the good of others involved he should back down and return to his old life.

Such is pure deception. It is exactly what Satan wants him (or her) to think. With God, the new saint is not tested beyond his strength, because he now has the power of God to help him. Further, the new saint is not the cause of the warfare now being waged internally. Therefore, his backing down will do nothing to lessen it. God loves him and wants to give him life. Satan hates him and desires to destroy him. Since Satan's ultimate plan is to injure him whether he does back down or not, his only real choice is to trust in God and to plunge onwards to full freedom.

Even the thought of returning to sin is exactly why God allows each saint to be tested. He wants each saint to know whether his (or her) decision to escape Satan and to serve God is firm or wavering, whether he truly desires to go back to the old life or to live in the new, and whether he will retreat or will proceed with Him. God also wants every Christian to know that as He saved each one from sin He can also deliver each one from the power of sin.

THE MIXED MULTITUDE

Every new saint's encampment at the spiritual Red Sea may find him (or her) in some disparate company. The Hebrews left Egypt with a group called "a mixed multitude" (Exodus 12:38). So too, each saint may find himself traveling with an odd assortment of people as he leaves the world of sin. These, led by curiosity or by the belief that they are somehow a part of the Lord's body, want to walk with the company of saints.

The Deceived

A portion of the mixed multitude may include those who have been deceived by faulty denominational or cultish teaching that declares them to be Christian though they have never been spiritually reborn, do not know Christ, and therefore cannot be called after His name. This group includes those who were labeled Christian after they followed the rules of their denomination and human traditions rather than the requirement of God for salvation. They feel that their choice of church or their faithful service to the religious organization that they were born into makes them a part of the Christian community. Or, they believe their "good" works put them in the express lane to heaven. Since none of these know God, they may travel in Christian society but they are not a *bona fide* part of it.

The Undecided

Additionally, some in this hodge-podge may have never made a decision to be free of Egypt or of their sin in order to serve God. They may have heard of the need for salvation and have been brought close to a place of decision for the Lord, but each time they are on the brink of a true spiritual breakthrough or a release from sin, they turn their back on God. They just will not repent, confess their sins, and ask for those sins to be forgiven. Yet, in spite of refusing God, they want to be accepted by Him and to enjoy the privileges that accompany His presence.

The Uncommitted

Another part of this mixed multitude may no longer want to remain under the mastery of Satan, but they refuse to commit themselves to the lordship of Jesus Christ. They may or may not have accepted Jesus as Savior but do not acknowledge Him as Lord. They have declared they hate Satan but have not yet learned to love or trust God. Once eager to be out of Egypt or released from their sin, they now demand more time to think about their position and their decision. This group hangs suspended, not knowing what to do or where to turn. Since they are not ready to follow Him, they end up stalled at the Red Sea.

For any in this mixed multitude, sometimes the delay at the Red Sea lasts indefinitely. Rather than a momentary pause to assess the situation and then to move on, many choose to set up camp. In confusion, they fight God and reject the freedom fighters who are trying to help them. They face continuous onslaught from satanic forces because of their own refusal to move or to escape on the path which God has chosen for them. Instead of deciding for God and following Him to freedom, they find themselves in the Valley of Indecision – under attack, left behind, thrashing about, and going nowhere.

GO ON!

It is God's will that all men and women everywhere be saved from sin and then be delivered from the power of sin. However, He will not force them to be. In His plan to reconcile humanity with God, He created them with a free will, allowing them to use His gift to make their own decisions concerning Him, their salvations, and every other aspect of their lives. Rather than controlling them as Satan does, God chooses to love and guide people, even if their decisions are wrong. He will not bypass or override people's decisions of will.

By an act of will, each man and woman decides for God or against Him. Each decides to overcome his (or her) fear, rejection, and doubt by the grace of God and to continue on his journey to freedom. Or, each continues to waver at every sign of trouble and to yearn to return to the past. It is each person's decision that decides the issue, not God's.

Salvation is provided for all who choose God and follow Him. His command for each, once saved, is to go forward. To go back, to reenter, or to continue to practice sin as a habitual way of life is blatant disobedience. God cannot honor such.

If each saint has made his (or her) decision by his spiritual Red Sea to refuse to fear, to reject or deny God, doubt, or to join the mixed multitude who don't truly know God, then the command for him is to proceed. Through a combination of the mercy and power of God and the leadership of men and women who are trying to help him, God will bring him into freedom. Whatever in his life is symbolic of the Red Sea will be the very thing that God will open to allow his escape from Satan. Whatever seems to be blocking his way or threatening him with death will be that which becomes his path to new life.

WATER BAPTISM

The Christian counterpart to the Hebrews walking through the Red Sea to new life is water baptism. By it, a new saint of God is dipped into water and then is raised out of it. This signifies the cleansing of the old carnal life and the resurrection into new life in Christ.

As myths concerning the depths of the waters of the Red Sea have to be blasted away, so must the misconceptions concerning Christian baptism. Denying any part of this rich experience because of ignorance or prejudice would cause a saint to miss a great blessing.

According to *Funk and Wagnalls Standard Dictionary*, the word baptize means to plunge or dip into. It means that something is submerged or is totally immersed and then is lifted out again.

As Christians, each saint is commanded to submit to water baptism (Matthew 28:19; Mark16:16; Acts 2:38). This means that each individual saint is being asked to immerse himself (or herself) in water and then to rise again. The Israelites could not go around the Red Sea or splash through a shallow spot. Instead, they had to plunge into and walk through the sea while walls of water towered over their heads. Similarly, every saint is to follow their pattern and to be totally immersed in God's waters of love.

Scripture supports the idea of complete immersion in baptism. Matthew 3:5-6 speaks of crowds being baptized **in** the Jordan River, and Acts 8:38-39 speaks of the Ethiopian eunuch going down into and coming up out of the water. Perhaps the best instructive example of immersion in baptism is that of Jesus Himself: *"After being baptized, Jesus went up immediately from the water"* (Matthew 3:16).

Identifying With Jesus' Death, Burial, And Resurrection To New Life

God has good reasons for being so particular about water baptism. By it, each Christian is totally identified with Christ in His death, burial, and resurrection (Romans 6:3-5).

The Bible refers to the crossing through the Red Sea as a baptism. By it, the Israelites were baptized into Moses (1 Corinthians 10:2). In a saint's baptism, his (or her) immersion in water baptizes him into Christ (Romans 6:1-7).

The Israelites had walked for three days and nights to the Red

Sea and then plunged into it as an act of faith in the LORD'S power of deliverance. Then, passing through the sea, the Israelites emerged victoriously to new life in a new land. Jesus, as an act of faith in God, allowed Himself to be crucified for the sins of mankind and then was buried for three days and nights in a grave; His body of flesh had been destroyed. On the third day, Jesus rose triumphantly from the dead to wonderful resurrection life.

Jesus died each saint's death as each one's Sacrifice and Substitute. He was buried in each saint's grave. He arose from death, raising each saint to new life in Him.

When the enemy pursued the Israelites into the Red Sea, God moved by bringing fear, inability, and ruin on the enemy, destroying every one of them. It was a total, complete defeat. Just so, by water baptism, each Christian announces that Jesus won victory over Satan and all of his forces. Satan has been totally defeated, and his power over each child of God has been totally destroyed.

By his (or her) water baptism, each saint is individually signifying that when Jesus was crucified, he died with Him. Romans 6:6 informs us: *"knowing this, that our old self was crucified with Him, that our body of sin might be done away with, that we should no longer be slaves to sin."*

By his (or her) water baptism, each Christian is acknowledging that when Jesus was buried, he was buried with Him. *"Therefore we have been buried with Him through baptism into death"* (Romans 6:4a).

By his (or her) water baptism, each saint is declaring that when Jesus arose to resurrection life, he arose to resurrection life with Him. Romans 6:4b-5 states,

> *so that as Christ was raised from the dead through the glory of the Father, so we too might walk in newness of life. For if we have become united with Him in the likeness of His death, certainly we shall also be in the likeness of His resurrection....*

All of this goes far beyond the forgiveness of sins. It reveals the total change or transformation in each saint's life. In dying with Christ or in being crucified with Him, each saint died to sin. In other words, his (or her) old adamic man, fleshly nature, and carnal life passed away. Sin, which once ruled him, forcing him to do all sorts of evil, no longer has control over his life. He is no longer a slave to sin (Romans 6:6) but is free to serve God.

As burial follows death in the natural, so it does in the spiritual. When Jesus was buried, each saint's old man was buried with Him, left to forever molder in the grave. Each who was made dead to sin is made alive to God (Romans 6:11). Once dead and buried, each saint's new man is raised up with Him through faith in God (Colossians 2:12). Each is resurrected to new, glorious life in Christ.

It is important to note that water baptism is not synonymous with salvation. While it is a sign of salvation, it is not salvation itself as it does not – cannot – save a Christian from his (or her) sins or bring him into right relationship with God. Since it is the outward expression of an inward change of heart toward God or a sign that a born from above experience has happened to a new saint, it can be deduced that salvation must precede baptism. Therefore, if there has been no change of heart, baptism is unnecessary, and those who are not Christians should not participate in it.

THE FEAST OF FIRST FRUITS

A saint's participation in water baptism is also his (or her) spiritual participation in the Feast of First Fruits. 1 Corinthians 15:20-23 declares that the death and resurrection of Jesus are the hallmarks of Christianity. It is not only the death of Jesus but also His resurrection which separates Christianity from all other religions. This resurrection, attested to by many (Matthew 27:52-55), tells the world that Christians serve a living God.

Jesus, the Passover Lamb, broke the power of sin over each saint's life. Jesus, the unleavened or sinless Bread of Life, separated each saint from sin and evil. Jesus, the First Fruit, is the first to rise from the dead or come out of the ground as the first fruit of the harvest. While the Israelites, once settled in the promised land, brought a sheaf gathered from the early harvest into the house of the Lord and waved it before God so the people would be accepted, Jesus rose to the Father and presented His blood in the heavenly Holy of Holies so that each saint might be acceptable to Him (Hebrews 9:11-12). He brings each reborn saint forth in resurrection life so that each may be among the first fruits of His creatures (James 1:18).

The Church should note that Scripture does not record lengthy delays between salvation, deliverance, and water baptism (Acts 2:41; 8:35-38). If the Church should present the gospel in such a way that all the ramifications of spiritual rebirth, separation, and cleansing are fully understood as part of one feast, then newborn saints will not desire delay but rather will be eager to be baptized – immediately.

Further, it should be noted that infants may be dedicated to God but not baptized. To dedicate an infant to God is a wonderful thing to do, but that doesn't make that baby a Christian. Only those old enough to understand the gospel message and to accept Jesus as Savior and Lord meet scriptural requirements for water baptism. Babies, who cannot make such a decision, are not among these. Each person must declare himself (or herself) for God and then be baptized in Him rather than be unwittingly baptized and then have someone else declare him a Christian.

Have you been baptized? Not according to ceremony or denominational tradition, but have you been baptized according to God's Word and will? If not, will you do so now? Ceremonies are fine in their place, but the important thing is just to submit to baptism. If you are a committed Christian but have not sealed your decision for Christ with a biblically proper baptism, there is no good reason not to lay aside this book and do so right now.

Scripture does not mention an elaborate ritual in baptism. It does not state that a pastor or priest is required to officiate, and it does not declare that an audience is required to watch. You could fill a bath tub, a Jacuzzi, or a backyard pool and immerse yourself in it. Or, you could find a lake or pond to plunge into that you may signify your death, burial, and resurrection to new life.

Please go now!

Declare your old man to be dead.

Declare that you identify with Christ in death and burial.

Declare that you identify with Christ in resurrection to new life in Him.

Declare that since you died, were buried, and rose with Christ, you are no longer carnal but Christian, no longer dead but alive.

Plunge in and arise. Know that you are a new creature in Christ.

And then, thank Him.

Salvation from sin, deliverance from the world of sin, and the cleansing of baptism have culminated in each saint of God being a new creature full of new life in a new land. The immediate result of all these miracles should be a healthy fear of God. It should be an awesome respect for who He is as well as for what He does. All that is left for any saint to do is to fall on his (or her) face and to worship Him. At last fully out of Egypt, each can sing a new song.

Chapter 9

THE RED SEA:

THE CHURCH'S DELIVERANCE FROM THE FALSE CHURCH SYSTEM

As the Hebrews' journey was not complete at Passover and as each saint's individual journey is not finished after his (or her) salvation and separation from sin, so the travels of the assembly of saints, the Church, are not ended with its deliverance and pulling away from the world. Like the Hebrews and like every spiritually reborn saint, the Church, as His body, is asked to walk through the waters of baptism. In so doing, it identifies with Christ in His death, His burial, and His resurrection. That means that it is dead to collective sin and is alive in Christ. It means that it has buried its past and is enjoying its present and future with Him. It means that the Church has been delivered from the old life and has been resurrected into the new.

PURSUIT BY THE ENEMY

As the true Church walks along, it will be visited by, inundated with, and led by the Holy Spirit, the visible presence and manifestation of God. The Church will need to know His holy presence and power, because as soon as it is launched on its journey into freedom, it will find itself being followed. It will be pursued by the false religious system from which it is escaping. Not content with defeat, the system will once again lift its hand against the true Church – to its utter destruction.

Fear And Terror

As Pharaoh chased the Israelites, so the false church system will pursue the true Church. This will not be done in order for the system to apologize or repent for its abuse. Rather, it will be because the system realizes that it has lost its laborers. Knowing it will be difficult to continue the system without them, it needs to get its former slaves back under its control.

Further, the system knows that once freed, the Church will, by the Spirit, spread around the globe, surpassing any fleshly or satanic network built by New Age slaves. It will work to defeat the age-old attempt to enthrone men and women by spreading the gospel of the kingdom of God. Then, backing up the Word of God by holy, miraculous manifestations of the power of God, it will set the stage for the greatest harvest of souls the world has ever seen.

The humanist system can't let that happen, so it will begin to pursue the true Church, intending to strike fear into the hearts of its brave leaders so that they will give up their flight into freedom. The configuration of the pursuing army may shock the Church, for it will be persecuted not just by the world but also by the counterfeit church. First, the shallow converts and much of the money raised for wrong reasons will be channeled into the effort to coerce the true Church to rejoin the system. Second, those who once called themselves brethren will call the true saints blasphemers and heretics.

Even worse, the false shepherds are leading the pursuing army or are at the head of the pack which is tracking down the true Church with hue and cry. As mentioned previously in chapter six, the story found in 1 Samuel 21 and 22 is a warning to the Church. Doeg was the chief of Saul's shepherds (1 Samuel 21:7). He told evil stories and made accusations to Saul about David and the priests of God who served the true King. Saul, a type of tyrannical leader like Pharaoh, was so angered at Doeg's report that he ordered the slaughter of the priests in spite of all protests of their innocence. When Saul's servants were cautious enough to be unwilling to slay the Lord's anointed, Doeg, the shepherd, turned on and killed the holy men (1 Samuel 22:18).

Similar situations are happening now. While the priests of the King serve Him, the shepherds of the false system will endanger and terrorize them. They will accuse them, slander them, turn on them, and even kill them in an effort to keep them from finding and serving in the true Church.

Rejection

The Church's journey away from the old and toward the new is stressful. Leaving familiar things, practices, and habits behind is stressful; leaving family and friends behind is stressful. As before, this separation presents a test for the true Church. First, it must choose to accept or reject the leaders that it views as causing so much upheaval. As the Israelites had to agree to follow or refuse to follow Moses no matter how difficult things became, so today the true Church must follow or refuse to follow the leaders which God has raised up to lead His Church out of the world religious system and into the kingdom of God. Further, it must choose to accept or reject Jesus, the One who brought it out of the world and the One who is its Head (Colossians 1:18).

Once again God's people will come to know their own natures better and will see if they will follow God at any cost. As they choose between past or present, tradition or being led by the Spirit, and slavery or service, they will also be choosing whether to accept Christ and be led by Him or whether to reject him and be led by a person or by Satan. If Christ, they will have to agree to accept His leadership in every test, at every time, for every reason.

Doubt

As the true Church is tried by fear and tempted to reject God, it will be also be tested by doubt. As fear in each individual can lead to doubt, so also fear in the corporate Church can lead to doubt. Nevertheless, it must learn to stand in the face of evil and to trust God.

When God led the Israelites out of Egypt, He did not take them on the shortest or most direct route to the promised land. In spite of all their doubts, they were still in His presence. In spite of all their concerns, unease, and apprehension, He was leading them where He wanted them to go. In so doing, He was exposing them to their own weaknesses so that those weaknesses could become strengths in His power. In the same way, today God is leading His true Church on unfamiliar paths. He is present with His redeemed every step of the way. When doubts surface, the Church must remember two things: 1) it is never, never, never to go back into Egypt; and 2) as God used the desert times to change a rag-tag group of untrained slaves into a powerful army that conquered the tribes occupying the promised land, so now He is raising up, training, and changing the slaves of the church system into a powerful fighting body that will resist and conquer any force on the face of the earth that defies and rejects their God.

As Satan, his demonic hoards, and human flunkies try to deceive, harass, threaten and pressure the true Church, it should become apparent that the dominant spirit behind all this evil is witchcraft. It is Satan's attempt to impose his will on God's church. The Church must stand firm in the knowledge that the power of Satan has been defeated, and, in spite of all bluster and threats, he no longer has any authority over the true Church. Rather than being mired in doubt, the Church must remember that Satan is an already defeated foe and must step forth with confidence in the Lord, who is forever victorious.

WATER BAPTISM

Long ago when Moses and the children of Israel realized they were trapped between the army of Pharaoh behind them and the Red Sea before them, Moses exhorted them, *"Do not fear! Stand by and see the salvation of the LORD which He shall accomplish for you today ... The LORD will fight for you while you keep silent"* (Exodus 14:13-14). The Israelites were then told to go forward on a path as yet not seen. As they were obedient to God, they found themselves walking through the sea on a path that led to safety and freedom.

This is exactly what God is now asking of His Church. It has come far on its journey, but there remains a long way to go. While continuing on its travels, it must not allow itself to be stopped by fear of the enemy. It must realize that sometimes, instead of all its frenetic activity, it is more appropriate to stand and allow the Lord to work. It must believe His promise that He will build His Church. The Church must trust Him enough to go forward at His command even if no visible path or way can be seen. It is only by such a commitment to obedience that the Church will realize its identity in Christ and will truly know that Satan is a defeated foe.

Has the corporate body of Christ truly understood that when Jesus died, was buried, and then rose to new life His Church, or the sum of the saints worldwide, died with Him, was buried with Him, and rose to new life in Him?

In His death, is the Church aware that as His physical body was beaten and broken He was suffering as a Substitute for His Church; that as His physical body was torn and mutilated He was sparing His spiritual body that agony?

In His burial, has His corporate body of Christ ever likened His interment and His long days and nights in a grave to its own burial of the past?

In His resurrection, has the whole body of Christ recognized that as Jesus rose bodily to new life and resurrection power by the power of God, so too will the Church rise bodily or as His body, full of His new life and His resurrection power?

If the Church of God cannot answer a resounding yes to all of the above questions, then it has not corporately undergone water baptism. It has not been delivered from its past. What has this failure meant to the Church? First, it has lost its sense of with whom it is identified. Second, it hasn't understood the meaning of its death and burial in Christ. Third, the Church doesn't walk in His resurrection blessings. In short, it has an identity crisis.

Identifying With Jesus' Death

For the Hebrew children gathered at the Red Sea, the Word declares: *"For I do not want you to be unaware, brethren, that our fathers were all under the cloud, and all passed through the sea; and all were baptized into Moses...."* [emphasis added] (1 Corinthians 10:1-2).

However, those in God's New Testament Church have been given a different, though equally concise, direction: *"Or do you not know that all of us who have been baptized into Christ Jesus have been baptized into His death?"* [emphasis added] (Romans 6:3).

In practical terms, what does this mean to the Church of the Lord Jesus Christ? It means the Church is not to be immersed into a man or a ministry. It means the Church is not to be dipped into a religious rite or ritual. It means the Church is not to be plunged into a denomination or a creed. It means **the** Church is not to be overcome by **a** church. It means the Church is to be identified only with its Head, Jesus Christ.

While some of the Church don't understand the significance of identifying with Jesus as its Leader, its Head, and its Lord, so also, some of the Church don't understand and therefore don't identify with the blessing of His death on their behalf. They don't know that by His redeeming work the body of Christ is free of the body of sin (Romans 6:6). They are unaware that since their old selves were crucified with Him they do not need to live by their carnal nature, but rather they are free to live in and to demonstrate their spiritual nature.

That carnal nature, also known as the flesh, includes all those things that express the adamic nature of mankind rather than the holy nature of God. It is the sum of the evil, sinful characteristics that became a part of human nature after Adam and Eve succumbed to Satan's temptation and sinned.

As revealed by Galatians 5:19-21, the deeds of the flesh or the adamic nature include *"immorality, impurity, sensuality, idolatry, sorcery, enmities, strife, jealousy, outbursts of anger, disputes, dissensions, factions, envying, drunkenness, and carousing."* Galatians 5:24 and 1 John 2:16 add to the picture by declaring that passions, desires, the lust of the flesh, the lust of the eyes, and the boastful pride of life are also characteristics of flesh. Revelation 21:8 includes the cowardly, the unbelieving, the abominable, murderers, immoral persons, sorcerers, idolaters, and liars among those with a carnal or fleshly nature. Is it any wonder then that Romans 9:8 states that the children of flesh are not the children of God?

Why is God so insistent that each saint and His whole Church be concerned about the flesh? The Bible answers this question by stating that the flesh concentrates on the outward rather than the inward (1 Samuel 16:7), reaps corruption (Galatians 6:8), fights against the Spirit of God (Galatians 5:17), and ultimately bears fruit to death (Romans 7:5). None of this is appropriate in His holy, chosen ones.

History books and the Bible reveal how the flesh gained such a foothold in the Church. After God's judgments on Egypt and the Israelites' salvation and deliverance, Pharaoh momentarily yielded to reality and allowed the Israelites to leave. Then he once more hardened his heart and pursued them, fully intending to annihilate them.

In like manner, Satan, in his rebellion against God, was defeated and was forced to release all those he had long held in the captivity of sin. Yet, even though their salvation was won, he determined he would not let God's children escape his clutches without a fight.

Multiplying his efforts against individual saints, Satan also attacks God's Church, that whole group of believers around the world who have been called out of the world system. This body was just barely established in the first century when it was viciously attacked. By satanic instigation, its leaders and members were pursued and dogged by both civil and religious enemies. Pressure mounted. Baby saints, seemingly as unprepared for such evil as the Hebrews had been in earlier days, no doubt felt they had their backs to the wall.

As He did to Moses and the Israelites and as He did to each saint, God tested the early Church. The first widespread persecution came at the hands of the Roman government. Though its evil and wickedness were so great that some new saints gave up their faith, others allowed themselves to be tortured and die rather than renounce their Lord. Even more importantly, as the persecution physically dispersed the saints, they used what was meant for evil for good: as they spread throughout the empire, they preached the gospel to the then-known world.

Shortly after this, the young Church faced a new enemy. Most new Christians had come from a Jewish background. As such, they had faithfully obeyed Moses and the law. With the coming of Christ and the establishment of the New Covenant, this allegiance to man and to legalism was broken. Since the Jews didn't like losing control of so many converts, the Jews came against the Christians, trying to re-impose their law on them (Acts 15).

Yet in both cases, the early Church understood and believed the truths of its identity in Christ's death and burial. It did not revert back to its carnal heritage. In remaining true to Him, in spite of their difficulties, they became known as those who turned the world upside down.

However, over time the Church began to show evidence of walking by flesh rather than by faith. By the fourth century, the Church was again under attack. It faced opposition by the Gentiles who compromised the Church with the introduction of pagan rituals and religious rites.

Throughout the ensuing Dark Ages, the Middle Ages, and into more modern times, the Church has been harassed, tormented, afflicted, and persecuted. Though sometimes it was strong enough to stand firm, at other times it yielded to ungodly pressure. When this happened, it floundered further and further from the true knowledge of God. Especially in recent years, the Church has grown weaker in its struggle. As a result, it has grown away from its identity with Christ and has become increasingly identified with the world, the flesh, the devil, and self to such a startling degree that it is oftentimes barely distinguishable from them.

Yet, just as the Bible can record the decline of the Church as flesh gained a greater and greater hold, so it can also state the good news: through identifying with His death, the Church can walk in victory over flesh because *"Now those who belong to Christ Jesus have crucified the flesh with its passions and desires"* (Galatians 5:24).

By His death, Jesus crucified the flesh, overcame Satan, and overcame the world for individual saints and for His whole Church. As more and more of the Church realizes that it was an active participant with Jesus in His death, that it was crucified with Him, it will realize that flesh and the world can no longer hold it in their grip. Flesh can no longer compel or force the saints of the Church to involve themselves in collective works of flesh. In Him, it can crucify the flesh.

Identifying With Jesus' Burial

The Church is blessed as it identifies with Jesus Christ in His death and His burial. To bury something is to lay it to rest; to entomb; to cover it; to leave it behind. Through water baptism, God is asking the Church to bury its old man and to leave him behind. He is asking the Church to acknowledge its new, cleansed state where sin has been washed away.

Years ago, Moses and the Hebrews walked through the waters of the Red Sea. This was symbolic of water baptism (1 Corinthians 10:2). Except for the divine intervention of God, they would have collectively plunged to their grave in the waters. Just so, God wants His Church to submit to and be immersed in water baptism as a sign of cleansing and of ensuring that collectively the old, fleshly, sinful man is buried.

It is not hard to imagine that as the Hebrews watched Pharaoh and his army advance toward them their fear and terror mounted. Then, when death was all but upon them, they watched with wonder and awe when God parted the waters of the Red Sea and Moses urged them to pass through it. It is also not hard to imagine that in their haste to escape the rages of the enemy, they dropped all their excess baggage as they ran, eliminating the things that weighed them down and leaving behind the things they would not need anymore. Similarly, the Church identifies with Christ in His burial by dropping all its excess baggage, eliminating those things that bog it down, leaving behind the things of the world that will not be welcome anymore, and plunging forward through the waters of baptism as a sign of its cleansing.

Identifying With Jesus' Resurrection To New Life

The Church is blessed as it identifies with Christ concerning resurrection to new life. When He died, He did not stay dead. Instead, by the power of God, He rose from the dead to a new and glorious life. In identifying with this resurrection, His Church is to rise to that new, pure, powerful life with Him.

After passing through the Red Sea, Moses and the Hebrews

walked out of the watery grave. As they stepped on the opposite shore, they were no longer the same. Delivered from Egypt, they were now a new people in a new land with a new life.

Just so, in identifying with Christ's resurrection, when the Church marches through the cleansing waters of baptism and emerges from them, it is no longer the same body. Delivered from the world system of sin, it is a new creation in Christ. It is a new people (the true Church) in a new land (the kingdom of God) with a new life (the life lived in the resurrection power of Jesus Christ). It has received the holy, heavenly nature of God and can move about freely acting as His agent of grace and glory, living in the world but not being of the world.

The Church will finally understand that it has already traveled from old to new, from sin to righteousness, from death to life, and from burial to resurrection. It will be a new body manifesting its inner change of nature by its outward actions of obedience which give testimony of the greatness of God. It will be a witness to the world that things can change – in Christ.

THE GIFT OF GOD

In all of this, the Church must understand that the blessings associated with salvation, burial, and new life apart from sin or the works of flesh are by the grace of God alone; they are not by works of men and women.

After saying (through Moses) to His Hebrew children, *"Do not fear! Stand by and see the salvation of the LORD which **He** will accomplish for you today ... **The LORD** will fight for you while you keep silent"* [emphasis added] (Exodus 14:13-14), He, with no help from Moses or the Israelites, saved His people. By the power of His own hand, He utterly destroyed the army of Pharaoh. In an exact parallel, Jesus faced the gathered forces of evil, and, with no help from any men or women, paid the penalty for the sins of humanity. Thus He saved His beloved Church by winning salvation for all who will call on His name. By His power alone, He totally, finally, completely, and eternally defeated the enemy of mankind.

Not on the basis of what the Church did for God but because of God's work on behalf of His people, His salvation and resurrection life are available to His Church. They are the love gifts of a holy, compassionate God to His children as they identify with Him.

God has said He will have His Church and that the gates of Hades shall not prevail against it (Matthew 16:18). Since God has said it, it is true. In order for the Church to rise to its full potential and to fulfill its part of God's plan, it must have a clearer identity of who and what it is. As the Israelites and as each saint had to learn that they could only succeed as they identified with their Lord, so too His Church must know that it exists and can succeed only as it remains separated from the world and identifies with Him.

As part of this separation and identification, the Church must take part in water baptism. Perhaps individually, some have discovered the blessing that such holy submission brings. Yet, has the body of Christ as a whole been so obedient?

THE FEAST OF FIRST FRUITS

Such activity will spiritually involve the whole Church in the Feast of First Fruits. Only as His Church allows itself to be totally immersed in the living waters flowing from its beloved Bridegroom can it see its old, fleshly nature dead and buried with Him. Only through water baptism can resurrection life once again be a testimony of the true Church of God.

The early Hebrews were a type of the first fruits of salvation. Jesus was the fulfillment of the type. The saints of the early Church were called the first fruits among His creatures (James 1:18). Should His present Church
be satisfied with any less?

Since the Church is the sum of the saints, it too, in baptism, was crucified with Him, was buried with Him, and has been raised with Him to resurrection life. Once it truly knows that and understands how it happened and what it means, it will begin to identify itself as one with Him, as a victor in Christ.

EGYPT

Abraham's Covenant
Passover
Outer Court
Enemy: Pharaoh
Slavery/Oppression/Bondage
Dead Works
Enforced Labor
Stationary/Going Nowhere
Poverty
Old Adamic Nature
Rejection
Leeks and Garlic
Death
Courtship
Lamb
Savior/Deliverer
Freedom
Salvation
Egypt

EGYPT

Abraham's Covenant
Passover
Our Door
Exodus – Passover
Slavery/Occult worshippers
Death
Enforcer's spot
"sabotaging young travelers
Buyers
Destination Danger
Freedom
Of Unseen Dangers
Deaths
Courier
Life
Transfer
Leaders
Lives
Trip

BOOK 2:

THE DESERT

BOOK 2:
THE DESERT

PART IV:

THE DESERT

Chapter 10

THE DESERT:

THE ISRAELITES' SANCTIFICATION OF A NATION

God's word to Moses had been, *"Go to Pharaoh and say to him, 'Thus says the LORD, "Let My people go*, **that they may serve Me**"'" [emphasis added] (Exodus 8:1).

Saint and sinner alike know what happened once those words were uttered. When Pharaoh refused to obey God, God did His part; He moved in power and delivered His people. Finding themselves free and safe on the other side of the Red Sea, the people did their part. They worshipped Him.

It is wonderful to read that the first act of a people set free from slavery was to honor and praise their Savior and Deliverer. Their song, sung from deep within thankful, awestruck hearts, thundered out. Its choruses, declarations of the wonder and power of the majestic LORD and all that He had accomplished, yet fill our souls and thrill our spirits in familiar verses:

> *I will sing to the LORD, for He is highly exalted; the horse and its rider He has hurled into the sea. The LORD is my strength and song, and He has become my salvation. This is my God, and I will praise Him; my father's God, and I will extol Him.* (Exodus 15:1-2)

The Israelites were right to recall the glories and power of God. They were right to recount the mighty deeds of sovereign God. Since God delivered Israel from captivity by means of a mass exodus from both the Egyptians and the land of Egypt, the repetition and magnification of such a phrase as, *"I am the LORD your God, who brought you out...."*

(Exodus 20:2) or *"The LORD brought us out of Egypt with a mighty hand and an outstretched arm...."* (Deuteronomy 26:8) are entirely appropriate.

However, as important as all of this was, the Israelites' story does not stop there. Neither did their journey. As soon as they passed through the sea, the people found themselves in a desert. Knowing that a desert was not the land flowing with milk and honey which had been promised and that the wilderness of Shur (Exodus 15:22) was not the land of Canaan, the children of Israel were faced with a decision. They had to choose whether they would stay where they were or follow God to the promised land.

A desert is a desolate wasteland. It is an area lacking an adequate supply of water, one without the plentiful rainfall needed to sustain abundant life. Therefore, it is a dry, barren, unfruitful land, one unable to be cultivated for crops. Also, a desert is an area that alternates in extremes of temperatures, hot by day and cold at night. Sudden violent storms are not uncommon in deserts. It is a land where few animals can survive, but, of those that do, many are capable of inflicting great pain and even death to humans, like snakes or scorpions.

Since the desert has such a harsh environment, it is almost impossible for large, concentrated numbers of people to live there. Those who do are often mobile. With families and tents, they are constantly on the move, ever traveling, never setting down permanent roots. They seem like pilgrims in a strange land. Yet, God led His people to this hostile environment!

Why? Why would God do this? When the children of Israel thought their problems were over, why would God introduce them to more? Was it because He was a capricious God who liked to see His children squirm? Was it so that He could squeeze them and press them and become another taskmaster over them? Or, perhaps, was it that His people had sought Him as Savior but not as Lord? Was it that, while He had promised them Canaan, He knew they weren't ready to go there?

While He had delivered their lives, He knew the Israelites' hearts were yet far from Him. He knew that a people who had been held so long in bondage serving another master would need an extensive period of adjustment, preparation, and training before realizing the fullness of His promise.

The Israelites didn't know how to survive; they didn't know how to fight the enemy; they didn't know how to follow leadership; they didn't know how to get along with one another; and they surely didn't know how to submit to or worship God in ways of His choosing. Therefore, it was not in hatred or mockery but in mercy and grace that God set them aside for a while. He led them into the desert so He could teach them.

The Israelites' decision whether to remain where they were or to go on in God was not long in coming. As the song of worship died out, Moses led the people into the wilderness. How appropriate it was that as the Israelites' final journey in Egypt was of three days duration, so now their first journey in the desert was one of three days (Exodus 15:22).

TESTING IN THE DESERT

The Israelites tested God to see how long they would have to put up with adversity. They examined Him to find out how to deal with a God who wouldn't bow to their every whim and demand. They tried Him to find if He would allow them to follow their own will or, if not, if they could revert to their old ways.

Yet in testing God, something else was happening about which the Israelites may not have known. While His children were testing Him, God was also testing them. He tested them to teach them that they were a rebellious people, denying both His authority and the godly authority exercised through the human leaders He had placed among them. He tested them to show them that their blessings from Him depended on their obedience to Him. He tried them to teach them to depend on Him as the source of all they needed. Whether it be for water, food, victory, government, ways to worship, order, placement, direction, leadership, or healing, He wanted them to believe that He would provide for them rather than, as they implied, that He would not. He proved them so they would learn to be more afraid of Him than they were of people.

Through testing, He proved who had a forward vision and a different spirit. He revealed those who wanted to break away and go back and those whom He could lead onwards. He tried them so the fear of God would keep them from sinning (Exodus 20:20). In short, He tested the Israelites to show them He was Lord.

Rebellion: Marah

At the end of the three days, trouble appeared. The Hebrews had no water. When they finally found some, it was so bitter they could not drink it. Appropriately, the place was named Marah, which means bitterness (Exodus 15:22-26).

Instead of trusting the God of their deliverance to provide for their needs, the Israelites tested Him. Soon the sound of murmuring, rather than worship, arose. In His mercy, God showed Moses a tree which, when cast into the bitter waters, made them sweet. To add a further blessing, the LORD promised, upon condition of their obedience to Him, to be Jehovah-rophe, the LORD their healer (Exodus 15:26). As such, He would not allow any of the diseases with which He had plagued the Egyptians to fall on the Israelites. While this healing was a miraculous blessing in the natural, it was also a type or shadow of future blessings in the spiritual.

The Israelites may not have been aware of it, but the experience at Marah was the birth of rebellion in the desert. While this was the first, it surely was not the last time they would test God. In fact, as time would tell, the Israelites had just joined battle against the Lord. When they grumbled and voiced their problems to Moses, God heard them (Exodus 16:8). When they directed their accusations against him, in truth they were complaints against God (Exodus 16:8). By going deeper into sin with each test, they acted much as Pharaoh had, defying God by hardening their hearts against Him.

Hunger

However, the children of Israel didn't learn quickly. Soon came another problem.

> *Yet they still continued to sin against Him, to rebel against the Most High in the desert. And in their heart they put God to the test by asking food according to their desire. Then they spoke against God; they said, "Can God prepare a table in the wilderness?"* (Psalm 78:17-19)

No longer thirsty, the Israelites were now hungry (Exodus 16:1-15). It didn't take long for the rumbling of stomachs to become the grumbling of mouths. Remembering the flesh pots and bread of captivity, the Israelites cried out:

> *"Would that we had died by the LORD'S hand in the land of Egypt, when we sat by the pots of meat, when we ate bread to the full; for you have brought us out into this wilderness to kill this whole assembly with hunger."* (Exodus 16:3)

Again, in mercy, God moved. Longing for bread, He sent them manna. Longing for flesh, He sent them quails. Although they had once again failed His test, He still loved and provided for them.

Thirst

A third test quickly followed. To see if they had learned from their earlier trial, the Israelites were again challenged with thirst. At a place called Rephidim, there was no water for the people or for their livestock (Exodus 17:1-7). Again, quarreling and grumbling broke out. Again, the people declared it would have been better to die in Egypt than to die of thirst in the desert. Growing in unbelief, they were quickly but erroneously convincing themselves that slavery in Egypt had meant life and that freedom in the desert was bringing death.

Once again, God's answer to their challenge was to extend His hand of mercy. At His command, Moses struck a rock with his staff and water poured forth. *"Behold, He struck the rock so that waters gushed out, and streams were overflowing"* (Psalm 78:20).

God didn't provide a trickle of water that would satisfy just the barest of needs. He sent overflowing rivers of water coursing through the desert to love His people unto Him. By so doing, He not only showed that He could provide water but that He could and would do so in a variety of ways. God's miraculous power was limited neither in quality nor in quantity. Surely this should have answered the question, *"Is the LORD among us, or not?"* (Exodus 17:7).

The Amalekites

While yet at Rephidim, another challenge presented itself (Exodus 17:8-16). The Amalekites, descendants of Esau, came against the Israelites. A fierce desert tribe, the Amalekites, were the first human enemy outside the borders of Egypt to try to impede the Israelites' journey to Canaan.

God's orders for this crisis may have surprised many. No longer commanding the Israelites to stand and see the work He would do, God now clearly instructed His people to participate actively in their deliverance from this enemy. If they desired victory, the orders no longer were to wait or stand; instead, they were to go and fight (Exodus 17:9).

Choosing Joshua as the military leader, Moses sent him to the field of battle to smash the physical enemy with troops and swords. While Joshua was doing that, Moses stood on a hill overlooking the battlefield and fought the spiritual battle by extending his staff, or the rod of God, over the scene.

As long as his hand remained up, or as long as Moses extended God's authority over the situation, the battle went favorably for the Israelites. When Moses weakened, the tide of battle turned to the Amalekites. Finally, supported by faithful servants, Moses upheld the authority of God long enough so that the spiritual foes were spiritually overwhelmed by the power of God, and Joshua prevailed so that the human foes were physically conquered by the power of God.

To celebrate such great victory, Moses built an altar and named it Jehovah-nissi. This name, meaning the LORD our banner, recognized that the LORD had carried the day for His people. (For more about Jehovah-nissi and other names of God, read the author's book, *Jehovah-Jesus*). Moses then heard the LORD declare that He would wage war against the Amalekites (Exodus 17:16). Though the Amalekites would dog the Israelites' footsteps in the desert and kill off the stragglers (Deuteronomy 25:17-18), a time would come when even the memory of the Amalekites would be blotted out (Exodus 17:14).

The Supremacy Of The Rod Of God

Tracing the spiritual journey thus far, one common thread appears: the rod or staff of God. God's rod is His symbol of authority. It is the way He extends His rule over His people. Sometimes in so doing, He acts alone, sovereignly extending His might and power to accomplish His own purposes. At other times, He trusts His authority into the hands of men and women for them to exercise in His name.

In either case, it is good to remember that it is the rod of **God** that is being discussed. It is the staff of Elohim, the righteous, holy, true God, Ruler of all the earth, lands, and people. As such, it is the symbol of holy authority and should be respected or used only in ways that reflect the character and intent of the owner.

God began His teaching about authority when He introduced Himself to Moses and taught him how to use His rod of authority. First, in the privacy of the desert, God commanded Moses to throw his staff on the ground. When he did so, it turned into a snake. When Moses obeyed God and picked up the snake by its tail, it became a rod once more.

Then Moses took his staff to the court of Pharaoh. Egypt was a land that worshipped many gods. Among these was a god called Set or Satan. As might be expected, the emblem of royal power was the serpent, which was crafted, molded, and worn on the crown of Pharaoh. When Moses arrived on the scene, he lost no time in showing everyone that he was God's instrument of judgment by establishing the divine authority of God over the false authority of Egypt's gods.

At first, Moses used God's rod to perform a few miracles which, through evil power, Pharaoh's magicians were able to duplicate. At Moses' command, Aaron cast down God's rod, and it became a serpent. When Pharaoh's ministers of evil did the same and their rods also became serpents, God's rod swallowed up theirs (Exodus 7:8-12), thus showing that God's power is greater than Satan's and that the Savior would overcome the serpent.

Continuing with his supernatural demonstration, Moses used the staff to strike the Nile, turning it to blood; to stretch over Egypt's streams and pools, causing frogs to overrun the land; and to strike the dust, causing gnats to plague people and beasts. After this, Pharaoh's magicians could no longer conjure enough satanic power to duplicate the extraordinary exhibition of the power of God. God further commanded Moses to raise his staff toward the sky, which led to thunder, hail, and fire flashing on the land of Egypt. Then He commanded Moses to stretch it over the land, causing locusts to come and eat everything left after the other plagues. Then God again told Moses to stretch the staff towards the sky, causing thick darkness to cover the land for three days (Exodus 7 – 10).

Soon after, when the Hebrews were at the Red Sea, Moses once again exercised God's authority by using his rod to open a path in the sea (Exodus 14:15, 21). When Pharaoh's army sought to use that same route, they, as their god had been, were swallowed up by the power of God when the waters closed over them (Exodus 14:26-28).

While in the desert, God continued to show His authority using His rod. At Rephidim, God told Moses to use the rod to strike the rock, and when Moses did so, water came out of the rock (Exodus 17:1-7). This was soon followed by the stunning victory over the Amalekites. Joshua led the warriors into battle while Moses stood on a hill and watched. When Moses raised the rod of God, the Israelites prevailed, but when he lowered the rod, the Amalekites gained power. Since Moses' arms grew tired, Aaron and Hur had to support his hands until the Amalekites were defeated (Exodus 17:8-16). With the battle against the Amalekites, the rod of God that brought such magnificent victories over sin, the world, the flesh, and the devil was again used to extend God's authority over the enemy of flesh.

THE COVENANT AT MOUNT SINAI

Time went on. Days passed while the Israelites marched. In the third month after leaving Egypt, they came to Mount Sinai (aka Mount Horeb, Malachi 4:4; Deuteronomy 9:8-9). On this very mountain Moses had met God and received his commission to deliver God's people (Exodus 3:1-10). On this very mountain God had prophesied that the people would come to worship Him (Exodus 3:12). Now, they were there.

In all of their conflicts, God had made it abundantly clear to all who would see that He was the Israelites' source of life. From Him would come whatever was needed to sustain life. Since the issue of the provision of physical necessities had been so clearly and miraculously determined, God now wanted to turn the Israelites' thoughts to spiritual matters. His chosen people, who visibly lived in His presence and power, were now to become His covenant people (Exodus 19; 20:1-17).

Soon after arriving at Mount Sinai, Moses went up to seek God. God called to him and said:

> "Thus you shall say to the house of Jacob and tell the sons of Israel: 'You yourselves have seen what I did to the Egyptians, and how I bore you on eagles' wings, and brought you to Myself. Now then, if you will indeed obey My voice and keep My covenant, then you shall be My own possession among all the peoples, for all the earth is Mine; and you shall be to Me a kingdom of priests and a holy nation.'" (Exodus 19:3-6)

Moses took this message to the people and reported their answer back to God: *"All that the LORD has spoken we will do!"* (Exodus 19:8).

Then God began to prepare His people for a most sacred event. He wanted to make a covenant with those who had pledged themselves to Him. So important was this covenant or agreement of relational commitment and so important did God consider this bonding of humanity with Himself that He personally came to deliver His word concerning it.

God ordered the people to consecrate themselves. He also gave them boundaries they were not to pass when they approached Him. For their own protection, God's people were to meet Him, yet they needed to keep a distance. On the third day when they heard the ram's horn sound, they were to assemble at the foot of the mountain to meet their God.

When the special morning arrived, accompanied by the rumble of thunder and flashes of lightning, by thick clouds of smoke, by the ever increasing sound of trumpeting, and by great quaking (Exodus 19:16-20), the LORD descended on Mount Sinai in fire and smoke. Claiming lordship over His people, His commandments rang out for all to hear (Exodus 20:1-17). In summary, these are:

1. I am the LORD your God who brought you out of the land of Egypt. You shall have no other gods before Me.

2. You shall not make, worship, or serve idols.

3. You shall not take the name of the LORD your God in vain.

4. Remember the Sabbath day, to keep it holy.

5. Honor your father and mother.

6. You shall not murder.

7. You shall not commit adultery.

8. You shall not steal.

9. You shall not bear false witness against your neighbor.

10. You shall not covet.

Pentecost

Later, God commanded a feast to commemorate the issuing of the Law be held in His honor. It was to be known as Shavuoth, the Feast of Weeks, or Pentecost (Deuteronomy 16:9-12; Leviticus 23:15-21). The word Pentecost means fifty. Seven Sabbaths plus one day, or fifty days, after Passover, the Israelites were to come before God to celebrate the end of the barley harvest and the beginning of the wheat season. According to rabbinic tradition, it was fifty days after the Israelites escaped from Egypt that they met with God at the foot of Mount Sinai and were given the Ten Commandments (Exodus 19-20). Thus, the feast of Pentecost became associated with the giving of the Law and the establishment of covenant. As with Passover or the Feast of First Fruits, this feast could only be celebrated once the Israelites settled in the promised land since no grain crop could be planted or harvested while the tribes were marching through the desert.

Rejection

Whatever the future celebration concerning the giving of the Law might be, God's majestic display of might rocked Sinai when He came to meet with His people. As the mountain quaked, so did the Israelites. Their reaction to holy God was not awe or worship – it was outright terror. They screamed at Moses: *"Speak to us yourself and we will listen; but let not God speak to us, or we will die"* (Exodus 20:19).

In effect, because they were still afraid that the worst thing that could happen to them was to die, they rejected the authority and personal leadership of God, their source and sustainer of life.

Giving The Law

When Moses communicated the extraordinary appeal of the fearful people, God did as requested. Asking Moses to be His messenger, He gave Moses the laws, ordinances, and statutes by which He would govern the people. He finished by stating His promise and His purpose.

> *"Behold, I am going to send an angel before you to guard you along the way and to bring you into the place which I have prepared. Be on your guard before him and obey his voice; do not be rebellious toward him, for he will not pardon your transgression, since My name is in him. But if you truly obey his voice and do all that I say, then I will be an enemy to your enemies and an adversary to your adversaries. For My angel will go before you and bring you in to the land of the Amorites, the Hittites, the Perizzites, the Canaanites, the Hivites, and the Jebusites; and I will completely destroy them. You shall not worship their gods, nor serve them, nor do according to their deeds; but you shall utterly overthrow them, and break their sacred pillars in pieces. But you shall serve the LORD your God, and He will bless your bread and your water; and I will remove sickness from your midst. There shall be no one miscarrying or barren in your land; I will fulfill the number of your days. I will send My terror ahead of you, and throw into confusion all the*

people among whom you come, and I will make all your enemies turn their backs to you. I will send hornets ahead of you so that they will drive out the Hivites, the Canaanites, and the Hittites before you. I will not drive them out before you in a single year, that the land may not become desolate, and the beasts of the field become too numerous for you. I will drive them out before you little by little, until you become fruitful and take possession of the land. I will fix your boundary from the Red Sea to the sea of the Philistines, and from the wilderness to the River Euphrates; for I will deliver the inhabitants of the land into your hand, and you will drive them out before you. You shall make no covenant with them or with their gods. They shall not live in your land, because they will make you sin against Me; for if you serve their gods, it will surely be a snare to you." (Exodus 23:20-33)

After Moses reported all of this, the Israelites confirmed this covenant. They agreed to do as God had said. Moses then wrote all the words of the LORD on a tablet of stone. Finally, to ratify the covenant, he built an altar, slaughtered some animals, and offered them to God. Taking some blood from the sacrifice, He sprinkled it on the altar and on the people saying: *"Behold the blood of the covenant, which the LORD has made with you in accordance with all these words"* (Exodus 24:8).

God must have been pleased with what He saw and heard. Moses, Aaron and his sons, and some elders of Israel were allowed to see God. As they beheld Him, they ate and drank in sweet communion (Exodus 24:9-11).

Rebellion: The Golden Calf

Even as Moses remained in communion with God in the cloud on the top of Mount Sinai, at the foot of the mountain, the camp sinned. *"They quickly forgot His works; they did not wait for His counsel, but craved intensely in the wilderness, and tempted God in the desert"* (Psalm 106:13-14).

First, under the direction of Moses' brother, Aaron, they made a molten, golden calf. Adding blasphemy to this iniquity, they declared their idol, not God, was their redeemer (Exodus 32:4). They became so carried away in their idolatry that they built an altar and ordered a feast day for worshipping the calf (Exodus 32:5-6).

God revealed this tragedy to Moses. Even as His anger kindled against His people, Moses interceded for them. He entreated God not to remember the acts of His rebellious people but rather to recall the promises He had made to Abraham, Isaac, and Jacob. When the LORD changed His mind about utterly destroying the sons of Israel, Moses went down the mountain. Seeing with his own eyes what had happened, his anger burned (Exodus 32:7-19). Realizing that the worship of the golden calf was idolatry and understanding that its creation violated the first three commandments, Moses knew that God's covenant with His chosen people had already been broken.

Acting justly, Moses shattered the stones upon which the shattered covenant had been written. Then, he ground the golden idol into powder, scattered the powder over some water, and forced the Israelites to drink it. Not accepting Aaron's lies, denials, and irresponsibility (Exodus 32:21-24), Moses called any who would stand for the LORD to come to him. When the tribe of Levi did so, he ordered them to go forth and execute brother, friend, and neighbor who had taken part in the rebellion against God. That day, three thousand people fell dead.

Then followed a wonderful manifestation of faithfulness and mercy. Moses returned to the rejected LORD. He didn't mince words or mouth excuses. He confessed the sin of the people before holy God and asked for forgiveness. In response, God sent him back to the camp to continue to lead the obstinate people (Exodus 32:30-34). At first declining to accompany the Israelites (Exodus 33:3), God later relented and declared that His presence would be among His people on their journey.

Soon, God wrote the same commandments on new tablets of stone and then honored Moses by giving him a glimpse of His glory. Passing in front of Moses, God revealed His name and His nature to him:

> *The LORD, the LORD God, compassionate and gracious, slow to anger, and abounding in lovingkindness and truth; who keeps lovingkindness for thousands, who forgives iniquity, transgression and sin; yet He will by no means leave the guilty unpunished....* (Exodus 34:6-7)

Instructions For The Tabernacle

Once again, God called Moses to the top of the mountain. God, who had chosen a people and been accepted by them, now wanted to live with them. Extraordinary as it may have seemed, He gave Moses explicit instructions for the building of a tabernacle that would house His presence (Exodus 25-27,30). He also revealed His plan for the priesthood that would serve Him (Exodus 28-29) and details of acceptable sacrifice and worship (Exodus 29).

Soon the Israelites began to build God's house. Everyone whose heart moved him (or her) to do so brought a contribution for the building of the tabernacle (Exodus 35:21). When it was finished, this dwelling place, built by the hearts of men and women for the heart of God, was dedicated. On the first day of the first month of the second year, it was erected and its furnishings set in place. Aaron and his sons were cleansed, clothed, and consecrated as God's priests.

Wonderfully, during the dedication ceremony, the glory of the LORD filled the tabernacle. In supernatural display of majesty, God indwelt His home with His presence (Exodus 40:34).

The High Priest

This special house of God was to have a special leader. Titled the high priest, the first one named in the Bible was Moses' brother, Aaron (Exodus 28:1). As the leader of Old Covenant religion and ritual, his function might be described as a go between, one who intervened between God and His people (Exodus 30:7-10). As such, Aaron led the Hebrews' religious rites by offering sacrifices to God (Hebrews 5:1). He was also a teacher (Leviticus 10:11) and an intercessor, the mediator who stood between the wrath of God and humanity (Numbers 16:46-48). He entered the Holy of Holies once a year to atone for both his sin and the sins of the entire Hebrew camp (Leviticus 16).

The Priesthood

A priesthood was then initiated to serve in the temple. It was composed of men who were descendants of Aaron, the first high priest (Exodus 29:9). Always busy, these men were charged to keep the sanctuary (Numbers 3:38), to offer sacrifices (Leviticus 1:1-17), to move the tabernacle when God moved the camp through the desert (Numbers 4:5-15), to carry the ark of the covenant (Joshua 3:6-17), and to teach the Law (Leviticus 10:8-11).

Offerings

God called Moses to attention once again. Resuming His

instructions, He taught Moses about acceptable offerings. Burnt offerings were for dedicating oneself to God, and peace offerings were to enjoy communion with God.

Now, added to these offerings and placed at the head of the list, was the requirement of a sin offering, the way in which atonement could be made for sin. Perhaps with Aaron's denial of and irresponsibility toward sin in mind, God made it clear that each Israelite was to be held strictly accountable for his (or her) own sin. Whether priest, leader, or commoner, when each sinned, each had to personally acknowledge that sin and make atonement for it by bringing an animal to the court of God to be sacrificed (Leviticus 4:27-28).

Further, when inspired to do so, the Israelites could go beyond the offerings required by law and could make offerings to God from their hearts. As an example, in addition to the animals for sacrifice, the leaders of the tribes of Israel brought offerings of gold and silver to be used in the tabernacle. When these platters, bowls, and pans were dedicated to the service of the Lord, worship in the tabernacle began (Numbers 7).

Rebellion: Nadab And Abihu

Unbelievably, rebellion once again reared its ugly head. As priests and as sons of Aaron, Nadab and Abihu were surely aware of the ordinances of God concerning worship. Yet they rebelled against God's will by deciding upon and then following their own ways of worship (Leviticus 10:1-3).

Not long before this, Aaron and these young men had been officially consecrated as priests. After the ceremony, they exited the tent of meeting and blessed the people. As they did so, fire came from before the LORD and, as a sign of God's approval, it consumed the offerings which were on the altar (Leviticus 9:24).

When the people saw this, they fell on their faces before God. Not so Nadab and Abihu! Instead of worshipping as holy priests, they took their firepans, put fire and incense in them, and offered strange fire before the LORD.

Instantly, judgment fell. Since they had followed their own way instead of God's way, Nadab and Abihu forfeited their lives. Fire once more came from the presence of God. However, this time, instead of honoring lawfully offered sacrifices, it consumed the unlawful priests.

While it must have seemed a very harsh way to do so, God was trying to teach His people a fundamental principle of worship: they must make a distinction between the holy and the profane (Leviticus 10:10).

THE CAMP

God then turned His attention from the people to the camp in which they lived. First, He numbered the camp by tribes (Numbers 1). Then, He gave Moses concise directions for the arrangement of the camp, whether it was at rest or marching behind the cloud of God.

This was no slovenly hovel or sloppy, disorganized group! While at rest, by God's order, the ark of the presence of the LORD was always to occupy the central position of the camp. The tents of all the tribes were to surround Him on the north, south, east, and west. Further, the tents of the Levites and priests were to be placed between the ark and the tents of the tribes. Each tribe, family, and individual was to remain in the place which God, not man, had designated. Starting with Judah on the east and ending with Naphtali on the north, the camp was never to deviate from its prearranged order. Visibly, while at rest the camp of God would look like the map on the following page (map credit to Alan Hiu at http://alanhiu.blogspot.com/2010/05/cross.html).

Seeing this from a biblical perspective reveals a wonderful truth. The formation of the camp at rest clustered around the ark bears a remarkable resemblance to a cross. The formation made the ark of God's presences the heart of the people.[1]

Positions

God had declared the Levites to be His servants. The sons of Levi, Kohath, Gershom, and Merari, were assigned places of encampment near the ark of God so that their works of service with the tabernacle could be easily and quickly accomplished. These families were particularly charged to transport the ark, the tabernacle, and all the holy objects and furnishings. Their duties were specifically given; nothing was left to chance or misunderstanding. Each servant not only had his place in the camp, but also his own God-given task (Numbers 3-4).

---

[1] More information on this topic can be found at https://www.biblestudytools.com/commentaries/revelation/related-topics/camp-of-israel.html.

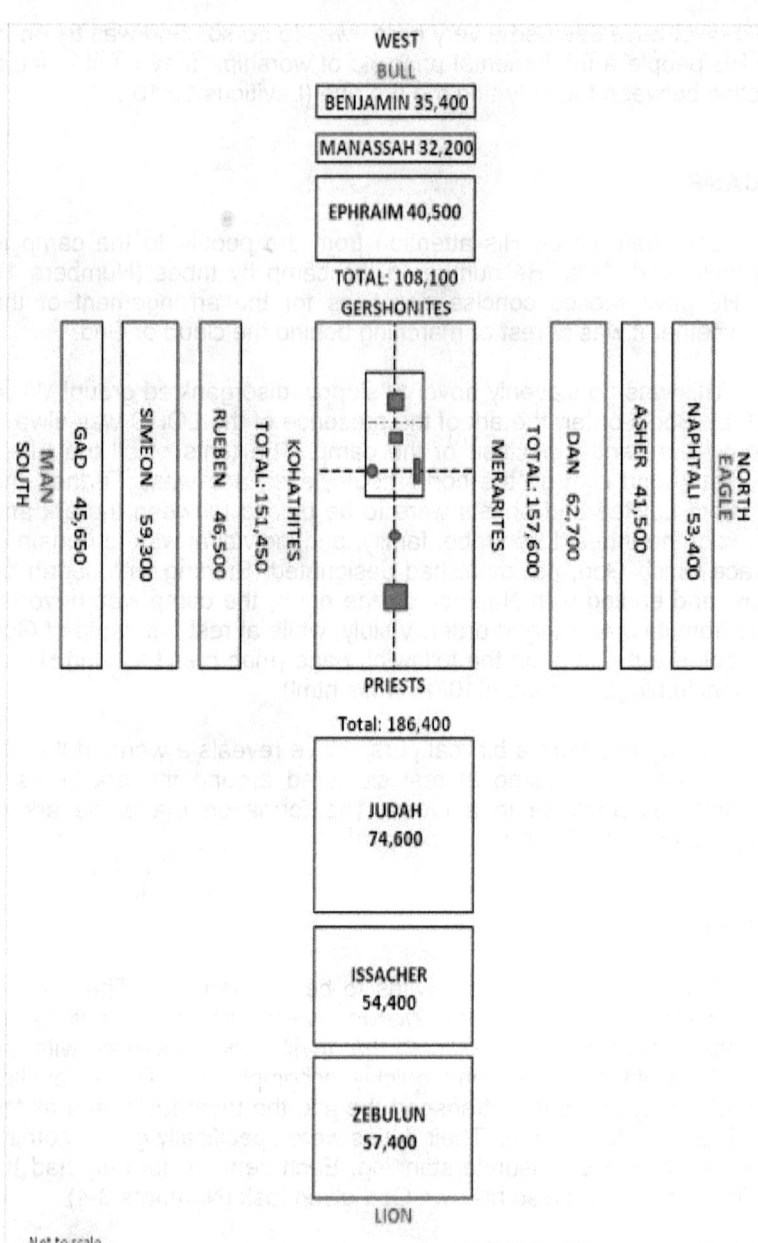

Not to scale.
Number Chapter 2
KOHATHITES, MERARITES & GERSHONITES BELONG TO THE TRIBE OF LEVITES

The Pillar And The Cloud

Then God taught the Israelites one of the most important lessons they could ever learn. He had introduced Himself to Moses at Sinai and joined all of Israel on their headlong flight to the Red Sea. By cloud or pillar of fire, He had led His children. Now, He intended to lead them through the desert in the same way that He had saved them – by His Presence as seen in His cloud of glory by day or His pillar of fire by night.

Already the cloud of His glory filled the tabernacle. When He wanted the Israelites to move, He lifted the cloud and removed His presence. As soon as He did so, the Hebrews were to break camp and follow Him.

When He moved, they were to move. When He stopped, they were to stop. Whether they remained in a particular place a day or a year was entirely up to God (Numbers 9:15-23). In this way, the Israelites would not only learn obedience, but they would always be where He wanted them to be.

Silver Trumpets

As a final preparation for their continued journey, God outlined a plan by which He and His people could communicate. He ordered the making of two silver trumpets.

The priests were to blow these trumpets (Numbers 10:1-10). If one sounded, only the leaders were to gather before the tent of meeting; if both were blown, all the Israelites were to assemble. The trumpets were to sound the alarm for war or to warn that the camp must prepare to move. They were to be blown to announce feasts and the first days of each month. Further, they were to be sounded over the sacrifices. It was up to the people to learn the meaning of the communication of the trumpets and to respond to them quickly and correctly.

Pause

What a first year it had been! In addition to all else, the Israelites had had leaders from their own people set over themselves (Exodus 18:21-22), had learned of war, and had learned to wait on God (Exodus 24:18). They had dishonored God by building a golden idol but had also honored Him by building Him a home. They had furiously and repeatedly rebelled against God but found they were still commanded to submit to

Him. They had yearned for old ways but had been told to learn and follow new ones. They had thought the desert would be but a temporary pilgrimage leading directly to Canaan, but as yet they were still walking through it. Now, in the midst of the trials and tumult came a short pause.

While the camp paused, it would be wise for us to do so too, so we can review several important observations. First, God placed great emphasis on the desert experience. From Genesis 46, when the children of Israel entered Egypt, until Exodus 14, when they left, our Bibles record 430 years of history in nineteen chapters. By way of contrast, the forty years of the desert journey are detailed in 136 chapters (Exodus 15 to Joshua 3). If God cared enough to ensure that these chapters were meticulously chronicled, we should read them and heed them.

Second, the desert experience was meant to bring a people and their God together. The covenant between God and the Israelites was cut in the wilderness after the Israelites' salvation, not in Egypt. Further, God announced His lordship, set forth His commandments, and asked His people to accept Him, submit to Him, fellowship with Him, and worship Him in the wilderness, not in Canaan.

Third, the Israelites had to learn to walk the talk in the desert. God's people had to put into practice the rules and commands they had been given. They were asked to live their love for and their faith in God. Having been in the desert little more than a year, they had no idea that their recalcitrance in doing so would cost them thirty-nine more years and that God would ultimately have to release not this but the next generation to enter the promised land. At this point, the Israelites were ready to leave Sinai, but they were not ready to leave the desert.

MOVING ON

Then it began. Little more than a year after leaving Egypt, the cloud lifted, and the Israelites set off (Numbers 10).

More Complaining

As soon as the camp began to move, the people began to complain again. As soon as the people began to complain, the discipline of the LORD fell on them. He sent fire to burn among the people, which consumed the outskirts of the camp (Numbers 11:1-3). Once again Moses had to intercede for the Israelites, and once again God had mercy on His people.

Raising Of Leaders

When he heard the people expressing their desire to return to Egypt and especially when he knew they were scorning God's provision of manna, Moses himself fell into grumbling, in utter despair at leading this stubborn people. He asked why God was so hard on him and why the whole burden of the people was on him. In addition, after informing God that leadership had not been his idea, Moses declared his inability to deal with the situation. In short, he was ready to quit (Numbers 11:4-15).

God immediately responded to this. He told Moses to gather seventy elders who were known among the people as leaders. He then promised: *"Then I will come down and speak with you there, and I will take of the Spirit who is upon you, and will put Him upon them; and they shall bear the burden of the people with you, so that you will not bear it all alone"* (Numbers 11:17).

When this happened, when God put His Spirit on the seventy, they began to prophesy. Prophetically, Moses yearned, *"Would that all the LORD'S people were prophets, that the LORD would put His Spirit upon them!"* (Numbers 11:29).

Rebellion: Miriam And Aaron

Yet a people who would not yet accept God would also not accept His governing them or the human vessels He chose as His leaders. The murmuring and faultfinding did not stop; like a wildfire, it swept through the whole camp. The people had complained of the LORD; Moses had grumbled to the LORD. Now, almost as an echo of earlier sibling rivalry between Cain and Abel, Ishmael and Isaac, or Esau and Jacob, Miriam and Aaron rebelled against God. They rejected the leadership of their own brother, Moses (Numbers 12).

Outwardly their complaint was that Moses had married a Cushite woman. In reality, the problem was an attempt to establish self-government. They were attacking the leadership that God had placed over them because they were ambitious enough to want that place for themselves. It was a case of the humble versus the proud. Miriam and Aaron could see the anointing of God on Moses. They knew that God had set Moses apart to lead His people, that He spoke to Moses face to face (Exodus 33:11), and that He had allowed Moses to see His glory (Exodus 33:18-23). Yet, they dared attack God's anointed.

Once more, God moved to put down rebellion. He personally and severely rebuked the errant pair, and His anger left Miriam a leper. As soon as Aaron saw her, he repented. Then Moses interceded, and Miriam was healed and restored to fellowship. However, neither Aaron nor Miriam reached the promised land.

Rebellion: The Israelites Refuse To Enter The Promised Land

What had been sporadic incidents of rebellion quickly became full-blown insurrection. The Israelites now reached the high water mark of their rebellion against the LORD (Numbers 13-14). Arriving near the border of Canaan, God ordered twelve men, one leader from each tribe, to spy out the promised land. Moses instructed the spies to evaluate the land, the people, and the strengths and weaknesses of the cities and fortifications. Also, if possible, they were to bring back some of the fruit of the land.

The men did just that. For forty days they spied, evaluated, and searched. Then they returned to the camp, bringing with them pomegranates, figs, and a cluster of grapes so large it needed two men to bear it.

The spies gave a positive report on the beauty and fruitfulness of Canaan. They declared it to be just as God had said it was, a land flowing with milk and honey. However, they then gave a negative report on the people and cities. They said the land was occupied by enemies who were too strong for the Israelites. They described fortified cities and announced that giants were in the land which were so large that the men had seemed like grasshoppers compared to them.

While the spies returned with fruit, they also returned with unbelief and fear. They earnestly urged the Israelites not to enter the promised land.

The Israelites knew that God was in the midst of them. Even the Israelites' enemies knew His presence dwelt there. God had made it clear to His people that He was going to give them the land. Yet God would not force them to do His will. He had given
each of them a free will and expected them to use it in making their own choices. In yet another episode of rebellion, the Israelites chose to ignore the will of God. It wasn't that they could not but that they would not enter Canaan.

Of the twelve spies, only two, Joshua and Caleb, passed this test. Of a different spirit, they urged the people to take the land. The other ten spies failed miserably. In spite of all of God's supernatural miracles on their behalf, these spies insisted on assessing the situation by their senses and their feelings. They saw trouble and felt fear. Soon the voice of the people was once again rising:

> "Would that we had died in the land of Egypt! Or would that we had died in this wilderness! Why is the LORD bringing us into this land, to fall by the sword? Our wives and our little ones will become plunder; would it not be better for us to return to Egypt?" So they said to one another, "Let us appoint a leader and return to Egypt." (Numbers 14:2-4)

Whatever else the desert did for the Israelites, it taught the faithful to pray. Time after time, Moses and Aaron interceded (Numbers 11:2; 12:13; 14:5; 14:13-18; 16:22; 16:45; 21:7), and time after time, God favorably responded. Even so, at this point, the people were ready to stone their leaders (Numbers 14:10). When God appeared on the scene and declared His intention to smite and dispossess the Israelites, Moses did a glorious and heroic thing. God had earlier revealed His name and His nature to Moses. Moses reminded God of that and challenged Him to be slow to anger and abundant in lovingkindness. He asked God to forgive the iniquity of His people (Numbers 14:17-19).

At the same time the LORD extended His mercy, His judgment also fell. Declaring that He had been tested enough by a rebellious people, He declared that those same people had forfeited their inheritance. Having persisted in rebellion too long, none of the people He had brought out of Egypt, except Joshua and Caleb, would ever step foot in Canaan. Their own insurrection had turned on them.

> So the LORD said, "I have pardoned them according to your word; but indeed, as I live, all the earth will be filled with the glory of the LORD. Surely all the men who have seen My glory and My signs which I performed in Egypt and in the wilderness, yet have put Me to the test these ten times and have not listened to My voice, shall by no means see the land which I swore to their fathers, nor shall any of those who spurned Me see it. But My servant Caleb, because he has had a different spirit and has followed Me fully, I will bring into the land which he entered, and his descendants shall take possession of it. Now the Amalekites and the Canaanites live in the valleys; turn tomorrow and set out to the wilderness by the way of the Red Sea." The LORD spoke to Moses and Aaron, saying, "How long shall I bear with this evil congregation who are grumbling against Me? I have heard the

complaints of the sons of Israel, which they are making against Me. Say to them, 'As I live,' says the LORD, 'just as you have spoken in My hearing, so I will surely do to you; your corpses shall fall in this wilderness, even all your numbered men, according to your complete number from twenty years old and upward, who have grumbled against Me. Surely you shall not come into the land in which I swore to settle you, except Caleb the son of Jephunneh and Joshua the son of Nun. Your children, however, whom you said would become a prey – I will bring them in, and they will know the land which you have rejected. But as for you, your corpses will fall in this wilderness. Your sons will be shepherds for forty years in the wilderness, and they will suffer for your unfaithfulness, until your corpses lie in the wilderness. According to the number of days which you spied out the land, forty days, for every day you shall bear your guilt a year, even forty years, and you will know My opposition. I, the LORD, have spoken, surely this I will do to all this evil congregation who are gathered together against Me. In this wilderness they shall be destroyed, and there they will die.'"
(Numbers 14:20-35)

Additionally, the ten spies who made the bad report about the promised land died by a plague before the LORD (Numbers 14:37).

That which the Israelites had feared the most was now going to happen. If they would not walk in God's power and see it consume their enemy, that power would now consume them. If they would not kill off their manifestations of flesh, that flesh would destroy them. They would now die in flesh.

God had pardoned the Israelites, but the people had yet to reap what they had sown. They had rejected the LORD. They had tested Him ten times (Exodus 15:22-26; 16:1-4; 17:1-7; 17:8-16; 20:18-21; 32; Numbers 11:1-3; 11:4-6; 11:10-34; 14:1-4), and He had tested them. It was not God's lack of provision but the Israelites' lack of thankfulness, not His inability but their rebellion that brought judgment. God didn't send them to wander in the desert to die; they sent themselves there.

Even Joshua and Caleb, God's faithful servants, had to march on the desert detour. They too had to share the punishment and suffer for thirty-nine more years. The difference was that though their entrance to Canaan was delayed, they eventually did enter it and receive their reward. However, that entrance was denied to everyone else. While the faithful ones gained their inheritance through vision and obedience, all the others forfeited it through fear and rebellion.

Presumption: The Israelites Attempt To Enter The Promised Land Without God's Command

Perhaps thinking that they could undo God's decision, the Israelites compounded the problem. Already judged for iniquity, they added to their list of errors. If rebellion is not doing what God has said to do, presumption is doing what God has not said to do. The Israelites now presumed on God.

The people of Israel had just rejected God's command to possess Canaan. They had refused to be obedient and enter the land He had promised them. Now, with no instruction from Him, they decided to reverse course and go anyway. They were going to do that which God had not commanded.

Moses warned them not to *"go up, or you will be struck down before your enemies, for the LORD is not among you"* (Numbers 14:42). They would not succeed for the LORD was not in their actions. Yet, the Israelites went anyway. With no ark of God's presence, they had no power. Without Moses, they had no leader. The inhabitants of Canaan struck and defeated them. Presumption cost them dearly.

Rebellion: Korah, Dathan, And Abiram

Yet sin continued to rage. Korah, Dathan, and Abiram conspired with 250 leaders of the congregation. Moses had recently delegated authority to other leaders, including Korah, Dathan, and Abiram. However, instead of being content with their positions of responsibility, they wanted more. They rose up before Moses and challenged the legitimacy of his leadership (Numbers 16). They claimed that all the congregation of Israel was holy and that Moses and Aaron had exalted themselves above everyone else. They claimed that Moses and Aaron had raised themselves to positions of leadership rather than God raising them.

Moses accepted neither the accusation nor the rejection hurled at him. He knew who he was and Who had made him such. Since people had had no part in placing him in his position of authority, he wouldn't allow people to displace him.

Once again the real problem was not with the accused as much as with the accusers. Sensing pride and jealousy, Moses said:

"Hear now, you sons of Levi, is it not enough for you that the

God of Israel has separated you from the rest of the congregation of Israel, to bring you near to Himself, to do the service of the tabernacle of the LORD, and to stand before the congregation to minister to them; and that He has brought you near, Korah, and all your brothers, sons of Levi, with you? And are you seeking for the priesthood also?" (Numbers 16:8-10)

As a Levite, Korah served in the tabernacle, so he possessed a heritage of honor and privilege; as part of the tribe of Reuben, Dathan and Abiram were men of renown. Yet they wanted more. They wanted what was not theirs. As Miriam did earlier, they learned that God chooses who **He** will and raises who **He** will.

The leadership that had been challenged now came into prominence. Moses directed the conspirators to bring censers full of fire and to offer incense before the LORD. Aaron was to do the same. Then God would choose whom He would honor.

Moses also talked with Dathan and Abiram. He gave them reason and time to repent. However, his efforts were met with complete refusal to yield and further hardening of heart.

God made His choice. Korah, Dathan, and Abiram and their wives, families, and possessions were swallowed up when the ground split open beneath them. Then fire came forth from God and consumed the 250 others who were offering incense.

Bronze is a symbol of judgment. The censers of these rebellious men had been made of bronze and their rebellious actions brought judgment down. Those who had asked for judgment to fall on the righteous themselves fell under the judgment of holy God. The Lord then ordered that their censers be hammered into sheets of plating which would cover the brazen altar.

Self And Flesh

It was during this challenge that a great truth became obvious. While interceding that God's judgment not fall on the whole congregation of Israel, Moses and Aaron appealed to the God of the spirits of all flesh (Numbers 16:22). This precisely described the problem of the people and gave the reason for the extended desert journey: from the rebellion at the Red Sea until that moment, the people had been acting for themselves, not God, and in flesh, not in spirit.

In the early stages of their journey, it was apparent that one of the main differences between the Israelites and God had to do with the flesh. The Israelites were awash with passions, anger, fear, resentment, divisions, and quarreling. To prove Himself to them, God tested them in order to overcome the power of flesh. However, progress was excruciatingly slow. Since entering the desert, another problem had arisen. While still exhibiting the sins of the flesh, a second transgression that needed to be overcome had become apparent: self.

As seen by their constant clamoring for adequate food and water and for protection from all enemies, the Israelites perceived their primary desert need as the sustainment of self. As they demanded these needs be met, the children of God involved themselves in expressions of self. Unbelief, grumbling, rebellion, pride, ambition, ego, arrogance, and self-promotion were evident in all their activities and responses to God.

While in Egypt, the Israelites had served sin. They had been freed from Egypt to go and serve God. They accepted the freedom, but they did not accept service to anyone but themselves. The Israelites knew God to be their Savior, but they would not acknowledge Him as their LORD. They would not agree that He was Master and that they were His servants.

Even at Mount Sinai, this defiance or insubordination was apparent. There, though God had met with the people and proclaimed, *"I am the LORD Your God"* (Exodus 20:2), the people quickly reneged on the covenant which declared His lordship and broke the commandments that they had agreed to obey in order to maintain their special relationship with God. They then chose other gods, the first of which was the golden calf. Although they carried other gods with them all the way through the desert (Acts 7:42-43), their real god at this point of their journey was self.

The Israelites wanted self-rule. The people wanted to pursue their own desires, do what was right in their own eyes, and do as they pleased. They wouldn't accept God's governance because they wanted to do only what they felt like doing. They wouldn't serve Him as Master because they chose to serve themselves. Psalm 106:13 sums it up: *"They quickly forgot His works; they did not wait for His counsel...."*

In refusing to serve God, the people had become their own gods. In rejecting the lordship of God and in trying to determine their own destiny, the Israelites had set a pattern that repeated itself throughout the desert trek. As God had judged Egypt for raising and serving false gods, so He now judged His own children for the same offense, the raising and exalting of the god of self. In both cases, the pronounced judgment was death. Korah, Dathan, and Abiram and their followers were raising themselves up and were seeking to replace godly leaders with selfish ones and to replace godly government with a fleshly one. Their attempted coup resulted in their deaths.

Rebellion: Moses

Soon after Korah's rebellion, more tragedy occurred in the Israelite camp: at Kadesh, Miriam died (Numbers 20:1). Instead of supporting Moses as he grieved for his sister, the Israelites contended with Moses because they had no water. They demanded to know why Moses "made" them leave Egypt and brought them to this wretched place (Numbers 20:5). As he usually did, Moses took his problem to God, and the LORD told him to: *"Take the rod; and you and your brother Aaron assemble the congregation and speak to the rock before their eyes, that it may yield its water"* (Numbers 20:8).

In exasperation and anger at the people for their continual evil and lack of trust in God, Moses did not obey God. Instead of speaking to the rock, he raised his staff and struck the rock twice. Water poured forth abundantly for the people, but Moses paid dearly for his transgression. He forfeited his entry into Canaan (Numbers 20:12).

The Edomites

As if Moses' loss triggered opposition, more problems arose. Moses sent messengers to the king of Edom asking permission for the Israelites to pass through his territory on the way to Canaan. The king not only refused but he came with a heavy force to keep the Israelites out of Edom (Numbers 20:20-21).

The people of Edom were the descendants of Esau. Esau and Jacob (whose name was later changed to Israel) had once been brothers. As brother had opposed brother in the earlier relationship, so now, brother opposed brother in the desert. The Edomites attempted to divert the Israelites and to keep them from walking on the king's highway on their journey to the promised land.

Fiery Serpents

Forced to walk around the land of Edom, the Israelites once

again complained about God, Moses, the wilderness, and the lack of food and water. As a result, the LORD sent fiery serpents among the people. The serpents bit the Israelites, and many of them died (Numbers 21:5-20).

This time, the people repented, and God relented. God commanded Moses to make a fiery serpent out of bronze and to set it on a pole. Then, when the wounded looked upon the serpent, they lived. If they didn't, they died. Once again under a bronze symbol of judgment, God taught His people that in facing their problems they would be made whole.

The Canaanites

The Edomites were not the only people to come against the Israelites. Soon there was conflict with the Canaanites. The Canaanites, the original inhabitants of Palestine, lived near the eastern shore of the Mediterranean Sea. Descendants of Noah through his son, Ham, they were described as a fierce, wicked, idolatrous people who defiled the land (Leviticus 18:24-27); Deuteronomy 29:16-17). While the Canaanites were one distinctive tribe, their name was also used to describe a combined group of tribes that included the Canaanites, Hivites, Hittites, Girgashites, Jebusites, Perrizites, and Amorites (Deuteronomy 7:1).

The land the Canaanites occupied was the land that God had promised to Abraham and his descendants (Genesis 12:1-5). Needless to say, when the Israelites showed up to claim their land, conflict arose.

The Amorites

The Israelites walked on. Having begun their desert journey by battling the Amalekites, now toward the end of their sojourn in the wilderness, they found themselves confronting the Amorites. The cloud of the presence of God was leading the Israelites on the path to the promised land, but to get there, they had to pass through the land of Sihon, the king of the Amorites (Numbers 21:21-30). Once again, they asked permission to continue on their journey, and, once again, they were refused. As the Edomites had done, the Amorites rallied against Israel.

However, this time the Israelites did not back down. They struck Sihon with the sword, defeated him, and took possession of his land and cities. As the Israelites continued on their journey, Og, king of Bashan, challenged them in battle. Hearing and heeding the LORD'S command not to fear, the Israelites struck him, conquered him, and occupied his land too (Numbers 21:33-35). These two victories finally seemed a taste of things to come.

The Moabites And Midianites

It is sad that the Israelites did not maintain their newfound courage and faithfulness. Soon they committed the worst possible offense:

> While Israel remained at Shittim, the people began to play the harlot with the daughters of Moab. For they invited the people to the sacrifices of their gods, and the people ate and bowed down to their gods. So Israel joined themselves to Baal of Peor, and the LORD was angry against Israel. (Numbers 25:1-3)

Even after God's judgment had fallen on those involved in this sin and after they had been executed for their sin, the Israelites clearly hadn't learned their lesson. Instead, they compounded the problem with further harlotry.

> Then behold, one of the sons of Israel came and brought to his relatives a Midianite woman, in the sight of Moses and in the sight of all the congregation of the sons of Israel, while they were weeping at the doorway of the tent of meeting. (Numbers 25:6)

One among the Hebrews continued to be zealous for God. One continued to feel as God felt and to see as God saw. One continued to understand God's heart, and he responded to this blemish on God's name. Phineas, grandson of Aaron, rose up, took his spear, and killed both the Israelite man and the Midianite woman as they engaged in harlotry. In so doing, he stopped the plague that had broken out among the Israelites.

One man responding on God's behalf could and did make a difference. One man's zeal and obedience changed God's heart toward a whole people. After Phineas had responded for God, God responded to Phineas, making a covenant of peace with him and his descendants forever (Numbers 25:10-13; see also Psalm 106:30-31).

In addition, Phineas's actions checked a plague that was ravaging the Israelites. This plague was another in a long line of plagues (Numbers 11:33; 14:37; 16:46; 25:8). God had once promised to keep the Israelites from the diseases of the Egyptians if they obeyed Him. Whether or not the diseases which afflicted the Israelites were exactly those which consumed Egypt, they were nevertheless God's judgment on His people. The Israelites hadn't obeyed God, so God hadn't blessed them with health.

A New Generation And A New Leader

Finally, after many long, hard years, the day came when the older generation had died off. Except for Joshua and Caleb, the leaders and the people of Israel were gone. A whole new generation had been established. The LORD commanded Moses to take a census of the new generation (Numbers 26). When it was complete, He informed Moses that he was about to die or be gathered to his people (Numbers 27:12-14). Moses was allowed to climb the mountain of Abarim to view the promised land, but he never stepped into it.

Realizing that his absence would create a problem, Moses asked God to raise up his successor. He asked for a man who would lead the people out and bring them in (Numbers 27:17), like a shepherd who takes good care of his sheep. God quickly responded to this request. Knowing that the Israelites' next job was to possess the land and that they would need a military man skilled in warfare in order to do so, God chose Joshua, a man in whom was the Spirit (Numbers 27:18). God told Moses to commission Joshua as leader in the sight of all Israel to provide continuity in the handing over of the leadership and to provide Joshua's governance with legitimacy. Moreover, after Aaron's death, new spiritual leader was needed as well, and God raised up Eleazar, son of Aaron, to be priest. As the old generation had been led by Moses and Aaron, so the new generation would be led by Joshua and Eleazar.

Inheritance Not In The Promised Land

On the border of Canaan, the Israelites once again fell short. The sons of Reuben and Gad looked around at the land that the Israelites had conquered and noted that it was highly suited for raising their livestock. They asked Moses that the land of the Amorites be given to them as their land inheritance. Disregarding the fact that it was not part of the promised land, they had decided to settle there (Numbers 32:1-5).

Thinking at first that these tribes didn't want to go to war and that this would make the rest of the people too fearful to enter the land like their fathers had been, Moses would not agree with their request. He thought their decision was about to bring more judgment on the Israelites. However, the sons of the tribes of Reuben, Gad, and the half-tribe of Manasseh assured him that they would cross into Canaan and fight with their brothers for as long as it took to possess and occupy the land. Only after that would they return across the Jordan River to settle their own land (Numbers 32:6-32).

They kept their word. Only after Canaan had been invaded and won did the sons of Reuben, Gad, and the half-tribe of Manasseh leave the promised land. They were the first tribes placed into their new inheritance. Unfortunately, years later, according to *Matthew Henry's Commentary* on 1 Chronicles 5:25-26, because they sinned against their God, intermingled with the nearby nations, and engaged in their idolatrous practices, they were also the first tribes to be displaced.

DESERT'S END

What a time it had been! For forty long years, the Israelites had wandered. Within the prescribed boundaries of the Red Sea to the Jordan River, they had repeatedly walked the same ways and circled the same mountains. Though it may have seemed that they had spent a lot of time spinning their wheels going nowhere or engaging in much labor but seeing little fruit, God always had a purpose. During this time, He had taught His people some hard and valuable lessons.

The desert had been a time of change. All who walked in it were affected by it. It is important to realize that by God's choice, no one had gone directly from Egypt to Canaan. Without exception, everyone – **all** leaders and people – had to spend time in the desert. The vast majority had died there. By the grace of God, they were not in Egypt when they died, but they were not in Canaan either. The cloud of the Spirit was slowly but surely leading them there.

The desert journey should have lasted eleven days (Deuteronomy 1:2). Instead, it took forty years. It has been wisely said that it took one night to get the Israelites out of Egypt but forty years to get Egypt out of the Israelites.

Yet, let it be remembered that the Israelites made their journey in the presence of God. God, who loved them, oversaw every step of the way. As the Shepherd of Israel (Psalm 80:1), He led His people like a flock (Psalm 77:20). Not only with the staff and rod of authority but also with a heart of love, God had guarded, guided, and kept His children, bringing them to the very edge of the promised land.

Chapter 11

THE DESERT:

EACH SAINT'S PERSONAL SANCTIFICATION

If the Israelites had not had a bloody Passover lamb, Pharaoh's power over them would not have been broken and they would not have been saved. Just so, if each saint did not have the Sacrificial Lamb, Satan's power over him (or her) would not have been broken and he would not have been saved. If the Israelites had not departed on an exodus from Egypt, they would not have been separated from evil. Similarly, if each new saint does not leave the world system, he will not be separated from sin. If the Israelites had not been bold and obedient to plunge into and pass through the waters of the Red Sea, they would have never reemerged as a new, free, full-of-life nation on the other side. Likewise, if each saint will not submit to water baptism, he will never truly know that his death to sin, his burial of the past, and his resurrection to new life make him a new creature, one able to sing to the Lord as he enters his new life in Christ.

The exodus is the story of the nation of Israel as it occurred several thousand years ago. Yet, as a child of God in the twenty-first century, each saint has the same story and faces the same journey. As the Israelites had to decide whether to sit on the far shore of the Red Sea or to rise and cross the desert, so must each saint. If his (or her) decision is to go forward, each must realize that he will meet with the same failures and successes, the same valleys and mountain tops, and the same enemies and friends that the Israelites did. He must recognize the fact that not one man, woman, or child of Israel walked directly from Egypt to Canaan; each had a desert detour, and so does each saint. In fact, he will find both journeys to be remarkably similar.

THE DESERT

Soon after a spiritually reborn saint has been forgiven of sin by the power, grace, and mercy of God and has passed through the refreshing waters of baptism, he (or she) finds himself in a strange and alien land. Not still in sin but not yet in the promised land of rest and inheritance, each finds himself, as the nation of Israel did, in a trying and confusing place. He is what is known as a carnal Christian, redeemed and reborn in spirit but still walking out the process of reclamation in soul and body.

This new land is the saint's place of passage. It is an area through which he (or she) must travel, adjust to, live in, and conquer while he is there even as he makes slow but steady progress toward the land of promise. It can be a place of torment as well as of great beauty. For each child of God, it is often a spiritually dry and barren place. It is a place where natural elements take their toll. It is a place where enemies without and within attack and sometimes destroy. It is a place where there seems little to sustain or keep those found there. It is a place where each often fails to cope with the new ways and is lured back to the old ways. It is the desert.

The desert is a place of testing and trial to show each saint the condition of his (or her) heart toward God. The trials that God used to test the Israelites in the natural realm are the very same trials He uses to test each new saint in the spiritual realm. In His foreknowledge, God already knows the thoughts, words, deeds, and attitudes of each saint. He knows what each has said and what he will say, what each has done and what he will do. Therefore, God does not test so that He may learn of His heart toward His children; He tests so that each child may know the condition of his heart toward God. Oh, that every saint could early and sincerely learn to pray as David once did in order to know the truth of his heart toward God: *"Examine me, O LORD, and try me; test my mind and my heart"* (Psalm 26:2).

The desert is so hostile to God's lambs and sheep and so devoid of fruit, milk, and honey that each saint knows in his (or her) heart that the journey does not – cannot – stop here. Therefore, as soon as his exuberant burst of worship unto Almighty God dies out, He is asked to set out or to continue his journey. Knowing that a long, difficult march lies between where he is and where God wants him to be and knowing that God is the only One who can successfully lead him to the place He has chosen for him, each must decide whether to cast his lot with God and to go on with Him or to remain where he is.

As he (or she) contemplates this decision, he must remember that even as he could not save himself, neither can he sanctify himself. God alone can break the power of sin, and He alone can separate the saints from sin. When a saint declares he does not have the strength to give up behaviors that dishonor God, he is right. Yet God is not asking him to do so by his own power. He's asking him to call out to Him and then to allow God's power to do it for him.

Similarly, as each saint cannot consecrate himself (or herself), neither can he sanctify others. Although saints may become frustrated or unhappy in seeing the need for sanctification in their spouses, parents, siblings, children, friends, neighbors, or bosses, they are not in charge of those people's exoduses. Only God is. Any unholy works by saints to sanctify others are all in vain. They end in control, not in conviction; they are of flesh, not of spirit; they are temporary, not eternal; and they are fraught with error, not perfect.

Each person has to decide for himself (or herself) whether or not to leave Egypt or the land of sin. No one is able to or should be allowed to make that decision for another. Likewise, each must decide to walk on God's chosen path at God's chosen pace. While a saint can surely pray and voice his concern about another to God, he cannot force a sluggish loved one to participate in an exodus.

For those living stones determined to follow the cloud of God's presence, the desert adventure begins. First come some challenges of flesh.

THE FLESH

To understand the problem concerning flesh it is necessary to know what the term means. Biblically, if the word flesh is used, it is a reference to the physical body. However, if the term **the** flesh is used, it is a reference to the inner part of men and women that was alienated from and is still in rebellion to God since the events in the Garden of Eden.

In an article titled "What Does the Bible Mean By 'The Flesh'?" Monseigneur Charles Pope writes the flesh is:

> the rebellious, unruly and obstinate part of our inner self that is operative all the time. It is that part of us that does not want to be told what to do. It is stubborn, refuses correction, and does not want to have a thing to do with God. It bristles at limits and rules.

It recoils at anything that might cause a person to be diminished or be something less than the center of the universe. The flesh hates to be under authority or to have to yield to anything other than its own wishes and desires. The flesh often desires something simply because it is "forbidden."

Further, he teaches:

The flesh is in direct conflict with the spirit. "The spirit" here refers not to the Holy Spirit but to the human spirit. The (human) spirit is that part of us which is open to God, which desires him and is drawn to him. It is that part of us which is attracted by goodness, beauty and truth, which yearns for completion in God and to see His face. Without the spirit we would be totally turned in on ourselves and consumed by the flesh. Thankfully our spirit, assisted by the Holy Spirit, draws us to desire what is best, what is upright, good, and helpful.

According to Monseigneur Pope, the flesh does not grasp spiritual teachings (John 6:63); is not willing to depend on anyone or anything outside its own power or control (Philippians 3:3-9); hates to be told what to do (Romans 7:5); is intrinsically hostile to God (Romans 8:5-7); demands to be fed (Galatians 5:16-17); and fuels sin (Galatians 5:19-21).

The battle to defeat flesh is a part of every saint's desert journey. The only way to deal with flesh is to crucify it as Jesus was crucified in the flesh on the cross. The only way to deal with self is to die daily, to die to the old man, and to come alive to God in Christ. Dying is not easy or fun; rather, it is difficult and painful. A half-hearted, partial attempt is useless.

TESTING IN THE DESERT

As each saint faces testing in the desert, he (or she) must remember the difference between tempting and testing: Satan tempts but God tests. Satan tempts to embarrass a saint in his weakness, but God tests to encourage him in his strengths. Satan tempts to tear him down, but God tests to build him up. Satan tempts to send him running back to bondage, but God tests to send him on to his inheritance. Satan tempts so he will cover up or deny his shortcomings, but God tests to show him things about himself that he must address.

Rebellion And Bitterness: Marah

God leads each saint quickly away from the Red Sea into the wilderness. It doesn't take many days in the hot, burning wasteland to reach a point of real thirst. The discovery that God has not only allowed His new saint to become dry but has then led him (or her) to bitter water puzzles him. Yet, as God did with the Hebrews at Marah, He has led His saint to the revelation of bitterness. This bitterness must be cured before the journey can resume.

In His infinite wisdom and mercy, is it not God's blessing that each saint be made aware as to whether or not he (or she) is bitter or angry toward those people, places, or things that once held him captive in the world? Is it not God's kindness for each new saint to understand there might be a lack of forgiveness toward those who, though calling themselves family or friend, could never lead the parched one to God? Is it not God's favor that makes each new lamb aware that his heart may not be right toward those, be they pastor, priest, teacher, or leader in the world's ungodly, religious system, who could see his thirst for holiness but time after time led him to an empty well, who saw him longing for the true God but never brought him to His flow of living water? Is it not God's goodness that allows each saint to hear the sound of his own voice caustically complaining so he can realize the sin of bitterness in his own heart?

Further, while God brings each saint to the point where he (or she) realizes the need for healing of the inner, emotional, or mental issues that tear at his heart, He blesses him to understand that He can heal the outer, physical ones too. At Marah in the desert, God revealed exactly how He would do that. As He led Moses to a tree that, when thrown into the pool of bitter waters, made them sweet, so He leads each saint to a new tree, one which has the miraculous power to mend wounded or broken hearts and to heal physical diseases. This special healing tree is the cross of Christ.

By applying Jesus' outpouring of love to the bitterness in his (or her) heart, each saint's inner pain can be healed, forgiveness for those who have hurt him will flow over and through him, his thirst will be quenched in Jesus' everlasting fountain of joy, and his heart will be healed in His balm of love. Additionally, by administering the on-going healing power found in Jesus' sacrifice at this cross, a saint's physical body can be healed. This is his first test.

Soon follows another test. Has each person who has been saved by grace and who finds himself (or herself) in the desert been well taught about life after salvation? Does each at this onset of his desert journey know the Lord well? Does each truly trust Him to care for him or does the lack of any visible means of spiritual sustenance frighten the newly reborn into unbelief?

Has each person who has been saved by grace been told that since he (or she) is a citizen of the kingdom of God, he is subject to His rule? Does he know that he is now expected to keep God's laws and obey His voice? When each finds this out, is he angry and does he rail against those who brought him out of the kingdom of darkness?

Therefore, is it a surprise that early in the desert walk, God's new creature, through fear and unbelief, sometimes rebels against the leadership of those who helped him (or her) to freedom, not knowing that his grumbling, complaining, and murmuring is really a sin against the God who saved him?

Hunger

Onwards each new saint must travel. Soon it becomes apparent in his (or her) desert walk that he is hungry; he has no food. In the world, he has not been nourished on holy bread. What meager provisions or foodstuffs he brought with him from his slavery to sin are quickly depleted. He is once again faced with the reality of his deep poverty.

Once more, the Lord provides. Waiting until a saint realizes his (or her) need of spiritual food and cries out to Him for help, He quickly moves to furnish him with nourishment. He sends him a limitless supply of the Bread of Life, Jesus (John 6:35), to fill him to overflowing.

As God instructed the Israelites concerning the gathering of manna, so He now instructs each saint to pick Him up and to feed on Him, the Word made flesh (John 1:14). Each saint is to fill his (or her) heart with holy Scripture every morning, as much as he needs for that day. As he does so, he is totally filled, nourished, and made whole by Him. And as he does so, he is tested to see whether or not he will follow God's instructions.

Thirst

Shortly after beginning their natural wilderness journey, the Israelites came to Rephidim, a second place of quarrelling and testing over lack of water. Each saint's spiritual journey quickly brings him (or her) to that same point. Often contentious because of the flesh within him rebels at constantly needing to seek both his supply and his Supplier, he rises up against God and demands that his needs be more quickly and automatically met. Even as God shows him the shortcomings in his temperament and in his desire to remain independent from God for provision, His fullness of love acts for each saint, blessing him richly.

To quench the Israelites' thirst, God told Moses to lift his staff and to strike the rock. When he did so, streams of water gushed out. Today, God shows that His Shepherd's rod or staff is still the authority by which the needs of His people are met and the demands of the flesh are conquered. By raising this staff and striking the Rock, Christ Jesus (1 Corinthians 10:4), living water will flow forth. As His provision was so abundant for Israel that it caused streams to flow in the desert (Psalm 78:16), so also His gift of the waters of life will be immeasurable toward each saint. His miracles on behalf of each of His beloved lambs should answer the question that the Israelites asked as they wandered in the desert wasteland: *"Is the LORD among us, or not?"* (Exodus 17:7).

Yet sometimes, they do not. Sometimes a saint is yet unconvinced of God's goodness. Soon more tests follow.

The Amalekites

The Israelites had come out of Egypt and found that they could not lead and keep themselves in the desert places. Therefore, with much grumbling, they had to maintain an attachment to God. So too, each saint or newborn Christian who has just escaped out of the world of sin, finds he (or she) cannot live through his barren, wasteland walk without the constant help and protection of God. He is bewildered to find that he is nothing without God; he is angry that he can do nothing without God.

The first human enemy that came against the Hebrews in the desert were the Amalekites. Some say that the early attack of the Amalekites on the Israelites is a type or figure of the attempt of the flesh to reemerge as the authority over people. Since it is true that flesh does not lightly accept its displacement in the governing of people and will immediately try to rise and reclaim its throne, this claim cannot be taken lightly. In fact, when tempted by such evil, each saint must face his (or her) enemy and refuse the resurrection of his old man by proclaiming the victory of the cross over the flesh.

The Amalekites were descendants of Esau, brother of Jacob. As known from their animosity toward the Israelites, they were a fierce people who displayed evil and lack of fear of God. They sought out the weakness of their enemy and used it as a place of attack. To gain victory in battle, they laid in wait to ambush, fight against, and destroy their foe, all to oppose their advancement toward the promised land.

Today, this same enemy challenges each new saint. As soon as he (or she) enters the kingdom of God, the modern-day forces of Amalek lie in wait. When they spot a weakness in a saint's faith, they attack. They assault his family or criticize his choice of friends. They invade his marriage. They attack his health. They savage his occupation. They assail his hopes, dreams, and plans. In short, they do all they can to discourage and oppose his advancement in God's plan for his life. If they are not successful in stopping it, then they try to destroy it.

However, just as God saved the Hebrews from the attack of the Amalekites, so also, He saves His saints. At Rephidim God changed His orders to the Israelites from, *"Do not fear! Stand by and see the salvation of the LORD which He will accomplish for you today"* (Exodus 14:13) to *"go out, fight against Amalek"* (Exodus 17:9). God is saying the same to each saint today. Having no authority or power to save or sanctify himself (or herself), each new saint must fight this enemy in and through Christ. His call from God, spoken through the apostle Paul, is: *"So then, my beloved, ... work out your salvation with fear and trembling"* (Philippians 2:12).

The Israelites fought the battle at Rephidim by prayer and the rod of God on the part of Moses and by military action on the part of Joshua. Although each new saint may feel unarmed, unprepared, and unequipped, that same two-sided approach of prayer and actively engaging in spiritual warfare will win his (or her) battle against self today.

In his (or her) warfare against the flesh, each saint must declare the legality of his position. *"I have been crucified with Christ; and it is no longer I who live, but Christ lives in me; and the life which I now live in the flesh I live by faith in the Son of God, who loved me and gave Himself up for me"* (Galatians 2:20).

By declaring this verse, each saint acknowledges that when he (or she) was crucified on the cross with Christ, the power of flesh that dominated his life was defeated by that cross. He also acknowledges that His old man of flesh died and his new man of spirit, which is occupied, led, and strengthened by Christ Himself, is now alive. The "I" of each saint's life has been replaced by Christ; he now lives for and through Him.

After declaring the truth of his situation, each saint must then apply that truth. While flesh has been legally dealt with at the cross, experientially it does not like being replaced. It will try to rise and regain its position of control over each saint. Therefore, it must be the subject of diligent watchfulness and constant warfare.

Centuries ago, Amalek was so loathsome that God swore to blot out even his memory. God is just as adamant in His determination for each saint today. His declaration through Moses that He would fight this enemy through generation after generation (Exodus 17:16) is a clear sign to each saint that he (or she) must fight the flesh until it is entirely wiped out.

The Supremacy Of The Rod Of God

God entrusted His rod to Moses, and Moses used it to display God's authority over and over again. Through the rod Moses performed miracles in Pharaoh's court, brought about the plagues in Egypt, parted the Red Sea, and provided water from the rock in the wilderness. During the battle against the Amalekites, the rod of God that had brought such magnificent victories over sin, the world, and the devil was again used to extend God's authority over this enemy of flesh.

The difference for each saint is that the rod of God is no longer a piece of wood. The rod of God is one of the many weapons that God gives each saint to help him (or her) fight in his spiritual warfare. To a saint, the rod of God is now the sword of the Spirit, the word of God (Ephesians 6:17).

In the New Testament, there are two fundamental words used for "word." The first is *logos*, which generally means the written Word of God or the Bible. The second is *rhema*, which is the spoken word of God. This special word that guides a saint through a trying circumstance may come through a prophetic word, a word of knowledge, a message released through a dream, or a passage in the Bible that seems to jump off the page. This rod of God, this *rhema*, is what a saint holds up and uses in his (or her) warfare. This word of God becomes a sword in the hand of every saint and, when spoken in faith, pierces the lies of the enemy, overcomes his attacks, and defeats the foe.

THE NEW COVENANT

Not too long after the desert journey begins, the purpose of his (or her) trials and hardships becomes evident to each saint. He has been saved and separated from the world in preparation for one of the highest honors he or any other person could hope to have: God wants to cut covenant with him. At a time and place of His choosing, God asks each saint to stop wandering, to come to His mountain, and to let Him establish His lordship over him.

A covenant is an agreement or a contract. It is a pact between two people or parties. Some covenants are unconditional, which means they have no obligatory clauses, restrictions, or stipulations attached. Other covenants are conditional. By these, one person makes a promise and agrees to keep it if the other person fulfills certain requirements or maintains obedience to certain provisions or demands.

As God brought the Israelites to a halt in the wilderness and made a covenant with them, so also He temporarily stops the desert wanderings of each saint; calls him (or her) to consecration; sets boundaries beyond which he must not pass; and then grants each, as His blessed, privileged, chosen one, the divine and holy honor of meeting with Him in order that He may establish each in covenant.

The proclamation of this covenant is clear: Jesus is Lord! As God came down to Mount Sinai to establish His Lordship and to issue His covenant to the children of Israel, so today God majestically approaches each saint, declares His Son Jesus to be his (or her) Lord, and brings him under the mantle of the New Covenant.

Pentecost (The Baptism Of The Holy Spirit)

While the New Covenant is an agreement of grace rather than Law, it is yet a declaration that Jesus is Lord and a command that He be obeyed. When Jesus ransomed and redeemed each saint, He bought him (or her) with the price of His blood. Since He did that, each saint became His. As the Owner and Master of each saint, He is Lord of his life in any way and for whatever reason He chooses. It is the privilege of each saint to submit to Jesus and, by his obedience, to allow Jesus to fulfill the will of His Father toward or through each saint.

The obvious question of each saint at this point may be, "But how can I ever do that? In my impotence and lack of experience, how can I ever keep covenant with God?"

The only way to fulfill the covenant of God is through the power of God. The power of God is His Spirit. The only way each saint is enabled to fulfill God's will or to keep His covenant is through the power of the Enabler, the Spirit of God, the Holy Spirit. To obtain this power, the baptism of the Holy Spirit is available to each one.

Long has the Christian world labored, fought, and divided over this baptism. Due to faulty teaching, error, and fear, many have become confused concerning this topic. Problems seem to center around four major areas: denial, delay, unholy demonstrations, and unnecessary pressures. Perhaps a quick digression will help in the search for God's heart in the matter.

Denial

Many denominations resist the idea that the baptism of the Holy Spirit is a valid Christian experience. They instruct the pastors or ministers under their authority to avoid, protest, refute, refuse, or prohibit this baptism. Often, they do so in such overblown, fear-producing ways that the saints are forever scarred on their journey toward God. As a result, they obey denomination rather than God.

This negative attitude is often the result of misunderstanding the various roles that the Holy Spirit plays in the life of the saints. The denominations do not differentiate between the indwelling presence of the Spirit of God and the empowering for holy service by His Spirit. They insist that the indwelling of each saint by the Spirit of God at the time of his (or her) spiritual rebirth and the empowerment of that saint by the Holy Spirit are one and the same. Then, through roundabout reasoning, they declare that if a saint already enjoys the presence of God through the indwelling of His Holy Spirit, there is no reason to repeat the experience by asking to be empowered by God through immersion into His Holy Spirit.

Yet, would it be repeating the same experience? Are indwelling and empowerment the same thing?

Without question, since Jesus and the Holy Spirit are two persons of the one triune God, they cannot be separated. At the time of his (or her) born-again experience, when a new saint asks Jesus into his heart, it is not Jesus in the form of a physical man but the Spirit of Jesus (John 16:7-13; Acts 16:7) who enters into and indwells that saint. It is this indwelling which makes the saint a temple of the Holy Spirit of God (1 Corinthians 3:16).

This Spirit of Christ (Romans 8:9) or abiding presence of God allows His attributes of love, joy, peace, indeed all the fruit of the Spirit, to mature the saint, to conform him (or her) more and more into the image of Christ, to allow him to be as or in the manner of his Lord.

On the other hand, empowerment is a different work of the Spirit within the new saint. It is asking the Holy Spirit, described by the Amplified Bible as the Helper, Comforter, Advocate, Intercessor, Counselor, Strengthener, and Standby (John 14:16), to enable each Christian to do what he (or she) has been told by God to do. It allows him to be a vessel of holy power through whom God can do His work. It provides him with the gifts of the Spirit so he is able to be like God is and to do as He does.

The words indwell and empower do not have the same meaning. Biblically, to indwell is to abide in, to direct, or to control (Romans 8:9); it implies a sense of containment. To empower is to come upon, to enable to act, to authorize (there's that rod again!), or to permit; it is the beginning of the process of releasing.

These words are not even close to being synonymous. In fact, they are almost opposites. Without question, when applied to the problem of the Holy Spirit and the believer, it must be made clear that there is one Spirit of God but He is easily capable of fulfilling two different functions or demonstrating two separate aspects of His work with each saint.

The early apostles understood this difference between infilling and empowerment. Paul, speaking to new converts in Ephesus, specifically asked: *"Did you receive the Holy Spirit when you believed?"* (Acts 19:2).

Paul knew that God indwelt believers at salvation, so he was not questioning them about that experience. In fact, when he learned of the lapse in their teaching which had led to the omission of the baptism of power, he went on to describe and differentiate between the two events.

> *And they said to him, "No, we have not even heard whether there is a Holy Spirit." And he said, "Into what then were you baptized?" And they said, "Into John's baptism." Paul said, "John baptized with the baptism of repentance, telling the people to believe in Him who was coming after him, that is, in Jesus." When they heard this, they were baptized in the name of the Lord Jesus.* (Acts 19:2-5)

Though Paul knew that the Holy Spirit indwelt these Christians, he led them through a second baptism, the baptism of the Holy Spirit. *"And when Paul had laid his hands upon them, the Holy Spirit came on them, and they began speaking with tongues and prophesying"* (Acts 19:6).

As Paul capably taught and showed, believers should have two experiences or two baptisms: the first is the baptism into Christ, which allows each saint to identify with the death, burial, and resurrection to new life of Jesus Christ; the second is a baptism or an immersion into His Holy Spirit which enables each saint to obediently and victoriously live that life through Christ in him (or her).

To the Jewish mind, Passover, the celebration of the breaking of the power of sin, and Pentecost, the original Spirit baptism, were thought of as two aspects of one overall experience. They were the beginning and end of one holy season with God, neither complete without the other. The basis of this belief is found in the Israelites' natural journey. They received the presence of God in the form of the shekinah cloud of glory during their deliverance from Egypt, and then, after traveling to Mount Sinai, they were immersed in His Spirit in the form of the fire that descended on the mountain. These were two separate experiences. Similarly, each saint should ask God to come into his (or her) heart or indwell his temple at the time of salvation and then ask his Lord for the baptism of the Holy Spirit.

Further, God wanted all the Israelites to receive His baptism of power because He knew how difficult it would be for them to cross the desert and to keep His covenant without it. Sadly, when the majority of the Israelites rejected it, this was proven true. A whole generation died.

So too with each saint. It would be extremely difficult to successfully survive his (or her) desert experience or to keep God's covenant without His power. No saint can fully obey in his own strength. Each needs His ongoing empowerment within to do His works without. Being baptized in His Holy Spirit is not a duplication or repetition of the indwelling experience but is instead a separate and necessary requirement for victorious Christian life.

For any who may still deny the need of the baptism of the Holy Spirit or for those who declare it to be optional, hear the Word:

> *As for me, I baptize you with water for repentance, but He who is coming after me is mightier than I ... He will baptize you with the Holy Spirit and fire.* (Matthew 3:11)

> [F]or John baptized with water, but you will be baptized with the Holy Spirit.... (Acts 1:5)

> Repent, and each of you be baptized in the name of Jesus Christ for the forgiveness of your sins; and you will receive the gift of the Holy Spirit. For the promise is for you and your children and for **all** who are far off, **as many as the Lord our God will call to Himself.** [emphasis added] (Acts 2:38-39)

Delay

Again, denominational theology has proved a burden rather than a help to saints. Some denominations teach that there must be a long waiting period, a tarrying time, between salvation and the baptism of the Holy Spirit. This time could extend for days, months, or even years as saints, desperately seeking all that God has for them, line altar rails or pray in small rooms, endlessly appealing to God to bless them with His baptism.

The truth is that God longs to give but bound saints aren't allowed to receive. Those listening for the voice of God often hear human words instead: "You aren't ready," "You're too young in the Lord," "You haven't tarried long enough," "You aren't holy enough," or "Our denominational rules state that you must wait longer."

All of these are nothing but human restrictions or ungodly restraints placed on a Christian. They bear no resemblance to scriptural commands that pertain to the baptism of the Holy Spirit. They are found nowhere in the Word.

Again, using the Israelites' natural journey as an example, it is apparent that they did not delay in receiving God's Spirit. As soon as they left Egypt, they proceeded straight to Mount Sinai, where the power of God rapidly came down upon them. God did not tell them to wait a while at the foot of the mountain while they matured; instead, He poured Himself upon them straightaway so they could mature.

So too with each saint. Rather than purposefully delaying through endless seeking, God would have him (or her) move quickly into closer relationship with Him. Salvation, which includes baptism in water, begins a saint's relationship with God. The baptism of the Holy Spirit then allows him to keep covenant with God through the exercise of the holy power of Christ in him. Though parts of one overall blessing, neither is complete without the other.

Unholy Demonstrations

Without question, legitimate claims of excess and abuse arise in matters concerning manifestations of the power of the Spirit of God. Without question, the bizarre and ungodly actions of some who claim to be baptized in the Holy Spirit foster negative attitudes and give poor testimony as to the greatness of God.

Perhaps two thoughts will help. First, God is a God of order who commands that everything be done "properly and in an orderly manner" (1 Corinthians 14:40). Further, the His Word states that the spirits of those manifesting His gifts are able to be and ought to be under the control of those people (1 Corinthians 14:32). If they are not, what is being manifested is not of God.

However, rather than disciplining those who are poor witnesses to the wonders of God or training up a saint in correct expressions of the fruit and gifts of the Spirit, some religious groups opt to eliminate the problem altogether. Forbidding any manifestation of the Spirit of God, they quench Him, prove poor stewards of His gifts, and shut down holy power in that body. They doom new Christians to an impotent existence.

Second, those strange demonstrations and bizarre behaviors may not expressions of the Spirit of God at all. They may be ways that self or flesh rises and demands attention. Or worse, they may be unrecognized examples or demonstrations of evil, satanic power.

One of the gifts of the Holy Spirit that would obviously be suppressed by a church that is uninterested in or that prohibits the work of the Holy Spirit is discerning of spirits (1 Corinthians 12:10). This gift helps a saint to know the presence of and to distinguish between holy, human, and evil spirits. If ever any gift is desperately needed in this final hour, this is it. How ironic that the very gift meant to help the Church has been rejected by so much of it.

Can every saint avoid all the visual and audial impact of unholy demonstrations purported to be from the Spirit of God? Probably not. However, can each saint recognize and protect himself (or herself) from them? Definitely yes! By receiving the baptism of the Holy Spirit, he is enabled to discern the holy from the profane and to learn and follow holy disciplinary procedures against those mocking God.

Unnecessary Pressures

A final area of controversy surrounding the baptism of the Holy Spirit concerns the pressures and demands that some place on those seeking this blessing. The false church system has been most successful in reducing the spiritual things of God to mundane ways and methods. It constantly strives to diminish the grace of God to a performance of works. At times, it has done so concerning the baptism into God's Spirit, first by preceding this baptism with human rules, regulations, and expectations and then by declaring exactly what results must follow. These pressures are not from God.

Let it be clearly stated that people have no say in the matter. God is the giver of holy gifts (James 1:17), not people. Therefore, **He** decides how, when, where, and to whom He will give His gifts, not people. That includes the gift of the baptism of His Holy Spirit. While the Bible does say that people can be used as a channel of blessing with the power of God working through them (Acts 9:17; 19:6), never doubt that Jesus is in charge (Matthew 3:11; Mark 1:7-8). Any and all manmade rules concerning this blessing are negated by His sovereignty.

Gifts of God can never be earned; they can only be received. To degrade His baptism to a set of rules, to make it a human work, will always end in disappointment or failure. Whatever a saint receives as the result of tarrying, pleading, or straining may not be the gift of God but a faked performance just to have the pressure of other people to subside.

Similarly, as people cannot dictate the way the baptism is administered, neither can they command specific results. Some denominations incorrectly teach that the presence of certain feelings or actions "prove" the baptism has occurred and the absence of them show it has not. The truth is that people can encourage those who are seeking the baptism, advise them concerning what the possible results might be, and instruct them to flow with any blessings that God offers, but they cannot demand that the same results happen to every person, every time, in the same way.

More specifically, how many times have those seeking the baptism of the Holy Spirit been told they need proof of that baptism? How many times are they informed that the baptism only occurs "as evidenced by speaking in tongues?" Is this scriptural? Is the phrase, "as evidenced by speaking in tongues" found anywhere in God's Word? Can those in the professing Church really have the effrontery to teach a saint to receive the gift of God by faith and then demand that the saint and God prove themselves by a human-inspired test?

Those who declare that speaking in tongues is proof of the baptism are fond of detailing a few Scriptures in which the baptism of the Holy Spirit is mentioned. In Acts 2:4, the Jews received the baptism and then spoke in languages that were unknown to them. Further, in Acts 10:45-47 and 19:6-7, the Gentiles received the baptism and spoke in tongues. Therefore, some conclude that a pattern has been set by which the baptism in the Holy Spirit must always be followed by speaking in unknown languages.

However, is this true? A few more Scriptures on the subject must not be overlooked. When Acts 8:17 states that the baptism of the Holy Spirit was being poured on and received by people, the verse does not mention a manifestation of the gift of tongues. While that does not mean there wasn't one, the obvious omission of reference to tongues denies the generalization that all who receive the baptism of the Holy Spirit must prove it by immediately speaking in tongues.

Another relevant verse is Acts 19:17, which declares that the apostle Paul received the baptism of the Holy Spirit, but it says nothing about Paul speaking in tongues on that occasion. Although Paul later declares that he spoke in tongues (1 Corinthians 14:18), nowhere does he say that he received the gift of tongues simultaneously with his baptism in the Holy Spirit. Tongues could have been a gift received at his baptism or one that God blessed him with at a time of His choice.

The Bible would indicate that there is no universal gift given to all who are born of the Spirit. As Paul writes about spiritual gifts, he asks the rhetorical question, *"All do not speak with tongues, do they?"* (1 Corinthians 12:30). In the same way he points out that not all Christians are prophets have the gift of healing. Then Paul adds, *"But one and the same Spirit works all these things, distributing to each one individually just as He wills"* (1 Corinthians 12:11). By his words, it is clear that the Spirit chooses each saint's gifts and that those gifts will vary. Saints are not Christian clones! God likes diversity. As 1 Corinthians 12:4-11 says,

> *Now there are varieties of gifts, but the same Spirit. And there are varieties of ministries, and the same Lord. There are varieties of effects, but the same God who works all things in all persons. But to each one is given the manifestation of the Spirit for the common good. For to one is given the word of wisdom through the Spirit, and to another the word of knowledge according to the same Spirit; to another faith by the same Spirit, and to another gifts of healing by the one Spirit, and to another the effecting of miracles, and to another prophecy, and to another the distinguishing of spirits, to another various kinds of tongues, and to another the interpretation of tongues. But one and the same Spirit works all these things, distributing to each one individually just as He wills.*

Further, the demand to speak in tongues in order to prove that the baptism of the Holy Spirit has happened lays the saint and the whole Church open to human and demonic activity. Many pressured saints will do anything, make any sound, move their mouth in any way, or even come up with a fake language just to get their tormentors, those "helping" them to receive the baptism, to stop harassing them. Worse, all the legitimate gifts of the Spirit can be counterfeited by satanic forces. If given an opportunity, they can and will speak a demonic language through a Christian who, casting all caution and discernment aside, is desperate enough to try anything in order to get his (or her) "evidence."

To sum up, it can be concluded that speaking in unknown tongues is a wonderful gift from God. Two thousand years ago on the Feast of Pentecost, a group of people had gathered together. Suddenly, a noise like a mighty wind filled the house they were in, tongues of fire appeared and fell upon each one of them, and, filled with the Spirit, they began speaking with other tongues (Acts 2). The party must have spilled into the street because soon the Jews who lived in Jerusalem and visitors from at least a dozen other lands who had come to the city to celebrate the Feast heard those who were filled with the Spirit speaking in the visitors' languages. Those speaking were speaking languages unknown to themselves but were clearly understood by those who languages were being spoken.

By the law of first use, those subsequently baptized in the Holy Spirit could look for the same manifestation, that of speaking in other languages and proclaiming the mighty deeds of God (Acts 2:1-11). Yet, this does not mean that those ministering the baptism should demand this result as a sign of blessing. Rather, it means that God will hear the heart's desire of those praying for the baptism and bless them with gifts of His choosing at a time of His choosing. Tongues is not a gift that a saint must prove that he (or she) has or fake that he has because of the unrighteousness demands of others. It is a glorious gift given by the Son of God that may be received simultaneously with a saint's baptism in the Holy Spirit or one that he receives and grows in as he goes from faith to faith (Romans 1:16-17) in his journey with God.

Who Is The Holy Spirit?

Since it is the baptism of the Holy Spirit, each saint must learn who this Spirit is. The Holy Spirit is the third person of the trinity. He is a person, not an it, a thing, or an impersonal force. He is wonderfully described in Scripture as the Spirit of life (Romans 8:1-2), the Spirit of truth (John 14:17), the Spirit of glory (1 Peter 4:14), the Spirit of grace

(Hebrews 10:29), the Holy Spirit of promise (Ephesians 1:13), and the Spirit of God (Romans 8:14). He is not the physical presence of Jesus Christ but the Spirit of Christ (Romans 8:9) within each saint. It is this majestic One who wishes to empower as well as indwell God's child.

What Is The Baptism Of The Holy Spirit?

To understand the baptism of the Holy Spirit, each saint must also know what a baptism is. With the events at the Red Sea as an example, a baptism is a dipping into, an immersion. It is also a consecration or an initiation into something. At the time of the baptism of the Holy Spirit, each saint becomes totally immersed into the Spirit of God, consecrated unto Him, and introduced into His power.

Baptism is a gift from God (Acts 8:20). It is so precious that He entrusts only His Son, Jesus, to administer it. Jesus determines when a saint shall receive it. Knowing that the longer a saint puts off the baptism the less likely he (or she) is to ask for it, He does not encourage delay.

As for method, there is but one way to receive this special, holy treasure: ask for and receive it from God. At his (or her) salvation experience, a sinner has to repent, confess his sins, ask Jesus to be his Savior, and believe by faith that he is redeemed and that Jesus has come to live within him. Similarly, at his baptism into the Holy Spirit, each saint must ask for and receive this gift by faith and then believe that Jesus has immersed him into the power and might of His Holy Spirit.

All of this is not for the personal benefit or aggrandizement of any saint. Each receives power from on high for the same reason that the 120 who were gathered in the upper room did: *"but you shall receive power when the Holy Spirit has come upon you; and you shall be My witnesses...."* (Acts 1:8).

Are you hearing this command? Then, are you ready? Dear saint, if you are convinced that you will fail unless the power of God both accompanies and enables you through your desert journey, you will find that Jesus is waiting to baptize you into His Spirit. This may mean leaving family and friends who choose to remain permanently encamped by the shores of the Red Sea or departing from those who choose to endlessly and fruitlessly wander through the barren wastes. It may mean separating from denominational demands and overcoming the fear of people. It will surely mean less of self and more of Christ.

Years ago, after the Israelites survived the Passover and the exodus, they journeyed to Mount Sinai. There, God introduced them to the feast of Pentecost. Known as the Feast of First Fruits or Weeks, the Israelites were to celebrate by making loaves of bread from their grain harvests, by waving them before the LORD, and by sacrificing animals for burnt offerings. It was to be a time that they, as the first fruits of the survival from Pharaoh's evil empire, were to be dedicated to God. It was marked by the appearance of God in fire and cloud on the mountain, by the LORD demonstrating His Lordship, and by the LORD giving His people the Law.

Today, after his (or her) salvation from sin and escape from Satan's evil kingdom, God invites each saint to celebrate a spiritual Pentecost. As part of a spiritual harvest of souls, he can, by desire rather than by law, immerse himself into God, consecrate or dedicate himself to the Lordship of Jesus Christ, and be empowered by His Spirit. He can ask for and by faith receive his personal baptism into the Holy Spirit. That is, each new saint who has already been indwelt by the Holy Spirit at the time of his salvation can, in a second celebration, honor God by allowing the power of His Holy Spirit to fall on him.

When he (or she) does so, his baptism may be accompanied by supernatural testimony. As each saint yields to the Lordship of Jesus Christ and as He slowly begins to possess each heart, each will feel awestruck. God's words may thunder in a saint's ears; His lightning arrows of truth may pierce a saved one's heart; His trumpeting voice may make a Christian's ears ring; the ground beneath a reborn child of God may shake as he truly comes to know that Jesus is **his** Lord. Further, he will be blessed with supernatural gifts.

Rejection

Shaking each saint away from the past into the present and thrusting him (or her) from his self-centeredness into commitment to his new covenant with God is not a pleasant experience for some. While they left Egypt because they wanted the presence of God, many are put off or frightened by the manifestations and power that accompany His declaration of Lordship. Like their ancestors in faith (Exodus 20:19), when God's Spirit gently moves to fill them, too many saints scream at God, "Stop it! I'm afraid of You! Approach me through others, such as my pastor, priest, or leaders, and I'll listen. But I reject personal relationship with You. I want no part of this Spirit stuff!"

These new saints do not yet understand that the display of the power of God, whether obvious externally or only dimly evident internally, was not meant to make them afraid of God. Rather, it was to give them a spiritual fear of God, an awe of Him, so that none would dare break covenant with Him either by sinning (Exodus 20:20) or by returning to their old ways.

Yet, some do break covenant with Him. Some, who have been saved, live as though they were still in the world. The apostle Paul recognized this dilemma in writing his epistle to the Christians in the Church at Corinth.

> *However brothers and sisters, I could not talk to you as to spiritual people, but [only] as to worldly people [dominated by human nature] ... You are still worldly [controlled by ordinary impulses, the sinful capacity] ... are you not unspiritual, and are you not walking like ordinary people, [unchanged by faith]?* (1 Corinthians 1:1-3 AMP)

Though the Holy Spirit indwells some saints, He receives little, if any, recognition or acknowledgement of His right to rule. Therefore, these particular saints may not heed the demand of holy God that His saints be holy (1 Peter 1:15-16), or they may not cleanse themselves *"from all defilement of flesh and spirit, perfecting holiness in the fear of God"* (2 Corinthians 7:1). The saints then walk in flesh, giving in to their lower desires, being ruled by body or mind rather than by spirit, and being worldly and immature. They may be heard cursing, gossiping, or lying; they may be seen carousing in bars or driving so poorly as to endanger others; they may cheat on their income taxes; they may honor what the world calls an "alternate lifestyle;" or they may live with their "partners" without benefit of marriage. They indulge in the deeds of the flesh, such as *"immorality, impurity, sensuality, idolatry, sorcery, enmities, strife, jealousy, outbursts of anger, disputes, dissensions, factions, envying, drunkenness, carousing, and things like these"* (Galatians 5:19-21).

For any new saint, decline sets in if he (or she) rejects the new, goes back to the old, or tries to serve God under Old Covenant Law. It leads to defeat if he honors God as Savior but rejects Him as Lord. It leads to failure if he accepts Him as God the Father and God the Son but rejects Him as God the Holy Spirit. It leads to impotence if he, like many evangelicals, teaches about God but refuses to walk in His power. It leads to hypocrisy if he, like many Pentecostals, goes out and preaches and proclaims that Jesus is Lord to others when it is painfully obvious He is not Lord to that particular saint.

Giving Grace

When God gave the Israelites the Law to guide, guard, and keep them, it was meant to be their blueprint for life in obedience to Him. Also, the Law was to be a tutor, bringing the Hebrews to Christ so that they might be justified by faith (Galatians 3:24). Jesus was the end or ultimate purpose of the law for righteousness (Romans 10:4). Under the New Covenant, no saint has to struggle to obey the law for his (or her) righteousness; instead, he has been given grace.

Grace is most often defined as God's favor. It is the gift of God's approval. No matter what any saint has done, with salvation God's grace unequivocally grants him (or her) forgiveness and approval. God gifts him with acceptance and validation. It is God's goodwill voluntarily showered on each believer so that he can live in the heart of God and walk in the love of God. It is a blessing unearned and immeasurable.

Rebellion: The Golden Calf

Even as God is settling the issue as to who is Lord and is amazing each saint with the promise of His presence within and of His grace, for some, the immediate result of losing the right to control his (or her) life and of being expected to submit to God is rebellion. Before God is even finished communing with them, some saints are breaking away from the covenant they made with God. They are choosing another god.

It may come as a shock to a new Christian that he (or she) now owes allegiance to God, not to self or to human traditions. If he has been asked by God to do a certain thing and he has not been obedient, he may have forfeited his reward because of his lack of response. Yet, like the permissive "snowflake" society he has come from, he may demand His blessing anyway, loudly badgering God to reward him for disobedience. Such evidences of sulkiness, entitlement, spoiled behavior, or demanding to be loved through gifts may work with doting grandparents but not with God. When He refuses to reward disobedience, an angry saint may challenge His authority. A pouting saint may ask Him who He thinks He is or what gives Him the right to tell him what to do. In short, instead of understanding that his anger ought to be aimed at his own stubborn heart, he rebels against God. Like the Israelites, he makes a new god that is more pliable to his demands. In so doing, he breaks covenant with true God.

The first god the Israelites made after coming out of Egypt was a golden calf. Early in each saint's desert walk, if he (or she) feels thwarted by God, he too may begin to honor the work of his own hands. Throwing off God's glory, he decides the shape, form, and being of the god he will honor. Then he molds it and makes it by the sweat of his own brow. By works of self-effort, he creates his idol, and then he worships it, calls it "God," and bows before it. Often, he doesn't see that his god is himself, his family, his job, his recreational activity, or even his ministry.

After rebelling against God's will and rejecting His Lordship, the saint then establishes his (or her) own lordship. He becomes the determiner of whom he will worship and when, where, and how he will do so. In short, he becomes lord of his own life. Self reigns once again.

When this happens, it doesn't take long for God to show His displeasure. To correct the situation with the golden calf on Mount Sinai, God commanded Moses to grind the idol into gold powder, to mix it with water, and to have the Israelites drink it. Similarly, to deal with each saint's plunge into idolatry and to assert His Lordship, God asks each erring saint to reduce and destroy his (or her) idols. Then He asks him to pick up the cup of His blood and to drink it as a remembrance of Him who is true God (1 Corinthians 11:25). This call to order, this call to return to covenant with God, jolts each saint into the awareness that Jesus shed His blood and died for him in order to purchase his freedom. This jolt should be more than enough to put down the insurrection of self in even the most hard-hearted of saints.

A saint can learn the depth of devastation that accompanies the loss of the manifest presence of God only through intense prayer. This is appropriately referred to as "a wilderness experience." By this deep communion he (or she) recognizes his own foolishness and understands there is no point in continuing his journey if he has turned away from His God. By seeking God, he learns that the only thing that distinguishes Christians from the world is the living presence of God within him. By a saint destroying all of his idols and confessing and repenting of his sins, God will reestablish the broken covenant and will continue with him.

Instructions For The Tabernacle

Before leaving this place of covenant, the Lord instructs each saint concerning His new tabernacle or dwelling place. God dwelt in the tabernacle of Moses throughout the Hebrews' forty-year journey in the wilderness. He was with them every step of the way. So, too, God also abides with each new saint throughout his (or her) desert experience.

How can this be? Scripture tells us that each saint is the ark, the dwelling place of God. God's tabernacle on earth is within the heart of each one of His children. 1 Corinthians 3:16 reminds us: *"Do you not know that you are a temple of God and that the Spirit of God dwells in you?"* Thus, everywhere a saint goes, God goes with him.

God's New Covenant tabernacle, each saint, is meant to spiritually resemble the Old Covenant tabernacle that the Hebrews physically carried through the desert. Like the tabernacle of Moses, each saint is made up of three parts. The Outer Court in Moses' tabernacle held the laver for cleansing and the brazen altar where the priests offered sacrifices for sin. This compares to the saint's outer being, his (or her) body, which is to be kept holy unto the Lord. As the apostle Paul reminds us, *"Therefore I urge you, brethren, by the mercies of God, to present your bodies a living and holy sacrifice, acceptable to God, which is your spiritual service of worship"* (Romans 12:1).

The Inner Court or Holy Place of Moses' tabernacle contained the candlestick, which shed its light to reflect the glory of God, the table of showbread, which was for the nourishment of the priests, and the altar of intercession, where the priests offered up prayer to God. This corresponds to each saint's inner being, his soul, through which he (or she) is to manifest the light or glory of God, be nourished by His Word, and engage in prayer.

The innermost area of Moses' tabernacle, the Holy of Holies, contained the ark of the presence of God. It was the abiding place of His glorious Majesty. This equates to the heart or spirit of each saint, which is the abiding place of the Holy Spirit.

Under the Old Covenant, only the high priest could move from the Outer Court to the Holy of Holies, where he would be near but not in the presence of God. In contrast, under the New Covenant, all barriers are down. The veil that prohibited entry into the Holiest Place was torn when Jesus died on the cross for our sins (Matthew 27:51). Unlike the Old Testament tabernacle, where the journey toward the presence of God was for atonement, in the New Testament tabernacle, the journey into the presence of God is for worship. As God's tabernacle, each saint is free to use every part of his (or her) being to worship Him. Each is free to enter the Holy of Holies, and, from his own heart, to worship God in spirit.

The unbelievable truth is that each newborn saint is God's earthly home. His presence and power resides within each of His children. Each who opens his (or her) heart to God becomes the castle of the King when He takes up residence.

Only when each saint is in covenant with God, only when each saint acknowledges that he (or she) is the tabernacle of God can he become involved in building the tabernacle. Each whose heart stirs him (or her) or who yearns to be anointed as God's holy dwelling place must heed the call to bring his contribution for the building of God's house (Exodus 25:1-8). Whatever he has of value and whatever treasure he is must be freely given unto Him so His temple will be one of sanctity rather than of self, of spirit rather than of flesh.

When the building is finished, each Christian must ask God to search the work. Each must dedicate his (or her) heart to Him and must bid Him to come, to take up residence, and to ascend His throne. Each must earnestly long for God's glory to fill his heart to such an extent that he can no longer stand in his own strength. Each must seek to be so full of God that all evidence of flesh and self is overshadowed by the glory of His radiant beauty shining from deep within his heart.

The High Priest

Knowing God changed both His covenant and His tabernacle in the New Testament, each saint may suspect that He made a corresponding change in those that serve Him too. As he (or she) inquires, he will quickly learn that God did indeed make changes in the person and in the role of the high priest. God wants all saints dependent on Him, not on another person.

Though given his office by God, in some ways Aaron proved he was yet a man. Displaying many human weaknesses, he allowed and even promoted idolatry (Exodus 32), he refused accountability for his sins (Exodus 32:21-23), harbored jealousy (Numbers 12:1-2), and failed to obey God fully (Numbers 20:1-13).

In the New Testament, a saint no longer has to rely on the imperfect ministry of an imperfect man ministering in the office of high priest. Each saint has a new and eternal High Priest, One who was tempted to sin but did not and One who is strong and not weak (Hebrews 4:14-15). His name is Jesus.

As High Priest, Jesus is now the mediator of the New Covenant (Hebrews 8:6). He is the only One to stand between God and each saint. No person's church, pastor, priest, spouse, brother or sister in the Lord, or friend is the one through whom he (or she) is to approach God; only Jesus is. He offered Himself as a sacrifice on each saint's behalf, and by that sacrifice He has and does reconcile the differences between God and men and women (Hebrews 2:17). Through His Holy Spirit, Jesus leads the sacrifice of worship unto holy God; He is the teacher (John 3:2); and He is the Intercessor (Hebrews 7:25).

As all religious life revolved around the ministrations of Aaron centuries ago, so now a saint's relationship with God is centered upon the ministry of Jesus Christ, the High Priest of the New Covenant. Before Him all must bow and, full of thanks and praise, declare Him to be the fulfillment and the perfection of the office of High Priest.

The Priesthood

As Jesus is the new High Priest in the New Testament, so also He is served by a new priesthood. Jesus is the Head of a whole group of ministering servants who are known as the royal priesthood (1 Peter 2:9). No longer composed of men who are descendants of the tribe of Levi, this royal priesthood is made up of **all** who have been reborn from above. It includes every individual saint who comprises the Church of Christ.

> *Coming to Him as to a living stone which has been rejected by men, but is choice and precious in the sight of God, you also, as living stones, are being built up as a spiritual house for a holy priesthood, to offer up spiritual sacrifices acceptable to God through Jesus Christ.* (1 Peter 2:4-5)

As God released the Israelites from Egypt to serve Him, so He releases each saint from sin to serve and worship Him. No priest can serve God as he chooses to. As a newborn saint who is still on the early stages of his (or her) journey, he has barely met his God. How could he know what would please Him? How could he know how to honor Him? The only way he can do so is to be instructed in worship by Jesus, the One who knows God best.

Some older saints may have adopted ungodly or stifling practices in worship. They may have added things that are not of or for God, or they may have rejected things that don't meet denominational approval or are said to offend people. To correct such errors, they can only turn to Jesus and ask Him to teach them to worship in spirit and in truth (John 4:24). If necessary, they must ask Him to break the shackles that bind them to traditional, humanist rituals, and then they must get on with worshipping God.

The sacrifices of worship under the Old Covenant are obsolete.

While God no longer demands or accepts offerings of slain animals in His New Covenant worship, He does yet require sacrifice. To participate in His new order of worship, each saint, as a priest of God, must bring to the altar of God the sacrifices of thanksgiving (1 Thessalonians 5:18), of praise (Hebrews 13:15), and of a broken and contrite heart (Psalm 51:16-17). God will accept these with joy and by them will extend great blessings.

As each saint progresses through his (or her) wilderness journey, he must truly come to know that he cannot mediate between Himself and God without Jesus, that he must practice a spirit of gratitude, that he must praise his Savior, and that he must bring all his brokenness to God for healing. Further, he must learn that since he is now a priest of God, no one else can serve in his place. He is individually responsible to participate in His priesthood and is personally required to worship his God.

Each saint has been cleansed, clothed, and consecrated to serve in God's priesthood. To sit back passively and to expect others to do his (or her) job for him is arrogance. Not to participate is sin, because it is not keeping covenant with God. Each saint must examine himself in this matter of priesthood. If he is convicted by the Spirit of God that he does not measure up, then he must repent, take up his role as priest, cast it at the feet of Jesus, and ask Him to teach him to minister unto holy God.

Offerings

The Sin Offering

Before any saint can truly walk with God, he (or she) must learn the principle of the sin offering. What a wonderful God of grace He is who knows that even after a saint is initially cleansed from sin, he will sin again over the course of his life. Even so, he will not lose the presence of God.

God gave the Israelites a law for the atonement of sin (Leviticus 4). By it, whoever had offended God had to bring an appropriate animal for sacrifice for his (or her) sin. Since no one could do this for him, this forced him to acknowledge his own responsibility for that sin. If he failed to do so, his personal sin was not atoned for.

Just so, in His foreknowledge, God knew His children would

sometimes be weak, miss the mark, and sin. After cleansing each from sin at the time of his (or her) salvation, God provided a way for him to be continually cleansed, as needed, through the blood of Jesus. 1 John 1:7-9 clarifies this by stating: *"[T]he blood of Jesus His Son cleanses us from all sin. If we say that we have no sin, we are deceiving ourselves and the truth is not in us. If we confess our sins, He is faithful and righteous to forgive us our sins and to cleanse us from all unrighteousness."*

Today, when any saint stands convicted of sin by the Holy Spirit (John 16:8), he (or she) must appear before God to make his wrongdoing right. Each must stop pointing fingers at someone else, humble himself, and say, "I have sinned, Father." He must repent, confess his sin, and ask his Father for forgiveness. He who is always faithful pardons and releases those who do so.

However, if any should say he (or she) has no sin, he is not being honest with himself. If he believes that, once saved and sanctified, he is always or fully holy, he deceives himself. Salvation and sanctification were complete works of grace concerning his past, but they also minister to the present. If he will not accept responsibility for sin committed today and will not repent before God, he is not acquitted of that sin. If he will not admit present sin and confess it to God, he is not forgiven of that sin. How long he carries his self-imposed burden of sin and guilt is up to him.

The Burnt Offering

While crucifying the flesh can be compared to the sin offering since it is inextricably connected with atonement, salvation, and separation, dealing with self can be more appropriately compared to the burnt offering (Leviticus 8). The burnt offering was that sacrifice by which dedication, commitment, and consecration led to greater submission to the will of God. Through it, each saint lays self on the altar and burns it with fire until it is totally consumed, leaving the saint free to be on fire for the glory of God. It is a sacrifice whose aroma is pleasing to God.

Free-Will Offerings

Each of the tribes of Israel offered gifts to God to help in the work of the tabernacle (Numbers 7). Oh, that each saint today would learn that it is more blessed to give than to receive. Oh, that each would learn that ministry is serving God rather than being served, that it is offering unto

Him rather than taking from Him, that it is giving up treasures rather than clinging to them. Whether speaking of objects of material value or of things dear to his (or her) heart, such as family, home, time, talent, or position, each saint must present all that he has as an offering to God rather than keep it for his own use. Since every good and perfect gift has come to him from the Father of lights (James 1:17), it is meant for the work of service in God's tabernacle.

Rebellion: Nadab And Abihu

Each saint must endlessly be reminded of the fact that he (or she) was released from sin and Satan to worship God. Knowing **who** he is to worship is one thing; realizing that God also gets to dictate **how** he is to worship is something else. If a saint is to fall before and worship the One who allows him to walk in His presence and power, it must by in ways of His choosing, not of the saint's.

Nadab and Abihu were sons of Aaron and priests of God who, by their own choices and behavior, became casualties in the war of self. They knew God's requirements for offerings and sacrifices, and they knew the requirements were to be followed exactly. However, instead of submitting their wills to His, Nadab and Abihu followed the desires of their own hearts and offered God false fire. The result was their deaths.

Learning from that tragic lesson, each saint, as a priest of God, must worship God in ways of His choice. He (or she) is not to worship by the rote and ritual of human tradition or the ego of flesh and self but according to the leading of the Holy Spirit. Rather than grabbing his censer and offering false fire, he is to worship God in spirit and in truth (John 4:24), expressing himself toward God through the obedience of the fire of holy love that God has kindled in his heart.

THE CAMP

While yet pausing in the desert, each saint must take time to examine his (or her) surroundings. His part of the Christian camp, his individual person, must be organized. He must be sure that he is in his proper place in relationship to both God and to his
brothers and sisters in the Lord.

Positions

Of utmost importance, each saint must recognize and acknowledge God's position as his (or her) Head and His place in his heart. God demanded to be the center of all life and activity in the camp of the Israelites. He demands no less central a place within the heart of each child of God. Each saint must check to see if God occupies the spirit of his being and if He is the reason for his existence. He must be sure God is the focal point of his thinking and service. He must be sure that no one and no thing takes God's place. He must honestly know he is not striving to be the central point of his own existence, competing with God for attention, serving himself, and expecting God and others around him to do so too.

Further, each saint, as a priest of God, must ascertain if he (or she) is in the same position the Levites were, near enough to the presence of God to make ministry unto Him pleasant and effective. He must ensure that the tents of others, such as family, friends, and circumstances, have not been placed between him and God so they take his eyes off God, take time from God, or otherwise hinder his worship of God.

As each saint becomes more fully aware of the position of God, he (or she) must know his own position or placement by God. Since God saved each saint to serve Him, He has a plan for each – a place, a role, or an assigned function in service. This position keeps him near the camp and connected to the body of Christ.

Each saint must come to believe that God has ordained his (or her) days. As God long ago had specific jobs for each Israelite, so He has specific responsibilities for each saint now. Each not only has an assigned place in the body but each has a specific function within that place.

First, God calls. If a saint responds, He saves and sanctifies him (or her). Then without exception, God begins to train each for work of His choosing. Once trained, He raises him and appoints him to a job. With His anointing flowing over him, God makes the way for that saint to exercise his gifts and calling. To **some** saints, Jesus gives Church offices: apostle, prophet, evangelist, pastor, and/or teacher (Ephesians 4:11). To **all** saints, the Holy Spirit gives gifts (1 Corinthians 12:4-11). These are for the service of God, not of people.

Here a saint must be careful not to offend God. First, he (or she) must never covet the place of another. Each saint cannot be all things to all people and so must minister only in the anointing specifically given to him by His Lord. Second, he must not seek to change his anointing. If he freely acknowledges that Jesus is Lord, he must just as freely submit to His choice for him. Third, as he cannot add to or fill roles that were not divinely ascribed to him, neither can he take from them. He cannot let other people keep him from fulfilling that place which God, not people, has assigned to him.

The Pillar And The Cloud

As each saint progresses in placing God in the center of his (or her) life and in learning to function where God placed him, he must also learn that he cannot be led in that role by flesh or by self. He must not serve the demanding of his body or the leading of his soul (intellect, will, or emotion). Rather, he can do what he is supposed to do only as he yields to and is guided by the Spirit of God.

God made a covenant of Lordship with the Israelites and set forth commandments they had to obey in order to honor that covenant. The many rules, regulations, ordinances, and statutes that governed the people were collectively known as the Law.

Likewise, God has made a covenant with each new saint. Since this is not a covenant of law but of grace, a saint cannot keep it by formality, fleshly tradition, or the rituals of organized religion. He (or she) can honor it only as led by the Holy Spirit.

God dwelt in and over His tabernacle in the midst of the Israelite camp. As the cloud or the shekinah glory, He led them through the desert. Now, as the Holy Spirit, He abides in the tabernacle or temple of each saint, communing with him (or her) and telling him what to do and when and how to do it. In so doing, God leads him through the wilderness.

God has one plan. To fulfill it, certain things must be done at certain times. Foreknowing all of this, God has prepared each saint for his (or her) part in His plan. As the Israelites learned, each saint must determine to follow the Spirit of God, moving when He moves and stopping when He stops. He is required to go as far as God goes (but no further).

When the cloud lifts and moves on, so must each saint, whether it is convenient or not. Not to do so causes him (or her) to be left behind. Not to do so causes him to forfeit the presence and power of God. Not to do so leaves him alone, lost, and aimlessly wandering in the desert.

Silver Trumpets

In the camp of Israel, when God moved the camp was to move. To alert the people that a change was coming, the Lord charged the priests to blow silver trumpets (Numbers 10:2-6). Even so today, each saint serves a living God who is not content to stay in one place. Each saint comes to know that if he (or she) establishes a permanent dwelling place in the desert, he will never arrive in the promised land. The only way he can know if the cloud or the spirit of God is about to move is to listen for the sound of His trumpets.

Today's trumpet is the voice of Jesus. Through Jesus, God speaks to His people. *"God ... in these last days has spoken to us in His Son...."* (Hebrews 1:1-2). Further, the apostle John heard Jesus speak and said He sounded like a trumpet. *"I was in the Spirit on the Lord's day, and I heard behind me a loud voice like the sound of a trumpet ... Then I turned to see the voice that was speaking with me. And having turned I saw ... one like a son of man...."* (Revelation 1:10-13).

Jesus fulfilled the type or symbolism of Israel's silver trumpets. He strode through Galilee and Judea sounding the alarm, *"Repent"* (Matthew 4:17). He assembled His followers with the call, *"Follow Me"* (Matthew 4:19). He spoke to hearts, and in so doing, He changed lives. He led and directed lives and gave them meaning. Since He walked in such close communion with His Father, He could then speak the mind of God.

As He did for His early disciples Jesus can and will do for each saint today. He will gladly reach, teach, direct, and speak forth the counsel of God to any who desire to hear.

Each Christian must understand that he (or she) **can** hear the voice of God. Since he must readily acknowledge that he hears the voices of flesh, self, and the enemy, why would he fail to believe that he also hears the voice of his Father? Further, he must understand that he **needs** to hear the voice of God. If he doesn't, how will he know where to go or what to do? How will he know how to serve?

Christianity is communion with God. It is the restoration and reconciliation of relationship with God in order to be near Him. It is talking and listening to Him in order to hear Him. It is knowing Him in such intimate fellowship that when a voice calls out, a saint will know whether or not it is His. Further, if it is His voice trumpeting forth, each saint will know how to respond to the sound.

It is up to each saint to listen for the trumpet. It is up to each saint to understand the message sounding forth. No saint can continue to fumble along by hearsay, by what faulty theology may have taught him (or her), or by what others have told him to think or do. Each is personally required to hear, understand, and respond to what God is speaking to him.

Pause

As those trained and skilled in the appropriate fields of study can testify, a desert, though seemingly barren, actually teems with life and with interesting things to ponder. A stroll through the desert cannot begin to uncover the vastness or the richness of truth found there.

So it is in the spiritual desert. A saint cannot allow flagging fortitude to hinder or hurry him (or her) through the treasuries of growth, understanding, and submission to God that can be found only in the desert experiences of life. Just as the desert experience was meant to bring the Israelites and God together, so too it is meant to bring each saint and God together. Just as the Hebrews were asked to live their love for and their faith in God, so does each Christian. Each one needs to take the proper time required to hear God's voice, to obey God's leading, and to learn the lessons God wants him to learn. Only then is it time to move on.

While resting, each saint must learn an important lesson: God's love and His Lordship are two separate entities even though both are parts of His nature. Each saint must clearly understand that God's love for him (or her) is distinctly different than His demand for obedience by him.

God's love is unconditional, a fruit of His mercy and grace. No child of God can earn it; he cannot add to it by his good behavior; he cannot diminish it by his disobedience. God, who is love (1 John 4:16), loves each saint whether he (or she) knows it, believes it, or even likes it.

On the other hand, God's rightful demand for obedience is conditional. He is allowed to establish rules and to demand that His child obeys them. Upon learning His will, if a saint obeys and serves Him, he (or she) is recompensed with both blessings and positive rewards (Psalm 62:12). However, if he defies or ignores God, he is not.

Though a saint wants to walk in God's love and to receive His blessings, sometimes he (or she) errs in his perception of them by thinking they are synonymous. Therefore, if he forfeits a blessing through failing to submit to God's Lordship or through disobedience, he also mistakenly believes he has lost God's love. He sees God's love as a control mechanism, a way He forces His children to "be good." The saint hasn't fully grasped the fact that God's love for him remains constant by God's choice, however obedience brings rewards by the saint's choice.

For too many saints, memories of a parent practicing human conditional love rather than holy unconditional love still evoke pain. How often did the words "If you aren't a good little girl Daddy won't love you anymore" link conditional love with conditional obedience. That may be an imperfect human father's harmful way, but it is not holy Father's divine way.

The truth is that if a saint breaks covenant with God, then God has the right to deny him (or her) his reward. If a saint has enthroned a false god in his heart, he has dethroned true God. Again, God's covenant is not an agreement to love a saint; He already eternally loves him. Rather, His covenant is the declaration of His Lordship over the saint and the assurance of His presence and power if that saint meets His terms. If any should irrevocably deny, reject, replace, or break it, God will continue to love him, but He is not required to reward him (Exodus 33:3).

MOVING ON

Though having paused in the desert for a while, each saint has been growing. Now it is time to choose whether or not to continue his (or her) spiritual journey at a slow but steady pace. In making that decision, he knows two things: 1) if he refuses God's tutorials, he will sentence himself to endless repetition of his tests and trials and he will remain in the desert until his lessons are learned; and 2) if he appropriates them quickly, he will soon be released to enter Canaan.

More Complaining

When the Israelites' journey resumed, so did the complaints against God. In spite of the passage of thousands of years, today there are still complaints. Each saint hears them because he (or she) is the one making them. So often he scorns God's provision: "I wanted a bigger house," or "I claimed a Cadillac, not a Ford." Or, he complains of His gifts: "I wanted healing power. Why am I stuck in this room where no one can see me and told to pray?" or "Who wants to live by faith? Why can't I prophesy?" If each truly listens to his surly heart and his snarly voice, he cannot then wonder why God sends fire down to consume (Numbers 11:1).

How often has even one child of God mocked the ancient Israelites or judged them to be stupid and stiff-necked only to find out that he (or she) is doing the very things that they once did?

Raising Of Leaders

As the journey resumes and as each saint walks along, God will raise up leaders for him. Moses was the deliverer of the Israelites, but Jesus is the Savior and Deliverer of each saint. As such, He is Leader or Head of His people. In turn, He raises up those who will take His place among His people, and He delegates them to walk in His anointing as they govern, guide, and guard His own.

To solve the problem of leadership among the Israelites, God said:

> "Gather for Me seventy men from the elders of Israel, whom you know to be the elders of the people and their officers and bring them to the tent of meeting, and let them take their stand there with you. Then I will come down and speak with you there, and I will take of the Spirit who is upon you, and will put Him upon them; and they shall bear the burden of the people with you, so that you will not bear it all alone." (Numbers 11:16-17)

When Moses did so, God fulfilled His word. *"Then the LORD came down in the cloud and spoke to him; and He took of the Spirit who was upon him and placed Him upon the seventy elders. And when the Spirit rested upon them, they prophesied"* (Numbers 11:25).

God is doing this same thing today. Each saint needs guidance and comfort on his (or her) journey. Since he has come out of the world, he cannot go to the world for help, advice, counsel, or guidance. Indeed, through Jesus and the Holy Spirit of God, he has a better way.

As God once said to Moses, so now He says concerning his saints: "Select those from among My family who are known to love God, those who have been faithful in little, those about whom it is obvious they will serve Me well. Bring them before Me. I will place My Spirit on them, and they will lead the saints and bear their burdens."

Without question, each saint is to be led. Each leader is to be one of God's children, one wise and spiritually mature in the Lord. Each leader is to be privately called and then publicly made known because the spirit of his (or her) heart is to serve. Each leader must receive God's power of service from the Holy Spirit in order to lead men and women in the service of God.

Rebellion: Miriam And Aaron

As soon as each Christian thinks he (or she) has learned about leadership, God tests him. He is given the opportunity to examine his heart to see if he harbors the spirit of Miriam and Aaron, to see if he has a problem submitting to leadership. Sometimes, he just doesn't like the person designated to be in authority over him because they clash in their personalities or in their ways of doing things. Sometimes he is jealous that God chose another for a position that he coveted for himself. In spite of the fact that God raised someone else, he still feels he could do a better job. Though he knows that a holy anointing is on a particular leader, he feels he is the one who should have been chosen to lead.

Miriam and Aaron were Moses' siblings. They knew God's call on Moses' life, but they came against him anyway (Numbers 12). It was a case of the arrogant attacking the meek, the proud coming against the humble.

Sometimes a saint's worst adversaries are his (or her) own brothers and sisters in the Lord, those who know God has blessed him, who can see the anointing of God on him, and yet, because of personal differences, covetousness, or jealousy, they do all they can to interfere with or bring down his ministry.

Let each saint learn that he (or she) cannot choose his leaders. God does that. Once His will is known, each saint must let His choice lead. He must be cautious not to follow the steps of Miriam and Aaron, whose pride and selfish ambition led them to try to usurp Moses' position. As God's judgment fell on them for such activity, it also can and will do so now on those who try to usurp their God-placed leaders.

Rebellion: Refusing To Enter The Promised Land

At some point in his (or her) desert journey, each saint must come to the heart of the matter. He knows he is not to go back to Egypt. Yet, because he is having difficulty in the sands and rocks of the wilderness, he takes his eyes or vision off Canaan. Suddenly, the call comes! *"Go up and check the promised land. Search carefully. Examine both the land and its inhabitants. Determine their strengths and weaknesses. Then report what you have discovered"* (Numbers 13:17-19).

All too often, when so commissioned, he (or she) fails, like his predecessors did. He, like the spies sent out by Israel, tells God what his natural eyes have seen or his physical ears have heard. He declares the smell, taste, and feel of the enemy. He sees giants and, allowing his flesh to arise, he becomes afraid. He fails entirely to ask God to show him the land from the spiritual point of view.

The Israelites faced and fought physical enemies. Since these human foes occupied the land that had been promised to the Israelites, they had to be dealt with. All too often a saint fails to understand that his (or her) enemies are spiritual ones, that the battle is *"not against flesh and blood, but against the rulers, against the powers, against the world forces of this darkness, against the spiritual forces of wickedness in the heavenly places"* (Ephesians 6:12). As such, his physical senses can't discern them and his natural abilities can't defeat them. Yet, they possess his land.

In the kingdom of God, warfare is spiritual. The battles are spiritual; the armor and weapons are spiritual; the enemy is spiritual, though perhaps being manifested through a person. Since evil occupies the place promised to God's child, it must be dealt with.

If a saint is one of those entrusted by God to spy out the land and to report back and if his (or her) report is full of fear and discouragement, he too has allowed his flesh to rise. Like the leaders of ancient Israel, he too has been led by flesh, not by spirit. If he is afraid of the enemy, if he is downcast about his own strength, if he feels weak in size and number and so will be defeated, he too brings a bad report.

Please don't misunderstand. Each saint must always speak the truth, even if that truth is sometimes unpleasant. However, an accurate report should not include – or incite others to – fear. God is in charge of all things. His wisdom and timing are perfect. If a saint is going ahead of God, it is good to hear counsel to wait. If he (or she) is out of order, it is good to know how to return to right standing with God. However, if God has designated him to fight a certain battle, has said that He would lead him, and has prepared him for it, it is nothing but outright rebellion to allow flesh and fear to rise up, gain control, and cause him to refuse to do so.

In the kingdom of God, flesh and spirit are enemies. They are eternally and actively in opposition to one another. If a saint allows fear to rise and tries to fight his (or her) spiritual enemies according to flesh, he is wasting his time and costing himself dearly.

The first loss that comes from battling in the flesh is failure. As soon as any saint becomes convinced that his (or her) enemy is a giant, is bigger than he is, or is bigger than the promises of God, he has lost the battle. Then fear turns to unbelief. Then unbelief leads to rebellion. That saint will not go where God says to go or do as He says to do.

The second problem that comes from battling in the flesh is the charge of irresponsibility placed against his (or her) account. Not only is he individually responsible if he finds himself identifying with the ten fearful spies, but he is also accountable if he leads others to do the same.

As a direct result of a bad report by ten spies, God's judgment fell on the entire camp. Of an estimated two and a half to three and a half million people, only two adults, Joshua and Caleb, lived to enter the promised land. The rest walked in the desert until they died. In considering this, today's saints should examine themselves. What results have their actions brought about? Have they given others good, honest, hopeful reports or bad, fearful ones? Are their fears keeping multitudes of others in the desert? Is their own hesitation to lead or refusal to obey God prolonging their own walks or keeping others out of the promised land?

Presumption: Attempting To Enter The Promised Land Without God's Command

Flesh and self are constant companions in the desert. The Israelites' refusal to go to Canaan when God had said to do so was a manifestation of flesh and rebellion. However, the Israelites' next decision, to go to Canaan when God had not said to go, was self-determination and presumption (Numbers 14:39-45). The result wasn't just failure, it was disaster.

Often, as a consequence of rebellious behavior, a saint falls under God's judgment. Then, rather than repenting, confessing sin, asking for forgiveness, and waiting on God for direction, he (or she) charges off, following selfish ways and doing self-ordained works to make things right with God again. He presumptuously acts by self-control or self-government, decides for himself what to do, and then does it with no direction from God. He does not stop to realize that to have refused to follow God's banner is one thing; to then take it up and carry it where and when he chooses despite God saying not to do so is quite another. To all such arrogant displays of self, God would say, *"Therefore humble yourselves...."* (1 Peter 5:6).

As warfare of flesh is ineffective and fruitless, so is that which is determined by self. What God does not originate, He will not honor. He will not share His glory with people. He will not let people supersede Him in prominence or purpose. He stands behind His word, saying, *"I am the LORD your God"* (Exodus 20:2). In any battle in which a saint is humanly led by Major Ego, the major is superseded by God, who is spiritually commander-in-chief. God still does, and always will, reign supreme.

Rebellion: Korah, Dathan, And Abiram

The tests that a saint faces in the desert sometimes seem both endless and repetitive. However, God always has something new to teach him (or her). For instance, while the lessons concerning Miriam and Aaron's challenge to leadership should have taught a saint much, learning from Korah, Dathan, and Abiram's attack will enrich him even more (Numbers 16). While the first challenge was jealous, dismissive remarks to a brother, the second was a deep conspiracy by other Israelite leaders. Similarly today, sometimes a brother or sister in the Lord attacks a saint, but sometimes the leaders in the Church are the ones attacking.

Each saint must recognize that, while some leaders in the Church are indeed in their positions by the call of God, others are not. Whether ignorantly or willfully, some Church leaders are in their positions by the call of man, not of God. These are a product of family heritage, of human appointment, or of misplaced zeal. Others are self-made and power hungry. In other words, even within Church leadership, there are ungodly leaders and ministries.

Therefore, any saint who is truly trying to be led of the Spirit is going to run into trouble with those who walk in their carnal natures of flesh or self. Every saint occupying a position of leadership given to him (or her) by God will, sooner or later, incur the wrath of those who want that position for themselves.

As it was for Moses, the important thing for him (or her) to know is who he is in Christ. When modern-day Korahs question "Who do you think you are?" and today's Dathans shout "Who gave you the right to do that?" and contemporary Abirams taunt "Why are you exalting yourself?" each saint must know that he is exactly who God said he is, that his authority is from God, and that he is not exalting himself but doing just as God said to do, even if it means rocking the boat or ruffling feathers.

Further, if someone deliberately challenges a saint with the intention of raising himself to that saint's place in God, the saint must be determined that, in Christ, such a thing will not be allowed to happen. He (or she) must stand his ground knowing that it is wrong to relinquish his rightful place in God to one with no godly call or anointing.

When sin challenges, a Christian's only recourse is to stand, seek God, and let Him fight for him (or her). He must give God the opportunity to show whom He will honor. Perhaps He will direct the saint to go to his challengers to see if their hearts are hardened or if they are open to repentance. In any case, as he seeks God, it will become evident who has heard His word and who is walking in His will. Just as the Lord's blessing fell on Moses and his judgment fell on Korah, Dathan, and Abiram, so today the Lord's blessing will fall on His chosen and His judgment will fall on the self-chosen.

Self

It may seem like the attacks against a new Christian all involve the flesh, but now it is time to introduce a new enemy on this desert journey. Unlike the outward, fleshly attacks, such as the search for sustenance, this enemy is the compilation of all the forces which seek to preserve and exalt people. This enemy is self.

Self is the inner essence of a person. It is his (or her) being. Made up of mind, emotions, character, personality, and abilities, it forms the identity of a person and distinguishes him from everyone else.

It is easy for a new saint to believe that, given the opportunity, he (or she) could take care of himself. He secretly thinks that now that he is free of the past, he is able to make the decisions by which he can guide, guard, and govern himself and to do the things by which he could provide for and protect himself in the present and the future. Despite having asked Jesus to be his Savior, he does not yet acknowledge or recognize Him as Lord. The very essence of self is the saint thinking that he will be his own master.

Self also seeks to convince every new saint that he (or she) wasn't freed from Satan in order to worship God, but rather was freed to serve and worship himself. It causes every person to place himself on the throne and to declare his right to rule. It is at the root of humanism. In 2 Timothy 3:2-5 the Bible identifies self thusly:

> *For men will be lovers of self, lovers of money, boastful, arrogant, revilers, disobedient to parents, ungrateful, unholy, unloving, irreconcilable, malicious gossips, without self-control, brutal, haters of good, treacherous, reckless, conceited, lovers of pleasure rather than lovers of God, holding to a form of godliness, although they have denied its power.*

Concerning character, those laboring under the evil of self are known for their pride. Their ego knows no bounds. They are constantly generating division by professing that they are right and all others are wrong. Though these people cannot see them, their manifestations of self are obvious to others: self-centeredness, self-absorption, self-gratification, self-pleasure, self-determination, self-effort, self-approval, self-praise, self-exaltation, self-idolatry, self-deifying, self-pity, self-tolerance, self-sustaining, and just plain selfishness. Perhaps this can by summed up by one more expression of self: self-will.

Concerning practice, expressions of self include all things that magnify one human, group, race, or people over another. On an innocent level, this can involve proclaimed preferences for the fourth grade over the fifth grade or Washington School over Lincoln School. It can also be seen in academic rivalries between various colleges or athletic contests between professional sports teams. On a less desirable level, the evil of self encompasses prejudice and racism. It accounts for the ungodly promotion of one religion or denomination over another. It incorporates the hatefulness of violent nationalism.

As God fought the battle of the carnal, adamic nature in the world and changed each saint from an old being of flesh into a new creature of spirit, so He uses the desert as His theater of war in the fight of self-centeredness versus Christ-centeredness. In addition to knowing Jesus as Savior, the desert is a time to establish Jesus as Lord. No saint is excluded from this conflict. Many will die in the desert before this stronghold is conquered. Yet, as always, victory comes through the rod of Christ, His cross.

Rebellion: Moses

At some point along the way, frustration will become the enemy of each saint in his (or her) ministry to God. Contending with the same problems over and over again might lead him to become impatient, abrupt, fed up, or burnt out. Without intending to, when he reaches the limit of his human endurance, he fails to tap into the limitless supply of God's patience and love. Then, in response to a crisis, he fails to believe God or to treat Him as holy in the sight of the Church (Numbers 20:12). He thoughtlessly does something that brings judgment down on himself.

Think back to Moses. When once more faced with a thirsty, quarrelsome people, he struck the rock twice instead of speaking to it as commanded by God (Numbers 20:8-11). In so doing, he disobeyed God and was severely judged for it. He was not guilty of backsliding or of a purposeful return to habitual sin, but he did sin. It is important to note that the result of Moses' act was not loss of salvation. He must have repented and received forgiveness of this sin, because he, along with Elijah, later appeared before Jesus when He was transfigured on the mountain (Matthew 17:1-3). Yet, while Moses did not lose eternal life with God for his sin, he did lose part of his reward. He never reached the promised land. Just so, a saint's sins of rebellion can cost him (or her) the fullness of his reward.

The Edomites

In working out his (or her) salvation, a saint discovers that his enemies are not always within. Sometimes outside forces try to distract him from his obedience to the Lord. As the Edomites, descendants of Israel's brother, Esau, came against the Israelites in their desert trek, so today some people, both in the world and in the Church, will attack new saints in their wilderness journey. As the goal of the Edomites was to divert the Hebrews or to prevent them from going toward the promised land, so today the goal of those hindering God's newly reborn saint is to divert, delay, and interfere. It is to put up barriers, blockades, and stumbling blocks that will cause him to take a long detour or that will stop the forward progress of his desert journey altogether. If threats or coercion fail, they will attack with force in order to drive the searching one off the path entirely. They don't want him to walk on the King's highway of holiness or to realize God's plan and place for him. Hindrance and obstruction are never-ending battles that must constantly be addressed and won by Christians.

Fiery Serpents

Tiring of his (or her) journey, each Christian is tempted into sin. It so often seems that he runs out of energy or zeal for holy obedience long before the enemy runs out of snares or pitfalls. When at last he is unwilling to endure any more hardship in the desert, his mouth once again becomes a source of trouble.

Ungratefulness is one of the most heinous of sins. This lack of response to God's goodness shows that the saint thinks He has failed to provide or satisfy. Or, it shows that the saint is ignoring God, assuming that His provision is a duty, something owed the saint, rather than a gift.

When a saint mocks, belittles, or scorns holy provision, God is aware of his (or her) wrong attitude. Every time he denies or rejects what God has done, fails to thank Him for it, and asks Him instead for what he wished He had done, he spits in God's face. Every time he argues for his choice of provision rather than thanking God for His choice, he manifests his inherent desire to control God.

In the garden in Eden, the serpent told Eve that God had not adequately provided for her, that He was holding back the best of His provision from her. Today, that same serpent, Satan, tempts a saint to scorn God's supply, to ask for more, and to fail to be grateful for what He has so bountifully and wisely given. The Israelites had to make an image of a bronze serpent, put it on a high pole, and look on it to be healed from the bites of the fiery serpents. Just so, when a saint comes under the fiery judgment of God, he (or she) must face his weakness and must ask God to heal his heart of the sin of ingratitude and his mouth through which he expresses it. He must look upon the cross of Christ, realize the cost of the things that God has freely given, repent, be healed, and then *"in everything give thanks; for this is the will of God in Christ Jesus for you"* (1 Thessalonians 5:18 NKJV).

The Canaanites

As the Israelites had to deal with the Canaanites as a people-to-people conflict or as physical combat in the natural realm, so each saint must deal with any Canaanite spirit that attacks him (or her) as he approaches the end of his spiritual desert journey.

A study titled "The Seven Types of Evil Spirits"[2] lists the seven tribes that make up the Canaanites and identifies a predominant spirit associated with each tribe. This study describes the Canaanites as

---

[2] Gage, Rick. "The Seven Types of Evil Spirits." *Petra 101.* 23 June 2009. http://rickgage.webs.com/apps/blog/show/1244319-the-seven-types-of-evil-spirits Accessed 31 Aug 2017.

lowland dwellers known for their addictions, perversions, and people pleasing. The Hittites were known as the sons of terror who affected whose around them with torment, phobias, fears, depression, and deceit. The Girgashites were clay dwellers, a reference to earthiness. The Perizzites belonged to a village, and as such they were seen as those of limited vision, laziness, and low self-esteem. The Hivites were villagers who loved the things of the world; in short, they were hedonists. The Jebusites were threshers, those who beat down or suppressed those exercising spiritual authority and who were known for legalism. The Amorites were mountain people who looked down on and domineered others and who loved fame and glory.

In spite of the long desert journey, the fatigue, and the struggles already endured, God commands each saint that each of these tribes, the present-day spirit of these tribes, or what these tribes represented has to be dealt with before the saint enters the promised land to receive the fullness of his (or her) inheritance. Each tribe is to be personally conquered and destroyed. None is to be shown mercy. No covenants are to be made with them, no intermingling allowed with them, and all of the places where they have become idols in the heart of any saint must be torn down (Deuteronomy 7:1-5).

Why? Because all who are born again and whose sins have been forgiven through the cleansing grace of the blood of Jesus Christ are holy to the LORD God; each has been chosen by the LORD for Himself; each is a special treasure above the people of the earth (Deuteronomy 7:6). Therefore, none are to bear the hallmarks of the Canaanites; instead, each must exhibit the distinctive features of his (or her) spiritual inheritance in Christ Jesus as members of the kingdom of God.

The Amorites

At the end of their desert journey, the Hebrews had to battle the Amorites. Descendants of Canaan, they were fierce warriors and wicked idol worshippers who lived in mountains (Genesis 15:16; Judges 6:10). According to an online article in the *Jewish Encyclopedia*[3], they were "the main representatives of heathen superstition," "an evil and sinful people

---

[3] Muller, W. Max, and Kohler Kaufmann. "Amorites." *Jewish Encyclopedia*. Jewish Encyclopedia.com. 2011. http://www.jewishencyclopedia.com/articles/1422-amorites?fb_comment_id=10150347823750905_24343673#f31441d88646918. Accessed 28 July 2017.

whose wickedness surpasses that of any other," and "symbolized by black water because of their black art, their witchcraft, and impure mysteries by which they contaminated Israel in the time of the Judges."

Likewise, today as each saint approaches the end of his (or her) journey, he finds that his pathway toward the presence of and relationship with God is attacked by those who want to spread unholy superstitions or outright lies about God. They hope to reduce his zeal for God and convince him to commit wicked acts against Him. They want him to seek power from another god.

If a Christian is determined to accept the challenge to conquer wickedness, God will bring him (or her) to the place or situation where the battle can be fought. The Lord will identify the many faces of wickedness within him, point out the strongman holding dominion, tell him how the battle can be won, grant him wisdom and strength, and then fight with and for him. In His time and in His way, victory can be won.

Too, if witchcraft occupies ground in a saint that it has no right to be on, tries to hold onto kingdoms within him (or her), or persists in clinging to unreleased areas of his heart, God is there to fight with and for him. All parts of a saint's being that he has held back from God's lordship and all areas he has not allowed God to reign over are hotbeds where the spirit of the Amorites can attack. This sin must be defeated.

When the Amorite within is defeated, the saint can take possession of those once alien lands in his (or her) intellect, will, and emotions and bring them under the authority of the King of kings. Further, his success in battle gives him a taste of victory. Though he knows other enemies lurk ahead, even giants in the promised land, he is assured they can be overcome through God.

The Moabites And Midianites

As each saint walks closer to God, each must be aware of the temptation to serve other gods. As the Israelites learned in the matter of Moab and Midian (Numbers 25:1-8), if he (or she) begins to fellowship with those who serve false gods, the chances are high that eventually he will be corrupted too.

A saint's false gods may be his (or her) constant insistence on wealth, prestige, cars, or homes. They may be his children, job, church, or ministry. They may be his television shows or athletic contests. Or, false gods may be the more blatant rulers of ungodly religions, the demands of humanism, the deities of cults, or the evil rulers in the occult realm. Whatever form they take, false gods are essentially those things that he serves, spends excessive time or money on, or worships instead of true God.

Whoever or whatever these false gods are, they are anathema to the Lord. He has commanded His child not to indulge in their rituals. He (or she) is not to intermingle or intermarry with those who serve them nor to play the harlot by sacrificing to or bowing down to these idols.

Would that each saint had as pure a zeal as that of Phineas! Would that each loved God so much that he (or she) would rise on His behalf and defend His honor with single-hearted fire and devotion! Would that each would raise a hand to stay the plague that is sickening and killing God's saint because of his indulgence in idolatry.

As each saint makes his (or her) way through the desert, he must remember that it is full of enemies – the Amalekites (or self), the Edomites (or hindrance), the Amorites (or wickedness), and the Moabites and Midianites (or seducers intoidolatry). While they are universal in their attacks upon each saint as he walks in the desert, through Christ they all can be conquered.

A New Generation And A New Leader

Like the Israelites, each generation of saints is asked to decide whom they will serve. When each new saint comes into the kingdom of God, a necessary change of leadership takes place in his (or her) life. Each has been brought out of the kingdom of darkness into the kingdom of light (1 Peter 2:9). Each is no longer ruled by Satan and his minions of death but by Jesus Christ.

How did this happen? When each new believer asked Jesus into his (or her) life as Savior, he was also asking Him into his life as Lord. That is, he asked Jesus to be his Master, his Leader, or the One in charge of his life. As Moses was the shepherd of the Israelites, so Jesus is the good Shepherd who leads each saint (John 10:11). His is the only voice that a saint should follow (John 10:4). Similarly, as Joshua was the military leader of the Israelites, so Jesus is the righteous Warrior whose end-time purpose is to judge and make war (Revelation 19:11-16). He has already defeated every enemy of mankind and is coming to establish his victory on earth.

Inheritance Not In The Promised Land

As the Israelites needed new leaders when they were going to a new place, so does each saint. New life situations require choices, and new leaders can give invaluable guidance when a saint is on unfamiliar ground.

The Israelites' inheritance was not in Egypt. Nor was it in the desert. It was gained in the promised land. Lessons should be learned from the Reubenites, the Gadites, and the half-tribe of Manasseh who chose their inheritance outside the boundaries that God had prescribed and who later suffered for it.

No saint can determine his (or her) inheritance. He cannot set its terms, and he should not seek it in places that satisfy his flesh but starve his spirit. What looks good may not actually be good for him. What others enjoy may not be in his best interest. Yes, he can make choices for himself, but they may not be in God's perfect will for him and may keep him from accomplishing God's purposes through him. Instead of veering off course and settling in a place of his own making, each saint should stay on course and follow God into his inheritance of the promised land.

DESERT'S END

The desert may seem like a wasteland to the natural person. However, to the spiritual person, it is a treasure. If he (or she) has been faithful to follow God, a saint's wilderness journey will one day come to an end. At this time, it is wise to take a census of all he has done and learned, to take stock of his person and position, and to count his blessings.

First, as his trek winds down, a saint has had many chances to learn to know the Lord. He (or she) should surely be aware that without God he is nothing.

When God redeemed him (or her), He placed him on solid ground. Psalm 40:2 says, *"He brought me up out of the pit of destruction, out of the miry clay, and He set my feet upon a rock...."* Only after a sinner has become a saint is he eligible for sanctification. The pit is sin, the rock is Jesus, and the lifting out is sanctification. Once out, a saint must agree to clean up his act. God's cleaning the dirt, grime, and mire off the saint is sanctification.

Second, a saint must realize that not all who were children of

Abraham were children of faith. Just so, not all who call themselves Christian are children of faith. Some still believe that works, rather than faith, will save them. Therefore, they are still in the bonds of slavery to works in Egypt. Others readily accept the presence of God but reject His power and Lordship. Therefore, they have come out of Egypt but have stopped on the far side of the Red Sea or have died off in the desert. Just a few have passed the tests, have crossed the desert, and are waiting for the order to go into the promised land.

Third, if he (or she) is determined to go on to Canaan, he is aware of his need for new leaders. Almost all those who, whether wisely or foolishly, led in the desert died there. Before crossing into Canaan, God set new leaders before the Israelites: Joshua was to lead them in military conquest, while Eleazar, the son of Aaron, was to be priest. For a saint, his (or her) military leader is Jesus. As Captain of the Host, He will lead His saints into the promised land and will conquer the enemy. Each saint's religious leader is also Jesus. As High Priest and mediator of the New Covenant, He will lead in sacrifice and in worship of God.

Fourth, in looking back over his (or her) life, a saint may suddenly realize that he's spent most of his Christian walk in the desert. He understands and acknowledges that, whether it has been days, weeks, or years since his spiritual rebirth, he's been wandering through wastelands. Yet has his desert experience been a waste of time? Does he realize that the desert is God's school or training ground? In truth, hasn't he learned some wonderful lessons as well as some hard ones?

Fifth, the desert has been a place for each saint to sort out his (or her) life. Its main purpose is to teach him that he is not the lord of his life. Only and always, Jesus is Lord. The sojourn in the desert has thus been God's choice of place where He teaches each saint to focus on Him, to depend on Him, and to live his life centered around Him. Until each has learned that and learned it well, God will not release him from the desert or to go and minister the joy of Jesus to others.

Sixth, can each saint also see that much of his (or her) desert struggle was of his own choosing? Haven't his own decisions and slowness to submit to Jesus prolonged the journey? Yet, if he is among those alive in Christ after a long, long time of wrestling with flesh, self, and rebellion, can he yet praise his Lord? Can he obey the Word? It states he is to:

> *Shout joyfully to the LORD, all the earth. Serve the LORD with gladness; come before Him with joyful singing. Know that the LORD Himself is God; it is He who has made us, and not we*

ourselves; we are His people and the sheep of His pasture. Enter His gates with thanksgiving, and His courts with praise. Give thanks to Him, bless His name. For the LORD is good; His lovingkindness is everlasting and His faithfulness to all generations. (Psalm 100)

Dear saint, have you come out of sin and victoriously crossed the desert? Do you realize that though you are tired, you are not at the end of your journey? God has commanded His children to go on to the promised land. Are you willing to go on?

Chapter 12

THE DESERT:

THE CHURCH'S SANCTIFICATION

Soon after its exodus from the world system and its passage through the Red Sea, the true Church also finds itself in the desert. If each individual living stone has to walk in the wilderness while God rearranges the order of their lives, then the sum of those stones, the Church (1 Peter 2:5), must make that same journey for the same reason. If each saint has to journey until he (or she) has either victory and life or defeat and death, so must the Church. The collective body of Christ must wander through dry places and barrenness until Jesus becomes the Head of the Church in more than name only and until the children of God, led by the Spirit of God, reach the Jordan River.

As the Israelites' desert journey began with the redemption of God's chosen people and their flight out of Egypt and as each saint's desert journey starts with salvation through the blood of Jesus and separation from the world, so also the Church, founded on the work of the cross and the blood of the Lamb, must begin to walk through the desert until it arrives at the promised land.

Please, Church, do not underestimate the importance of the journey that awaits. To explain, the Israelites, God's chosen people, were separated from or called out of Egypt. However, in spite of the miracles wrought by the mighty hand of God, a problem arose. As the Israelites faced crisis after crisis, instead of approaching God they grumbled and asked Moses what to do (Exodus 15:24). To compound their sin, they declared that they were wrong to have left Egypt and that they wanted to go back.

The Israelites had left Egypt, but the memory of that land was luring them back. They were being enticed by false memories of the past and by hard times in the present to return to old places and old ways.

What had been horrible in reality was now being pleasantly remembered. What had once threatened their lives now seemed the way to save their lives.

Like the Hebrews freed from the power of Pharaoh and from the land of Egypt thousands of years ago, the Church is also a called out body. It's name, Church, means the called out ones. As such, it is an assembly of those who have been delivered from the power of sin and separated from the world. Yet doesn't the Church have the same problem that the Israelites did? Hasn't the Church been tested to see if it would compromise God's standard by accepting the rules, rites, behavior, morals, and ethical values of the world? During times of trial, hasn't the Church been subjected to an endless barrage of voices inviting it back into sin or its old, worldly life? In some ways, hasn't the Church listened to this unholy seduction and responded to these enticing voices? To some degree, hasn't it compromised its relationship with the Lord and become so like the world that it is sometimes hard to tell the Church from the world?

Like the Israelites, the Church was supposed to have been a distinctive body. It was supposed to be a light in a very dark world. It was supposed to shine as the bride of Christ so the greatest possible difference could be seen between it and the world and between it and the harlot or counterfeit bride, the false religious system. It was supposed to have proudly carried the banner of the Lord Jesus, and, as His betrothed, to have prepared itself in purity and holiness for marriage to Him.

Has this happened? Is that what we now see? Is the Church separate and holy or is its splendor muddied from being too close to the muck pits? For instance, has its government copied world government or has it submitted itself to God's? Are its schools godly ones or mere imitations of worldly ones? Is the fruit of the Spirit seen in its children, or do they act like the children of the unsaved? Are its finances entangled in civil government, its people dependent on government welfare programs, and its saints reliant on humanist, worldly social programs? Is it involved in human, worldly projects, or is it totally devoted to the commands of God? Is its ministry of healing body and soul executed in godly ways or in human or even evil ones? Is its practice of justice an extension of the righteousness and justness of God, or is it an ineffective repetition of the world and its ways? Are its laborers trained in secular, worldly ways by ungodly teachers from ungodly texts, or are they thoroughly schooled in the biblical principals of God? Does it administrate divine love, life, and law in a dying world, allowing people to see the difference between God's ways and those of people?

The list could go on. The Church was called out of the world, but to what extent has it been lured back into the world? To what degree has it opened its doors to readmit the world and to give it access to its once holy body?

The answers to questions such as these can only be answered in the Church's response to the trials of the desert.

TESTING IN THE DESERT

When the Israelites left Egypt they discovered that they were not magically transported to Canaan. Instead, a long journey separated the two lands. Similarly, the true Church is discovering that, though born again and called out of the world, it has not been magically sent to the land of promise. It too faces a journey in which there are tests, trials, beauty, hardship, adversity, comfort, change, growth, defeat, and victory. It too finds itself in the midst of a desert.

The Israelites' journey began with the redemption of God's chosen people, their flight out of Egypt, and their journey through the desert. Each saint's journey starts with salvation through the blood of Jesus Christ and his (or her) separation from sin. So too, the whole Church, redeemed from sin and called out of the world, must walk out its salvation by making a journey through the desert to the banks of the Jordan River.

As the Israelites and as each saint discovered, the desert is a place where God tests His own (Psalm 11:5). In school, students are often tested to see how much or how little they know about a subject and then retested after a concentrated course of study to see how much they have learned. Similarly, in the desert God tests His Church to see how much or little it knows about Him, and then, after teaching His Church, He retests to see what it has learned. The Church may be surprised to find out that it is not as smart as it thinks it is. Quite often, it has failed His initial tests.

Each saint brings individual strengths and weaknesses, talents or inabilities into the local and universal Church. The desert is the place in which God tests these and turns them around. He makes the weaknesses strengths in His strength and the inabilities areas of anointing from Him. He asks the Church to surrender its strengths and talents to Him so He can cleanse them of flesh and self. If it does so, He allows them to be used in His service. If it does not, He won't allow the profane to be used in service or worship to Him.

God tests His Church to see if it will rely on Him or on others for provision, protection, and leadership. Further, God tests His Church so that it may discover for itself the things He already knows about it but what it must learn about itself. He tests His Church to give it an identity or to show it who it is. He tests His Church to let it learn if He or another is Lord. He tests His Church to see if it will walk under His command as one body or split up into several camps (called denominations) under human command. He tests His Church to see if it will go back to Egypt, endlessly wander in the desert, or follow Him to the Jordan River. He tests His Church to see if this generation is the one to go on or if it is simply one more that must die off in the desert so a new one can arise (Deuteronomy 8:15-17).

Rebellion, Hunger, And Thirst: Marah

The Lord considered the Israelites to be His flock, and He led them through the wilderness as their Shepherd (Psalm 78:52). Just so, He is the personal Shepherd of each of God's lambs and is the true Shepherd of the whole flock of God's sheep, the body of Christ (1 Peter 5:4; John 10:14).

According to Psalm 23, God not only supplies His flock's needs, but He leads, feeds, guards, and guides it. Jesus makes His Church lie down in green pastures where it can contentedly munch its food. He leads it to still waters where it can drink of Him deeply and be restored. He leads it on the paths of righteousness and through the valley of death, governs it with rod and staff, protects it from its enemies, anoints it with oil, and promises it a dwelling place in His house forever as the bride of Christ.

Would any truly rebel against such loving, merciful leadership? To some degree, the answer seems to be yes. As the Israelites' journey began with their redemption and their flight from Egypt, and as each saint's journey starts with his (or her) salvation through the blood of Jesus and his separation from the world, so too, the whole Church, redeemed from sin and called out of the world, must walk in its salvation through the desert to the banks of the Jordan River. Somewhere on its journey the Church will come to Marah. Here, though God may be testing His Church, His Church is also testing Him (Exodus 17:7).

As soon as it begins to pull away from the world system, the Church faces its first enemy: flesh. Soon after leaving the Red Sea, the Israelites and each newly saved Christian were tested by the scarcity of natural and supernatural water and food. As soon as the shortages became known, desperate cries and angry complaints rose up to God. While shouts of, "Find us water!" and "Feed us, or we shall die in the desert!" were heard, the real question everyone was asking was, "Who's going to take care of ME?" The same trials face the Church; the same comments are heard; the same questions are asked.

As those who have gone through these tests had to learn that God is their Provider, so too His Church must learn that apart from Him, there is no holy provision. God's Church cannot supply itself. Even in the most basic necessities, such as food and drink, Jesus alone is Jehovah-jireh, the LORD who provides (Genesis 22:14). He gives to His Church out of the abundance of His storehouse. The Church dares not rely on itself, on people, or on another power to be its source of supply. The Israelites could not; individual saints cannot; the body of Christ cannot.

Pride makes the Church think it can self-sufficiently supply its own needs. Arrogance makes it believe it can provide for or help others independently of God. It is sin for the Church to accept provision to meet its needs from a source other than God.

As the Church must acknowledge that the Lord is its Provider, so it must recognize and confess that He is its provision. Only Jesus, both the Living Water and the Bread of Life, can enable the Church to survive in the desert. Water from any wellspring other than His deep pools will not quench thirst; rather, it will quicken it. Spiritual food or teaching that is from a root or basis different or apart from His Word will not fortify or strengthen His body; rather, it will sicken it. Jesus is all His body must eat and drink from in order to remain alive and healthy throughout the desert walk.

Has the Church heard this? Has it accepted, been indifferent to, or rejected His provision? Is it dependent on Him, self, or a different god to sustain its life? Is it still bitterly complaining about the quality and quantity of its provision at the brackish waters of Marah? Is it still wandering hungry and thirsty in the desert? Or, has it moved on, safe in His provision and love?

The Church dares not underestimate the significance of this message. Things are not repeated in the Bible to bore the reader but to underscore their importance. If the writer of Exodus twice wrote of the Israelites' reaction to a shortage of water, the Church as much to learn – and heed – from it.

Further, Marah has an additional blessing for the Church. Arriving at this place of tainted water just after salvation from the world of sin, it corporately discovers healing in the atonement. Here it begins to understand that God's Son, Jesus Christ, is not only the source of spiritual healing through forgiveness of sins but also the source of physical healing through the blood He shed while suffering at human hands for the benefit of mankind.

When the Old Testament prophet Isaiah (53:5) says, *"But He was pierced through for our transgressions, He was crushed for our iniquities; the chastening for our well-being fell upon Him, and by His scourging we are healed,"* he is revealing healing for both the inner and outer person. Further, the pronoun "our" indicates the plural. Jesus did not suffer and die to provide healing for just one person; He did so for everyone.

Just as each saint finds himself (or herself) in mental or physical need of healing and can go to the cross, ask for, and receive that healing, so the Church, as a corporate body, finds itself in need of healing and can – and must – go to that same cross, ask for, and receive healing. The provision was made two thousand years ago; now is the time to seek and apply that provision not only for our own healing but also to use the blessing of healing to extend the kingdom of God here on earth.

The Amalekites

In testing the Israelites and in bringing them to an awareness of problems in their attitude and behavior toward Him, the LORD allowed them to meet an enemy called the Amalekites. He repeats the same test for the body of Christ. Freed from the mastery of Satan, the Church isn't long in the desert before it decides that it wants to be its own lord. Thus begins the battle of flesh.

Recognizing and dealing with the Amalekites was a concern for the Israelites. Similarly, recognizing and dealing with the flesh is an on-going concern for each saint. Recognizing and dealing with the Amalekites is now a battle for the whole Church. As every saint progressively learns that he (or she) died to sin in order to live to God through Christ, so the sum of those individual saints, the Church, must learn and affirm this (Romans 6:11). That means fighting and gaining victory over the flesh.

When any unbeliever is individually saved by grace he (or she) becomes a saint, one who is holy, separated, sanctified, and dedicated to God. As a saint, he should not remain a lone sheep in a distant field but should become a part of the flock of God. Often, however, rather than understanding his place as part of the body of Christ, he tries to retain individual relationship with God. He is a saint saved by God but fellowshipping with flesh.

Whatever degree of flesh each saint carries about individually is exactly the same degree of flesh that he brings into the Church. If he is lean of flesh, he adds no carnality to God's flock. However, if he is bulging with the evidence of frequent indulgence in egocentric activity, he adds his accumulation of the sins of the flesh to the whole body, producing a carnal, humanist body of Christ.

As the Israelites were called to face and fight the Amalekites, so the Church must engage in battle with flesh. God would never release His holy authority or unleash His mighty power to a Church so full of flesh that it would expend it on people, situations, or ways of its own choosing. It is only as traces of flesh are defeated and driven away that God will empower His body to do His works.

God demands that the Church fight the battle of flesh. The Church must remember that at the battle of Rephidim God changed His orders to the Hebrews from *"stand and see"* to *"go and fight"* (Exodus 14:13; 17:9). Having been saved and brought out of Egypt by His great power, they were now to engage the enemy themselves. In like manner, the members of the Church, under God's direction and in His strength, must fight the enemy of flesh themselves.

Too, Scripture shows a definite extension of the singular to the plural in the matter of saints dealing with flesh. While the words of Romans 6:6, *"knowing this, that our old self was crucified with Him, in order that our body of sin might be done away with...."* refer to the death in Christ of each individual saint, the words of 2 Corinthians 5:14-15 [emphasis added] include the whole Church:

> *For the love of Christ controls **us**, having concluded this, that one died for **all**, therefore all died; and He died for **all**, so that **they** who live should no longer live for **themselves**, but for Him who died and rose again on **their** behalf.*

These words were addressed to the Christian Church at Corinth. Its saints were to understand that Christ had died for all, and when He died, so did they. In response to this magnificent victory on their behalf they were no longer to live for themselves but for Him. They were to put down the flesh, to die to self-centeredness, and to live as Christ-centered Christians in the community of God, the Church.

To help the twenty-first century Church better understand its death to flesh and its restructuring from a group of individuals into a corporate body, the teachings of Jessie Penn-Lewis are very instructive[4]. In her exposition of 2 Corinthians 5, she sheds light on the Church's position toward death. The writer of this epistle, the apostle Paul, uses the Greek word *apothnesko* to declare the Church's death as something consummated and finished. This word means to die out, to expire, to become quite dead. This firm and settled position of death to sin, the world, the flesh, and the devil is the central identification of the Church which it must recognize and acknowledge before the Holy Spirit can make this position of the Church the experience of the Church.

Apothnesko is not the only Greek word used to describe the Church's death. Others clarify the outworking of this death and the Church's responsibility toward it. For example, in another epistle, Paul uses the word *thanatoo* when he writes, *"but if by the Spirit you are putting to death the deeds of the body...."* (Romans 8:13). This scripture makes it clear that the saints must cause the doings of the body to die, to take away their life, or to bring the deeds of the flesh under the power of that death. Therefore, though dead, the Church must subdue the unholy deeds of the corporate body or of its corporate expressions of flesh.

Further, Paul uses a third word for death. In Colossians 3:5, he states, *"Therefore consider the members of your earthly body as dead...."* Here the Greek word *nekroo* is used, and, in reference to the members of the body, it means to deprive the members of the body of the activity of the old life. Thus all the members of the body or the whole Church must die until they are no longer energized by the fallen life of Adam but are brought under the power of the cross. They are thereby made "dead to sin" and alive to God for His service.

Finally, 2 Corinthians 4:10-11 declares that Christians are, *"always carrying about in the body the dying of Jesus, so that the life of Jesus also may be manifested in our body."* Here, the apostle Paul uses the Greek word *nekrosis,* which means to put to death. In the present tense, it is expressive of the action being incomplete but in progress, a daily dying. It shows that there will never be a point during the Church's sojourn on earth in which it will not need to apply the death of the cross if it is to die to the flesh and to live for Christ. Therefore, though the Church has died with Christ through a mighty, powerful act of God, it must act on its own behalf to continually put to death its flesh in order to grow to

---

[4] Penn-Lewis, Jessie. *The Centrality of the Cross*, Fort Washington, PA: CLC Publications. 1993. pp. 14-17.

maturity in its new resurrected life.

Yet, is the Church doing so? Is it fighting the battle with flesh with a determination to win? Has the flesh hurt its service to God and kept it from rest? Is the Church responding to the attack by the Amalekites? As Moses did at Rephidim, is it consistently and effectively wielding the twin weapons of godly authority and intercession in its spiritual warfare against the power of the flesh so spiritual victories will be manifested in physical ways?

In order to fight this battle with flesh, the Church is to judge itself. While the Lord has said that the Church is not to judge the world because that is His job (1 Corinthians 5:12-13), it is definitely to judge itself (1 Corinthians 5:11-12). The Church dares not point fingers at others for the very things it tolerates within its own body. If it will not judge itself, it is indicating that rather than subduing the flesh, it craves to indulge it to its own destruction. If the Church will not judge itself, it causes God's judgment, which is much greater judgment than its own, to fall on it (1 Corinthians 11:32; 1 Peter 4:17-18).

The Israelites could not go on until they had faced and defeated the Amalekites. Neither can the Church. It is God's wish that even the memory of expressions of the flesh be blotted out. It is also His warning that stragglers or those who separate from the true body of Christ will meet with continuous harassment from this enemy. Without question, some in the Church will succumb to the heat or the scorpions of the desert, but many will also fall by the wayside or be killed because of the failures of the flesh.

The Supremacy Of The Rod Of God

As the rod of God was given to Moses to break the power of Pharaoh and to free the Israelites from his deadly grip, and as it has been given to each saint for use in his (or her) personal spiritual warfare, so also God gives His rod of authority to the whole New Testament Church. This rod is the rod of Elohim, the strong, powerful, covenant-keeping God. It is His holy authority given to His Church to accomplish His will in the kingdom of God on earth.

Authority is jurisdiction, command, and dominance. It is sovereignty and supremacy. In the vernacular, it is clout. For the Church, it is God's permission to move in power.

God is the source of all power (Romans 13:1). His Son, Jesus, moved in authority when He walked on the earth as a man, commanding unclean spirits to obey Him (Mark 1:27), forgiving (Luke 5:18-26), and ruling over all unlawful authority and power (1 Corinthians 15:24-26). After His death and resurrection, Jesus delegated holy authority to the disciples. Speaking to them as a group or as the fledgling disciples of His Church, He told them to use that authority to do the will of God on earth (Matthew 28:18-20).

This authority always goes back to the cross. All those who are bathed in the blood that Jesus shed on the cross are given authority to walk in the ongoing power of the cross. These Christians are urged to deny themselves, to take up their crosses, and to follow Him (Mark 8:34). These, the Church or the most powerful people on the earth, are urged to discover their authority in Christ and to use it to rebuke and overcome their enemies (Titus 2:15) and to carry the love and nature of God existent within that authority with them as they extend the kingdom on God on earth.

THE NEW COVENANT

Shortly after God brought the Israelites out of Egypt by the power of His outstretched arm (Passover), He led them to Mount Sinai for the purpose of making a covenant with them (Pentecost). Shortly after each new saint was forgiven of his (or her) sin (his spiritual Passover), God called him into covenant with Him and introduced him to the baptism into the Holy Spirit (his spiritual Pentecost). So too with His Church. After its Passover or its salvation and deliverance from the false religious system in the world, Jesus leads His separated body of believers to a place where He will meet with it in order to enjoy the blessings of His New Covenant and to learn of and walk in the enabling power of His Spirit.

A covenant is an agreement or contract between two parties. According to *Smith's Bible Dictionary*[5], two principle types of covenant exist. The first is a covenant of works whereby God promises to bless His people upon condition of their obedience. The second is a covenant of grace whereby God promises to save men and women on condition of their believing in Christ and receiving Him as Savior and Lord.

The covenant God made with the Israelites is an example of a covenant of works. When it was given, God declared His Lordship to them. His proclamation, accompanied by supernatural signs of wonder

---

[5] Smith, William. *Smith's Bible Dictionary.* Iowa Falls, IA: Riverside Book and Bible House. 3rd Printing. p. 127.

and power, was followed by a lengthy list of commands, rules, and ordinances that were to govern every facet of life and worship. All of these items in the Law had to be kept to maintain the covenant. After receiving the Law, Moses wrote it down, and the covenant was then inaugurated when he sprinkled the blood of sacrificed animals on the book of the Law and on the people (Hebrews 9:18-20).

The Law, as given to the Hebrews, was perfect (Psalm 19:7). However, though it was holy, righteous, and good (Romans 7:12), imperfect men and women could not keep it. The Law could neither perfect them (Hebrews 10:1) nor make them righteous. While it could reveal people's sin to them (Romans 7:7), even the most strenuous works or most exact observance of religious ritual could not provide the right standing with God that was needed because of that sin.

For 1500 years, the ministry of law continued to prove that mankind could not earn salvation through works of flesh (Romans 9:31-32). A better way had to be found. So it was in Jesus. Jesus was the end of the law for righteousness (Romans 10:4). He took on Himself the sins of all mankind, suffered and died for us, and, in a glorious expression of God's power and majesty, was raised from the dead. Seen on earth by His disciples for forty days after His resurrection, He indicated that although He was about to leave this world, His work on earth was to continue through His disciples. His orders to them included:

> *All authority has been given to Me in heaven and on earth. Go therefore and make disciples of all the nations, baptizing them in the name of the Father and the Son and the Holy Spirit, teaching them to observe all that I commanded you; and lo, I am with you always, even to the end of the age.* (Matthew 28:18-20)

> *Go into all the world and preach the gospel to all creation.* (Mark 16:15)

> *....repentance for forgiveness of sins should be proclaimed in His name to all the nations, beginning from Jerusalem.* (Luke 24:47)

The promise that would follow His disciples' obedience to His commands was the evangelization of the world, a massive harvest of souls for Christ. This harvest would be accompanied by some extraordinary signs:

> *These signs will accompany those who have believed: in My name they will cast out demons, they will speak with new*

> tongues; they will pick up serpents, and if they drink any deadly poison, it will not hurt them; they will lay hands on the sick, and they will recover. (Mark 16:17-18)

However, a problem arose. Jesus' death had ended the need of animal sacrifice for sin. It had declared the old ways obsolete. Further, Jesus Himself had ascended into heaven, so He was no longer physically on earth to minister. With no Old Covenant, no ritualistic religion, and no physical presence of Jesus, how were the disciples supposed to do what they were asked to do? All work had to be carried out under the authority of an Overseer, and He was gone.

The answer to this dilemma was the second type of covenant, a new covenant, the covenant of grace, which Jesus gave to those who would become His Church. The night before He died,

> When the hour had come, He reclined at the table, and the apostles with Him. And He said to them, "I have earnestly desired to eat this Passover with you before I suffer; for I say to you, I shall never again eat it until it is fulfilled in the kingdom of God." And when He had taken a cup and given thanks, He said, "Take this and share it among yourselves; for I say to you, I will not drink of the fruit of the vine from now on until the kingdom of God comes." And when He had taken some bread and given thanks, He broke it and gave it to them, saying, "This is My body which is given for you; do this in remembrance of Me." And in the same way He took the cup after they had eaten, saying, "This cup which is poured out for you is the new covenant in My blood." (Luke 22:14-20)

This New Covenant was to be much different from the old one. It represented Mount Zion, not Mount Sinai (Hebrews 12:18-24). It was initiated with the blood of Christ rather than that of an animal. The dwelling place of God was to be in the hearts of men and women rather than in an ark in a manmade tabernacle (1 Corinthians 3:16). The High Priest of the covenant was Jesus, not man (Hebrews 7).

It cannot be stressed enough that God did not give His new Church the Old Covenant; that was a gift to the Hebrews. The new Church did not and does not have a covenant of animal sacrifice for the forgiveness of sin. The new Church did not and does not have a prescribed, ritualistic, religious service of worship that can occur only in a certain place, at certain times, and under the leadership of a certain group of men. The new Church did not and does not have a covenant of laws, rules, and legalisms. Instead, it has been given the New Covenant of God and is expected to accept, appropriate, and apply its provisions.

The Bible makes it clear that in this dispensation, the law for righteousness is finished because it was fulfilled by Christ. His Church now serves Him under a banner of grace (Romans 6:14) and by His Spirit. When Jesus died to the Law, all who died with Him also died to the Law. The Church is in no way bound to the law of Moses, but instead it is blessed by God's grace in order that it may serve Him in the newness of His Spirit.

> *Therefore, my brethren, you also were made to die to the Law through the body of Christ, so that you might be joined to another, to Him who was raised from the dead, in order that we might bear fruit for God. For while we were in the flesh, the sinful passions, which were aroused by the Law, were at work in the members of our body to bear fruit for death. But now we have been released from the Law, having died to that by which we were bound, so that we serve in newness of the Spirit and not in oldness of the letter.* (Romans 7:4-6)

The Israelites wandered in the desert under the Law. In contrast, the Church should be walking through the desert in grace. If instead it is forsaking God's grace and following in the footsteps of the Law, its desert trek will turn out to be an expression of futility and impotence under the covenant of law.

The Israelites slid into a ritual of flesh in order to keep the Law. To some degree, the Church, following the practices of the Old Covenant rather than obeying the New, has also reduced its ministry or its worship to works of flesh performed by ritual, human tradition, and religious law. Rather than walking in grace, it is mirroring the ancient Israelites and the present world society and is reverting to endless laws and legalisms. Rather than serving by the Spirit, it is reverting to the slavery of flesh. It does not seem to understand that as a ministry of flesh, the Church can never please God.

> *For those who are according to the flesh set their minds on the things of the flesh, but those who are according to the Spirit, the things of the Spirit. For the mind set on the flesh is death, but the mind set on the Spirit is life and peace, because the mind set on the flesh is hostile toward God; for it does not subject itself to the law of God, for it is not even able to do so; and those who are in the flesh cannot please God.* (Romans 8:5-8)

If the Church is not charged to abide under law, why does it spend so much time making and enforcing rules and regulations? Why does each denomination have non-Biblical rules that, if followed, make people a member of that denomination rather than of His Church? Why do local churches put saints under obligation to manmade laws in order to remain in good standing with that Church? Why do so many pastors spend so much time ordering saints to follow rules rather than to love God? How often does the Church fail to hear about Jesus because its leaders are too busy issuing human restrictions?

Aren't regulations and demands such as "Thou shalt not wear jewelry (or make-up or bright colors)," "Thou shalt not dance (or smoke or play cards or go to the movies)," "Thou shalt worship God only by singing hymns while accompanied by an organ" common in the Church? Hasn't the Church imposed laws concerning food, drink, and days of worship (Colossians 2:16)? About such manmade rules the Word says:

> *If you have died with Christ to the elementary principles of the world, why, as if you were living in the world, do you submit yourself to decrees, such as, "Do not handle, do not taste, do not touch!" (which all refer to things destined to perish with use) – in accordance with the commandments and teachings of men? These are matters which have, to be sure, the appearance of wisdom in self-made religion and self-abasement and severe treatment of the body, but are of no value against fleshly indulgence.* (Colossians 2:20-23)

Do not misunderstand. No society can exist without authority and order. The kingdom of God is no different. While the Church is not under Old Covenant law or humanist regulation, it most definitely is subject to the law of God and the laws of Christ (1 Corinthians 9:21). He, not people or denominations, is in charge. In His kingdom, God the Father sets the rules, Jesus builds His Church by them, and the Holy Spirit enforces them while making them known to the saints.

While all things done by saints in God's service must be done properly and in order (1 Corinthians 14:40), there is a vast difference between this and the nit-picky, stifling, ungodly requirements of human law that have nothing to do with salvation, holiness, and the ministry or extension of divine government by God's Spirit.

Perhaps this can be understood better if it is approached from another, more personal angle. Suppose you are in love with a woman and she is in love with you. Mistakenly thinking it will help or enhance your relationship, that sweet someone begins to give you rules to follow. All you hear is, "Call me at seven," "Bring me some flowers," "Take me to my favorite restaurant," "Don't touch that vase," and "Don't keep me waiting." Soon, so caught up in keeping the rules so as not to offend her, you're too busy for relationship. Love quickly cools, and the slavery of trying to please or appease overwhelms, stifles, and then deadens your love.

The Church is supposed to be having a love affair with Jesus. Its heart should melt at the thought of Him, and its voices should be calling out to Him. Whoever heard of passing laws to regulate a love affair?

The Church cannot and should not even try to regulate devotion and passion. People cannot set forth rules to govern the worship of God. Under the Old Covenant, laws for worshipping God were given by God Himself. They were then written down so the Hebrews would never forget or deviate from them. Under the New Covenant, God set forth no such rules. Why then do people do so?

The Church cannot tell its members that the proof of their love for God is perfect attendance at Church services. It cannot make laws telling people to love God by giving the Church all their money – and then cursing them if they don't. It cannot demand that people devote themselves to ministry and then proceed to tell them exactly which ministry they are allowed to do and which are forbidden to them. These laws should not – cannot – govern love for Christ. If saints don't love God just because they love Him, all the rules in the world won't make any difference. Obedience can't produce love; rather, obedience is a fruit of love.

The Church has been given a covenant of grace so it will carry His name around the world through love, not through the ministry of law. It is a covenant of relationship, not of ritual; of inspiration, not of tradition; of life, not of death. The Church should keep covenant by allowing that grace to work within it so it can bring others unto Him, so others can share His great love. In so doing, it will discover that the New Covenant is truly better than the Old.

Pentecost

The Church is not able to keep covenant with God without divine assistance. Thus, the Holy Spirit of God has blessed it with grace. Defined as unmerited favor, grace was introduced into the Church by Jesus (Romans 5:2). It is the source of salvation (Ephesians 2:8-9), justification (Romans 3:24), and forgiveness (Ephesians 1:7). God's grace is glorious (Ephesians 1:6), abundant (Acts 4:33), and all-sufficient

(2 Corinthians 12:9). This holy grace accompanied the Holy Spirit when He descended upon the Church at the Feast of Pentecost.

In Greek, the word Pentecost means fifty. In Hebrew, its name, *shavuoth*, means weeks. It was called such since it was to be perpetually celebrated seven weeks and one day (or fifty days) after the Passover Sabbath (Leviticus 23:15-17). The Feast of Pentecost was also known as the Feast of the Early Harvest since it took place between the grain harvest and the ingathering of fruit. God ordered that during this feast an offering from the grain harvest was to be brought before Him (Exodus 23:16-19).

The most well-known significance of Pentecost was as a commemoration of the giving of the Law. Fifty days after leaving Egypt (Exodus 19:1), the Israelites gathered at Mount Sinai. There, God broke forth on them and made His covenant of law with them. To remember this crucial period in history, God commanded that as soon as the Israelites reached the promised land they were to begin celebrating Pentecost and were then to observe this holy day every year from that point onwards.

Obediently, hundreds of years later, Jews in the first century were gathered in Jerusalem and were ritualistically celebrating the Feast of Pentecost when God met with a small, separated, called-out group of them and taught them the true, spiritual significance of the feast: He sent the Holy Spirit among them. Just before Jesus had ascended to heaven, He had commanded His disciples: *"And behold, I am sending forth the promise of My Father upon you; but you are to stay in the city until you are clothed with power from on high"* (Luke 24:49). Luke goes on to explain what this promise was in Acts 1:4-5:

> *Gathering them together, He commanded them not to leave Jerusalem, but to wait for what the Father had promised, "Which," He [Jesus] said, "you heard of from Me; for John baptized with water, but you will be baptized with the Holy Spirit not many days from now."*

Fifty days after the Lord's resurrection from the dead, the Holy Spirit descended on this small group. In supernatural manifestation of God's power by rushing, violent wind and tongues of fire, the Holy Spirit met with the disciples and poured Himself out on them. This coming of the Holy Spirit upon them, both male and female, is, by common consent of Bible scholars, referred to as the beginning of the Church.

Those early saints became the first fruit of a harvest of souls.

They were the human manifestation of the Spirit of God, the means through which the Church would serve God not by law but by the power of His Holy Spirit until the fruit of its labor was brought in and the ingathering of the harvest of souls from all over the world was complete. The power of the Holy Spirit would enable the disciples to take His name, word, and testimony all over the world (Acts 1:8).

According to rabbinic tradition, the exodus was not complete until the Law was given. Therefore, Passover and Pentecost were seen as the beginning and end of one holy season. Today, the Church's separation from the world is not complete until the place occupied by the world is filled with the Spirit of God. As Passover meant freedom and Pentecost meant the Old Covenant of Law to the Hebrews, so today the Church's Passover is its corporate salvation into one body and its Pentecost is its empowerment for service through the power of the Holy Spirit. Neither is complete without the other.

Rejection

As there was an unpleasant aftermath to the presence of God at Mount Sinai, so too there has been an unwelcome reaction to His Spirit in the Church. As the Israelites once cried out in fear of God and rejected His presence, so too the Church, in not understanding its absolute dependence and need of the Holy Spirit, has erred in its negative reception of God's Spirit.

It is sad but true that the Church has brought enormous problems on itself by not meeting the terms of God's covenant. It has thought that the call to accept Jesus as Lord and to worship Him in the way He commands was an option. It is not! If it has been saved by Him, it knows Him as Savior. If it is to serve Him, it must submit to Him as Lord. That means it must walk with Him by His Spirit.

Yet is there not a group in the Church who accepts Jesus as Savior only? They know, teach, and preach the Word, but they do not experience the reality of it because they have denied the Holy Spirit. They are known for their in-house fellowship gatherings but seldom see a new face in their midst because they try to evangelize without the Holy Spirit's power to do so. These saints truly love Jesus, but because they will not accept His Sprit, they are powerless. Their lives and ministries are good hearted but impotent.

Often these evangelicals are so overly concerned that their members will get "fleshly" if they walk in the grace or manifest the gifts of the Holy Spirit that they shut any such manifestations out of their fellowship. They fail to realize that it is only the working presence of the Holy Spirit which can keep them from getting fleshly or which can allow them to discern the difference between flesh and spirit.

An opposite extreme can be found in the born-again Church that also violates the spirit of the New Covenant. These are saints who have accepted Jesus as both Savior and Lord but then pay no heed to Him as such because they have been corrupted by the lust for power, power, power. Rather than deny that the Holy Spirit is the power through which they are to do the work of God, they readily acknowledge it. However, they want His power for their own self-determined purposes, to gain a reputation for having supernatural ministry, and to glorify themselves rather than God.

When God refuses to allow power-hungry Pentecostals to illegitimately use His name and strength for their own purposes, they grow angry and use them anyway. Rather, they misuse them. They speak prophetic words that have not come from God, they declare untrue healings, they claim to walk in faith when they really walk in presumption, and they allow unholy excesses in worship and in the use of the gifts of the Spirit which bring offense to both the body of Christ and the Christ of the body.

The austerity of those who deny the power of the Spirit is matched by the excess of those trying to control it for their own use. The truth is that both are wrong. God has sent His power to **His** Church; that power is to be accepted and used to serve **Him**. Rather than reject His power or crave it for the wrong reasons, the Church must learn balance. It must admit the Holy Spirit and welcome His gifts and graces even as it allows their expression only for godly purposes and in godly ways. It must walk in the fullness God intends for it but do so without offending God, the saints, or the unsaved.

Does the Church realize that in rejecting the Holy Spirit of God it is, in effect, rejecting God? Does the Church understand the full extent of its error? While evangelicals and Pentecostals have been quarreling with each other about God's Spirit, they have not carried His message to a dying world. In short, because of foolish infighting, the Church has not performed the task it was given to do. It has offended the various parts of the body and the Head of the body, Jesus. It has been disobedient in attitude as well as in behavior. It needs to approach its Lord for forgiveness.

Giving Grace

As God gives each Christian grace, so also He gives the whole body of Christ the gift of grace (Romans 5:15). For the Church, grace is the manifestation of the approval of God. It is His acceptance, respect, and good will toward all believers. It is that adornment or enhancement or enrichment that sets the Church apart from the world. It is not found on tablets of stone but is imprinted on the hearts of believers.

Rebellion: The Golden Calf

While loving and granting grace to His Church, God is also in authority over it. He therefore has every right to ask it to obey Him or to walk in His ways. Obedience is the Church's positive response to His will. However, if the Church is not fully convinced that Jesus is Lord and that He is the only God it must serve, it may end up doing some foolish and futile things. As the Israelites once did, it may rebel by fashioning false idols or golden calves. To more fully understand the temptation to rebellion, God's Church must learn the difference between love and obedience.

Concerning love, one of God's holy attributes is love, *"for God is love"* (1 John 4:8). From His limitless supply of love, He perfectly and eternally loves. Therefore, love is who God is as well as what He does. Further, God's love is universal; He loves everyone, saint and sinner alike. God's love is unconditional; His love is unqualified, unrestricted, unequivocal, and unlimited by what men and women do or don't do. God's love is not subject to people's wills; He loves whether they want Him to or not. God's love does not offer or result in reward or punishment; it remains constant no matter what a person's behavior. Blissfully, wonderfully, eternally, it just is.

In direct contrast, obedience is not a description of God's attributes, nature, or character. Nowhere does the Bible say, "God is works." People's obedience to God is not universal, perfect, and eternal; some people obey God and some do not. People's obedience to God is conditional, often limited or restricted by the maturity of the individuals or by their emotions and feelings. People's obedience to God is subject to their will; some people obey God, some obey Him sometimes, and some refuse to obey Him at all. Some obey Him without question, while others do the things God asks them to do if they like the assignment but refuse to comply if they don't. People's obedience to God does produce reward or punishment; it is subject to His judgment. Saints who obey or those whose works are tested by fire and yet remain faithful to Him receive rewards; those whose works are burned or destroyed by fire suffer loss of reward (1 Corinthians 3:12-14).

From this it can be seen that God's New Covenant of love is different than His Old Covenant of law and obedience. His New Covenant is not an agreement to love His Church if it obeys Him; He loves His Church whether it agrees with Him or not. He loves His Church with no strings attached. It is not dependent on works since His Church cannot earn His love by works.

Why then does the Church seek God's love? It already has it. Why does it try to earn His love? It already has it. Why does it not realize that its problems stem from lack of obedience on its part, not on lack of love from God? Why does it walk in rejection and then reject the One who loves it by creating and worshipping false gods? Why are its golden calves so often a means of self-worship?

The Church must learn from the Israelites' mistakes concerning their sin with the golden idols. While Moses tarried on the mountain, the Israelites saw smoke but no visible substance of God. In stubborn rebellion, they then decided to create with their own hands the form of the God they could not see. Instead, they made a false god.

It is highly probable that the Israelites made their idol with the gold they brought out of Egypt. Since it was an idol to a false god and since God did not order its building, the calf was a heinous work of evil whose presence brought dire consequences. Fashioning such an Idol allowed Satan access to the Israelites. It brought him, in the form of a false god, back into the Israelites' camp. It gave him a foothold or legal access to work his evil among the people.

Has any part of the Church rebelled in like manner even to a small extent? Though disciples who lived in the first century saw Jesus, who was the exact image of God, saints in the world today have never seen His physical substance. Barring a supernatural revelation, they have never seen, heard, tasted, smelled, or felt Him. Yet, because the Church wants a God it can physically relate to, it ignores the Scriptures that declare God is Spirit (John 4:24) and tries to build an unseen, unknown, imperfect image of Him. From the treasury of things it honors, from its limited imagination, and from the inability of its own hands, it creates a golden god. Usually in the form of a church leader or a ministry, it idolizes it, worships it, and calls it God.

The Church must learn that golden calves are always an idolatrous expression of humanism. They are always a product of the work of people's hands, minds, or the lust of their eyes or flesh. Since these idols also allow Satan a foothold within the body of Christ, they must be gotten rid of immediately.

Instructions For The Tabernacle

In addition to inaugurating a New Covenant with His Church, God indicated that He wanted changes in the way He was to be worshipped. One such revision involved His tabernacle.

God once dwelt among the Israelites as the shekinah glory. He gave Moses His plan for His tabernacle, oversaw its construction, and then in a wonderful, overwhelming presentation of Himself, occupied its innermost chamber.

Later, God dwelt among men and women when Jesus was born as a man and walked on earth. When He did so, He was the temple of God (John 2:19). After His death, burial, and resurrection, Jesus ascended to His Father in heaven, taking His physical presence out of this world. Knowing His children could not exist without His presence, God sent Another, His Holy Spirit, to dwell within and among them. As the Hebrews once had His tabernacle and as Jesus became each saint's temple, so now there exists a different sanctuary that is home to His special, spiritual presence. That sanctuary or holy dwelling place is His Church.

God has chosen that His Spirit should abide in the body of Christ. As He resides in each saint, so He dwells in the sum of the saints who make up the local and universal Church. It may have been with hesitation and amazement that each saint learned and then agreed that he or she was the sanctuary of Holy God. It is just as astonishing – and just as true – that the body of Christ is now God's earthly tabernacle (2 Corinthians 6:16).

Sadly, all too many Christians have been indoctrinated with the deception that the Church is a manmade building of wood or stone or that it is a place where saints go rather than who they are. Both of these errors are totally contrary to Scripture. The truth is that God is not concerned or impressed with buildings; He does not dwell in a physical sanctuary made with human hands. Solomon was wise enough to know that the glory of God could not be contained in even the most beautiful building (1 Kings 8:27).

God's true house is a spiritual one. He dwells in a place that He raised for Himself by His divine power. He lives within the saints, the Church, the body of His creation. *"but Christ was faithful as a Son over His house – whose house we are"* (Hebrews 3:6).

God has saved and sanctified a body. He has built and furnished His house (Hebrews 3:4). In an honor given only to born-again saints, He indwells that body, His Church, to its eternal blessing and joy.

The High Priest

The changes in the temple of God foretell the need for changes in the servants who worship in the temple.

Aaron was the first high priest of Old Covenant religious ritual. As such, he offered sacrifices, taught, and was the intercessor and mediator between people and God. Jesus Christ is the High Priest of the new religious order (Hebrews 7:11,22). He is the High Priest of each saint and the High Priest of the corporate body of saints, the Church. He became High Priest, not through the choice of any person, but by the appointment of God (Hebrews 5:1-5).

Concerning sacrifice, Jesus is qualified to be High Priest of the Church because He alone was without sin, and therefore He alone was able to offer Himself as a perfect, unblemished sacrifice for sin (Hebrews 5:9-10).

As mankind's Substitute, Jesus took the sins of all men and women on Himself and suffered and died for them. When He rose from the grave, He ascended into heaven and entered the heavenly sanctuary, where He sprinkled His holy blood to atone, once and for all time, for those sins (Hebrews 9:11-14). Any time the Church falls from His standard, Jesus is able to cleanse His Church through His own blood.

As High Priest, Jesus is **the** mediator or go-between for the Church in its new and better covenant (Hebrews 9:15; 12:18-24). He is **the** One whom God places between Himself and humanity (1 Timothy 2:5). He is **the** One to whom the Church must turn in its search for God. He is **the** One who settles the differences between God and the Church.

As High Priest, Jesus is the Church's instructor. He is its Rabboni or Teacher. Since He is the Word, He is the only foundation and standard of holy instruction. Further, since He was the perfect Servant, He is the only One who can teach God's body to be a servant unto their

Lord.

As High Priest, Jesus is the Intercessor or the One who stands in the gap or God's Church (Hebrews 4:14-15). He is the One who mediates, negotiates, intervenes, or pleads to God the Father on behalf of the Church when the Church has fallen into difficulties. As both Savior of and Head of the Church (Ephesians 5:23), He reaches out to heal the wounds of the body of the Church. Jesus ensures that all things that once caused a severance of relationship within the Church are reconciled (Romans 5:10).

The Priesthood

As each saint must minister under the authority of God, so must the corporate body. The purpose of the Church is to know, love, and serve God. Obviously, if it does not know Him or if it does not hold Him dear to its heart, it cannot effectively serve Him. Its activities become duty, not love.

One thing that God's priesthood must clearly understand is that Jesus is the Bridegroom and the Church is His bride. He, who is perfect, is not washing spots and ironing wrinkles out of His garments to prepare for His marriage; His bride is. He is not His bride's submissive manservant; His bride is His maidservant. He is the Light of the world, but His priesthood or body of servants has been commissioned to be a light in the world. His Church radiates or reflects or manifests His glory.

God's priesthood is to minister in His tabernacle under the authority and command of Jesus Christ. It must do as He says and must worship in ways of His leading. If it does not, then instead of worshipping, it is just going through ignorant or rebellious motions, which are meaningless. Too, if it does not, its sacrifices are not accepted by God. They are not the sweet aroma of the burnt offering of total dedication but rather are the stench of burned flesh.

The simple fact is that if the Church or His holy priesthood will not worship God, no one else is going to. The world doesn't worship Him. False cults and their false gods do not worship Him. The counterfeit religious system only pretends to worship Him. The only worship God wants or will accept is from His own. The only sacrifices He will accept are from His Church as offered through its High Priest, Jesus Christ.

Is the priesthood God-centered, Jesus-taught, and Spirit-led in its worship or not? Is its version of service the same as His? Is its idea of praise and worship a reflection of His will or its own? Does He receive many sacrifices from His body, or have the fires on once-holy altars burned low? Is the priesthood yet in the desert in its worship?

In Old Testament times, service and worship were almost synonymous. Religious service consisted of obedience to the laws of worship as given to Moses on Mount Sinai. This service of worship was seen in the outward forms of religious ritual, ceremony, and conformity to religious law on Sabbaths and feast days. Perhaps a more personal aspect depicting service or obedience as worship is the example of Abraham who worshipped God by offering his son, Isaac (Genesis 22).

However, today, people have separated the two. This is evidenced in many Christians who think worship is something someone leads them through on Sunday mornings while service is their calling or ministry or the way they are later seen and heard doing "godly" works.

The mistakes in this belief are evident. Worship is not works. It is the declaration of the worth of God. It is reverence, honor, and awe for who He is. It is obedience to the command to commit body, soul, and spirit into the blessing of praising the one true God. The difference between Old and New Testament worship is the expression of it, not the meaning of it. Under the Old Testament, worship was by prescribed order; under the New Testament, worship is by spirit. God is searching for those who will worship Him but will do so in a new and different way. *"God is spirit, and those who worship Him must worship in spirit and truth"* (John 4:24).

God still calls His Church to serve Him by worship. In the quiet moments of worship His priesthood begins to know and love Him. Then, from this private altar, He calls this body to represent Him to others or to minister more publicly on His behalf. Kneeling before Him at His altar must always precede rising and going for Him.

A praying Church is a powerful Church. A praising priesthood is a powerful priesthood. As soon as God's people learn that worship is service, they will become the mighty Church that the gates of Hades shall not overpower.

Offerings

It was only after the Israelites' golden calf had been destroyed that the people were called upon to bring offerings for the building of Moses' tabernacle. The contrast is clear. In the first case, people asked people to bring gold to build their own false god. In the latter instance, God called His children to offer their substance to Him while He built His house. The first had to be destroyed; the latter endures.

The Church cannot truly build the house of God if it is being fashioned as an idol. The true Church cannot be built from the same substance once used to create graven images. Using provision to form and fashion a false idol depletes the supply of that which than can be offered to the building of the true house of God.

Only when the Church's idols are destroyed will God ask His people to contribute toward the building of His sanctuary. Only when the Church offers back to God those things that He, not people, has provided for His body will the work created honor true God and be a fit place for His glory to indwell.

Rebellion: Nadab And Abihu

One way the Church builds the tabernacle of God is through worship. Therefore, it must be aware that there are true ways to worship and false ways to worship. As the Church is not to create false idols, so also it is not to participate in false worship. It is not to follow the example of Nadab and Abihu.

Nadab and Abihu were the oldest sons of Aaron (Exodus 6:23). They were blessed to be among those who were called up Mount Sinai to worship the LORD from afar (Exodus 24:1). Yet, despite growing up in a holy family, despite taking part in their people's worship of God, and despite being personally blessed by God's favor, they chose to eschew proper worship in favor of improper. Even while the tabernacle was being dedicated, even while *"the glory of the LORD appeared to all the people, even while fire came out from before the LORD and consumed the burnt offering and the portions of fat on the altar"* (Leviticus 9:24), they threw off God's chosen command of worship and "worshipped" Him after the flesh. They *"took their respective firepans, and after putting fire in them, placed incense on it, and offered strange fire before the LORD, which he had not commanded them"* (Leviticus 10:1). So serious were their actions of flesh and so serious was their affront to God that *"fire came out from the presence of the LORD and consumed them, and they died before the LORD"* (Leviticus 10:2).

On their forty-year desert trek, the Hebrews had to learn to worship their one God in the manner of His choosing. Similarly, each saint's wilderness journey includes learning to worship true God while overcoming the problems, the prejudices, and the judgments formed against others who do not worship in the same way. Surely then, while learning to worship its one true God, the job of the Church, at both local and universal levels, is to avoid the pitfalls of flesh which plunged true worship into error.

The Church is not to offer its worship to Satan or to self but unto God. Since He is holy God, He will accept only holy worship. Since praise and adoration of God is a foundation stone of the Church, the Church must learn more about it.

Worship is often associated with music. Long ago God created beings called angels. To lead them, there were three arch or chief angels: Michael, the warrior, Gabriel, the messenger, and Lucifer, the worship leader. Today Lucifer is known as Satan. Satan, still persistent in efforts to defy and defeat God, was once in charge of worshipping Him.

The Bible states about Satan:

You were the seal of perfection, full of wisdom and perfect in beauty. You were in Eden, the garden of God; every precious stone was your covering ... The workmanship of your timbrels and pipes was prepared for you on the day you were created. (Ezekiel 28:13 NKJV)

Since no human king could claim to have been in Eden or to be the anointed cherub who covers, many Bible scholar believe this to be a dual prophecy; that is, it refers to both the human king of Tyre and to Satan. Further, the Word says: *"Your pomp and the music of your harps have been brought down to Sheol"* (Isaiah 14:11). Again, this dual prophecy refers to both the human king of Babylon and Satan.

Timbrels are similar to tambourines. They are percussion instruments that create beat and rhythm. Pipes are wind instruments. They create harmony and chords. Harps are stringed instruments. Since percussion, wind, and string instruments were a part of Lucifer from his creation, he was like a whole orchestra. He was a master musician. Through his gifts, he was to worship God. Bible scholars believe that his description as the *"anointed cherub who covers"* (Ezekiel 28:14) means in part that he was created to cover the glory of God with worship and praise through music.

However, something happened. Lucifer took his eyes off God and placed them on himself. He declared:

> "I will ascend to heaven; I will raise my throne above the stars of God. I will sit on the mount of assembly in the recesses of the north. I will ascend above the heights of the clouds; I will make myself like the Most High." (Isaiah 14:13-14)

Rather than worship, he wanted to be worshipped. As a result of his iniquity, he was cast out of heaven.

> You were blameless in your ways from the day you were created until unrighteousness was found in you. By the abundance of your trade you were internally filled with violence, and you sinned; therefore I have cast you as profane from the mountain of God. And I have destroyed you, O covering cherub, from the midst of the stones of fire. Your heart was lifted up because of your beauty; You corrupted your wisdom by reason of your splendor. I cast you to the ground. (Ezekiel 28:15-17)

> How you have fallen from heaven, O star of the morning, son of the dawn! You have been cut down to the earth, you who have weakened the nations! (Isaiah 14:12)

When Satan fell to earth, his music and his desire to be worshipped came with him. Even today, he is doing all he can to direct people's worship toward himself. Failing that, he seeks to pervert it. If he cannot dictate who will be worshipped, he tries to control the ways of worship. Evidence of his success in the world can be seen with the ease in which he has turned some forms of music into earthly, demonic, sensual tools of satanic worship. In addition to his influence in the world's music, his guns are trained on the Church in an effort to pervert its music of worship as well.

The Church must remember that worship was once Satan's reason for being. It was his area of strength. By it, he tried to overcome the world. He is now trying to use his power and expertise to gain a stronghold over the true body of Christ.

In His Word, God has stated which sacrifices are acceptable and pleasing to Him and which are not. Offering Him anything else is false sacrifice. In His Word, God has also described ways of worship that are acceptable and pleasing to Him. Offering Him anything else is false worship.

Under the Old Covenant, worship was a ritual. It was always offered in a set, formalized way. Today, because the Holy Spirit directs all true worship (Philippians 3:3), it need not be offered in a repetitious way. Individual saints can seek His order of worship and follow it in private moments of love, worship, and waiting on Him. Should the corporate Church do any less? Rather than the ritual and formality that marked Old Covenant worship, the Church should enjoy worshipping Him as He chooses to be led: after the Spirit.

If the Holy Spirit asks His Church to fall on its face before Him, it must not dance. If He asks it to dance, it must not sit. Worshipping in the midst of a whole body that is on its face before Him or that is singing, shouting, waving, clapping, leaping, dancing, crying, and lifting holy hands and hearts in praise to God in harmony with one another and under the anointing and direction of His Spirit is an unspeakable joy for those who are freed in spirit to participate. If it is such to the Church, is it not to Him?

While God always allows true expressions of spirit in worship, He does not tolerate manifestations of flesh or self. He will not honor those who, like Nadab and Abihu, grab their censers, add false fire, and engage in rebellious acts of false worship. In other words, He will not respond to those who prefer to keep worship of holy God a human practice rather than a spiritual one.

Those engaging in such should be stopped before the whole body is hindered in its holy communion. If they are not disciplined by the Church, they will be disciplined by God because they are keeping His Church away from the full beauty of His presence. Even more seriously, they are preventing God from truly being glorified.

THE CAMP

Both the Israelites and each saint had to take time in the desert to learn some fundamental principles of God. So must the Church. Both the Israelites and each saint have had to examine their position in relation to God in order to ensure that He was at the center of their lives. So must the Church.

The Church, in seeking its place, has been blessed by warnings from God about those who will try to lead the saints away from Him. 1 Timothy 4:1-2 states: *"But the Spirit explicitly says that in later times some will fall away from the faith, paying attention to deceitful spirits and doctrines of demons, by means of the hypocrisy of liars...."* Further, 2 Peter 2:1 says, *"But false prophets also arose among the people, just as there will also be false teachers among you, who will secretly introduce destructive heresies, even denying the Master who bought them."* Having been warned, the Church must be on the lookout against such deception.

One of the specific doctrines that denies the Master is currently becoming more and more prominent: the glorification, magnification, and, in some cases, the deification of the Church itself rather than of the Head of the Church, Jesus Christ. It is seen, at least in part, in the ungodly teaching that, once saved, saints are to be raised and praised like God. It is also made known by the claims that a specific denomination within the church system is "the faith" or the means through which souls are saved. It is seen in the error claiming that obedience to the Church or to any of its affiliated or extra-church meetings and organizations rather than obedience to God is the goal or highlight of saintly existence.

By some, God is no longer the desired and acknowledged center of the camp; He is no longer the heart of the Church. Instead, a religious system is being raised to a place of such prominence that it now competes with God for attention, for service of worship, and for placement at the heart or at the most important point of the saints' lives.

The error and deceitfulness of this doctrine should be obvious. The Church is not the Light of the world; Jesus is. It is **a** light to a dark world but not **the** Light. The light that shines from it is not light from its own source; rather, it is the radiance and reflection of His light. For the Church to raise itself or to allow itself to become a focal point is to allow itself to become an idol. For the Church to engage in worshipping itself is idolatry.

It is time to acknowledge that some leaders at both the universal and local levels of the Church have led the body of Christ astray. They have not led saints to God but to a human institution which they have erroneously labeled as the Church. They have taught saints to serve not God but people and ministries – especially the false leader's particular ministry. In no way does this place God in the center of the camp.

As He demanded of the Israelites and of each saint, so He now commands His Church that He be allowed to abide in the heart of the assembly of saints. God must be placed in and allowed to occupy the middle of His camp even as He is surrounded by His called out body of saints. Since He must be in the heart of each individual tabernacle, He must be in the heart of the whole tabernacle. His Church must gather around Him and, as His holy priesthood, must worship and serve Him rather than itself. All direction must be from Him, all activity must honor Him, all worship must magnify Him.

The Church cannot compete with God for attention. Neither can it be self-serving. Its tents must be placed so close to the heart of its love that nothing and no one comes between it and God, the object of its worship.

The Church must remember that it is being prepared as the bride, not the Groom. It is not the Lord but the maidservant of the Lord. It does not cover Jesus but asks Him to cover His bride (Ruth 3:9). It does not give Jesus its name but accepts His since it is the bride of Christ, and its individual members are known as Christians.

In earlier days, scientists thought that the sun revolved around the earth, thus making the earth the center of the universe. Later, revelation showed how erroneous this belief was. If the Church has fallen into that same error, believing that the Son revolves around it and that it is the center of life, it is not in the position God has chosen for it. Revelation from the Word of God will show how erroneous this belief is and teach the Church its true place.

Positions

Any time a person interviews for a job, his (or her) resume is reviewed and then he is hired to fill a particular position. That is, on the basis of his credentials, the people interviewing him believe he could work well in a certain spot or placement. So it is with the Church. God has granted gifts and blessings to particular saints of His choosing in order that they, individually serving from their own places or positions in the body of Christ, form one glorious whole in the Church's service of worship to God.

Having established God's preeminence as the center or Head of the Church, the body of Christ must learn its duty concerning Him. It may sound repetitious, but as the Israelites and as each saint had much to learn about service to God, so does the Church as a whole.

Before any saint can successfully serve the Lord, he or she must die to self. That is an absolute requirement for the Church too. The Church cannot serve Him if it is looking out for its own best interests. It cannot serve Him if it is entangled with the world. As each saint had to make the decision for self-denial, so must the whole body of Christ. Following Jesus' example of dying to self in order to serve God, the Church must also die to self in order to worship Him (2 Corinthians 5:14-15).

As God has ordained the days and ways of each living stone, so He has done for the whole Church. The purpose of the Church is to be the agent of God on the earth, the ones called out to love Him and to do His will.

The Church's supreme example of such service was Jesus. He was sent to earth by His Father (John 7:28-29), and He was candid that His reason for coming was to serve Him. He said, *"I can do nothing on My own initiative ... I do not seek My own will, but the will of Him who sent Me"* (John 5:30; see also John 6:38).

Jesus was not acting independently but as an ambassador for God. His life was not an expression of His own will but of His Father's. He did not do His own works but those the Father sent Him to do.

Then, before ascending into heaven, Jesus made an astonishing declaration: *"Peace be with you; as the Father has sent Me, I also send you"* (John 20:21). In other words, He commissioned those whom He had taught to do as He had done. The twenty-first century Church is now those disciples, and its commission is to do the will of God. Its living stones, as ambassadors of Christ (2 Corinthians 5:20), are to carry His message throughout the world.

Knowing that its adequacy, ability, or sufficiency to administrate the New Covenant is not from self but from God (2 Corinthians 3:5-6), the Church is to serve God by His Spirit. Those who serve in Church offices are to equip the saints for the work of ministry (Ephesians 4:12-16). The saints are to exercise the gifts of the Spirit for the common good (1 Corinthians 12:7) and to do good works, *"For we are His workmanship, created in Christ Jesus for good works, which God prepared beforehand so that we would walk in them"* (Ephesians 2:10). In all of this, the Church is to recognize that it is building God's house:

> *And coming to Him as to a living stone which has been rejected by men, but is choice and precious in the sight of God, you also, as living stones, are being built up as a spiritual house for a holy priesthood, to offer up spiritual sacrifices acceptable to God through Jesus Christ.* (1 Peter 2:4-5)

Additionally, in serving God, the Church must bind and loose (Matthew 16:19). It is to extend the kingdom of God on the earth (Matthew 28:19-20). It is to prepare for marriage to the Bridegroom (Revelation 19:7). It is to pray (James 5:13-18).

Individual saints can do these works. However, the united body of Christ can do them much more powerfully and effectively. When all eyes, mouths, arms, hands, and lips are working in coordination with the Head, when each part of the body realizes the need of every other part in order to do a complete work, the job will get done.

The fact is that doing the will of God covers all areas of life. It affects saint and sinner alike. No other body can do this work. No other body has been commissioned to do it.

The Church needs to understand that the only reason for it to exist is for its service of loving and doing the will of God. Further, when the Church has completed its job, it won't be here any more. When Jesus finished His earthly work, He ascended to His Father in heaven. So too, when the Church is done with its earthly work, it shall rise to meet its Lord.

Is the Church's calling, doing the will of God, impossible? Does it sound like too high, too glorious, or too difficult a mission? Is it one that the Church cannot obey? Would God ask the Church to do so if it were unable to do so?

In its early history, God called the ignorant and fearful to follow Him through His Son, Jesus. Those disciples who witnessed Jesus's words and actions became the Church that saved, healed, loved, and delivered even unto death. Jesus' disciples today have the same call. As His Church is led by His Spirit and does His will, His saints can also be known as those who turned the world upside down (Acts 17:6 AMP).

The Pillar And The Cloud

It cannot be emphasized enough that the Church was saved to serve the Lord. It also cannot be emphasized enough that it can only do so as it is led by God's Holy Spirit.

The Israelites once moved through the desert following the shekinah or glory of God. As a cloud by day and as a pillar of fire by night, the people of Israel were led by the Spirit of God.

However, after the Israelites rejected God at Mount Sinai, the majority of the people did not know His personal presence. Therefore, a contradiction arose. The Hebrews were under orders to follow wherever and whenever the shekinah led them, but they were also a people walking in flesh with a priesthood which degenerated into works of flesh.

Then Jesus came. Full of the Holy Spirit (Luke 4:1), He ministered among men and women, and He suffered and died for them. He gave the Church the New Covenant, a ministry of grace that was and is empowered by the Spirit of God rather than by human efforts of flesh. He sent His Holy Spirit on all, not just on some, of those gathered in His name in Jerusalem. Therefore, all of His priesthood, which was baptized by one Spirit (1 Corinthians 12:13), is to be led by His Spirit (Romans 8:13-14).

The Church is not to follow a denomination; it is to be led by His Spirit. The Church is not to follow one person; it is to be led by His Spirit. It can only truly worship God and do His will as it is led by His Spirit.

Silver Trumpets

In the midst of their desert trek, God ordered the Israelites to make two silver trumpets (Numbers 10:1-2) so that messages could be quickly and universally communicated to the entire camp. The Israelites had to train their ears to distinguish the meanings of the sounds they were hearing. One sound meant that just the priests and leaders were to gather; another meant that all the people were to assemble. One blast was an announcement of a Sabbath, a first day of the month, or a feast day; another was an alert to prepare for war.

Of greatest importance, the trumpets were blown to announce that God was on the move. Throughout their desert journey the Hebrews were dependent upon the cloud or the shekinah of God for their direction and protection. They knew they were to rest in camp when the cloud was at rest and to follow the cloud whenever it moved. At the first sign of movement, the priests blew a trumpet to alert the camp to pack up and be ready to move.

Centuries later, Old Testament prophets were men and women to whom God revealed His secret counsels. These gifted people were not only to hear the heart of God but were also to speak forth or to communicate God's message to His people. They were to set the trumpets to their mouths and to blow long and hard (Hosea 8:1), assembling the people or warning them of coming events.

The Church must learn to discern what the cloud or the Spirit is saying to the Church (Revelation 2:29). The sound of the trumpet is still heard in the voice of Jesus Christ (Revelation 1:10). He speaks to hearts, calling His body to assemble or come together in unity. He makes special announcements or sounds the alarm for spiritual warfare. He gives fair warning that He is about to move and His camp or His Church must be prepared to go with Him.

Jesus' voice is speaking to His Church even now. Sometimes He does so personally; sometimes He does so through His chosen vessels, His prophets.

However, some problems afflict the Church. Some of His human prophets are not sounding a clear signal. Through this human error, the unclear sound causes the Church to be uncertain as to what message is being communicated. Therefore, it is difficult for the saints to respond correctly (1 Corinthians 14:8).

One problem with prophecy involves what is being said, or the message itself. God has given the Church criteria that enables it to judge the messages of its prophets. For instance, God usually speaks first to individual hearts. What a prophet then speaks should be a confirmation of what God has already said, not an initial instruction or direction. Too, **the** Word of God is the authority over **a** prophetic word. If **a** "word of God" does not line up with **the** Word of God, it is not a true, godly, prophetic message.

Further, God has one mouth. Since He is not a hypocrite, He speaks with one voice. He does not say one thing to one part of His Church and something totally contrary to another. Therefore, if two groups are causing great dissension within the body of Christ, each claiming to speak the whole truth of God but saying different things, the Church can be sure that one or both of them are wrong.

A second problem with prophecy involves who is saying it, or the messenger. The Spirit of Christ does not go from body to body uttering false prophecy. He is perfect and does not have to guess the will of the Father. If there is a problem with prophecy, it is not with Jesus but with His imperfect vessels, the saints or those who prove to be immature or false prophets.

While Jesus was a perfect Prophet, His followers are not. Some misunderstand their call. Some don't know or don't act like they are crucified with Christ or dead to flesh and self, so they operate in human or ungodly ways. Some who claim to be prophets are merely self-made men and women whose every word throws the Church into deeper error and confusion.

Without question, abuse has taken place in the prophetic office. Without question, the Church is at least partially to blame for this.

However, the answer to this dilemma is not to reject, throw out, or deny a God-given office. Instead, it is to correct the offense and to use the gift of God for the edification of the Church body.

The Church must not tolerate ungodly prophets or those who would falsely sound the trumpets. It must learn to discern or ascertain whether a message claimed to be a word from God is in fact of God, flesh, or Satan. It must judge the prophetic word (1 Corinthians 14:29), obeying it if it is from God and rejecting it if it is from any other source. If necessary, it must institute Church discipline (as outlined in Matthew 18:15-17 and Acts 15) to those in its midst who repeatedly diminish or abuse the prophetic word.

The Lord said He would do nothing without first telling His servants, the prophets (Amos 3:7). Long ago, He spoke to the Israelites through His prophets, telling them of their apostasy and coming dispersion (Amos 9:1-10; Isaiah 22). Thankfully, He also spoke of their re-gathering (Jeremiah 23:3-8; 30:3). Later, He sent a prophet, John the Baptist, to prepare the world for the coming of Christ (John 1:6-34).

The Church is now hearing the call of the trumpet or the voice of God through its prophets. He is speaking His counsel to the Church and announcing to it the imminence of the second coming of Christ. God's trumpets are sounding to gather all leaders and members of His true Church. The Head is revealing His message to His prophets; in turn, they are carrying His word to His body. They are sounding an alarm to His kings and priests: gather or assemble together! Worship only Me! Prepare for spiritual warfare! Prepare to move!

Pause

The Israelites paused for nearly a year in the desert in order to accept, submit to, fellowship with, and worship God. Each saint pauses to learn to hear God's voice, to obey His leading, and to learn the lessons He wants him or her to learn. So too must the Church pause.

When in the desert, the Israelites found fault with God. Rather than turning to Him, they turned away from Him. In their anger and dissatisfaction, they rebelled against Him (Hebrews 3:8), fell into unbelief in the God who had saved them (Hebrews 3:12), and entered disobedience (Hebrews 4:6). As a result of such sin, God declared they would not enter His rest (Psalm 95:8-11).

While this is a fact in the history of Israel, it is also a challenge to the true Church today since *"there remains a Sabbath rest for the people of God"* (Hebrews 4:9). It is imperative that God's Church stop testing Him and begin trusting Him. As the Lord asked the Israelites before, so now He asks His saints to bow down in worship of Him, to kneel before their God, and to acknowledge that the Church is His flock, not its own. It must refuse to rebel or harden its heart against Him and refuse to be known as the ones whose hearts go astray or the people who have not known His ways (Psalm 95). Unless it will do all these things, it will simply become one more generation excluded from all that He has for it; it will be another people who will never know His rest. Therefore, Church, *"let us fear if, while a promise remains of entering His rest, any one of you may seem to have come short of it"* (Hebrews 4:1).

MOVING ON

More Complaining

If murmuring (dissatisfaction, grousing, and griping) and complaining (objecting, criticizing, and finding fault) against God led to problems for the Israelites and for each saint, how much more so for the entire Church? Even when there seems to be a justifiable provocation or cause, the Church must come to realize murmuring or complaining is not an option. While those in the world may be free to murmur, those in the Church have received a different command: *"Jesus answered and said to them, 'Do not murmur among yourselves'"* (John 6:43).

Raising Of Leaders

When God released the Israelites from the sojourn at Mount Sinai to march to the promised land, it didn't take the people long to grumble and become unmanageable yet again. Nor did it take Moses long to realize that he was one man among many and that he could not do the job of governing all the malcontents by himself (Numbers 11:10-17). In response to his cry for help, God called, raised, and anointed others who were to share the burden of leadership (Numbers 11:24-25).

Today, a similar problem confronts the Church. Almost since the day the New Covenant was given, God's body has, in spite of all of His blessings, remained quite quarrelsome. It has severely tried and tested its leaders.

As in the first century, today there is only one true body of Christ:

the Church. All the parts of the body or the many members found in various geographical locations make up the local churches, the sum of which forms the universal or worldwide Church of God. Each local branch, as well as the whole body, needs the leadership of those who have been called and anointed to govern it by the standard of God's Word to honor its founder, Jesus; to direct it; to oversee it; to draw others to it; to teach it; and to train it by the direction of the Holy Spirit. One person cannot do all these jobs.

Jesus is the Head of the Church. In the first century when He walked on the earth, He chose a specific group of disciples, trained them, and then sent twelve of them out to do His work in the Hebrew community (Matthew 10:1-5). Later, when the numbers of disciples had grown, He sent out seventy more (Luke 10:1-23). In the twenty-first century, Jesus is still the Head of the Church. Although He is now seated in heaven (Ephesians 1:20), He has commanded that His work on the earth must continue (Matthew 28:18-20). To assist His Church in this herculean task, He still gathers His disciples around Himself, qualifies them, anoints them, and commissions them or sends them out to His work.
Gather

First, God will call His leaders. The number He raises into the supervision, management, and government of the Church is entirely up to Him. In His divine foreknowledge, He knows exactly the right number needed to minister to each part of His body. For the Israelites, He was precise in calling seventy to assist Moses (Numbers 11:16). For the local and universal Church of today, in His divine wisdom, He will be no less exact. He is aware of the number needed to do the work required. Those raised up are of His choosing, not people's. Their job is to obey Him, not people, and to do His will, not people's.

Qualify

God's qualifications for Church leadership are different than men and women's. They do not include a minimum or maximum chronological age but spiritual maturity. They do not include a certain number of years in ministry but a heart for true service of God. They do not include a degree from a Bible school or a relationship to a prominent member of ministry. They do not include self-sufficiency, arrogance, or rebellion.

The Church often thinks of qualifying its leadership in terms of training its leadership through courses, classes, and seminars. However, God thinks differently. He is primarily concerned with the character, nature, and being of those He chooses to represent Him on the earth. He looks at their hearts, not their heads. He examines who they are rather than how much they know.

According to God's Word, leadership in the Church is comprised of the ministries of apostle, prophet, evangelist, pastor, and teacher (Ephesians 4:11) and those known as elders or overseers (1 Timothy 3:1-7) and deacons (1 Timothy 3:8-13). Including both men and women, His governors are those whose godly qualities are apparent within his (or her) heart, spirit, and being as well as without, those in whom God can be seen, and those who walk in His presence. While qualifications for elders and deacons are listed in the Word, the Church must be careful to understand that entitling someone as elder will not give him these qualities; instead, he must have them, be them, and be known for them before God raises him up.

Anoint

When God has called and qualified His leaders, His Spirit will indwell them, giving them His presence, and will come down upon them, giving them His power. They are to be so immersed in the anointing of His Holy Spirit that they will lead His body, not by flesh but by the Spirit of God.

Commission

When all is in order, God will send out His new leaders. They may serve in this country or around the world. They may serve in home groups, Bible studies, prayer groups, or ministries in the local church. They may serve at bus stops, in bars, on fishing trips, or as part of a tour group. Those called, qualified, and anointed will go wherever He says to go and do whatever He sends them to do, all to promote the kingdom of God and the God of the kingdom.

The Church needs to trust God in the matter of its leadership. Instead of allowing a precious few to preside over the whole and to keep a death grip on all offices, gifts, positions, and titles, the Church should ask God to increase the numbers of those in leadership. It should ask Him to sort out those He has raised up as leaders and then honor His choices. In addition, it should ask Him to remove those who have selfishly or illegally gained positions of authority so that those He has chosen can occupy them. He should be allowed to bring forth those who will serve Him well. The Church should expect these to be anointed in His Spirit in order to share in the care and burden of His people.

The result of responding to God's raising of leadership is a properly functioning Church. Many bear the burden of the people so one does not bear it alone (Numbers 11:17).

Multiple leadership is not threatening or confusing. It is a threat only to those who want to maintain iron control of a body. It is confusing only to those who are already in error. To others, it is a protection against dictatorship within the Church and is a means of checks and balances against error.

Oh, that the Church had more men with Moses' mindset: those who know their limitations; those who realize that one leader at a local church level or one minister at the universal Church level cannot bear the burden of the whole body; those who realize that Church administration should not be under domination of a single, fallible human being but under a plurality of leadership; those who understand that people cannot humanly fulfill spiritual need.

Oh, that more leaders would emulate Moses' actions: that more would humble themselves and, instead of grabbing for even more authority and power, ask for help, for shared responsibility, for the gift of relief from the full-time pressure of leading a fleshly, selfish, complaining people. Oh, that they would cry out as Moses once did: *"I alone am not able to carry all this people, because it is too burdensome for me"* (Numbers 11:14).

As always, when God hears such a heart's cry, He will respond. When He sees leaders willing to have the power of the sin of centralized control broken and to be separated or delivered from it, He will quickly move to help.

Was Moses upset at losing some of his responsibility? NO! Was he jealous that others were made leaders? NO! He said: *"Are you jealous for my sake? Would that all the LORD'S people were prophets, that the LORD would put His Spirit upon them!"* (Numbers 11:29).

Rebellion: Miriam And Aaron

As soon as God places His leaders in the Church, problems arise. Just as the Church has to deal with battles against the flesh in its desert journey, so also it must face and win victory over the challenges of self. Within a congregation a sanctuary of self will always defy a minister of spirit.

Miriam and Aaron were the older sister and brother of Moses. Miriam had watched over Moses when, as a baby, he had been cast into the river to die. She was a prophetess and led the women in music and dancing (Exodus 15:20). Aaron was the first high priest; was commissioned by God, along with Moses, to deliver the Israelites from Egypt (Exodus 6:13); and was honored to see the glory of God on Mount Sinai (Exodus 24:9-10). Yet, even with this amazing history, these two conspired against Moses. They wanted to be recognized as co-leaders of the Israelites.

The first confrontation with godly Church leadership may come from the Miriams and Aarons in the body of Christ. These are the self-ambitious or those who want a slice of the pie for themselves. Rather than being related by a physical family, they are brothers and sisters in the Lord, who desire top billing for themselves while claiming to serve God. Their way to achieve that goal is to put down or try to suppress any they see as higher on the sacred ladder than they are.

The Church is made up of all who have had a born-again experience. Within that body are many whom God has genuinely called to leadership. Yet, also within that group are those who would raise themselves up to rule. In spite of the fact that an obvious anointing is on another, they claim a position God did not intend them to have.

All men and women are called upon to choose between Satan and his kingdom of darkness or Jesus and His kingdom of light. However, once that decision is made for the Lord, they are not asked to make any more decisions concerning their choice of leader. They are only asked to submit to and obey God's choices.

The Church does not choose its leadership; instead, from His perfect knowledge, God does. While those not chosen may disagree with His choices or accuse and slander His choices behind their backs, no amount of popularity, insinuation, manipulation, or unpleasantness can force God to make a minister of flesh a leader of God.

Yes, the self-raised can occupy Church offices if the Church is weak enough to let them. Yes, the self-called can assume leadership if the undiscerning let them. Yes, the self-ambitious can set themselves up in illegal authority if the passive allow them. However, the self-raised, self-called, and self-ambitious are not leaders of God.

The Church must be aware that criticism, jealousy, or aggression toward God's chosen leaders brings down God's judgment. In Miriam's case, she was left with leprosy. Although God did heal her, the whole camp was held up by her actions. In Aaron's case, he never entered the promised land.

If the Church can agree it has offended God in complaining about, grumbling against, accusing, or persecuting His chosen leaders, its hope for help is in the love of God. It must confess its sin (Numbers 12:11), and then offender and offended alike must intercede for His mercy. Only in this way can the body be healed and move on.

Rebellion: Refusing To Enter The Promised Land

As works of self and spirit are opposite in nature, so are those of fear and faith. The estrangement between fear and faith is so complete that if one of these predominates, it effectively cancels the other. Therefore, where fear rules, faith is crushed, and where faith rules, fear is crushed.

Fear is a powerful emotion. It is produced by threatened harm or pain and is usually accompanied by an earnest desire to avoid or escape the threat.

Unholy fear that plagues mankind is not from God (2 Timothy 1:7 NKJV). It is an evil that inhabits people's minds and inhibits their behavior. It is anathema to God. This type of fear is a symptom of flesh and self.

Not only a personal scourge, unholy fear is a highly contagious blight that can quickly spread from person to person until a whole body is infected. This type of fear is a weakness. Those in its snare are a danger to those around them. They cannot be counted on to help another, to act righteously, to resist compromise, or to hold ground in the face of the enemy. In fact, this fear is such a danger to the army of God that it was considered a reason to be sent out of active duty (Deuteronomy 20:8; Judges 7:3).

Contrary to fear found in the mind is the fear found in the spirit, which leads to faith in God. This fear is a reverence of or an awe of God; it is to honor the One in authority.

The Bible says that people are not to fear other people (Numbers 14:9; Hebrews 13:6) or other gods (2 Kings 17:38). On the other hand, God clearly desires that men and women should fear and revere Him.

Oh that they had such a heart in them, that they would fear Me and keep all My commandments always, that it may be well with them and with their sons forever! (Deuteronomy 5:29)

Tremble before Him, all the earth.... (1 Chronicles 16:30)

Fear God, and give Him glory ... worship Him.... (Revelation 14:7)

The Israelites' had to determine whether they would fear God or fear people when, in the midst of their desert journey, God commanded Moses to choose twelve men to spy out the land He had promised them. The spies, all leaders of Israel (Numbers 13:1-3), were to evaluate the land, the cities, and the people.

For forty days, their feet caressed Canaan as they walked and observed in the hills and valleys and then returned to report. They started by presenting a good report, declaring the land to be as fruitful as God had promised. Then, wavering a little, they stated the cities and those who inhabited them to be strong and fortified. Next, with the exception of Joshua and Caleb, the spies stopped reporting by faith and spoke by fear. They ended their report by giving a bad account, reporting information not ascertained in spirit but through the reasoning of their minds, wills, and emotions.

Their faulty reasoning of mind stated: *"The land through which we have gone, in spying it out, is a land that devours its inhabitants; and all the people whom we saw in it are men of great size"* (Numbers 13:32).

Their decision of will was: *"We are not able to go up against the people, for they are too strong for us."* (Numbers 13:31).

Their controlling emotion was fear: *"There also we saw the Nephilim ... and we became like grasshoppers in our own sight, and so we were in their sight"* (Numbers 13:33).

The fear of the ten spies became contagious. Instead of just remaining among the leadership, it spread throughout the whole congregation. The results were tragic.

The people did not believe the word of God concerning this land: *"spy out the land of Canaan, **which I am going to give to the Israelites**"* [emphasis added] (Numbers 13:2). Instead, they rejected it and chose the word and council of people who said, *"We are not able to go up...."* (Numbers 13:31). Unbelief then led to the now familiar procession of grumbling, complaining, and disobedience. Led by the ten false leaders, the people once more rebelled.

> *All the Israelites grumbled against Moses and Aaron; and the whole congregation said to them, "Would that we had died in the land of Egypt! Or would that we had died in this wilderness! Why is the LORD bringing us into this land, to fall by the sword? Our wives and our little ones will become plunder; would it not be better for us to return to Egypt?" So they said to one another, "Let us appoint a leader and return to Egypt."* (Numbers 14:2-4)

Despite pleading by their faithful leaders, Moses, Aaron, Joshua and Caleb, when the Israelites would not listen to or respond to the exhortation to follow God they brought great problems upon themselves. When they confused human and holy fear and believed the false report rather than trusting God, the result was failure and judgment.

In the first century, the New Covenant was given. Those who accepted it were to accept the authority of God the Holy Spirit and to understand their identify as God's called out ones, His tabernacle, His priesthood, His Church.

As did the Israelites before it, the fledgling Church had to learn to walk and experience its covenant with God rather than just to hear of it. With that walk came tests. God tried His Church to see if it would walk in faith or fear; He tried it to see if, like the Israelites, it would confuse the types of fear and walk in fear of people rather than fear of God. In great part, the natural journey of the Israelites and the spiritual journey of the Church have run a parallel course.

One of the tests to face the Church came around the year 400 AD. The Church had received its New Covenant and had started to walk in it. Over the years, as it more and more desired to make God its focus and to serve Him only, the Jewish-Gentile world began to persecute it for doing so. Toward the end of the fourth century, the Church sent leaders to search out its spiritual promised land and then listened with growing fear while these spies presented a bad report to it. A small, though powerful, group of Christians saw the wickedness and power of the Roman Empire with their natural eyes rather than the wonder of the love and power of God for His Church with their spiritual eyes. Due to persecution by this empire they viewed the Church as weakened, rather than glorious, and as defeated, rather than victorious. The giants they saw were Roman emperors who demanded to be called gods. Then, as a result of the spies' bad report, the Church focused its eyes on these giants rather than on God and His promises. Fear of people then spread from its leaders throughout the whole Church, and the bad report was magnified: "They outnumber us. They are stronger than we are. They are bigger than we are. We cannot overcome them. The church is a grasshopper; Rome is a giant. Don't confront it. Compromise!"

The compromise of Christianity with the pagan religion and ritual of Rome under the Emperor Constantine is the very thing which sent the Church into the desert. However, this time in the wilderness lasted not just for forty years but for seventeen hundred years, not just for one generation, but for a generation of generations.

While the Israelites were fearful, God was angry (Hebrews 3:10). As a direct result of their choice to disobey Him and to respond to the fear of people instead of God, He sent the Israelites back into the desert. They had to reap as they had sown. This was not penance or an attempt to placate an angry God; rather, it was living out the consequence of rebellion.

The Israelites' disobedience to a command of God because of fear of people also led to their deaths. When God sent a plague among the fearful Hebrew spies, they died immediately (Numbers 14:37). The rest of the congregation met a different fate. Bearing their guilt one year for every day they had spied out the land (Numbers 14:34), the Israelites wandered in the wilderness for forty years. During that time, all the unbelieving men, the men of war who had proved they were not men of war, died off. They were never able to see the promised land they had rejected. In other words, the Hebrews sent themselves to die. They sent themselves to wander in the wilderness until all who lived by the flesh died in the flesh. They sent themselves on a forty-year walk until, under the burning sun, they became a totally consumed burnt offering.

The consequences of failing to obey and fear God are just as startling to the Church. First, the Church has lost its direction. Wandering in the wilderness for years and years, it has never come to the place God has for it. Spinning its wheels in the desert, it has not gone as far as God wanted it to go. Circling in the waste places while endlessly ministering to people, it has watched while generations of believers and unbelievers have died off.

Also, the fear of people leads to death in the Church. God has judged leaders who bring the error of unbelief and fear to the Church. Without question, nationally and internationally known men, women, and ministries have died off. When they've wandered from the truth and their errors have brought tragic consequences to the body, they have been removed.

The Church must also realize that the majority is not always right. Sometimes, rather than leading the saints into truth, many loud, raised, human voices lead them into error. The Church must learn to follow one voice and one voice only: God's (John 10:4). It must throw in its lot with those who hear what He is saying to it, who share His vision, and who are willing to pursue that vision even if the majority of those who have come out of Egypt, but who are still in the desert, do not. Individually, this may cause painful discernment of relationships with spouses, parents, children, siblings, neighbors, co-workers, or friends. As a whole body, it may force rejection of leaders, denominations, or whole assemblies of the shortsighted and apprehensive who allow fear to cancel faith and who keep so busy in the flesh that they can't walk by the Spirit. If the Church allows the erroneous to lead it into error, it will share their fate.

Like the Hebrew nation, some consequences affect more than just those who set themselves against God. In the Church wonderful leaders and innocent saints filled with holy fear have had to endure the hardships of the desert as they stay in company with those who led them astray. Since what affects one part of the body of Christ affects the whole body (1 Corinthians 12:26), they have suffered for the unfaithfulness of others. Though there have been sporadic outbreaks of revival to give the faithful hope and vision, such as occurred with the Reformation, the Great Awakening, Azuza Street, the Welsh Revival, and the Toronto Blessing, they've walked in the shoes of the unfaithful through some hot places for a long time.

What the Israelites failed to realize is that their collective will could not supersede God's will. Their desert sojourn was a result of their choice, not God's. It was a result of their willful contrariness, not God's. Their reward or punishment was by their own choice, not God's. That is the same lesson that the Church must learn.

Presumption: Attempting To Enter The Promised Land Without God's Command

The sins of pride and fear often lead to the further sin of disobedience. If disobedience is not doing what God said to do, presumption is doing what God did not say to do. If disobedience is rejecting the will of God, presumption is deciding the will of God. They are two sides of one coin, and they add up to rebellion.

More specifically, in relationship, presumption is acting overconfidently, self-assertively, or with too great a familiarity. It is passing beyond acceptable bounds. It is taking for granted. In behavior, presumption is to act without authorization or permission or to act when motivated by assumed or conjectured divine knowledge.

For the Church, presumption is to make a judgment and act on it without a word from God. It is to decide what God wants done and then to do it without His permission or say so. It is to express and follow its own will even while declaring that it is His will. It is to indulge in all sorts of unauthorized works which human, traditional religious practices dictate rather than waiting on God and doing what will please Him.

Immediately after the fear-inducing report of the spies and the Hebrews' refusal to obey God and to enter the promised land, they compounded their sin by acting in presumption. With no command from God, no ark to accompany them, and no Moses to lead them, they charged into the hill country of Canaan and were soundly defeated.

The history of the Church reflects a similar pattern in its desert walk. The Church has indulged in presumption; it has refused to obey God and then decided to obey itself. Every time it engages in works not authorized by God, it presumes on God. Every ministry that overconfidently calls on the name of the Lord but denies His presence and power presumes on God. Every time someone calls out an untrue healing in order to force God to bring it to pass, he (or she) presumes on God. Every time the Church treats His majesty with too great a familiarity, it presumes on God. Every time the Church self-assertively makes up God's mind for Him and then acts according to what it has decided, it presumes on God.

To this, the living Word would say:

> "Not everyone who says to Me, 'Lord, Lord,' will enter the kingdom of heaven, but he who does the will of My Father who is in heaven will enter. Many will say to Me on that day, 'Lord, Lord, did we not prophesy in Your name, and in Your name cast out demons, and in Your name perform many miracles?' And then I will declare to them, 'I never knew you; DEPART FROM ME, YOU WHO PRACTICE LAWLESSNESS.'" (Matthew 7:21-23)

Rebellion: Korah, Dathan, And Abiram

If the challenge for leadership doesn't come from close brothers and sisters in the Lord, it will yet come. If it does not involve quiet challenges about the leaders it will involve open, combative confrontation with them. The two, Miriam and Aaron, had complained about Moses. Then the three, Korah, Dathan, and Abiram, challenged Moses, and the whole congregation came against him (Numbers 16).

So it is with the Church. First, godly leaders are challenged by close brothers and sisters in the Lord, then by the covetous, and finally by the very ones they had raised to lead. Therefore, all Church leaders are fairly warned: no matter who rises up to do so, challenges to leadership will come. If they don't involve quiet challenges about the leaders, they will involve open, combative confrontation with them. If they don't involve disputes over the vision of the Church, they will involve friction about how the Church spends its money.

Korah, Dathan, and Abiram were leaders of the Israelites. The two hundred and fifty they conspired with were also leaders and men of renown. Gathering before Moses and Aaron for face-to-face combat, they accused God's chosen leader of error and self-exaltation. They also tried to raise themselves up. In so doing, they too rebelled.

Moses easily discerned the crux of the matter. These men already had responsibilities in the camp, but they were not satisfied. They wanted more and were willing to sin to obtain it.

Does this sound like today's Church? Aren't there those who, not content to be a part of the body, want to be the head of the body? Aren't there those who have been placed in rightful positions of authority but who want someone else's job?

In the body of Christ some not only refuse to serve in their designated place but they also try to steal or usurp the place of others. The motives for such sin are greed (having much but wanting more), jealousy (wanting what someone else has), or pride (feeling one deserves more). The method of attack is often intimidation or the ungodly raising of large numbers of like-minded rebels to snarl, howl, and snap at the heels of the godly to force them to comply to their wishes. These types of behavior indicate ignorance and arrogance rather than godliness. Amazingly, the rebellious cannot see that greed, jealousy, pride, and domination with attempt to control are not the best qualifications for leadership.

The Church must place rebellion against its leaders in the proper light. It is not just human ears but divine ones that hear unjust accusation (Numbers 12:2). Rebellion is not an attack against another person but against God (Numbers 16:8-11). The Judge of all men and women does not look upon it with favor.

Korah, Dathan, and Abiram were swallowed up in God's judgment (Numbers 16:31-33). When the two hundred and fifty others challenged God's chosen leader, they met with instant judgment: the Lord's holy fire consumed them (Numbers 16:35). If the challenge to godly Church leadership met with such disastrous results then, it will also do so now.

All believers in the Church are ministers of God. However, while all leaders are servants, not all servants are leaders. Only those called, commissioned, appointed, and anointed by God as leaders are in fact true leaders. The rest, the self-raised, are impostors.

Many who call themselves God's leaders are not. Of those who truly are God's leaders, it should be obvious that a supernatural hand has raised them up. Those who they lead should be able to discern that they have the authority of God, not of people; they have been called by God, not by people; they fear God, not people; and they choose to serve God, not people.

The Church has the right – in fact it has the obligation before God – to test all things and to discern His will. Once His will is clearly known, it has no right to challenge Him or to rebel at His choice.

If a person or a group of people challenge a Church leader, let God prove His choice. Let the Lord show who is His, who is holy, and whom He will bring near Himself (Numbers 16:5). Those not of God will not meet His test nor receive His approval. Those who are of God will.

God's people have never liked discipline. At times, if they find it hard to acknowledge that they must discern good or evil from His point of view rather than their own, sometimes a need to discipline arises. To further complicate the issue, they often don't truly believe their errant behavior will bring judgment upon themselves. Though they know the world will be judged by God, they refuse to acknowledge that the Church will be judged too (1 Peter 4:17).

When the congregation complained against Moses and Aaron and blamed them for bringing death to the camp (Numbers 16:41), they were not discerning that the source of such tragedy was their own willful decision to sin. They were disagreeing with God's righteous act of judgment and telling Him He had no right to punish sin. They were looking for someone to bear the brunt of their displeasure. Sadly, rather than at the sinners themselves, they pointed their fingers at their righteous leader.

The Church is facing the same dilemma. God's Church is His flock, and those sheep are ruled by the rod of their Shepherd, Jesus. At times, they are a rather contrary lot who don't like to be told what to do by their Head, much less by His anointed leaders. When those leaders do something that does not meet with the flock's approval or when they don't allow sin in the camp, the sheep bleat their disapproval. When God's leaders establish and enforce righteous discipline, shout the need for repentance, or teach the need of accountability before God, the sheep bleat even louder. They sometimes make it quite clear that they would rather suffer false leaders than submit to the true.

When it gets to the point that the sheep reverse the righteousness of God by promoting or sticking up for sinners and by complaining about God's holy justice, they bring judgment on themselves. Often such sheep will cover up their attacks on their leaders with false counsel or euphemisms, such as, "Don't make waves," "Don't rock the boat," "Look the other way, and if you don't see it, it isn't happening," and "Ignore it, and it will go away." This denies the whole purpose of the cross, because Jesus died for righteousness's sake or for the forgiveness of sin, not for the denial of it.

God was patient with the Israelites; the reason for His patience was to bring about repentance (2 Peter 3:9). However, Korah was unrepentant; Dathan was unrepentant; Abiram was unrepentant; the two hundred and fifty were unrepentant. Not one of them confessed his sin. Therefore, their sins were not forgiven. Sin requires justice. The wages of sin is death. Since these sins were not covered, they met with God's wrath.

God has also been patient with the Church. He has revealed His standard, been merciful to sinners, and given time for repentance. Now, *"it is time for judgment to begin with the household of God"* (1 Peter 4:17). If the Church supports the unrepentant, it denies the importance of the cross. If it complains about the just rather than the unjust, something is wrong. Proper Church discipline for both saint and leader always leaves time and room for repentance. If a saint stubbornly refuses it or pridefully dismisses it as irrelevant, judgment falls.

In like manner, those feeling sorry for the disciplined, those who support them in sin, those who agree to cover up rather than deal with sin, those who allow emotions or feelings rather than spirit to rule are walking according to flesh and self. If they go too far, they too bring down judgment.

When God has judged, He will then show who carries His rod of authority. His leaders will be known by their fruit. The evidence of such holy anointing should put an end to all grumbling (Numbers 17:10).

One example of that fruit is that godly leaders will pray for those who challenge them. They are ever interceding for those under their charge. Due to the presence of God in their lives, they are able to disentangle themselves from any root of bitterness, to forgive, and to go forth in His love.

The saints should follow their leaders' godly example. Instead of coming against or challenging the leaders that God is raising up for His twenty-first century Church, they should honor and pray for them.

Flesh

For those truly seeking God as to whether flesh or Spirit is leading or empowering them, one fact becomes clear: flesh and spirit are total opposites. They are completely incompatible with one another (Romans 8:5-8).

Flesh is the work of people's hands. As such, it is weak, imperfect, and temporal. If people don't know or don't care to know the will of God, they won't have the power of God to fulfill it. They substitute their own will and follow it instead. They are found striving by their own strength to accomplish their own will in their own way. Sometimes they call this ministry. However, God is not mocked! He calls using human effort (flesh) to accomplish human goals (self) by its real names: humanism and rebellion.

Being led of the Spirit of God is much different. It is waiting on God until His will is known and accepted. It is then offering oneself as a channel through which the power of God may work out or accomplish God's will. It is God-inspired at the beginning, God-empowered in the doing, and God-finished to completion. As such, it is strong, perfect, and eternal.

Can evidence of the ministry of flesh in the Church be found? Are endless, unproductive committee meetings of people or of God? Are hearing the same sermons, following the same format, and singing the same songs signs of being led by flesh or by Spirit? Is giving all prayer requests to the pastor because he's expected to do all the praying (and teaching and preaching and....) a sign of being led by flesh or by Spirit? Is following one's own will or that of another person being led by flesh or by Spirit? Is blindly following a particular human creed or perpetuating a specific traditional religious system being led by flesh or by the Spirit? Is grinding away week after week in a formal, ritualistic religious service being led by flesh or by the Spirit? Is praising the Lord louder than all others or in ways designed to draw attention to self being led by flesh or by Spirit? Is delivering a doubtful prophetic message followed by an even more questionable "thus sayeth the Lord" and then whirling around and dropping to the floor with a dramatic thud so all eyes are on the messenger rather than on judging the message being led by flesh or by the Spirit? Is constantly referring to even the smallest service unto God as "**my** calling" or "**my** ministry" being led by flesh or by the Spirit? Is not yielding place when Church leaders believe the anointing of a position one has served in has fallen on another being led by flesh or by the Spirit?

The results of ministries of flesh in the Church are troublesome. Among these, two should be noted. First, as a result of flesh, ministry itself takes precedence over the One ministered to. In any ministry of flesh, since no fresh anointing of life and power occurs, ritual sets in. People think if they do something one way or repeat it often enough they will become good at it. Perfecting ritual through endless repetition, they ultimately declare themselves independent of the need of direction or power from the Spirit of God. Soon, tradition reigns. As rigidity sets in, people worship the form or the ceremony rather than God.

A second evil result of the ministry of flesh is that it allows only a small part of the priesthood to minister actively. Often only a few people or particular ministries are aggrandized. When they, at the expense of the whole Church, are heard shouting, "I'm the only one who can save the world," "I've got broadcasting equipment," "I've got connections, and "I've got influence," they are wholeheartedly engaged in the ministry of self, not of God. Then comes the clincher: "Send money!" Even the most naive should know this ministry is nothing more than a work of flesh, and, as such, it is evil in the sight of God.

No ministry of flesh in any form will save those in the world. Only the ministry of the Spirit will accomplish that. God has never asked one person or ministry to do it all. God has commissioned the whole body of Christ and empowered it by His Spirit to carry His message to the world. No amount of money paid to any ministry of flesh will make right in the eyes of God the Church's laziness, sluggishness, and passivity in obeying His command. God doesn't want guilt offerings but repentance. He then wants action by each and every member of the Church.

It is possible that what are now works of flesh began as a work of Spirit. By way of example, suppose a Church group needed funds for a

God-initiated project. It sought God, and He indicated that He would anoint a certain means to finance it. The Church followed His plan and blessings followed. Then later, perhaps the need for further money arose. The Church, without approaching God again, thinks back, remembers what brought success before, and repeats its actions. Soon, if there is even small success in so doing, the "third annual" fundraiser is initiated. The Church, now locked into a method, perpetuates the work, not the God of the work. The work has lost life, but it is religiously performed anyway.

The key to all of this occurred the second time the need for money arose. Instead of seeking God for a fresh word, the Church thought. Reasoning is a function of the mind, not of the Spirit. Therefore, the result of solely reasoning is a work of flesh, not of the Spirit.

If a clearer understanding of the ministry of flesh and its stranglehold on the Church has been reached, it is time to compare it to the ministry of the Spirit and power. Power, as given by God to men and women, is the ability to carry out the works of God by God acting through His people. After Church members have been given God's authority to work in a certain area, the power of God enables them to accomplish that which God authorized them to do. After the Commander-in-Chief has given an order, they are to exercise this holy power so that later they may return to God, salute Him, and announce, "Mission accomplished, Father!" That power is the Holy Spirit of God (Acts 1:8).

By way of contrast, a work of flesh starts with a man's (or a woman's) idea. He assumes authority and works in his weakness to bring it to pass. However, a work of spirit **always** starts with God. It begins with a revelation of the will of God from God's Spirit into a person's or some people's spirit. God then raises, anoints, and assigns those who have authority to do His will. He arms them with a word or a *rhema* concerning it, and His power works through them to fulfill His purpose.

Further, people's works of flesh are weak and immature, but the works of God are mighty and complete through His Spirit. If the ministry of flesh yields a sparse harvest with temporary results, the ministry of power by God's Spirit generates a huge harvest that is eternal. That which is ordered by eternal God and empowered by the eternal Holy Spirit is forever.

Scripture says that all power belongs to God (Psalm 62:11). It also says that the kingdom of God does not consist of words but of power (1 Corinthians 4:20). This means the Church has no power of its own. Oh, yes, surely, it can gain a measure of human power or control through such fleshly works as manipulation or intimidation. Just as surely, it is being tempted to accept and manifest unholy power from demonic sources. However, neither fleshly nor evil power is acceptable for work in the kingdom of God. Holy God demands holy power for holy works. The only holy source of that holy power is the Spirit of God.

Here the Church must be careful. It must not tolerate the presence of an evil spirit like Elymas, who wanted God's power for his own use, did (Acts 13:6-11). The Church cannot ask for nor accept power to do with it as it desires. It can only walk in the power of the Spirit if it has surrendered its self-will so completely that God knows He can trust it to accomplish His will. It is only as the Church becomes less self-serving and more committed to ministering to God that He can grant a greater and greater release of His power to His body.

As each saint had to do in order to be led of the Spirit, surely the Church must learn more about God's Spirit. As noted in the previous chapter, the Holy Spirit is neither an impersonal force nor a by-product of grace. He is God, the third person of the Godhead. He is the presence of Christ in each saint, the Church's hope of glory (Colossians 1:27). He is God at work in His children *"to work for His good pleasure"* (Philippians 2:13). He is the pledge of the saints' inheritance (Ephesians 1:13-14). Further, as 2 Corinthians 3:17 declares: *"Now the Lord is the Spirit, and where the Spirit of the Lord is, there is liberty."*

The fact that the Holy Spirit is invisible does not make Him any less real. His works are continuously manifest.

The Holy Spirit is here for the world (John 16:7-9). He leads everyone to Christ. God is not asking the Church to infiltrate or take over the world but to save souls out of the world by spreading the love of God and the message of the good news of Jesus Christ throughout the world by the power of His Spirit. Fleshly ministries dedicated to ruling the world by working to conquer and restore its systems are both tiresome and out of order. On the other hand, spiritual ministries dedicated to overcoming the world by releasing its hostages and depriving it of its power are delightful to the heart of God.

Further, the Holy Spirit is here for the Church. He's not here to harm it but to guard it. He's not here to lead it into error but to guide it into all truth.

Have some in the Church reduced the Spirit of God to the role of servant, one under the control of the Church? Do some in the Church teach that men and women can conjure up the power of the Holy Spirit through mental exertion or by human demand? Has the Spirit's role in healing been reduced or deleted altogether because some teach that healing is not a gift of God but a product of correct methodology? Do some in the Church who lack holiness and integrity still hold seminars which instruct others on how to produce miracles, believing that they can force God to manifest them? None of this is being led by the Spirit.

Healings are not limited to human ways, methods, or traditions; rather, they are an expression of God's infinite power and lovely grace through His Holy Spirit. Miracles are not human performances that can be taught or ungodly displays that can be commanded or controlled by people; rather, they are demonstrations of the divine sovereignty of God. Jesus said that signs and wonders would follow those who believe (Mark 16:17). Therefore, the Church must know that manifestations of His power are based on belief in and submission to God as His saints are led by His Spirit.

Jesus spoke the truth. When the early disciples went out into Jerusalem and the world, they did not assemble people to teach them power-seeking techniques. Instead they presented the gospel and acquainted sinners with Jesus, their Savior and Lord. As they did so, His power fell, amazing people and changing their lives forever (Acts 2:43; 14:3). So it should be today.

From approximately 1500 BC to 33 AD, the Old Covenant of law was in effect. Intended as a ministry to worship God, it dwindled into a ministry of flesh in which human traditions supplanted God's love and commands. From 33 AD until today, the New Covenant has been in place. It is meant to be a ministry of grace and Spirit. Yet much of the Church is yet serving under law rather than walking in grace as led by the Spirit of God.

Under law, the Israelites walked in the desert while serving God. That law was made weak through the ministry of flesh (Romans 8:3). Under grace, the Church is now walking in the desert. God's desire for His people is for them to pass through he desert quickly. However, like the Israelites, the Church has become delayed there while its ministries of flesh are revealed. God's grace has been weakened because many Church leaders and saints have insisted on perpetuating the ministry of flesh rather than turning to the Spirit of God. Due to this, a large part of the Church now serves man, not God.

Does the Church not know that Jesus was put to death in the flesh but was resurrected or made alive in the spirit (1 Peter 3:18)? Does it not know that in His flesh He abolished the Law (Ephesians 2:15)? Does it not know that Jesus inaugurated the New Covenant of grace by sending His Spirit upon His Church?

The Church needs to recognize and admit how much of its ministry closely resembles Old Covenant religion with its law-centered, ritualistic acts of flesh; its endless ministrations; and its constant doing, doing, doing, which never reaches perfection. Such didn't work before, and it won't work now. It has been tried; it ended in failure. It must now yield to a better covenant: the New Covenant. It must now yield to a better way: empowerment by the Holy Spirit. As long as any part of the Church works, talks, or acts as if it is still under the Old Covenant, that part will remain in the desert. As long as the Church continues in the ministry of flesh, it will never reach the promised land or arrive at the place to which God is leading it. (See Hebrews 9:1-8.)

God does not want His Church to return to the world. Neither does He want it to remain under law in the desert. The Israelites could not serve God without keeping the Law. The Church cannot please Him if it does keep it.

The true Church must realize its absolute poverty. It must let only God be its power and His grace be its gift. It must learn to wait on Him for the infusion of strength that is needed to do all He says to do. It must ask Him for a greater vision, not of who it is but of who He is.

> He is the Most High God.
> He is Almighty God.
> He is the all-sufficient One.
> He is the strong and powerful One.

The Church is not to walk by fleshly might or by human power. It is to be led and to do by His Spirit.

Rebellion: Moses

After their disobedience and presumption, the Israelites and their leaders were not yet done with rebellion. Having moved to the wilderness of Zin, the people again had no water. In their frustration they again contended with Moses and Aaron, blaming them for the lack of provision, declaring the desert a place they had been brought to die, and comparing their present situation with their memories of Egypt.

Moses approached God with the problem, and God promptly

gave directions to solve the problem:

> "Take the rod; and you and your brother Aaron assemble the congregation and speak to the rock before their eyes, that it may yield its water. You shall thus bring forth water for them out of the rock and let the congregation and their beasts drink." (Numbers 20:8)

At this point, Moses' vexation in dealing with this recalcitrant people exploded. Starting out obeying God's word, he took the rod and assembled the people. However, he then sinned before God and all the Israelites. Angry, impatient, and boiling over with frustration, he did not speak to the rock to bring forth water as God had commanded him to do. Instead, he lifted his rod and struck the rock twice as he had decided to do.

While the congregation of Israel was blessed in the abundance of water that flowed forth, Moses and Aaron paid a great price. Their unbelief and their not treating God as holy led to immediate judgment (Numbers 20:12).

Moses was a man, and he had his weaknesses. When faced with a defiant, ungrateful people, he was severely tempted and fell into sin. His transgression was not an act of apostasy but a careless, emotional, spontaneous explosion of frustration. Without question, today's Church and its leaders continuously have to deal with those who complain that God is not providing all their needs; who don't understand that they, not their pastor, have to overcome their sins of flesh and self while on the desert journey; and who are being lured step by step back into the world and into the false religious system. No wonder these godly leaders become frustrated. No wonder there are times they act out their aggravation in similar outbursts of anger.

However, when Church leaders occasionally sin they are accountable to God for that sin, just as Moses was. All of their works will be judged by fire. Those of gold, silver, and precious stones that survive the fire will receive a reward. Those of wood, hay, or straw will be destroyed by fire. *"If any man's work is burned up, he will suffer loss; but he himself will be saved, yet so as through fire"* (1 Corinthians 3:15).

Like Moses, Church leaders are human beings, tempted into and not always victorious over sin. When they fall, God's limitless grace yet blesses them. God is not a tyrant who demands instant perfection immediately after salvation or who will fitfully sweep His Church into hell if such is not forthcoming. Rather, He is a loving, patient God who saves sinners and sanctifies saints, walking with them on their journey to maturity and completion. Such is not achieved overnight. Along the path to maturity, each saint must face many desert storms and walk through or around the sand traps.

Church, be assured that the desert struggle to walk in spirit by dying to self is not an easy one. It often involves admitting bad choices and wrong behavior. Yet as long as the strugglers continue to grow and mature in God, to deny self, to rise and remain out of the slime pits, to go from strength to strength and from glory to glory, and to conform more and more to the image of Christ, then God will remain faithful to His own. By His Spirit, He will lead and guide them. He will be Captain of the Host for the army of the Lord. He will be the Rock, Fortress, Deliverer, and High Tower when the war gets rough. He will be Companion and Comforter to His loved ones. He will lead His Church through all the heat, sandstorms, and harmful animals of the desert.

As a final note in the matter of Moses at the rock, God is the Judge. He created the heavens, earth, nations, and men and women. Therefore, He is the Judge of them. He judged Moses, and He judges the leaders and saints in the Church today.

Saints have no command to condemn their brothers and sisters in Christ who no longer conform or perform according to Old Covenant Law. Bodies and denominations can no longer declare that those who don't think like they do are going to hell. Saints have no authority to indulge in self-righteous condemnation. Saints do not know and are not asked to decide the condition of other's souls.

God alone is the Judge. He alone knows people's hearts. He alone knows where each man and woman stands in relationship to Him. Only He is aware if a saint has left the world and is making steady, even if unnoticeable progress, toward Him. Only He knows if one has never left the world or has truly turned back toward it. In such judgments as these, the Church must let God be God.

When even Moses, the faithful one, failed, he joined all the congregation of Israel who were under God's judgment. He too was among those sentenced to walk in the dusty desert until the whole generation died off. He too was now among the number who would never set foot in the promised land.

The experience of Moses has profound application on God's leaders and His Church. There are no perfect Christians. Even Church leaders sin. Even Church leaders sometimes reach a point where they are fed up with the whining, quarrelsome sheep in their flock and, in a moment of exasperation, lash out. Sometimes they find that in using their rod of authority as a club, they lash out not at the sheep but at the Shepherd and that in aiming their blows at the Rock they are not maintaining the sanctity or holiness of God. Yet, what joy to know that God can read the heart of those who desire to repent from desert sins and that He is more than willing to draw them back to Himself.

The Edomites

Life in the body of Christ is not always peaceful or uneventful. One of the saddest commentaries on contemporary Christianity is that saints have not been taught that choosing God and His kingdom over Satan and his kingdom makes the Church an enemy of Satan or that spiritual warfare is a normal and on-going part of the life of the Church.

Satan has been warring against God for ages and generations. He has no love for any person who chooses God over him, so he wars against individual saints. Neither has he any love for the corporate body of saints, so he wars against the Church even though the gates of hell shall not prevail against it (Matthew 16:18).

While in the desert, the Church fights the enemies of flesh and self within, even as it is also attacked by other enemies without. It must learn to gain victory over foes such as hindrance, provocation, rebellion, immorality, and idolatry before it leaves the desert.

Soon after leaving Egypt, the Israelites were attacked by the Amalekites, who tried to interfere with their journey toward the promised land. With God's blessing, the Hebrews soundly defeated their foe. Forty years later, the Israelites were confronted by the Edomites, descendants of Esau, Israel's brother. To go to Canaan on the designated route, the Israelites had to pass through the Edomites' territory. When they asked for permission to do so, the Edomites rebuffed them. The second time the Israelites asked, the Edomites came against them with such a mighty force that the Israelites turned away and refused to engage them in battle (Numbers 20:14-21).

On its journey to the spiritual promised land, the Church also walks on the path God has chosen. It too meets enemies which interfere with God's armies, foes which refuse it access to the King's highway, or challengers whose purpose is to keep it from its destination.

Some of the Church's enemies are those close to it. Some are even former brothers and sisters. As the Israelites once learned, for the Church to deal with this situation by appealing to a sense of past loyalty, to a reasoning process, or to feelings is useless. Rather than using opinion or emotion as weapons, the Church must fight its spiritual wars with spiritual weapons: the name of Jesus, the Word of God, the victory of the cross, faith in God, and prayer. If its highway leads it to enemy territory where some would try to stop its forward march, it must go through that enemy territory (Psalm 68:4). If instead it hesitates or retreats, the enemies of hindrance, interference, and distraction will only cause future hardship.

Fiery Serpents

Sometimes the enemy the Church faces on its journey to the promised land is not an outside enemy; it is an inner foe; it is itself. The source of the Israelites' complaints against God was discouragement. First, they had to walk around Edom, and they became tired and disheartened on the way. Second, they decried their perceived lack of provision (Numbers 21:4-5). Similarly today, sometimes the Church becomes discouraged. Perhaps as a result of believing that its leaders have led it into another battle with another enemy, it finds itself dispirited and low in heart. Perhaps since it believes it doesn't have enough resources to do the job it is being asked to do, it complains. When God's judgment falls on this unfaithfulness, the Church must repent. When it does so, God will send the remedy to the problem. He counseled the Israelites to make a bronze serpent and to lift it high so that any who looked on it might be healed. That bronze serpent was symbolic of the cross of Christ, and lifting it up was a foreshadowing of Jesus' death on the cross. Any Christian or any church body who looks upon the cross will be lifted out of its discouragement, will find itself in renewed fellowship with Jesus, and will be given new life. It will be saved and healed spiritually.

The Canaanites

Next in the desert, the Israelites were attacked by the Canaanites (Numbers 21:1-3). These wicked sons of Ham fought with them and took some Hebrews captive. Thoroughly provoked, the Israelites did not again back down. They promised God they would destroy the enemy's cities if He would deliver the Canaanites into their hand. True to their word, when He did, they did.

In its spiritual journey through the dry, desert places, the Church is constantly being beset by those who attack it. Worse, it is plagued by those who take its people captive. When an enemy cult or the cares of the world ensnare the people of God, the Church must act. It cannot just abandon its own to the enemy and go on without them.

The Canaanites were a group of seven tribes, and the spirits of the seven Canaanite tribes still affect the Church today. According to Rick Gage[6], the spirit of the Canaanites or lowland people emphasizes unholy concepts of freedom and grace over thought, truth, and judgment and brings earthly passions and addictions, such as alcoholism and sexual perversions, into the Church. It is not by accident that the Bible describes Sodom and Gomorrah as Canaanite cities (Genesis 10:19).

As can be inferred from the name, "sons of terror," the Hittite spirit introduces fear into the Church. This is not the healthy fear of God; rather, it is the human emotion of fear. The spirit can be seen behind nightmares, phobias, despair, depression, and torment. In an aggressive form, it manifests as a form of terror leading to suicide. This spirit manifests in the Church by preying on emotions, and it seems to delight in attacking those with a prophetic calling (1 Kings 19:1-3). It does its work in the dark, so it can be responsible for the whisper campaigns, rumors, and verbal attacks that destroy churches.

The Girgashite spirit delights in earthly, temporal things while denigrating the spiritual and eternal. It tries to hold saints in the mental realm, so they overanalyze and base decisions on what they understand and see rather than on the voice of the Spirit or on the wisdom of God. The members of a local church affected by this spirit may be natural men and women who cannot receive the things of the Spirit because they seem like foolishness (1 Corinthians 2:14). This spirit is the very antithesis of the phrase, *"the just shall live by faith"* (Galatians 3:11 NKJV).

The spirit of the Perizzites tries to make the Church think small or to have a limited vision as to the breadth and depth of its spiritual influence on the community in which it dwells. It demeans big dreams and mocks the idea of financial success. It causes those under its influence to debase the hopes and ambitions of each new generation, resulting in generations of spiritual and financial poverty.

Like the Perizzites, the Hivites were villagers. However, their

---

[6] Gage, Rick. "The Seven Types of Evil Spirits." *Petra 101*. 23 June 2009. http://rickgage.webs.com/apps/blog/show/1244319-the-seven-types-of-evil-spirits. Accessed 31 Aug 2017.

spirits come against the Church in a different way. While the mantra for the Perizzites is "think small," the Hivites' slogan is "live it up." Unconcerned with limitation, abasement, or stifled propriety, they tend toward hedonism, privilege, and the pleasures of life while doing little or nothing to advance mankind.

The name Jebusite means thresher. For the Church this means those who stomp on other people, who put down and humiliate others, who see others as small and themselves as great. It is a divider, classifying some in the Church as gifted and important and others as of little or no value. It labels some as ministers and others as laymen whose only function is to sit, listen to, and obey their "spiritual authority."

The spirit of the Amorites attacks the Church through pride and self-exaltation. As fame seekers, they become dictators or those who want to dominate and control in the Church.

In spite of salvation, does the Church have problems with addictions and sexual sins (Canaanites)? Does it exhibit a spirit of fear, have a high teen suicide rate, or see its prophets constantly under attack (Hittites)? Do its members rely on seminars, instruction, classes, books, lectures, and other mental learning tools to know God rather than seeking the Spirit who knows God and imparts His wisdom (Girgashites)? Contrarily, does the Church base its knowledge on the subjective knowledge of feelings and emotions? Are small, local churches devoid of vision; have they given up their hopes of being a place where the glory of God will come to dwell; are they always in financial trouble (Perizzites)? Or, has Church become a place where the latest sound equipment, the biggest steeple, the newest carpet, or the most fun picnics and parties "liven" things up, a social paradise where living for every cause except the gospel of Jesus Christ is allowed and tolerated (Hivites)? Are there divisions in the Church that cause separation both within the local bodies and among the local communities (Jebusites)? In the Church, are there those who want to grow big just for the point of dominating the scene, who are always challenging authority, whose lust of the eyes and the pride of life won't let them be second best for any reason at any time (Amorites)? Perhaps the ancient spirit of the Canaanites is attacking the Church.

The Israelites had to come to the place where they knew that constantly trying to compromise with or giving in to the enemy would never solve the problem. They had to learn to be concerned as a whole body for the whole body. They had to realize that an attack on even one of the Hebrew people should be considered an attack on all of them. Further, when provoked, they had to agree that doing nothing was not the answer. The whole camp should respond in unity for the good of all.

For the Church, too, backing down doesn't pay. The Church is responsible for the Church. When one member suffers, all suffer (1 Corinthians 12:12-26). If an enemy provokes war on one, he provokes it on all. The Church, fighting in unity to defend the one or the many in God's body, will win great victory.

The Amorites

Another desert enemy the Israelites faced was the Amorites, a rebellious people steeped in evil and wickedness. Like the Edomites, the Amorites refused to allow them to pass through their land. However, this time, when the enemy defied the Israelites, the Israelites did not turn away. Instead, they engaged the Amorites in battle, defeated them, and possessed their cities.

While on its desert journey, the Church is also confronted with wickedness. Sometimes the battle is waged against an internal foe, such as sinfulness, baseness, wrongdoing, and dishonesty, and sometimes it is against an external one, such as villainy, depravity, immorality, and corruption. In a letter to a New Testament Church, the apostle Paul spoke of wickedness: *"For our struggle is not against flesh and blood, but against the rulers, against the powers, against the world forces of this darkness, against the spiritual forces of wickedness in the heavenly places"* (Ephesians 6:12). From this, several truths can be learned. First, wickedness is an active force about which God warns the Church. Second, the struggle to defeat wickedness is an on-going one; it is not over after just one battle. Third, since the enemy is not flesh and blood, it cannot be defeated using natural weapons. It is a spiritual enemy, so it must be defeated using spiritual arms.

The Moabites And Midianites

Finally, in the desert, the Israelites faced a coalition of Moabites and Midianites. These enemies succeeded in seducing the Israelites into spiritual and physical harlotry. They led the Israelites to bow to Baal, to offer him sacrifice, and to mingle or sin sexually with unsanctified women. As a result, the Israelites brought themselves under the judgment of God (Numbers 25:1-3).

In the midst of their sin, God sent a plague among His children that killed twenty-four thousand of them (Numbers 25:9). Then, before they left the desert, they were commanded to take full vengeance on the Midianites (Numbers 31:1-10). When they did so, they killed every king, every male, and every female who was not a virgin; burned their cities and camps; and took much spoil.

Today's Church is in desperate need of the priesthood of Phineas. It is in desperate need of those who, upon seeing sin in the camp, will rise up on behalf of the Lord, take up their spiritual weapons, and use them to rid the Church of those who blatantly practice their harlotry in the Church. Such zeal will turn back the anger of God and bring peace to those who so honor God (Numbers 25:3-14).

In today's battle with the spirit of Midian, some would lead the Church into idolatry, pollute it with false gods and ways of worship, and infiltrate it with immorality. At first this may be passively passed off as "just" an intermingling of the holy with the unholy or a compromise necessary for unity. But make no mistake. Idolatry and immorality by any name are still idolatry and immorality. They are always anathema to God, and they always lead to trouble.

Idolatry in the Church can actually involve the worship of pagan gods by those who call themselves Christians. For example, some Christians are members of the Freemasons, an organization that serves and worships Jah-bull-on. This name is a corruption of the names of three deities: Jehovah of the Hebrews, Bul or Bel, the supreme god of the pantheon of ancient Canaan (and therefore of Moab and Midian), and On, the god of the underworld and death in ancient Egypt.

Christians cannot associate with and serve unholy gods without bringing false worship into the Church. Since Christians are to read God's Word, they should be aware that long ago true God judged Baal (1 Kings 18:17-40) and the gods of Egypt (Exodus 12:12) and won great victories over them. The Church should be aware that, as happened to the Israelites, tolerating idolatry will bring sin and therefore judgment on itself.

False gods are not limited to pagan deities. They can also be leaders of cults or well-known people such as pastors, relatives, or bosses. False gods could be possessions, such as one's home or car, or addictions, such as work, sex, drugs, alcohol, computer games, gambling, or the lust for money. False worship could be the coveting and flaunting of a job, title, or position, whether in or out of the body of Christ. In short, to the Church, false gods are whatever it honors, seeks, follows, or places above God.

God gave the Hebrews the battle plan for defeating the Midianites. His words ring out to the Church today, detailing his plan to defeat idolatry and the harlotry that accompanies it: *"Be hostile to the Midianites and strike them...."* (Numbers 25:17).

The enemies the Hebrews and each individual saint faced in the desert while it rid itself of the flesh and self are no different than the foes the Church had to engage in during its own war against the flesh and self. The body of Christ can gain victory over hindrance, provocation, rebellion, idolatry, and harlotry by seeking God and by fighting against them in His strength until they are destroyed from its midst.

A New Generation And A New Leader

A sign that the Israelites were coming to the end of the desert experience was the appointing of new leaders and the issuing of laws concerning the settlement of the forthcoming inheritance. When God chose Eleazar to replace Aaron (Numbers 20:25-28) and Joshua to succeed Moses (Numbers 27:15-20), He was making it clear that it was necessary for both a spiritual leader and a military leader to bring the people into Canaan to possess the land. The boundaries of the promised land were set, and once the new generation of Israelites conquered and possessed the land the territories were to be distributed by lot according to population (Numbers 33:50-54).

It is exciting to see the beginnings of the same thing coming upon the Church today. The old generation, those who ensconced the body of Christ in sin, have been dying off either literally or in terms of their ministerial influence. Sadly, like Moses and Aaron, these leaders in the Church have fallen on their desert journey. Some have claimed that their loss of control, power, or authority was a result of enemy attack. In reality, discernment would show that lack of repentance, excess of flesh, satisfaction of self, or the welcome of human or satanic power to administrate false ministries caused the blessing of God to be removed from them.

Yet, while there is a time to tear down, there is also a time to build up (Ecclesiastes 3:3). New leaders have been rising in the Church. Saints have accepted Jesus as High Priest and have been responding to His call to priesthood. The New Covenant is being accepted and the old one, while honored, is being set aside; more and more of the flock are being taught the true Word of God. Intercessory prayer is arising. Further, saints have accepted Jesus as the Captain of the Host and have been answering the call to war: they are more and more willing to engage in spiritual warfare until victory is won through Jesus Christ. For the Church, too, military leaders as well as spiritual leaders will take it into the promised land.

Inheritance Not In The Promised Land

As the Israelites had to decide whether to obey the command of God and move into the promised land or to give in to the impulse of flesh and remain in the desert worshipping false gods, so must the Church choose. Without question, a large part of His body will elect to stay where it is. Since it is comfortable, since it has had its own way for too long to want to change now, since some of its ministry was established there and its leaders don't want to let go, and since it has come to a place that looks good to the flesh, the false church system will want to remain in the desert.

In making such a choice, it will reveal it is not God's holy Church at all but a religious organization looking out for its own welfare. Like Reuben, Gad, and Manasseh, in choosing to settle outside the boundaries of the promised land, it will take itself out of God's perfect will. Having been so deceptively successful in counterfeiting the true Church in private, it will now be forced to choose for or against the will of God in public. When heard declining God's invitation to move into His land and urging other saints not to accept either, the truth about the false church system will be known: those who for so long have accused the real Church of division are the real dividers.

In direct contrast to the false church system, the true Church, having come so far and endured so much, will never settle for less than its whole inheritance. No matter now it looks to the natural eye, the desert is not God's promised land, His provision, or His place of peace. Deceptively green valleys will not hold it; coming short of the will of God will not satisfy it. God's true Church will never choose to dishonor God by stopping short of His full will, distaining His land of promise, or giving up its full inheritance.

At the end of the desert journey the Church has reached another point of decision. It was led into the desert by God. While such a journey was a necessary part of its maturing process, it was not meant to be the Church's permanent home. The body of Christ must choose whether to stay in the desert or to continue to the promised land.

DESERT'S END

From all this description of the difficulties during the passage through the desert, several truths emerge:

To begin with, when an unruly, unarmed, untrained mob of Hebrews left Egypt they were called an army. In the desert, they became one. So too with the true Church. Through the centuries it may have resembled a rebellious, disorganized mob walking in dissention and strife rather than in solidarity and unity, but its desert experience is causing the true Church to grow strong and to become the army of God.

Also, the Amorites lived in the hill country, while the Canaanites dwelled in the valleys. Just as the Israelites had to defeat their foes in every circumstance, so the Church must learn to deal with its highs and lows, its peaks and valleys before it enters the promised land.

Too, the pardon of iniquity follows the confession of sin and the asking of forgiveness in prayer. As Moses interceded for the Israelites and God pardoned them, so His Church must repent; confess its sins of compromise, unbelief, and rebellion; and ask Him for forgiveness.

Further, the desert is the place where God sends His people until they learn that when Jesus died, was buried, and rose from the dead they died, were buried, and rose from the dead with Him, that through His sacrifice flesh and self were defeated, and that they are new creatures in Christ who must appropriate and begin to walk in His unparalleled victory. If the Church is still in the desert, such understanding, belief, and application is still in progress.

Fifth, the desert is the place where unbelieving people send themselves. It is for those who see with their eyes and not with their hearts. It is for those who are locked into the false church system and who want to stay where they are or even go back to the world rather than to go on with God. It is for those happy in their church social cliques and ministries of flesh. It is a place where those who won't die **to** flesh die **in** flesh. It is a place where human will decides if the smell of burning flesh is simply the stench of death or the pleasing aroma of sacrifice.

In addition, leaders are not always right. Leaders are not gods; rather, they are fallible men and women. They make mistakes. For the Israelites, two out of twelve of the spies saw and believed God, but ten out of twelve did not. If the Church's leaders lead it astray through ignorance or fear, it must reject their counsel. If necessary, it must remove them from their positions. The Church must not allow the fearful to speak for it or let their decisions become its decisions.

Seventh, unbelief leads to lack of rest. Concerning the Israelites, God said:

> "For who provoked Him when they had heard? Indeed, did not all those who came out of Egypt led by Moses? And with whom was He angry for forty years? Was it not with those who sinned, whose bodies fell in the wilderness? And to whom did He swear that they would not enter His rest, but to those who were disobedient? So we see that they were not able to enter because of unbelief." (Hebrews 3:16-19)

Those words also apply to His Church. His body should refute those who declare that disobedience and compromise will bring peace. Often those crying the most insistently for unity, harmony, or peace are in reality rebels crying out for the Church to compromise with the false church system or to lay down its arms and to declare a truce with the world. It is rebellion, not obedience, that causes division. It is compromise, not belief, that destroys peace. It is unbelief, not rest, that causes the march through the desert to go on and on. As long as the Church wanders in unbelief, it will never come to its rest.

Finally, God singles out and rewards those with a visionary spirit. The Israelites' leaders and priests had been anointed, and some had even seen God. Of them, God singled out and honored Caleb because he had a different, visionary spirit. Today, the Church's leaders and priests are anointed men and women of God. Of these, God will single out and honor those who dare to have a different, loyal, visionary, edifying spirit, those who give good reports, and those who seek to cross into and take the promised land.

By now the Church should clearly see the parallels between the Israelites' desert journey, each saint's wilderness trek, and its own meandering in dry places. Israel was a nation within the nation of Egypt. It separated itself to worship the one true God. The Church is a people within a people, the world. It has separated from the world to worship its one true God. Like Pharaoh and the Egyptians, leaders in the world fear the day when the Church awakens to its destiny and calls to God to be released fully from its lingering bondage to the world and its systems. The leaders in the world can see the Church has the potential to establish holy leaders who will bring godly change to those areas of life that dominate society: religion, family, education, government, media, business, arts and entertainment, politics, finances, and medicine.

Since the world fears the separation of the true Church that it once controlled and since it wants to bind the Church to its low moral standards and unholy laws, it fights to bring the Church back under its influence. It is not going to work. In whatever manner the world mocks the true Church, disparages it, condemns it, or aggressively attacks it, the Church is now the army of God, willing and able to repulse all invasions and to destroy all enemies as it marches onward, always toward God, always toward the promised land.

God allowed the Israelites to go through the desert because it had lost sight of its place and power in God's Old Covenant. God has allowed the Church to wander in the desert because it had lost sight of its place and power in God's New Covenant. Like the Israelites in the desert, the Church has become a burnt offering, burned by the fires of conflict and the heat of its desert walk until flesh and self have been completely consumed on the altar and the Church has become totally dedicated, consecrated, and loyal to only God.

It is now ready to continue its journey into the promised land and into its rest.

PART V:

INTERLUDE

Chapter 13

INTERLUDE:

THE ISRAELITES' TIME TO REMEMBER

And so it came to pass on the first day of the eleventh month in the fortieth year that Moses called a halt to the Israelites' desert wandering (Deuteronomy 1:3). Gathering the tribes together east of the Jordan River in the land of Moab, he began to prepare the people for the long-awaited moment: their entrance into the promised land. Though insistence upon returning to Egypt had delayed them and the ministry of flesh and of self under the law had diverted them, the Hebrews were at last ready to enter Canaan.

Of the approximately six hundred thousand men from the earlier generation who had entered the desert, only two, Joshua and Caleb, left it. Of the multitudes who journeyed through the burning sands over a period of forty years, only two men survived the trial by fire. Perhaps with this in mind, perhaps with own imminent death approaching, and perhaps in an attempt to prevent another such disaster, Moses gathered the Israelites into a camp meeting and spoke with them rather than hurrying onwards to enter the promised land.

During these last days of his life, Moses addressed the Israelites in five main areas. First, he reviewed the past, reminding the Hebrews that God had brought them out of Egypt by the power of His outstretched arm (Deuteronomy 26:8). Next, Moses recalled for them the laws, statutes, and ordinances which God had given them (Deuteronomy 11 – 26). He then spoke forth the promises of God concerning the future (Deuteronomy 33). Fourth, he gave the Lord's instructions about these promises (Deuteronomy 29-30). Last, he issued clear warnings to the Israelites, explaining to them that, by their own choice, blessings would fall on them as a result of obedience to the Lord or curses would fall on them as a result of disobedience.

A TIME OF REMEMBRANCE

Moses began this quiet interlude between the desert and the Jordan River with a review of the Israelites' recent history. He began by recalling where they had been and by reminding them it was God's wish that they leave that place. *"The LORD our God spoke to us at Horeb, saying, 'You have stayed long enough at this mountain. Turn and set your journey, and go....'"* (Deuteronomy 1:6). They were to go to and possess the land of the Amorites, the hill country, the lowland, the coastland, the land of the Canaanites, and even as far as the Euphrates River.

Continuing his discourse, Moses reminded everyone that sin had kept them from doing so forty years earlier. Sin (idolatry) had molded and shaped the golden calf, sin (rebellion) had caused the Hebrews to refuse to enter the promised land when He commanded them to do so, and sin (presumption) had caused them to go there when He had said not to go.

Further, Moses spoke of the Israelites' journey from Horeb (Mount Sinai) through the great and terrible wilderness until they came to Kaddesh-barnea, and he reminded them how tenderly God had carried them, as a man carries his son (Deuteronomy 1:31).

Declaring that their own fear and disobedience had led to God's judgment falling on them and that the Israelites had sent themselves into the wasteland instead of the promised land (Deuteronomy 1:40), Moses explained why the desert experience was necessary.

> *"You shall remember all the way which the LORD your God has led you in the wilderness these forty years, that He might humble you, testing you, to know what was in your heart, whether you would keep His commandments or not."* (Deuteronomy 8:2)
> *"Thus you are to know in your heart that the LORD your God was disciplining you just as a man disciplines his son."* (Deuteronomy 8:5)
>
> *"In the wilderness He fed you manna which your fathers did not know, that He might humble you and that He might test you, to do good for you in the end."* (Deuteronomy 8:16)

As Moses reminded them, the Israelites had circled Mount Seir without going anywhere (Deuteronomy 2:1). They had encountered the Edomites and Moabites. They had wandered for years until *"all the generation of the men of war perished from within the camp"* (Deuteronomy 2:14). Then, as a new generation with a new attitude emerged, they had been challenged to fight the Amorites.

Encouraged by God's words, *"This day I will begin to put the dread and fear of you upon the peoples everywhere under the heavens, who, when they hear the report of you, will tremble and be in anguish because of you"* (Deuteronomy 2:25), the challenged and chosen Hebrews defeated Sihon, king of Heshbon, and Og, king of Bashan (Numbers 21:21-35). They not only defeated them as a new generation of warriors, but they also captured their cities and destroyed all of the men, women, and children. Since they had so honored God, in turn, He would honor them. *"See, I have begun to deliver Sihon and his land over to you. Begin to occupy, that you may possess his land"* (Deuteronomy 2:31).

As a direct result of both battle and blessing, the captured cities were given to Reuben, Gad, and Manasseh (Numbers 32:33). Though they were east of the Jordan River and not in Canaan, they nevertheless became a part of the inheritance of the Israelites.

THE OLD COVENANT

The second major topic Moses dealt with at the camp meeting was that of law or authority. Moses knew the key to the Israelites' past lay in their obedience or disobedience to God's covenant. He also realized the key to their future lay in the same choices. Therefore, he carefully and painstakingly commanded the Israelites to hear and heed the Law and laws of God.

Gathering the Israelites around him, Moses restated the Ten Commandments as the LORD'S Law or authority over His people (Deuteronomy 5:1-21). Additionally, as he once communicated to the older generation the more general laws, statutes, and ordinances involving idolatry, sacrifices and offerings, and Sabbaths and feast days, so he did to the new. As he once spoke forth to those at Mount Sinai the more specific rules governing clean and unclean animals, sanitary and health codes, morality, divorce, relations with each other, and relations between themselves and God, so he spoke them to those sojourning in Moab.

The summary of the Law was:

> Now, Israel, what does the LORD your God require from you, but to fear the LORD your God, to walk in all His ways and love Him, and serve the LORD your God with all your heart and with all your soul, and to keep the LORD'S commandments and His statutes which I am commanding you today for your good? (Deuteronomy 10:12-13)

Considering the Israelites' past, of particular importance was the affirmation and application of two familiar laws:

> You shall not put the LORD your God to the test, as you tested Him at Massah. (Deuteronomy 6:16)

> Moreover, he shall not multiply horses for himself, nor shall he cause the people to return to Egypt to multiply horses, since the LORD has said to you, "You shall never again return that way." (Deuteronomy 17:16)

Moses followed these up with the LORD'S laws concerning warfare. The Israelites had been warned that their enemies lived in Canaan. Therefore, they knew that in making the promised land their own, they were facing certain warfare. Concerned with the upcoming battles, God had great interest in His soldiers.

First, as Commander-in-chief, God assured His warriors of His presence in war.

> "When you go out to battle against your enemies and see horses and chariots and people more numerous than you, do not be afraid of them; for the LORD your God, who brought you up from the land of Egypt, is with you." (Deuteronomy 20:1)

Then, perhaps taking them by surprise, He declared that some of His people were not eligible to serve in His army. Three things, all involving external circumstances, disqualified men from military service (Deuteronomy 20:1-7). Any man who had built a house but had not yet dedicated it, who had planted a vineyard but had not yet eaten of it, or who had become engaged but had not yet married would have his heart in another place. Since he would be easily distracted or diverted, since his mind would not be on the task at hand, and since he would not be wholly dedicated to serving God, it was best for him to return to home and family.

Of equal importance, a fourth reason, this time the internal circumstance of fear, disqualified men from being soldiers (Deuteronomy

20:8). If a man was afraid, he was to depart. The fainthearted were to return home in order to keep their fear from spreading and infecting others and to prevent soldiers in the front lines from entrusting their lives to those who might break under stress and abandon both their positions and their orders.

In the first three cases, the presence or absence of extenuating circumstances decided whether a man was approved or disapproved for military service. In the last case, the condition of heart was the deciding factor. Each man had to judge himself or search his own heart to determine whether he was fearful. He was then required to act on his own judgment and either remain or depart. No one else could to this for him.

In giving the Law to the Israelites, it is important to note that Moses had summoned all of them to hear it (Deuteronomy 5:1). Therefore, no one could say he (or she) did not know the commands by which God's covenant endured. The laws were not obscure, nor were they hearsay. They were the present, powerful statutes of God. Since all had heard, all were accountable.

Also, the Law was not obsolete. The new generation had not been given a new law but the old one. Since the Law was perfect as originally given, it did not need to be changed. It was not the Law but the attitude and behavior of the people toward it that needed changing. The people were not given permission to change the Law according to individual desire, taste, or want, or because of individual or corporate circumstances. God had given one absolute Law to govern His people until the coming of Christ brought a New Covenant.

Finally, in re-giving the Law, Moses wanted to teach everyone that the wisdom and understanding manifested in keeping God's ordinances would set the Israelites apart as a nation and would be a testimony of God among the heathen (Deuteronomy 4:7-8). Small wonder then that He insisted the Israelites keep His Law.

THE PROMISES OF GOD

Next during the interlude, Moses spoke forth the promises of God. The Hebrews' experiences in Egypt and in the desert had happened for a reason. Each experience had prepared them for something. Now that something was to be more fully revealed.

Until this point, the Israelites had not yet realized the full blessing of God (Deuteronomy 12:9). Now they were to receive the fulfillment of God's promises and, once in possession of them, they would enjoy their rest.

Legacy

To show the Israelites God's authority in this area of their lives too, Moses reminded them that, as a result of their redemption by God, they were God's own possession (Deuteronomy 4:20). Purchased of God (Deuteronomy 32:6), His desire was to bless the people whom He held dear to His heart with a bountiful inheritance. The legacy was to be given in two ways.

First, as His heirs, the tribes of Israel were to be given the land of Canaan. Canaan was not like the slime pits of Egypt, nor was it similar to the parched desert sands. Canaan was a land of beauty and grace prepared by a special God for His special people.

> *Then it shall come about when the LORD your God brings you into the land which He swore to Your fathers Abraham, Isaac and Jacob, to give you, great and splendid cities which you did not build, and houses full of all good things which you did not fill, and hewn cisterns which you did not dig, vineyards and olive trees which you did not plant, and you [shall] eat and be satisfied.... (Deuteronomy 6:10-11)*

> *For the LORD your God is bringing you into a good land, a land of brooks of water, of fountains and springs, flowing forth in valleys and hills; a land of wheat and barley, of vines and fig trees and pomegranates, a land of olive oil and honey; a land where you will eat food without scarcity, in which you shall not lack anything; a land whose stones are iron, and out of whose hills you can dig copper. (Deuteronomy 8:7-9)*

The promises of God included not just the giving of the land but the taking of it as well. The Israelites already knew the land was occupied by giants. Therefore, God's declarations and assurances of victory in taking the land were most welcome.

> *"You shall not dread them, for the LORD your God is in your midst, a great and awesome God. The LORD your God will clear away these nations before you little by little; you will not be able to put an end to them quickly, for the wild beasts would grow too numerous for you. But the LORD your God will deliver them*

before you, and will throw them into great confusion until they are destroyed. He will deliver their kings into your hand so that you will make their name perish from under heaven; no man will be able to stand before you until you have destroyed them." (Deuteronomy 7:21-24)

"For if you are careful to keep all this commandment which I am commanding you to do, to love the LORD your God, to walk in all His ways and hold fast to Him; then the LORD will drive out all these nations from before you, and you will dispossess nations greater and mightier than you. Every place on which the sole of your foot shall tread shall be yours;" (Deuteronomy 11:22-25)

As a final promise concerning this part of the inheritance, God pledged that as long as the Israelites remained under the authority of the Word of God their days would be multiplied in the land (Deuteronomy 11:18-21).

The second part of God's legacy was quite different. One of the tribes, the Levites, had been set aside as priests and servants in the tabernacle of the Lord. Unlike the other tribes, which were to receive a portion of land as an inheritance, the Levites were to receive something much more special. As the Lord's portion was His people, so the portion for the Levites was the Lord.

At that time the LORD set apart the tribe of Levi to carry the ark of the covenant of the LORD, to stand before the LORD to serve Him and to bless in His name until this day. Therefore, Levi does not have a portion or inheritance with his brothers; the LORD is his inheritance, just as the LORD your God spoke to him. (Deuteronomy 10:8-9)

The Levitical priests, the whole tribe of Levi, shall have no portion or inheritance with Israel; they shall eat the LORD'S offerings by fire and His portion. They shall have no inheritance among their countrymen; the LORD is their inheritance, as He promised them. (Deuteronomy 18:1-2)

Finally, Moses summed up the intent of God's promises to His people:

"So Israel dwells in security, the fountain of Jacob secluded, in a land of grain and new wine; His heavens also drop down dew. Blessed are you, O Israel; who is like you, a people saved by the LORD, who is the shield of your help, and the sword of your majesty! So your enemies shall cringe before you, and you will tread upon their high places." (Deuteronomy 33:28-29)

Instructions Concerning The Promises

Coinciding with the announcement of inheritance came the pronouncement of instructions regarding the securing of them. First and foremost, the Israelites were to possess and then occupy the land (Deuteronomy 11:8,31). They were not to waffle any more. They were not to be fearful any more. They were not to be rebellious any more. They were to enter and take the land.

When they did so, the Israelites were to show no mercy on the heathen, depraved, idolatrous nations they were displacing. The enemies of God were to be annihilated utterly. Also, since the Israelites were a separated people, they were not to make any covenant with, intermarry among, or serve the gods of the pagans and unbelievers (Deuteronomy 7:2-5). Finally, they were to tear down all altars, destroy all high places, smash all pillars, and burn all images of false gods (Deuteronomy 12:2-3) so that these things would not be a snare to them.

When the Israelites had accomplished the occupation of Canaan, God had further instructions for them: the priests were to administer the law of God in settling all disputes among the people (Deuteronomy 21:5), and the Israelites, when at rest from their surrounding enemies, were to blot out forever even the memory of the Amalekites (Deuteronomy 25:19).

How could a fledgling nation become a triumphant, militant invader of God's enemies? It was possible only through the power and might of God.

If they would recall....

If you should say in your heart, 'These nations are greater than I; how can I dispossess them?' you shall not be afraid of them; you shall well remember what the LORD your God did to Pharaoh and to all Egypt. (Deuteronomy 7:17-18)

If they would know....

Know therefore today that it is the LORD your God who is crossing over before you as a consuming fire. He will destroy them and He will subdue them before you, so that you may drive them out and destroy them quickly, just as the LORD has spoken to you. (Deuteronomy 9:3)

If they would fear God....

You shall not dread them, for the LORD your God is in your midst, a great and awesome God. (Deuteronomy 7:21)

You shall fear only the LORD your God; and you shall worship Him, and swear by His name. (Deuteronomy 6:13)

If they would obey....

Then Moses and the Levitical priests spoke to all Israel, saying, "Be silent and listen, O Israel! This day you have become a people for the LORD your God. You shall therefore obey the LORD your God, and do His commandments and His statutes which I command you today." (Deuteronomy 27:9-10)

....then they would succeed. Victory would be theirs.

Warnings Concerning The Promises

Finally, to emphasize the importance of God's promises and instructions, Moses sternly warned the Israelites. He repeated the fact that dishonoring God would bring disaster upon them.

First and foremost, Moses warned the Israelites to keep their relationship with God holy. Therefore, they were not to honor false gods (Deuteronomy 6:13) nor to make graven images (Deuteronomy 4:23). Furthermore, all forms of witchcraft were strictly forbidden (Deuteronomy 18:9-12).

Also, the people were warned not to indulge in pride. God was not giving them the promised land because of their righteousness but because of the wickedness of the heathen and because of His love for their forefathers (Deuteronomy 9:4-5).

In addition, Moses warned the Israelites to honor His covenant. God had already judged one generation for disobedience, and Moses wanted it well understood that He could and would do so again, if necessary. His admonition that the Israelites' future depended on their choice for obedience rang out:

"You should diligently keep the commandments of the LORD your God, and His testimonies and His statutes which He has commanded you. You shall do what is right and good in the sight of the LORD, that it may be well with you and that you may go in and possess the good land which the LORD swore to give your fathers, by driving out all your enemies from before you, as the LORD has spoken." (Deuteronomy 6:17-19)

"See, I am setting before you today a blessing and a curse: the blessing, if you listen to the commandments of the LORD your God, which I am commanding you today; and the curse, if you do not listen to the commandments of the LORD your God, but turn aside from the way which I am commanding you today, by following other gods which you have not known." (Deuteronomy 11:26-28)

If the Israelites kept covenant, God's blessing would include health, length of days, increased numbers of people, and His presence and power. If they broke covenant, God's curse would fall on both the land and the people.

Concerning the land, Moses warned that if God's wrath broke out, the land of milk and honey would dry up and be afflicted with plagues (Deuteronomy 29:22-23). Concerning the people, if God's judgment fell, He would uproot the people in His great fury and cast them into another land (Deuteronomy 29:28). He would scatter them, drive them away, and see them perish from the land.

When the people failed God (Deuteronomy 31:16), they yet had a choice. Moses warned that if they wanted to be whole, they had to recall the blessing and the curse, repent of their sins, and return to the LORD. If they wanted to be restored, re-gathered, and revived and to repossess the land, they had to obey the LORD and observe all His commandments (Deuteronomy 30:1-8).

Again and again Moses warned that the Israelites' choices made the difference between life and death. God had given a covenant, and the Israelites had to choose obedience or rebellion. From Moses' point of view, there was only one choice: *"I call heaven and earth to witness against you today, that I have set before you life and death, the blessing and the curse. So choose life...."* (Deuteronomy 30:19).

THE SOUNDS OF THE TRUMPET

The Feast Of Trumpets

This desert interlude brings to mind the Feast of Trumpets. As noted, the Israelites were required to celebrate three feasts every year. The first, Passover, was a three-part feast: 1) Passover itself, in which the blood of the sacrificial lamb covered the sins of the people (or the Church's salvation from sin by the blood of the sacrificial Lamb); 2) Unleavened Bread, which commemorated the Israelites' exodus from Egypt (or the Church's separation and sanctification from evil); and 3) First Fruits, which remembered the Israelites' journey through the Red Sea that led to new life (or the Church's water baptism through which it identifies with the death, burial, resurrection, and new life of Jesus Christ).

The second annual celebration was the Feast of Pentecost, which honored the time God appeared to and met with the Israelites in a new relationship, gave the Israelites the Old Covenant, and led the Israelites via the shekinah cloud (or the Lord appearing to His disciples in a manifestation, giving them the New Covenant, and leading them by Holy Spirit).

Finally, all the Israelites were to celebrate the Feast of Tabernacles. This was another three-part feast whose days included the Feast of Trumpets, the Day of Atonement, and then the actual Feast of Tabernacles or Feast of Booths (Leviticus 23:23-43). It occurred in the autumn at harvest time.

The Israelites had two calendars. While the Feast of Passover marked the beginning of the sacred year, the Feast of Trumpets announced the beginning of the civil year. The Feast of Trumpets was therefore a type of New Year's celebration. It was a time of great anticipation.

This feast was celebrated by blowing trumpets over a period of forty days. Beginning with the first day of the sixth month of thirty days and continuing on for the first ten days of the next month, their sound rang out. Their purpose was to cause the Israelites to pause, reflect, and prepare for the most holy day of the year. Specifically, the Feast of Trumpets was for magnifying the kingship of God (Psalm 98:6), causing the people to remember and to return to God (Hosea 14:1-2) and to awaken spiritually.

Other Soundings

Trumpets were an inseparable part of the Israelites' history. Long centuries before the desert interlude, God introduced the ram's horn to His chosen ones. When Abraham was prepared and committed to sacrifice his son, Isaac, on Mount Moriah, God stayed his hand. He then showed Abraham the real sacrifice, a ram caught by his horns in a thicket (Genesis 22:1-14). The horns of rams such as these became the trumpets of Israel, the shofars. Then, while the Hebrews were in the desert, God ordered Moses to make two silver trumpets. In addition to the reasons listed in Numbers 10:1-10, these horns were to be blown to proclaim the year of Jubilee (Leviticus 25:8-10) and to praise and worship God (Psalm 150:3).

While the desert interlude did not correspond to the timing of the Feast of Tabernacles according to the Hebrew calendar, the meaning of this celebration was in every way applicable to the camp of Israel as it sojourned near the Jordan River. Since Moses called the Israelites to a halt on the first day of the month, a trumpet would have sounded. Further, during the interval, the trumpets would have blown to assemble the people, bringing them together to hear of God. The shofars would have blared out the reason for the prolonged encampment. They would have brought people into awareness that God was their King, caused them to remember His greatness, and asked them to renew their commitment to Him. Finally, since the trumpets were used to announce the camp was to move out during the time in the wilderness, surely those trumpets would also have announced that the camp was to move into Canaan.

When Moses finished his exhortation, he paused. He had led the Israelites in song after leading them out of Egypt (Exodus 15:1-18). He now sang a song at the end of the desert experience (Deuteronomy 32:1-43). Then, after pronouncing his blessing on each tribe, he climbed Mount Nebo and died. In a place unknown to mankind, he was buried by the hand of God (Deuteronomy 34:6). The interlude was over and the people of Israel would finish the journey without him.

Chapter 14

INTERLUDE:

EACH SAINT'S TIME TO REMEMBER

The desert crossing had been a long, hard experience for the Israelites. So it is for each saint. For each who has endured spiritual windstorms and burning fires, who have survived predators, and who have finally learned to face and defeat enemies along the way, settling into an interlude, a temporary respite, is a welcome relief.

A TIME OF REMEMBRANCE

As Moses met with the Israelites in this interval of love, God will meet with any saint whose heart longs to go on. At that time, in a slow, thorough revelation, He will help each saint recall who He is and will show the saint who He expects him (or her) to be. He will recount what He has done for each saint and what He expects him to do for Him. Then, He will repeat His covenant, disclose His promises, and give instructions that will enable each saint to fulfill the promises. Finally, God will warn each saint that judgment on all his works is forthcoming. Rewards of blessings will fall on the obedient, but they will not fall on the disobedient.

God will remind each saint of the dark and utterly hopeless days of his (or her) slavery to sin in the world and then, by way of comparison, firmly affix in his mind the glories of his rescue and redemption, his salvation and his sanctification. Many a saint can pinpoint the time or details of the moment his heart was changed toward God; another whose journey was more gradual in nature may not remember the process of his or her salvation as clearly. If any has forgotten, he or she can ask God prayerfully, and that wisdom will be granted to him (James 1:5).

God will also gently show each saint the steps of his (or her) path with the Lord. Many times they have been in His steps; oftentimes they have not. When God knows it is necessary, He will reveal to each saint the idols that he had made with his hands, set up, and worshipped or particular areas of rebellion and presumption that continuously have to be dealt with. These, if repented of and confessed to God, are forgiven by the blood of Jesus. However, they serve as a warning to each saint not to go back to them or to go that way again. (See also Psalm 19:13).

Renewed Faith In God

The truth is that each saint finds the interval not only welcome but necessary. First, when events threaten to overwhelm him (or her) in the course of his life, it is not unusual for eyes to be drawn to the problem instead of to the answer to the problem. Similarly, after a long journey filled with dangers, toils, and snares, it is not uncommon for a saint to magnify his (or her) situation rather than the One who has power to lead him through it. The interlude is a special time in which this saint can get back to basics, once more learning to look for and depend on Jesus.

Preparation

A second reason to pause is that when the Lord is ready to move a saint into a new land or a place of service or into a greater depth or breadth or height in Him, He often first calls him (or her) aside. In ways beyond description or by means personally tailored to each saint's need, God declares His will for this new phase of the saint's walk. He then asks if that saint will obey Him even though, like Abraham, he may not know the particulars of where he is going. If the saint agrees to follow Him, while he is temporarily resting from the desert, God strips him of his past to prepare him for his future. He removes old habits, forbids old ways, and even takes away old companions. He exposes idols, destroys human dependencies, and sees that each saint, as Jesus once did, becomes of no name or reputation. When all that remains is a belief and a faith in God, God will meet with him.

Weeding Out

A third reason for the interlude between the desert and the promised land is to give God time to sort His flock. As noted, it is a staggering fact that of the hundreds of thousands of Hebrew men who entered the desert, only two of the same generation left it alive. Similarly, it is also possible that the vast majority of new saints who have been saved and delivered and who have endured the hardships of sanctification are yet in or have died in the desert. Only a small percentage of saints proved themselves in the wilderness, arrived at the banks of the Jordan River, and declared themselves willing to cross into Canaan.

Sometimes this reluctance to proceed is a result of disillusionment. A new saint may be shocked that he (or she) cannot be his own boss. Too often, discovering that truth and fighting against it take an enormous toll. Or, this hesitation may be a result of poor instruction. In many cases, a new saint has been taught by his own Church that this bleak desert existence is all there is, that once saved he won't face any new challenges. His whole reason for being is summed up in the sad, joyless, duty-without-love words: "Do and then die."

Separation

A fourth reason to pause is so that the saints can separate themselves into two groups: those who want to stay and those who want to press on. If a saint is used to the desert and is content to stay there, so he (or she) shall remain. However, among the flock some are not content to remain in the middle of nowhere. These are heard crying out: "This is not all there is! This is not as good as it gets! This is not God's full inheritance! There has to be more. I've come too far to give up or turn back now. Lord, do what You have to do to lead me forward. Do it perfectly and completely until it is truly done because I do not want to pass this way again." When God hears these words, He will begin the preparation within each heart that will ultimately allow that saint to cross into Canaan.

Establishing Jesus As Lord

A final reason for the interlude is that each saint needs to establish Jesus as Lord firmly in his (or her) heart and mind. No one leaving Egypt or the world is fully submitted to God. Without question, every saint, released from the horrible pressure of slavery and of doing what someone else said he must do secretly wishes to live his own life. Desiring to do what he wants to do, a part of him calls for freedom from any yoke, whether it be other people's, Satan's, or God's. Each saint must learn about the two kingdoms spoken of in the Bible – that of Satan, which is sin, evil, darkness, and death, and that of God, which is obedience, righteousness, light, and life (Acts 26:18). God does not recognize a third kingdom of self-rule. Therefore, to give each saint time to choose to submit to Him, God designed a desert experience to humble him, to test his heart, and to discipline him even while God teaches him to serve Him.

While the process of settling the lordship of Jesus is on-going, each saint spends much time tramping in dusty desert ruts or walking on human paths rather than God's. While being humbled and tested, each saint circles mountains or sets up and then disassembles any number of camps as he (or she) continues his way, such as wandering from one local church to another or supporting a certain ministry only to change and follow another. While being disciplined, each saint is hardened, strengthened, and tempered until well able to face and defeat his enemies. The desert makes a carnal, selfish saint a spiritual child of God, and the interlude leads him to understand that change.

THE NEW COVENANT

Then, after a review of the desert experience has allowed each saint to see the changes it has made in his (or her) character and in his heart, God brings up the matter of covenant. He reminds His own of the New Covenant of God and of the God of the New Covenant.

A Blessing From God

Sometimes a new saint is too little aware of the glories of his (or her) God. Without God, the power of sin over mankind would not have been broken. Without God, no one would have been redeemed or separated from the world. Without God, no one would be able to deal with flesh or deny self. Without God, no one would have been kept in food, clothing, or health in the desert (Deuteronomy 29:1-6). Without God, the New Covenant would not exist.

Universal

God is pleasant and powerful; He is lovely and lively, and so is His covenant with each saint. As Moses made all the Israelites aware that each person was accountable to keep the Old Covenant of law, so now every saint is required to keep the New Covenant of grace. There are absolutely no exceptions. Anyone purposefully distancing himself (or herself) from the New Covenant and repeatedly violating its words and principles is also walking outside the will of God. Therefore, he is outside the glories of God's presence and power as well.

Available

God's New Covenant has not been kept a secret. God has made His agreement and His will known to all. Whether available in Bibles, reference books, newsletters, preaching, teaching, audio or video tapes, or the electronic media, His Word abounds. In some lands where the message of the good news in not so obviously available, God has still made His name, covenant, and message known to the heart of men and women (Psalm 19:1-4; Romans 1:18-20).

Unchanging

God has never given His New Covenant to one saint, one Church, or one generation and a different one to another. Yes, a personal *rhema* may differ, but not a universal principle of His Covenant. He has spoken one absolute, unchanging pledge that He will not alter.

Holy

God's divine covenant is holy, setting those who choose to obey it apart from the unsaved in the world. Jesus is the Light of the world (John 8:12); each saint, radiating His glory, is a light to the world (Matthew 5:14). As each saint shines in the reflected glory of his relationship with God his (or her) light shines out more brightly, making him a beacon of light in the surrounding darkness. As he walks in covenant with God, he walks in deeper and deeper levels of dedication, consecration, sanctification, and holiness unto God.

Perfect

After declaring the universality, availability, constancy, and holiness of His New Covenant, God also makes each saint see that His promise is perfect. Since it is inerrant, each and every saint is accountable to obey it. Since it is flawless, any problem in keeping it is not with God's unrealistic expectations or overburdening demands on people; rather, the problem is with people's attitude and behavior toward His divine command and intent.

THE PROMISES OF GOD

After remembering the desert experience and discussing the covenant in this interlude between the desert and crossing the Jordan River, God declares His wonderful promises. Like the Israelites of old, slavery in the world never brought a sinner into his godly portion, and continuous wandering through the desert's works of flesh and self never brought a saint into godly peace. The promises of God have to do with the two things each saint is lacking: His legacy and His rest. The promised land is the place of the fulfillment of those promises.

Legacy

The experience in and the escape from Egypt was part of a natural journey for the Israelites. It was an actual event that happened to a real people. In a parallel manner, for each saint, salvation and deliverance were the beginnings of a spiritual journey by those reborn into the kingdom of God. Similarly, the Israelites' trip through the desert was an actual forty-year ordeal endured by a self-centered nation until they became the people of God. Just so, each saint's desert experience is a spiritual journey to the end of flesh and self. In a land marked by spiritual hills and valleys and dotted with spiritual parched lands and plains, he (or she) finally learns who he is in Christ.

In the world, an inheritance is that property, possession, or title that passes from one generation to the next within a family. Succession depends on the death of the one originally possessing it.

In His kingdom, God wills that each saint be His heir or an inheritor of His estate (Galatians 4:7), a co-heir with Christ (Romans 8:17), and a beneficiary of all His riches and treasures. Here, too, God's legacy is available only through death.

First, inheritance requires the death of the rightful owner of the treasures, Jesus, who is His Father's heir (Hebrews 1:2). In dying on the cross, He made provision for each saint to receive His inheritance. Second, it requires the death of the saint. Only through his (or her) born-again experience can he become a relative of God, an adopted son or daughter, and thus eligible to receive the family treasures of heaven.

In other words, those who receive God's inheritance must have died too. No one who is alive to the world is mentioned in God's will. A saint can only be given his (or her) inheritance after his own death to the world, the flesh, the devil, sin, and self. Only after he dies with Christ and is reborn to new life can he receive the indwelling Holy Spirit as a pledge of his full legacy. As each saint grows in resurrection life, he comes into greater and greater portions of his promised land or his spiritual inheritance.

God's Legacy Is Spiritual

When the Israelites crossed the Jordan River and entered Canaan, they received their enemies' physical lands as an inheritance from God after fierce warfare. Following the established pattern of relating the natural to the spiritual, when each saint enters the promised land, he (or she) does not receive an actual plot of ground as his inheritance, but he does gain the spiritual places where he can abide in strength and rest as promised to him by his Father.

It is not God's intention to give any saint anything of permanence in this world. One reason for this is that the earth itself is not permanent. The Israelites' natural inheritance was to last as long as the heavens remained above the earth, but each saint's spiritual legacy is forever (1 Peter 1:4). The present heavens and earth were created by a word from God. At His command, they will soon pass away (2 Peter 3:5-10). If any saint's heritage was of things of this earth, that too would pass away. However, since it is a spiritual legacy, it will last forever.

God's Legacy Is Otherworldly

God's kingdom is not of this world. Therefore, neither is that of any saint who, after being born from above, becomes part of the kingdom of God.

Do not misunderstand. Saints have physical bodies, and they live in a physical environment. Yet, while they are in the world, they are not of the world (John 17:14-15). In their natural habitat, God gives them those things that are needed to sustain life and to make existence on earth bearable. Yet the food, clothing, and shelter that God provides are not the permanent possession of any saint. They belong to God, and a saint is but a steward of them (Deuteronomy 10:14; Psalm 24:1; Luke 16:1-13). Whether God's provision is to be kept in storehouses, used, given away, or released to the care of a different steward is entirely up to the direction of the Spirit of God.

No saint is to be trapped by the cares of this world. The things in it are not to hold him (or her). Lands and possessions are not to ensnare him or delay him because of his failure to release them. Nor are they to concern and preoccupy him so much that caring for them takes precedence over seeking God.

Each saint must remember that his (or her) earthly dwelling is not his permanent home; God is preparing another one for him (John 14:2-3). His natural family is not his permanent one; God's family becomes his eternal one. He is not to be content with this world and the things in it, for they are not a true legacy. Jesus said His kingdom was not of this world (John 18:36), so His promised legacy is also not of this world.

God's Legacy Is Jesus

The greatest inheritance any saint receives from His Father is the Father's Son, Jesus. *"For God so loved the world, that He gave His only begotten Son, that whoever believes in Him shall not perish, but have eternal life"* (John 3:16).

In the Old Covenant, the Levitical priests were not given a physical inheritance like the other tribes. Instead, *"the LORD is their inheritance"* (Deuteronomy 18:2). Today, those who believe in Him are saints or the priests of God (1 Peter 2:9), and their inheritance is the Lord Jesus Christ. Through Jesus the fullness of that legacy is realized. This inheritance includes the kingdom of God (Matthew 25:34), eternal life (Matthew 19:29), the fulfillment of promises (Hebrews 6:13-20), and, ultimately, all things (Revelation 21:7). Further, each saint receives a personal legacy. According to the promises of Jesus, God will enable him (or her) to do greater works than Jesus did, God will answer his prayers, the Holy Spirit will be a constant indwelling Companion, the Father and Son will love him, and Jesus will give him peace to bless him with an untroubled heart (John 14:12-27).

Ultimately, the most wonderful blessing any saint could receive is Jesus. Every saint who understands God's inheritance is the dearest thing God has to give him (or her) and who delights in that legacy can only agree with the psalmist: *"The LORD is the portion of my inheritance and my cup; You support my lot. The lines have fallen to me in pleasant places; indeed, my heritage is beautiful to me"* (Psalm 16:5-6).

Rest

If earthly possessions do not constitute a permanent inheritance, what then should a saint look forward to in his (or her) Canaan? What are the promises he will receive from God? A saint receives a portion of territory that he must invade and conquer through Christ. Today, territory does not necessarily mean land. It means any area a saint has authority or influence over, such as family, friends, jobs, neighborhoods, workplaces, and organizations. God gives each saint his place in the territory and then tells him he must it take from the enemy, possess it, and occupy it.

Receiving the promises of land and of the Lord is one thing. Securing them is quite another. As God gave the Israelites instructions to follow in gaining their portion, so He now gives them to each saint. The commands concerning securing each saint's godly inheritance include:

> When the LORD your God brings you into the land where you are entering to possess it, and clears away many nations before you ... and when the LORD your God delivers them before you and you defeat them, then you shall utterly destroy them. You shall make no covenant with them and show no favor to them. (Deuteronomy 7:1-2)

> For you are about to cross the Jordan to go in to possess the land which the LORD your God is giving you, and you shall possess it and live in it. (Deuteronomy 11:31)

All spiritual warfare is to be fought under God's express command. When so led, each saint has the promise of God that God will precede him (or her) in battle and conquer the enemy by the power of His great might (Deuteronomy 9:3; Isaiah 45:2). Yet, it is up to the saint to take up his weapons of warfare, to join the battle, to defeat and destroy the enemy, and to possess his territory. In other words, he must cooperate with God in spiritual warfare.

No saint is authorized to fight those he (or she) chooses, when he chooses, or where he chooses. God and He alone knows how to direct the battle in order to manifest the greatest victory. He is El Shaddai, God Almighty; a saint is not. He is Commander in Chief of the armies of heaven; a saint is not. He is all wise; a saint is not. He has the whole plan; a saint has only a part of it.

Following the example of the Israelites, each saint must annihilate and dispossess the spiritual enemies, showing them no mercy. The Israelites' enemies in Canaan were deeply involved in the grossest of sins. Their idolatry, harlotry, perversions, and licentiousness are legendary. Leviticus 18 contains a long list of sexual perversions, and verses three and twenty-four of that chapter declare them to be the common practice of the Canaanites. Since these practices were forbidden to the Israelites, the Israelites, rather than becoming familiar with them or ensnared by them, were to destroy the Canaanites utterly and completely.

So it is in a Christian's warfare. The enemies of God are not to be spared. They are filthy and gross. They cannot be coexisted with. They cannot be reasoned with. They cannot be tolerated. They are to be defeated and then utterly destroyed and driven away. Their lands or areas they occupy must be possessed and submitted to the sovereignty of God.

The only possible way to follow these instructions is for each saint to fear God more than he (or she) fears people, to know the wrath of God is greater than the wrath of people, and to know the reward of God is greater than the reward of any person. In fearing God, each saint must acknowledge that his inheritance is not an automatic blessing but is conditional upon obedience. Obedience and blessing are a cause-and-effect relationship.

As each saint accepts his (or her) territory, conquers and dispossesses the enemies entrenched there, fears God, and realizes that his most precious possession is the presence of the Lord, he will come into rest. As he walks in God's way, he endures no more defeat, no more struggle, and no more wandering. He finds rest in God's everlasting arms.

Warnings Concerning The Promises

Finally, after recalling, reviewing the covenant, and learning of His promises, the interlude serves to warn each saint. Each who understands that the fulfillment of God's promises depends on following God's instructions must also be aware that it depends on heeding His warnings as well.

Life on the earth often seems to be a collage of signals. For instance, in driving, signs and traffic directives such as "Stop," "Yield," or "No U Turn" seem omnipresent and are intended to keep drivers from having an accident. Just so, in the spiritual world, God has given signs or warnings to direct each saint and to keep him (or her) from spiritual wreckage.

Witchcraft

Of utmost importance to each saint is his (or her) relationship with God. No saint is to dishonor the God of covenant in any way. No saint is to place anyone or anything above God. To ensure God remains as God in each Christian's life, the Bible warns that any and all forms of witchcraft are absolutely, totally, permanently forbidden to or by any saint.

No saint is to indulge in any form of spiritism at any time. Each saint must understand that only one Holy Spirit exists. However, profane spirits also exist: unholy, human spirits are those under the authority of people, while evil, demonic spirits are those under the authority of Satan.

Satan's downfall was his desire for worship and power. Saints should never seek the same. Witchcraft starts with a search for power. Its goal is to control people or situations. If someone asks for something from God and does not receive it, he (or she) may seek an unholy source of power to provide him with what he wants. If human power with its weak works of flesh fails him and he is yet determined to pursue his course, he may seek out and accept demonic power. This is entering the world of the occult.

Any occult activity places the one seeking power under the authority of the evil spirit which manifests the power that he (or she) has been seeking. It opens the door to that power or gives it legal access to use that person and to do through him the things that the evil spirit has been commanded to do by Satan.

Any "innocent" dabbling in the occult, such as horoscopes, fortune telling, hypnotism, water witching, acupuncture, Ouija boards, occult computer games, and demonically-inspired music is anathema to God. Whether indulged in because of ignorance, curiosity, deception concealing the dangers involved, or a need to get demands met because God wouldn't perform, all are absolutely forbidden.

Satan knows he cannot undo the work of the cross; he irrevocably lost that battle with Jesus. However, that doesn't stop him from demonstrating his evil power or deceiving people into accepting his power. Nor does it stop him from trying to establish a point of legal access by which he can control people's lives. He already has control of the life of everyone in the world, and he wants to take back or reestablish control of those who have escaped his world and have become citizens of the kingdom of God. Through the occult, if he is even mildly successful in so doing, he can weaken, block, and hinder a saint's relationship to

God.

Every saint should now understand God's warning against witchcraft and should see why the defeated enemies of God must be totally destroyed. They bring terrible offense to holy God, and, if left alone, will ensnare, turn on, attack, and try to destroy God's children.

Pride

A second area of warning concerns pride. God is all, and every saint is totally dependent on Him for all things. By his (or her) own power no saint can do what needs to be done. None can keep covenant without God's help. None can honor God without His help. Therefore, any heart claiming personal honor as their means by which they can walk closer with God is on dangerous ground. Anyone swelling in vanity and vainglory over his own accomplishments has not heeded God's warning against pride.

After the older generation of the Israelites had died in the desert, Moses ordered a census. The results indicated that the new generation of numbered almost exactly the same as the old (Numbers 26:1-51). This is a classic case of God raising someone up for a blessing, and when he (or she) abuses or refuses it, even through fear, it is given to another. Each saint must understand that God's purpose will be carried out with or without him. A saint uses his will to determine his behavior. If his will doesn't line up with God's, it doesn't change God's plan, it just changes the saint. By choice, he can be in God's will or out of it. If, for whatever reason, he chooses the latter, the blessing, reward, and rest meant for him will go to another.

The key to any saint's relationship with God has always been following Jesus' example of *"Your will be done"* (Matthew 26:42). If a saint tries to force God to do his (or her) will or if he refuses to do God's will, God will not compete with him. He will set him aside as He did the older generation of Israelites. Sadly, the saint will see others raised up in places meant for him even as he dies in the desert far from his journey's end.

Only pride makes a saint think that God's love towers over His justice. Pride blinds him (or her) from seeing that it is precisely because of His love for a saint that His judgment must fall (Hebrews 12:5-10).

The Future

A third warning concerns the future. Even after entering the promised land each saint can yet sin. If he (or she) does, even there he is accountable. The promised land is not a place severed from temptation or sealed from sin. In it, each is to keep moving towards perfection (Matthew 5:48), but he has no automatic guarantee of a holy walk. Each is yet dependent on obedience to be victorious.

The Israelites were warned that persistent disobedience could cause loss of blessings, even to the extent of being uprooted and scattered. Unfortunately, they did not heed this warning, and they were uprooted and scattered throughout the Assyrian Empire. This warning holds true for each saint. If a saint should persist in disobeying God, he (or she) could lose his blessings. Should that happen, he must remember that the way back is through repentance (Deuteronomy 30:1-4).

THE SOUNDS OF THE TRUMPET

While encamped in the interlude near the Jordan River, each saint can clearly hear the sound of blowing trumpets. The one, sure, prophetic voice that each saint must listen to is the trumpet-like voice of Jesus (Revelation 1:10). Jesus never ceases to call out to His own. His blasts and flourishes constantly establish for each saint a feast of trumpets. In part, they are a reminder of His kingship, a call to remember, an admonition to awaken, a warning to prepare for war, and a call to move on.

To Announce Jesus' Kingship

In the natural world, when a king walked before his people, his arrival was announced by a trumpet fanfare. When Jesus was born, He was acknowledged as King of the Jews (Matthew 2:2). His nativity was announced by a multitude of angels trumpeting the praises of God in heaven and peace and good will toward men and women on earth (Luke 2:13-14). Although He was King in the world, He said, *"My kingdom is not of this world"* (John 18:36). When Jesus died, the Roman governor, Pilate, also affirmed that He was King (John 19:19).

Now, centuries later, all Christiandom is warned to watch for the second coming of the King. He who created the heavens and the earth and who is sovereign over all is about to return. This monumental event will include the sound of a trumpet announcing His arrival.

> *And then the sign of the Son of Man will appear in the sky, and then all the tribes of the earth will mourn, and they will see the SON OF MAN COMING ON THE CLOUDS OF THE SKY with power and great glory. And He will send forth His angels with A GREAT TRUMPET and THEY WILL GATHER TOGETHER His elect from the four winds, from one end of the sky to the other.* (Matthew 24:30-31)

To Remember

Jesus always calls His saints to remembrance. A trumpet can be a sound of joy or a sign of judgment. For the Israelites, the Feast of Trumpets was a time of joy, but it led to or was a reminder of the coming Day of Judgment. For ten days, all of the Israelites were to spend time in self-examination remembering their thoughts and actions and, if found wanting, to heed the call to repentance on the quickly approaching Day of Atonement.

Similarly, each saint must examine his (or her) heart, not on a special, holy day but as a part of his daily Christian experience. While no saint is to become overly preoccupied in soul searching or self-examination, he must still be enough in touch with his inner being and with the Holy Spirit to hear the trumpet of alarm if God has been offended and if the saint is in need of repentance and reconciliation with God.

To Awaken

Third, to the saints who are all but asleep, the blasting voice of God would cry out to awaken, to come alive, to rise up from slumber. *"Awake, sleeper, and arise from the dead, and Christ will shine on you"* (Ephesians 5:14).

If ever there was a time in New Testament history when a great awakening would be welcome, this is it. In the Old Covenant, King Josiah heard the sounding alarm of apostasy and inaugurated one of the greatest reformations in Hebrew history (2 Kings 23:1-25). In the New Covenant, John the Baptist (Luke 3:2-14), Peter (Acts 10:34-48), and Paul (Acts 13:14-52) all began spiritual awakenings when they were inspired by the promptings of God to do so.

As were the Israelites, a saint of God must be attentive to the sound of God's trumpets. If a saint will but listen, he (or she) will hear the command to awaken from his deep slumber, apathy, indifference, and lack or concern and to obey God. While God has assigned each saint a ministry, that work is often stifled by the abundant "one man shows" in local churches. The result has been a scattered, impotent flock which the world takes delight in despising. Now God is saying to come together, to assemble as His one body, to receive His commands, and to be strong and bold enough to function corporately in God-given tasks despite human opposition.

To Prepare For War

Trumpets have been of great value for thousands of years in military warfare throughout the world. It is common to see films depicting buglers leading cavalry charges or to read stories of soldiers being guided in battle by the sounds of bugles. Even today people are moved at funeral services by the haunting sound of "Taps" played over the graves of those who have served their country.

No saint can hear the trumpet and not hear a call to warfare. Some saints yet mistakenly (and dangerously!) believe that if they are nice to Satan he will return the favor, that if they leave him alone, he will leave them alone. Such is not the case. His goals are still to steal, kill, and destroy (John 10:10). While he is now on the attack, many a saint is yet refusing to put on his (or her) armor or to learn the tactics of war. Young sheep, listen to the urgency of the sound. Hear the warning of the trumpet. God Himself is warning you. Prepare for war! Put on your armor (Ephesians 6:10-17); declare your *rhema*; stay in close ranks with those fighting with you; have faith in God (Mark 11:22; Romans 1:17).

To Move On

Further, it doesn't take too much imagination for any saint to know that his (or her) journey is not finished. Though he has followed his Lord to the bank of the Jordan River, he is not in Canaan. Any saint listening to the voice of the Lord will occasionally hear the command to move away from familiar ground and to follow God once again. When warned by the trumpets of a coming move, each saint must be prepared to pack his tent and to move on, even if other dear ones choose to remain where they are. No saint is to be a camp follower; rather, he is to be a God follower.

As a saint follows God, he (or she) must safely make his way through life's perils. Today, panic, fear, and stress are taking a frightful toll on both the saved and the unsaved. Jesus alone can guide each saint through the earth's perilous times into heaven's eternity. He alone can prepare each holy one to be ready in season and out (2 Timothy 4:2) or to lead him from one season of life to another. All of this requires each Christian to be in constant communication with his Lord. It demands time spent with the Lord, deep contemplation, fasting, prayer, and worship so that the saint can clearly hear the sound of the Lord's trumpet directing him.

So, saint, having come this far, you must remember that although you are on the border of the Jordan River and are ready to enter Canaan, you are still in the desert. So near and yet so far. You must choose whether to say there or to go on. When the call comes to move, will you be approved for such a journey, or, like Moses, will you be allowed to see the promised land but, because of disobedience, not be allowed to enter?

Chapter 15

INTERLUDE:

THE CHURCH'S TIME TO REMEMBER

As the Hebrews and as each individual saint had to pause before entering the promised land, so must the true Church. As the Israelites and as each saint of God had to assess the past and to discuss the future with the Lord, so must the Church. As God's chosen ones and as each child of the holy Father had to seek God concerning the covenant, the promises, the instructions, and the warnings of blessings or curses, so must the Church. It has learned from past experience before and must again do so now.

A TIME OF REMEMBRANCE

New Leadership

During this time out at the end of the desert journey, the Church needs to ponder several things. First, in this interval between ending the desert journey and entering the promised land, the Church finds itself, as the Israelites did, in the midst of a transition in leadership and a corresponding transference of power. When Moses struck the rock rather than speaking to it at Meribah, he forfeited his privilege of entering Canaan. Knowing all too well that the Israelites would need someone to lead them, Moses sought God. God then selected Joshua as the new leader and placed on him the same Spirit that was on Moses (Numbers 27:18). Later, on the banks of the Jordan River, the transfer of leadership was completed as Moses spent a few last days among his people exhorting them to follow God, and then he climbed Mount Nebo to die.

Similarly, at times the Church has been led by those who strike out at God rather than those who speak to Him. In various places it has been governed by those who insist on binding it under the Mosaic Covenant that God gave to the Israelites but not to the Church. It has been held in bondage by those who insist on daily repetition of the already perfect sacrifice of the cross, by those who encourage ritual and formality as a way of worship, by those so locked into manmade tradition that the Holy Spirit has been stifled.

Now, the torch of leadership is passing into new hands. As the men, women, and ministries that symbolize or carry on the rites and traditions of the Old Covenant die off, new leaders are arising. With God's anointing and authority on them, they are walking in obedience to Him. They are not looking back to or following the Old Covenant of law; they are bringing the true Church into the New Covenant of grace. They are no longer binding the Church under the dead weight of tradition but loosing it to walk in faith.

Back To Basics

A second reason for the Church to pause is that it is on the brink of the greatest wave of holiness, power, and justice that it or the world has ever known. To be part of such a tidal wave of sanctity, the Church must pause long enough to seek God, to get back to basics, to yearn for the holiness of His presence and the might of His power, and to learn of His ways, not just of His acts.

In an outpouring of love, God will allow His true Church to enter into a greater height, depth, and breadth of relationship with Him than it has ever known before. In ways designed to minister to the Church and to testify to the world, He will take time for His own to give it a deeper schooling in His Word and a deeper journey into His heart.

Such intimate times call for full compliance to the will of God. As the Church grows in maturity, God will strip it of excess baggage, of outmoded habits of worship, of things of the world that have crept in, and of its name and reputation. Like an old, derelict building that needs refurbishing, all the dead, decayed, rotted, warped, and tottering human superstructure of the Church will be torn down. When God is all that is left, He can build His true Church on its one true foundation, Jesus.

Separation

A third reason for the church's pause is that God is weeding His garden. He is extracting the occult that has ferociously attacked and pushed back the lines of defense of His Church. He is pulling out cults that deify people or promote human theology. He is uprooting entire denominations that are founded on salvation by works rather than salvation by faith through grace. He is removing the mantle of power from those who strip Jesus of His names and give them to humans, such as those who take His name Intercessor, give it to His mother, Mary, a deceased mortal, and then pray to her and raise her in such honor that she takes praise and glory from Father and Son.

The list of errors could go on and on. However, unlike other times, God has drawn a line while this present generation is still living. As the Israelites excelled in the land of Goshen in contrast to the decay of Egypt, the light of the true Church will begin to shine brighter and brighter in contrast to the deepening darkness all around it. Some which have been so sure of themselves and which have been thriving on error and deception for centuries will discover their lamp is being extinguished by God's judgment. Others, after years of feebly flickering fires, will allow their wicks to be trimmed and their lamps to be cleaned and will then, perhaps for the first time, be seen as a flame of truth for Christ.

Exposure Of Sin

God will use the pause at the end of the desert trek to expose the sin that has marked the Church from earliest times until the present day: its rebellion by refusing to fully acknowledge Jesus as Lord; its presumption by promoting those doctrines that minimize what God has done for people and maximize what people will do for themselves (such as those who follow the name it and claim it, positive thinking, and prosperity movements); those that command God to perform their will; and those that deny holy justice. All of these come under the umbrella of "Christian" humanism.

As God has recalled the problem, He has also declared the solution. Although the false church system has remained unbelieving, arrogant, aloof, stiff necked, and hard hearted, the true Church is humbling itself under the mighty hand of God. Even though the false church system will not admit error or ask for forgiveness, the true Church has fallen on its knees, is calling out to God, is repenting, and is confessing its sin. As a result, it is seeing the shadow of sin replaced by a mantle of glory.

Grace

As God reviews the past with His Church, He brings up the matter of covenant. The Church of God has never been, is not now, and never will be under the covenant of law. Its relationship with God is not based on rules and regulations; rather, God's covenant with all believers, whether Jew or Gentile, is a covenant of love and grace.

Grace is God's good will. Grace is realizing His good desire. Grace is clemency or full and free forgiveness. Grace is unmerited favor, the receiving of things not deserved. Grace is the love or favorable regard of God. Grace is a service or gift freely bestowed rather than earned, a given gift rather than a granted right. Summed up by the acronym of some wise saint, grace is **G**od's **R**iches **A**t **C**hrist's **E**xpense.

Grace is also a regenerative blessing. By grace, Christ ransoms, redeems, and then sanctifies saints. Then, in extending the process, Christ, the Spirit of grace, manifests Himself through those saints to bring even more sinners to regeneration, life, salvation, and holiness. Therefore, it is not law but grace that extends the kingdom of God. It is not law but grace that sends forth workers into the harvest. It is not law but grace that accompanies the word of God to the ends of the world and gives saints the ability to do all they have been commanded to do.

Grace does work in individual saints, but to do the work of worldwide evangelism, grace works best in the whole body of saints, the true Church. Grace does bless individual spiritual soldiers, keeping them, protecting them, and guiding them, but to do the work of conquering, possessing, and occupying, it works best in the whole body of warriors, the army of God.

As has been learned, it is not God's love that distinguishes the Church from the world since, *"God so loved the world"* (John 3:16). It is both obedience to the covenant of grace and submission to the Lord of the covenant that sets the Church apart, making its light a shining witness to an evil world. This covenant of grace can only be kept by an infilling of grace to the heart of each saint and to the spirit of the sum of the saints, the Church.

God's grace is available to **all**. God sent His Son to die for **all** men, women, and children. Jesus' sacrifice paid the price for **all** sin. He took on Himself all the sins of **all** people of **all** times and suffered and died for them. Then, He arose from the dead in glorious triumph, His sacrifice having paid the full penalty for sin and having made available salvation for **all** who would call on the name of the Lord. By grace it was wrought; by faith and grace it is to be accepted. At the final accounting, no one can give the excuse that Jesus suffered for everyone but him (or her). Since **all** sin was accounted for, grace is available to **all**.

THE NEW COVENANT

At the time when every saint is born again or receives salvation, he (or she) is brought under the jurisdiction of the New Covenant. This blessed, universal, available, unchanging, holy, and perfect agreement that applies to every individual believer is also God's guarantee, pledge, and commitment to His whole Church, affecting it in at least three ways.

First, since the Church is no longer under the Law but under grace (Romans 6:14), it is no longer required to slavishly perform rites and rituals so that sin will be covered or atoned for through the blood of an animal or so that the Hebrews' unique connection or bond with God will be maintained. Under the New Covenant, the relationship with God that humanity lost in the garden of Eden is restored and sin is forgiven through the blood of Jesus. Jesus informed his disciples: *"This cup which is poured out for you is the new covenant in my blood"* (Luke 22:20).

Second, while this New Covenant restores the relationships of all redeemed believers with their God, it also changes their hearts and spirits. The Church no longer has a covenant written on stone but one inscribed in the hearts of redeemed men and women (Jeremiah 31:33). Therefore, it causes saints to obey their God because they love Him, not because they are terrified by Him. Moses, who gave the Israelites the Old Covenant, foresaw a time when *"The LORD your God will circumcise your heart and the heart of your descendants, to love the LORD your God with all your heart and with all your soul, so that you may live"* (Deuteronomy 30:6).

Third, in addition to a new heart, God gives His Church a new spirit. The words of Ezekiel 36:26 reveal this blessing to the Church: *"I will give you a new heart and put a new spirit within you...."* This quickening of people's spirits draws them closer to God's Spirit so they are enabled to know and to do His will. Thus, through the New Covenant, God's Church, firm in its relationship to Him, enlarges the kingdom of God on earth because it loves Him and is enabled to do the works that Jesus did.

THE PROMISES OF GOD

During the holy interlude in which the Church pauses to catch its breath from the desert experience, God also declares His promises. One of those promises concerns the Church's inheritance, even if it is not necessarily the one the Church is seeking or desires. The Lord is giving the Church the inheritance of spiritual land or territory, the gift of Himself, and rest.

In Western nations the Church has truly become spoiled. For far too long it has considered God its sugar daddy. It has developed the attitude that any time it makes a request, He should jump to do its bidding. It seems to have forgotten that its purpose is to love and serve Him. All too often, the Church's measure of its affection for God is not in who God is but in what He will do for it, will provide for it, or will make it to be.

It is sad but true that the Church has turned a deaf ear to the promises of God. Instead of attending to God, it has made promises to itself and then tried to tease, appease, manipulate, or control Him into accomplishing them. Now, He is commanding the Church to understand the correct order for how things work. God gives; the Church receives. God commands; the Church obeys. God executes that which **He** ordains; the Church thanks Him. God is not obligated to satisfy the Church's fleshly desires, wants, or demands. He will bring about His promises concerning the Church's inheritance, but He is not obligated to fulfill the Church's demands concerning it.

Legacy

To some degree, the Church has tried to declare and pursue its own inheritance. It has loudly screamed for such things as prosperity rather than provision and reputation rather than character. It has tried to pick and choose its legacy rather than to accept that which is offered to it by the grace of God.

And what is the Church's legacy? First, it is land. For the people of Israel, their earthly inheritance was the physical plot of ground that God had promised to Abraham. It was a natural inheritance filled with hills and valleys, fruit trees and pasturelands, meadows and streams.

However, physical, geographical land is not the Church's legacy. The Lord said saints were not to love the world or the things of the world (1 John 2:15). He declared that His kingdom was not of this world (John

18:36). He commanded His followers not to lay up treasures on this earth (Matthew 6:19). Therefore, it must be acknowledged that as God rejected the world and the systems, name, titles, or possessions it could offer Him, so must the Church.

Unfortunately, through the years some of the Church has gone into deep error. God is not interested in His Church conquering this world and then presenting it to Jesus. God has not commanded His Church to infiltrate and overcome the systems of this world, to bring them to their knees, and to cleanse them for Christ. They merely represent temporal, world order, not eternal, holy order.

God also does not want His Church immobile through unholy dedication to earthly treasures and pleasures. He wants it unattached to things of this earth. He wants it willing and ready to go anywhere at any time to serve Him. While He will graciously provide for His Church, it is not to be possessed by possessions.

God's Church must realize that while asked to live in the natural world, it is not of it. It is not to be attracted to the things of the world. It must come to know that the kingdom of God is a spiritual kingdom. Therefore, for the Church, the things it is to possess are spiritual. Like Jabez, the Church should be seeking God's blessing and seeking to enlarge its borders (1 Chronicles 4:10). Since the spiritual kingdom of God is to be extended, the Church must engage in spiritual warfare until enemy strongholds are defeated. It must then possess and occupy them until Jesus, as described in the book of Revelation, comes to take the land and to establish His kingdom.

To enable its warfare, God has given the Church a second legacy. The priesthood of God is to have the Levites' portion or God Himself as a heritage. To understand this, long ago, God created the earth as a suitable habitat for a creature called man, and He gave the first human, Adam, authority to rule it (Genesis 1:26-28). Though Adam lost this dominion to Satan when he sinned in the Garden of Eden, Satan in turn lost dominion of the earth when he killed an innocent man, Jesus. When Jesus conquered death by rising to new resurrection life, all authority was given to Him (Matthew 28:18).

While Jesus walked as a man on earth, He chose, trained, and sent out disciples into the world. They did not carry God's authority to attack and defeat the oppressive Roman government but to cast out demons, to heal the sick, and to proclaim the kingdom of God (Luke 9:1). So, too, today's disciples are not to war against other people but against demonic rulers, powers, world forces, and spiritual forces of wickedness

(Ephesians 6:12). It can only do this through the authority and power of Jesus, who is present in the Church as its heritage and strength.

God once gave His Son **for** the world (John 3:16). However, He has given His Son **to** the Church. The Church did not receive ways or methods of service as an inheritance; it did not gain forms and traditions of worship as a legacy. Instead, God gave it Jesus, the One who is to be served and worshipped.

The Church's portion is not land or buildings. Rather, its portion is the One served in these places. Its portion is not the rites and rituals by which it approaches Him. Instead, its portion is the One approached: the Lord.

Rest

As a consequence of possessing its lands and Lord, the Church will realize another portion of its inheritance: rest. God had promised rest for the Israelites when they reached the promised land (Deuteronomy 25:19). After Joshua divided the conquered territory, the Israelites did indeed enjoy a time of rest (Joshua 21:44). However, this was not the rest promised to the Church. Later, David spoke about a coming rest (Psalm 95:11), but it was not fulfilled in his day either. The writer of the book of Hebrews explains this and then tells of a rest for believers (Hebrews 4).

God worked for six days and then entered His rest (Genesis 2:2). Despite knowing of this godly example, many who heard this often failed to believe it or heed it; therefore, they did not follow God into rest. It is this rest that is awaiting the Church.

> *So there remains a Sabbath rest for the people of God. For the one who has entered His rest has himself also rested from his works, as God did from His. Therefore let us be diligent to enter that rest, so that no one will fall through following the same example of disobedience.* (Hebrews 4:9-11)

Warnings Concerning The Promises

With the review, the discussion of the covenant, and the promises of inheritance ringing in the Church's ears, God draws the desert interlude to a close with instructions and warnings.

Acknowledge God

The Church must always be aware that God is the Head of His army. Therefore, He is the commander of spiritual warfare. In these present times, if the Church is going to do as it has been instructed, it must enter into whole new realms of trust, obedience, and power. To overcome today's challenging circumstances, it needs its Lord more than ever. To cross the Jordan River, its first instruction is to:

> *Know therefore today that it is the LORD your God who is crossing over before you as a consuming fire. He will destroy them and He will subdue them before you, so that you may drive them out and destroy them quickly, just as the LORD has spoken to you.* (Deuteronomy 9:3)

Overcome Enemies

Additionally, the Church must realize that all who are not for God are against Him. Evil can present a deceptively beautiful or innocent face. No matter how things look to the natural eye or how they are heard in the natural ear, it is God's strictest command to show no mercy to any enemy.

God's enemies are not people. They are the demonic forces, followers of Satan, who hate the Lord. No Church of God is to feel sorry for these foes; rather, they are to utterly annihilate them. No covenants are to be made with them, no favor is to be shown to them, and no intermingling is to happen with them for any reason. The enemies of God are to be destroyed, not entertained.

However, it is also true that these enemies of God sometimes manifest themselves through people. Therefore, in going about its Master's business, the Church must be careful to bear in mind that it is not out to harm or destroy men, women, or children. While it hates the sin, it must love the sinner. While it disciplines and draws errant saints to repentance, it must maintain an attitude of love toward them. While it must attack and defeat the evil forces of Satan by the power of the Lord, it must be concerned for all those bound or oppressed by them.

The Occult

Further, as each individual saint was warned against witchcraft, so is the whole Church. As discussed, witchcraft is an illegal attempt to gain ungodly authority or control. It is an attempt by Satan, whether through subtlety, outright assault, or the manipulation of people, to gain unlawful supremacy over the kingdom of God.

It is sad but true that many saints at some point in their life have become ensnared by witchcraft. Whether foolishly playing with a Ouija board, having "innocent" séances, or attempting to levitate something at pajama parties, or whether knowingly and willingly seeking out fortune tellers or being guided by horoscopes, much of the body of Christ has come under the influence of and has been weakened by evil power (Galatians 5:19-21).

Unless each and every instance of involvement in witchcraft is repented of, confessed as sin, and forgiven and cleansed by the blood of Jesus, it remains an area of weakness in a saint. To the slightest or greatest degree that it affects one child of God, it affects the whole family of God. To the exact measure that it binds or hinders one saint, it binds or hinders the sum of the saints, the Church. If one or some are disabled, crippled, undermined, devitalized, debilitated, or paralyzed by witchcraft, all are.

Only the most foolhardy would deny that witchcraft is a threat to the Church. God's solemn warning against it must be heeded.

Pride

Another warning to the Church concerns pride. God hates pride. Surely then it is unwelcome and unbecoming in His bride. The Church has not been chosen because of its righteousness but because of His. It has not been called out because of what it has done but because of what He has done. It is not His body because of its superiority but because of His. The Church has no reason for pride.

Yet, in spite of God's warnings, the Church has sinned. The only way it can maintain its holiness is to exhibit behavior totally opposite the nature of pride: die to self, confess shortcomings, and ask for God's forgiveness. The strength gained from doing that will so unify and identify the Church with Christ that its enemies will know they do not face a human religion but the Lord, who has already defeated them.

THE SOUNDS OF THE TRUMPETS

It is easy to see the parallels between the Feast of Trumpets in ancient Israel and the trumpeting voice of Jesus as He speaks to each saint (Revelation 1:10). It is just as easy to see that years later, trumpets became a prophetic voice crying out to God's people in the wilderness (Isaiah 58:1) and that today they are, by inspiration of the Holy Spirit, sounding their alarm to the whole Church. Trumpets are now the voices of men and women who have been ordained into the godly office of prophet and through whom Jesus speaks to bring the message, the word, and the will of God to His people. In every way that trumpets once spoke to the Hebrews, so now He speaks to His Church.

To Assemble The People

Long ago, God sounded forth His message that His leaders were to assemble. He wanted them to lay aside differences and assemble as one body. They refused. Instead of calling God's Church into unity, they divided it by group, sect, denomination, and even personal preference in order to carry on their own sectarianism and prejudices. Perhaps Methodists would meet to iron out the differences within the many branches of their own camp or Baptists would come together to solve denominational dilemmas. However, all leaders of all denominations would not assemble, lay aside human tradition, and unite as one body under Christ. They would not meet with colleagues from other denominations or consider them enlightened if they thought or acted in a way contrary to their church system theology and doctrine. Nor would they give up manmade power bases, positions, or titles.

When earlier leadership failed the Church, God sounded both trumpets, calling all His people to assemble. After the tempering experiences in the desert, the true Church does not need to be forcibly gathered. Saints are willing – even eager – to gather, to lay down arms once raised against each other, to ask for forgiveness for their alienation and estrangement from each other, and to become one flock under the care of the Chief Shepherd.

This united assembly is not a worldly organization raised to dominate the religious community; it is not another facet of the false church's counterfeit governmental structure; it is not the false unity promised by the world that does not know God; it is not the fruit of compromise or the illusion or deception of global religious harmony under the dominion of one unholy ruler. Instead, it is the gathering of saints unified by salvation through the blood of Jesus Christ who together obey the greatest commandments: *"You shall love the Lord your God with all your heart, and with all your soul and with all your mind"* and *"You shall love your neighbor as yourself"* (Matthew 22:37,39).

This expression of holy unity evidenced in the assembly of God is a oneness of heart, a singleness of spirit. It is the merging of the Head, Jesus, and the body, the true Church, in total integrity. It is by God and for God, not by people for people.

Those in true unity are identifiable to one another by the Holy Spirit, not by organizational charts, membership rolls, and tradition. Their oneness increases as they allow Him to heal all their differences. It approaches perfection when they choose to be in agreement with God rather than just with other people.

The Church will soon realize that it is the grace of relationship to God, not to other people, that will bring it into holy unity. It will soon understand that its fleshly efforts at harmony using deception or coercion to falsely unite its branches under a worldly banner or to pressure it to conform to manmade, religious rules are absolutely useless. The hidden and as yet unperceived fact is that when the Church is in divine, graceful unity, when it truly begins to fulfill the covenant of grace, no force on the earth will be able to touch it for strength, power, and ability. It will then smash the gates of hell and send the enemy reeling. It will go on the offensive, attack the enemy, break down his strongholds, and possess and occupy his territory until Christ returns.

To Alert The People To Be Ready To Move

Another purpose for blowing trumpets was to warn of an upcoming move. Long ago in the desert, whenever the trumpets announced that the glory cloud was about to move, the whole camp prepared to move. Today, prophetic voices are alerting the Church that God is moving. The Church has too long been camped in the desert spinning its wheels in various ministries of flesh. Yet Pentecost is not all there is. Pentecost is not God's fullness. God's cloud is moving from the desert to the promised land, from Pentecost to Tabernacles.

That means it is time for the Church to choose. Those entrenched in wilderness ministries can remain in them; God will force no one to move with Him. However, for those wishing to remain in the desert, remember the Amalekites! They killed off the Israelites' stragglers. Today they are ready to do the same to the Church.

To Sound The Alarm

Also, through the blowing of trumpets, the Israelites heard the alarm for war. Today, the Church's trumpets are loudly and clearly sounding that it is time to prepare for war!

Although God gave Canaan to the Israelites, it was not an empty land. Their enemies dwelt there, some of the cruelest, filthiest, most perverted people ever to populate the earth. If that wasn't bad enough, giants also lived in Canaan.

The Church's inheritance is no different. It also must conquer enemies and face giants in its promised land. That means war. That means spiritual warfare. That means pulling down strongholds and wielding the sword of the Lord.

To Announce The Season

The Israelites also heard the trumpets announce times and seasons. They charted the feast days, and since ancient Israel was an agricultural community, they kept track of the progression of plantings and harvests.

So too with the Church. The voices of godly prophets are calling the Church to a holy season. The trumpets are signaling a time of reflection and remembrance that should lead to repentance and atonement. The Church is being brought to a season on its knees as determined prayer, fasting, and meditation brings the exposure of its error, sin, and compromise.

All of these comparisons of the Feast of Tabernacles with the prophetic voices speaking out during the interlude of the Church lead to one inescapable conclusion. God is preparing all who will hear. Something new is in the wind. Something is about to come upon both the false church system and the remnant that is the true Church.

If anything, the trumpets should make the Church aware that it is in the end season or times. The end of the ages is upon it. Long ago in Israel, the Feast of Tabernacles followed the final harvest of the year. For the Church, the final and largest harvest ever reaped is near. For that reason, the Church is facing the greatest satanic opposition ever mounted against it. Despite this, the Lord of the Harvest is still in charge.

The Church now stands on the threshold of history. No other generation has been so poised for eternity. The question is, will it arise? Will it obey? Will it submit to its Lord and do His bidding? Will it go in, possess, and occupy? Or will it, like so many earlier generations, have to be succeeded by a new generation which loves its Lord enough to do as He says – to leave the desert and to enter the promised land?

EGYPT	DESERT
Abraham's Covenant	Moses' Covenant
Passover	Pentecost
Outer Court	Inner Court
Enemy: Pharaoh	Enemy: Self
Slavery/Oppression/Bondage	Immature Freedom
Dead Works	Works of Flesh
Enforced Labor	Busy-ness
Stationary/Going Nowhere	Wandering in Circles
Enemy Over	Enemy Within
Poverty	Earnest or Down Payment
Old Adamic Nature	Fleshly/Soulish Nature
Rejection	Acceptance
Leeks and Garlic	Manna and Quail
Death	Burial
Courtship	Betrothal
Lamb	Lord
Savior/Deliverer	Master
Freedom	Carnality
Salvation	Sanctification
Egypt	Mount Sinai

BOOK 3:

THE PROMISED LAND

BOOK 3:

THE PROMISED LAND

PART VI:

CROSSING THE JORDAN

PART VI

CROSSING THE JORDAN

Chapter 16

CROSSING THE JORDAN:

THE ISRAELITES ENTERING INTO THE PROMISED LAND

For the first time in their wanderings, the children of Israel were without their old leader, Moses. They had wandered in the wilderness for forty years, and during that time the unbelieving generation died off. However, they had finally safely arrived at the Jordan River, and they were preparing to cross it.

LET GO OF THE PAST

They had arrived there as a result of following their leader, Moses. Yet, Moses had just died. The Israelites took the time to mourn his passing and to adjust their thinking to follow God's choice for his replacement. The Lord chose Joshua, a leader, warrior, and faithful spy (Deuteronomy 3:28; 31:23) as the one who would lead His people into the promised land.

Then the LORD spoke to Joshua, His new leader, and said:

Moses My servant is dead; now therefore arise, cross this Jordan, you and all this people, to the land which I am giving to them, to the sons of Israel. Every place on which the sole of your foot treads, I have given it to you, just as I spoke to Moses. (Joshua 1:2-3)

READ GOD'S WORD

He then began to issue a series of commands, all of which were vital to the success of the venture of crossing the Jordan River. First and foremost, God reminded Joshua that His Law was always to be his guide, that time was to be spent studying that law, speaking that law, and obeying that law. He also declared that all prospective prosperity or success depended on compliance to that law.

> *"This book of the law shall not depart from your mouth, but you shall meditate on it day and night, so that you may be careful to do according to all that is written in it; for then you will make your way prosperous, and then you will have success."* (Joshua 1:8)

FOLLOW GOD

Then God issued more orders, and as a good field marshal, Joshua relayed them to his officers. He first instructed them to prepare themselves, because in three days the Israelites would be crossing the river. To aid in this preparation and to alert them concerning what lay ahead, he sent spies into Canaan. Unlike those who examined the promised land a generation earlier, these men returned with a good report and an exhortation to enter in. *"They said to Joshua, 'Surely the LORD has given all the land into our hands; moreover, all the inhabitants of the land have melted away before us'"* (Joshua 2:24).

Then the camp of Israel journeyed from Shittim to the banks of the Jordan River to lodge there before crossing. At the end of three days, the orders went out: *"When you see the ark of the covenant of the LORD your God with the Levitical priests carrying it, then you shall set out from your place and go after it"* (Joshua 3:3). In so doing, the people were to keep two thousand cubits' distance from the ark so they could clearly see it and could follow wherever it led them since they had not passed that way before.

As a final preparation, Joshua commanded the people to consecrate themselves (Joshua 3:5). Only a holy people could walk in and fulfill a holy purpose, the entering of the promised land.

Then the marvelous morning arrived. The moment the Israelites had long awaited was finally upon them. The priests took up the ark and carried it ahead of the camp to the Jordan River. There, Joshua spoke to his priests: *"When you come to the edge of the waters of the Jordan, you shall stand still in the Jordan"* (Joshua 3:8).

There, Joshua spoke to his people, revealing to them that their entrance into Canaan was to be a supernatural event.

> *"By this you shall know that the living God is among you, and that he will assuredly dispossess from before you the Canaanite, the Hittite, the Hivite, the Perizzite, the Girgashite, the Amorite, and the Jebusite. Behold, the ark of the covenant of the Lord of all the earth is crossing over ahead of you into the Jordan. Now then, take for yourselves twelve men from the tribes of Israel, one man for each tribe. It shall come about when the soles of the feet of the priests who carry the ark of the LORD, the Lord of all the earth, shall rest in the waters of the Jordan, the waters of the Jordan will be cut off, and the waters which are flowing down from above will stand in one heap."* (Joshua 3:10-13)

As God said, so it happened. As God had once divided the waters of the Red Sea so the Hebrews could pass from Egypt to the desert on dry ground, so now He stopped the flow of the Jordan River so the Israelites could pass from the desert to the promised land on dry ground (Joshua 3:16). As the priests entered the river, miles upstream the flowing waters were miraculously cut off and stood up in a heap so that the priests, who didn't even get wet, were able to hold the ark of the LORD until all the Israelites passed over.

After God's promises to Abraham and Moses, after four hundred and thirty years of slavery, after forty grueling years in the desert, at long, long last, God's chosen people finally entered Canaan.

THE DAY OF ATONEMENT

Many years ago God instituted the Day of Atonement among the people of Israel (Leviticus 16; 23:26-28), According to Hebrew tradition, after the disastrous affair with the golden calf, when Moses descended Mount Sinai the second time with the rewritten tablets of the Law, he found the people of Israel fasting, praying, and repenting. This humbling day became the Day of Atonement.

This sacred day was observed every year. It was a day in which the iniquity of the people was removed. As the second part of the Feast of Trumpets, it was their most solemn day of the year. This holy day was celebrated on the tenth day of the seventh month of Tishri, which was in the fall near the time of the final harvest. It was the climax of the pondering, reflecting, and remembering that had begun with the blowing of the trumpets.

The Day of Atonement is unlike all other holy days. Rather than occurring in the home, it took place in the temple. It was a time of fasting, not feasting, and a time of penitence, humbleness, and sorrow, not of joy or celebration. It was a day of judgment, since all people, with stripped and fully exposed consciences, had to appear before holy God. It was a day of returning, since the confession of sin and the actions of the high priest reconciled the people with their God.

It was also a day of sacrifice. The law demanded sacrifice and the shedding of blood as a means of atoning for sin. To satisfy the law, on the Day of Atonement the high priest would atone for his personal sins and then, after overseeing the sacrifice of animals, make atonement for the sins of the sanctuary and altar, of the priests, and of the people. In undeviating, holy ritual, he passed through the veil between the Holy Place and the Holy of Holies, burned incense before God, and sprinkled the blood of the sacrificed animals on the mercy seat.

At first glance, this day may not seem to have any connection with the passage into the promised land, but as the Feast of Trumpets has application to the desert interlude, so the Day of Atonement has application to the crossing of the Jordan River. Looking deeper, one can see the parallels between this holy day and the Israelites' journey. The Israelites began their journey in Egypt, the land of sin. the shedding of the blood of the Passover lamb (which later took place in the outer court), they marched through the desert (which symbolized the Holy Place), crossed the Jordan River (which symbolized the veil), and entered Canaan (which symbolized the Holy of Holies).

Just as the Jordan River was a barrier that the Israelites could not go past during their forty years in the wilderness, so the veil was a barrier that the priests could not go past during the rest of the year. Since they were barriers, they both prevented the Israelites from fully worshipping God. Only after the river and the veil were passed through could free and full worship take place.

Through Moses, God had commanded Pharaoh to release His people so that they could go to worship Him. Now, in Canaan, they were free to do so. He had truly brought them out to bring them in.

Chapter 17

CROSSING THE JORDAN:

EACH SAINT ENTERING INTO GOD'S PROMISES

As all the Israelites crossed the Jordan River passing from the desert to the promised land, so must each saint who wants to be in the presence of God. As the Israelites made the dramatic change from sand and scorpions to milk and honey, so must every child of God who wants to be held in his (or her) Father's arms. However, while the journey of the people of Israel was an outward, physical passage from one land to another, the journey of each saint is an internal, spiritual one from flesh and self to spirit.

LET GO OF THE PAST

Before actually crossing the Jordan River, each saint must take a short time to prepare body, mind, and spirit for this move. As part of that preparation, he (or she) must acknowledge his leaders. He would not have been camped on the banks of the Jordan River had he not been led there by God's chosen leaders. Without question, many saints were lost in the desert: some died from harsh conditions; some would not stay with the camp and were taken by predators or scorpions; and some decided to follow their own way and are still aimlessly wandering. However, some did safely arrive at that river, and their intention is to cross it.

Some Christian leaders have been very good. Unfortunately, others have been very bad. While both varieties have taught saints about life and God, at this point in time many of the old leaders have died. Some are physically dead. Some have broken under the strain and are no longer able to lead. Some are no longer walking with God. In many cases then, a spiritual break in relationship has come about.

For many, it is time to reconcile themselves to the fact that Moses, or the old leadership, is dead. For each saint to go where God wants him (or her) to go and to do what God wants him to do, forward vision is a prerequisite. Therefore, it is occasionally necessary to allow old relationships to die or to bury the spirit of the past in order to move on to the future. If any former leader's own disobedience has forfeited his entry into a new land, he obviously cannot lead others there. Before entering the promised land, it is necessary to let God choose new leaders, bury the old in heart and mind, and then move on.

READ GOD'S WORD

While preparing to cross the Jordan River, Christians need to pay careful attention to the commands of God. Any new experience requires both diligence and obedience.

First and foremost, God commands each saint to get into and read His Word. It is there that he (or she) will learn the will and ways of God.

God gave the Israelites the Old Covenant of law, but He has given the saints His New Covenant of grace. The principles of both are found in the Bible. God wants – demands – that every saint familiarize himself (or herself) with His Word. He can only do that by personal attention or time spent reading and studying it. Many saints learn about God from a variety of other sources, such as their pastors' preaching on Sunday mornings; Christian TV or radio shows; and teaching in books, CDs, or podcasts, and they call this good enough. While these methods are helpful, they do not fulfill God's command that each should **personally** read, ponder, memorize, and meditate on His Word. No person's instruction or opinion should be a saint's primary source of knowledge about God. God desires each saint to read, learn, enjoy, and act upon His Word on a One-to-one basis.

As each saint learns the Word and, through it, the principles of the kingdom of God, that Word is always to be on his (or her) lips. It is to be the guiding light behind every conversation, the basis for every decision, and the supreme, absolute authority of life. Only as it is spoken, meditated on, and acted upon is there assurance of a blessed and successful Christian walk.

FOLLOW GOD

As God gave the Hebrews plans for their entry in to Canaan, so also He gives strategies to each saint. First, He tells each to prepare himself (or herself) for the passage. Where he is going is nothing like where he has been, and each must get ready for massive changes in his life.

Each saint who desires to follow God closely must be consecrated. Consecration means a setting apart; it is sanctification or holiness. Sin and sanctity are total opposites. Before entering the promised land, each saint must avail himself (or herself) of the continuous cleansing power of the blood of the Lamb in order to become a holy vessel fit for holy use.

This means spending time in meditation and reflection, which should lead to repentance of sin where needed. This is not the tongue-in-cheek, insincere verbal declaration of "I'm sorry" by an unbroken heart which is hoping that the undiscerning will feel sorry for him (or her) and restore all his responsibilities and privileges so he can go on sinning. True repentance is the realization of error and the desire to make it right as declared from a broken and contrite heart or spirit.

Those saints who want to follow God also experience testing. As He did with Abraham, sometimes God will ask a saint to walk by faith, not knowing where he (or she) is going (Genesis 12:1). At other times, God will allow the saint to spy out the land, so to speak, to give him a glimpse or vision of the future. His purpose in doing so is to inform each saint where he is going and what awaits him there. It is also to see if any rebellion remains that would cause a saint to refuse to enter once again. Those who see the new land with God's eyes and who are anxious to go there pass the test.

Those who have passed God's test and who are ready to cross the Jordan River must then let God go ahead of them. God commanded all the Israelites that when they saw the ark of the covenant move they were to set out and follow it (Joshua 3:3). He now declares that when a saint sees the Lord move, he (or she) is to set out and follow Him.

First, each saint must **set out.** If God is moving, anyone who chooses not to follow Him will lose sight of Him. When He moves, no matter how delightful or comfortable a saint's present circumstances or how much control he (or she) has over them, he must either give them up and move on with God or find himself out of the presence of God. This means that there is no point in staying behind and hallowing a spot where God was. Each saint who reverences His presence must walk right behind Him in order to be where He is, to maintain his place, and to keep in living relationship to God.

Next, each saint must **follow**. In any journey, God must always go ahead. The priests of Israel carried God in an ark and the people followed; today each saint or priest carries Him in his heart. If God does not lead the way or precede a saint to those places he has never been before, that saint should not go there. If God is not in a place, neither should His child be. The order from God has never been, "Lead Me!" Rather, it has always been, "Follow Me!" (Matthew 16:24; Luke 9:59; John 10:27).

Finally, each saint must follow **Him**. One particular denomination advances the error which declares that one man, known as the pope, is infallible. To those who believe this, it means that he can make no mistakes concerning doctrine. On a much smaller scale, that same error is creeping into the born-again Church. Saints are now being told that one person, usually the pastor of a local assembly, can do no wrong. He (or she) has been given all authority, makes all decisions, and often dictates all religious as well as personal decisions of his people. Saints are instructed to do whatever he says, to go wherever he leads, and not to question him. Yet, nowhere in Scripture is such total power or control given to a person. In fact, the Bible clearly says that saints are to obey God alone if a person, even a powerful religious leader, is leading him into error (Acts 5:29).

It should be apparent to even the most timid of saints that if a so-called leader does not bear the presence of God and does not lead saints into the presence of God, that person is a counterfeit or a fraud. No matter now well known, manipulative, or intimidating he (or she) is, no matter how closely he resembles an angel of light, if a saint cannot by his spirit sense God in Him, he (or she) should never, never follow him – and he will be accountable before God if he does so. The order is to follow God and none other.

When preparations are complete, it is time for each saint to step forward. The work of salvation and deliverance marked by his (or her) exodus from sin and water baptism through the Red Sea at the beginning of his journey is now followed by the blessings of death to self marked by his passage through the Jordan River at the end of his desert trek. Thus, as God leads, so each saint must follow Him, cross his Jordan River, and emerge on the far side into the outstretched arms of the everlasting and merciful God.

THE DAY OF ATONEMENT

All of this should remind Christians of the Day of Atonement. It was the day the high priest passed through the veil into the Holy of Holies to atone for the sins of the people.

Under the New Covenant, although no longer a yearly ritual, atonement is yet a required biblical principle. It is so important it cannot wait until one particular day of the year; instead, it must be ever ongoing. Nor can it be bound to the imperfections of a human high priest; instead, Jesus is now the perfect High Priest of each saint's atonement.

For the Israelites, the Law declared that atonement for sin required the annual shedding of blood of a sacrificial animal and the sprinkling of that blood by the high priest before the mercy seat in the Holy of Holies. Jesus is the fulfillment of both requirements. He was the sacrificial Lamb slain for the sins of all people (John 1:29; Revelation 5:6). His blood was shed in a sacrifice so complete that any further attempt to repeat or imitate the sacrifice of the cross became the grossest of sin (Hebrews 10:12). He, as High Priest, also carried His blood to the Holy of Holies in God's heavenly sanctuary and sprinkled it there for the cleansing of flesh (Hebrews 9:11-14). (See also Hebrews 7-10).

The symbolism of passing through a veil is highly significant to those who are born again. In the Old Testament, the high priest had to pass through a veil of cloth to enter the Holy of Holies in the tabernacle or the temple to be in the presence of God. In the New Testament, each saint must still pass through a veil to enter the presence of God. However, rather than a veil of cloth, this veil is the flesh or the sacrificed body of the High Priest, Jesus. In other words, Jesus is the veil (Hebrews 10:19-20). He is the only entrance or passageway into the presence of God. He is the only entry into Heaven.

For each saint to follow Him, he (or she) must pass through that same veil of flesh. This is called dying to self. It happens when each saint has come out of the world of sin, has crossed and reached the end of the dry, barren desert of flesh, and has come to the end of himself on the bank of the Jordan River. There, having willingly decided to cross, he steps into the water and walks to the other side. Spiritually, this is symbolic of his passage through the veil of flesh. When he turns in repentance to the Lord, the veil is stripped off and taken away in Christ (2 Corinthians 3:14-16), and then he finds himself in the presence of God.

For those who would flippantly eliminate the requirement of repentance and dash to the Jordan River for a self-determined cleansing and presumptive entry into the promised land, please remember that all of the Israelites had to follow God. They had to follow when, as, and where God, not self, led. Dear saint, self cannot instigate a death to self; only God can. Wait on Him with prayer and fasting. When He moves, follow Him. Let Him lead you through your Jordan River.

It is significant that Jesus was baptized by John in the Jordan River to fulfill all righteousness (Matthew 3:13-17). At that same time and place the Holy Spirit visibly descended on Jesus in the form of a dove. In like manner, when each saint is baptized in water he (or she) is cleansed and receives the righteousness of Christ. When he is baptized in the Holy Spirit, he receives the earnest or down payment of his inheritance in the Holy Spirit. As he then proceeds, crosses the Jordan River, and enters the promised land, he comes into the fullness of life in the Spirit.

The passage through the Jordan River is meant to be a special time for each saint. Just as the crossing was a supernatural passage for the whole nation of Israel, so it is a divine and holy event for each saint. It is passage from flesh to spirit. It is death to self in order to live for and serve God. It is passing through the veil and being so awestruck and overcome in the presence of God that a saint can only fall on his (or her) knees, humble himself further by falling on his face, and cry out to his Lord, "Not my will, but Yours be done!"

Chapter 18

CROSSING THE JORDAN:

THE CHURCH ENTERING INTO GOD'S PROMISES

By now the pattern should be firmly established. What the Israelites did, each saint and the Church must do. The Hebrews were commanded to cross the Jordan River; each saint has to cross the Jordan River; and the Church or the assembly of saints must also cross the Jordan River.

At this point in Church history, there does not seem to be a large, jostling crowd assembling on the bank of the river. Long ago, by taking a census, it was noted that approximately six hundred thousand Israelites marched into the promised land (Numbers 26:51). Much later, God called a small number of people out of the Jewish-Gentile world to follow Jesus. Although He touched the lives of everyone around Him, only one hundred twenty disciples were praying when the Holy Spirit launched the Church. Over the years and centuries, God has watched as a counterfeit church system has developed, grown, rivaled, and then surpassed His own Church in numbers. It has been such a successful deception that the true Church is but a remnant in comparison. Yet this remnant must cross the Jordan River.

Numbers have never threatened God. He is able to save the few as well as the many. In fact, He has several times decreased numbers rather than increased them in order to find that true, dedicated, committed body of servants whose total dependence is on Him (Judges 7:1-8; 2 Chronicles 25:5-9). It is this dependent remnant that is now coming together at the Jordan River to begin final preparation for crossing over.

LET GO OF THE PAST

First on God's agenda is for the Church to realize, as each saint had to do, that the past is dead. Some of its members will indeed choose to continue to wander in the desert and some will come to the Jordan River and refuse to cross. However, for those willing and determined to go on, yesterday is gone. God is doing a new thing with and among His people. The Church cannot indulge in prolonged reminiscences about past glories. Its instructions are to look and to move forward. Lot's wife didn't make it because she looked back (Genesis 19:26), and neither will the Lord's bride.

One thing which the Church must release into oblivion is its traditional obedience to Mosaic law. Although Jesus came to bring a New Covenant, a great number of those calling themselves by His name are yet chained to the old one. The priestly vestments, the church buildings' floor plans, the Sunday morning worship rituals, and the leaders' lack of Christ-like grace confirm this fact.

The Mosaic Covenant was the vehicle which maintained the status quo, caused everyone to worship ritualistically in one way, established tradition as the norm, and controlled the religious community. While it served its purpose admirably in the dispensation it was meant for, its carryover into the Church has brought spiritual death.

Those insisting on remaining locked in the past have kept the Church from moving forward. They have kept it from entering the promised land. Unless the true Church renounces obedience to the Old Covenant of law under the leadership of the disciples of Moses as its primary reason for being, and unless it accepts both the New Covenant and the new leadership whose every intention is to follow God across the Jordan River into the new land, it will never arrive at the place where God wants it to be. If it will not yield or give up old ground, it will never be given new. It is the Church's Joshuas, not its Moseses, who have been chosen by God to lead it in new ways and in new power to new places.

READ GOD'S WORD

When the Israelites had gathered at the banks of the Jordan River, it was the only obstacle left before they could cross over into the promised land. To keep and protect them once they got there, they were commanded to be in constant touch with God through His Word. That same instruction applies to the Church. Concerning His Word, John 1:1,14 says:

In the beginning was the Word, and the Word was with God, and the Word was God ... And the Word became flesh, and dwelt among us, and we saw His glory, glory as of the only begotten from the Father, full of grace and truth.

God has sent His Word, Jesus, among His people, the Church. Jesus is the living embodiment of God's written Word; everything in the Bible points to Him. He who is the living Lord is also the living Word who abides as the authority over every Christian and over all the Church.

It is important to note that the Bible is **God's** Word. While many godly versions or translations of that one Word exist, each version is the whole and complete Word of God. If any group claims its has its own separate Bible, has a sectarian, humanist version of the Bible, or has received later revelations that it then added to the Bible, it either is in grievous error or is a cult. If any group wants to prove its theology using its own study books or "bible," that group may be presenting or promoting **a** word, but it is not **the** Word of God. It is therefore false.

God's Word is truth (John 17:17). Its purpose is to teach, reprove, correct, or train in righteousness (2 Timothy 3:16). It is living, active, and sharp, it divides soul and spirit, and it is able to judge the heart (Hebrews 4:12). In addition, the Word of God is not imprisoned (2 Timothy 2:9).

While space prevents but a cursory glance at the wonder, depth, grandeur, and glory of the Word of God, it must be stated that God's Church must live by His Word. The Bible is to be read, studied, sowed, and preached. It is one of the chief weapons against the wiles of Satan (Ephesians 6:11-18). Without it, the Church cannot stand. It is no wonder that one of God's strongest commendations came to the Church that kept His Word: *"I know your deeds. Behold, I have put before you an open door which no one can shut, because you have a little power, and have kept My word, and have not denied My name"* (Revelation 3:8).

FOLLOW GOD

For two millennia God has been forming, fitting, arranging, developing, training, qualifying, and readying His Church. The Church's ultimate purpose has always been union with God, the bride with her Bridegroom. As long as the Church has been content to dally in the desert, marriage has not been possible. Now those from His body who have been sent ahead to check the land are returning to report that the time is right, that all is ready. The Church is now shutting its ears to the world and to the false religious system whose voice has for so long discouraged it from crossing. However, now it is opening its ears and hearing the voice of the One who is encouraging it to cross into Canaan. Putting its fears and rebellion aside, it is determining to honor God by coming into His presence.

God's remnant has learned it cannot lead itself. History has proven and re-proven the fallacy of that. The change in the true Church is quite startling as it learns the joy of yielding. It is content to let God lead. It is listening for the voice of its Beloved and watching for His signal to come unto Him. For years, it has heard itself called the bride of Christ but never experienced the reality of it. Crossing the Jordan River is a way the Church has not passed before, and every moment on the adventure is precious.

Yet, in its excitement, the Church must be careful; it must follow only Him. Many voices of false gods, teachers, and prophets are seeking to deceive it, and many ministries of flesh are trying to divert it. All of this is an attempt to keep the Church from union with Jesus. It must turn its eyes upon Him and follow only Him.

THE DAY OF ATONEMENT

Best of all, the Church is learning the value of consecration. As the bride of Christ, the Church knows it is not fully prepared to approach its Bridegroom if it bears even the hint of spot or wrinkle (Ephesians 5:25-27).

A bride is often adorned in a lovely white gown and veil, which are symbols of her purity. However, her true concern in preparation for marriage should not be with the externals of dress or flowers, food or music. Her true preparation should be an internal readying of herself for her groom. This means a willingness to submit and obey. This means a readiness to forever honor and revere her beloved. This means an eagerness to take his name, to bear it proudly, and to love and serve him in whatever way she can.

God has long been watching His bride prepare herself. She has endlessly stood preening before a mirror, admiring her own reflection. Gowned in splendor and adorned in precious jewels, she is lovely to look at. The problem is that her eyes have been on herself rather than on her Beloved. She has kept her heart for herself rather than offering it to Him.

For the bride of Christ to be as beautiful inwardly as she is outwardly, two things need to happen. First, she must make a deliberate determination, a choice of will, to take her eyes off herself and to seek her Lord. Second, she must die to self. She, the bride of Christ, must enter the Jordan River and allow Jesus to lift the bridal veil, that which has covered her eyes and dimmed her vision. Only by doing this can she enter the presence of her Beloved.

This preparation for marriage leads the bride, the Church, directly to a day of atonement. To the Israelites, the Day of Atonement was a time of corporate cleansing. It was the day that the high priest went beyond the veil, entered the Holy of Holies, and sprinkled the sacrificial blood before the mercy seat to atone for his sins and those of the whole congregation. To the Church, a day of atonement is a time of cleansing in preparation for its marriage to the Lord. The Church as a whole needs to repent and atone for its sins through the cleansing blood of Christ. It also needs to cleanse its sanctuary and make it ready for its Lord. As long as the Church remains weak, apostate, materialistic, sexually promiscuous, and idolatrous, there will never be divine union.

Each saint has to allow God to cleanse his (or her) temple. Likewise, the sum of the saints or the Church, as the dwelling place of God, must also permit itself to be cleansed. That requires a solemn time in which all its sins are repented of, confessed, and forgiven. It also requires that the Church avail itself of the sacrifice of its High Priest, Jesus, who has entered through the veil and sprinkled His blood on the mercy seat. When the Church has done that, it will see its own veil of flesh removed so that it can see to freely enter the presence of God.

This humble walk does not seem to be the path that much of the Church has chosen. The counterfeit church system is so engrossed in boasting of triumphant, sweeping, personal glory that it cannot hear God's still, small voice. It has forgotten one of God's principles, that death must precede life. As the grain of wheat has to drop in the ground and die before resurrection to new life (John 12:24), so must the Church. It needs to stop seeking glory and to realize that victory and holy life do not come by self-proclamations of greatness but by yielding self to the death of the cross.

This means that preparation for life as a bride is really preparation for death to self. This is a death in which the bride foregoes all desire to be served but instead chooses to serve, in which she no longer competes with her groom but magnifies Him, in which she ceases trying to subjugate Him but instead submits to Him. It is a death in which her present barrenness will yield to fruitfulness.

The Church must die to all things that have kept it in the desert: self-government, self-will, self-service, self-gratification, self-confidence, self-adulation, and self-ambition. It must die to all things which keep it concerned with itself rather than with God.

What a special day it will be when the body of Christ gathers at its spiritual Jordan River! All over the world, those in one spirit with God will unite as one body and cry out for the veil of flesh to be removed. At God's command, holy leaders and priests will lead the true Church to the river, across the river, and into the promised land. By prayer, fasting, and repentance, by willingness to go forward, the Church will be in the presence of God.

Then, as the Church proceeds on its journey, it will suddenly discover its victory is that it no longer cares for self anymore. Its every thought, dream, and action will center on the Lord. Its every desire will be for Him.

By walking in His footsteps, by humbling itself, by dying to self, by giving up its life for His, the body of Christ will be brought into deeper relationship, a more manifest presence of God, and greater resurrection life. it will truly become a bride without spot or wrinkle. When the veil is taken away, God's bride will truly be one with Him.

It must also be remembered that crossing the Jordan River was a supernatural event for the Israelites because God caused the river's water to pile up so the people could cross on dry ground. Just so, when Jesus died in flesh to flesh, supernatural occurrences accompanied His sacrifice that bless each saint. For instance, after His death, the curtain or veil of the temple was torn in two, literally and symbolically allowing each child of God into His presence (Matthew 27:51). Therefore, the whole Church's passage from self-life to death to life in the spirit will also be a supernatural occurrence. The world will look on in amazement and the false church system will look on in mockery and distain as the true Church or bride of Christ enters the presence of her Lord.

Church, hasn't the betrothal dragged on an awfully long time? Haven't we held things up long enough? Can't we call out to Jesus and ask Him to remove our veil? Don't we realize that when He does so our vision will improve, that we will be able to view things more clearly, that the very first thing we see will be the wonderful, beautiful face and the deep, wise, lovely eyes of our Beloved?

Isn't it time to cross the Jordan River?

PART VII:

THE PROMISED LAND

PART VII.

THE PROMISED LAND

Chapter 19

THE PROMISED LAND:

THE ISRAELITES' UNION WITH THE LORD

And so, the unbelievable happened. That which had long been dreamed of, promised, and sought after actually occurred. The Israelites entered Canaan. A people long used to wandering finally came home.

In order to understand the magnitude of the difference between life in the desert and in Canaan, it is necessary to comprehend just what the promised land was. To begin with, Canaan was the **promised** land. It was a land promised to Abraham and his descendants through Isaac by none other than God Himself. God is the Creator of the heavens and the earth, therefore He is sovereign over all. All residents of His creation are subject to His authority. He has every right to place nations and peoples wherever He so chooses. It was God, not people or governments, who gave Canaan to the Israelites as an everlasting possession.

> *Now when Abram was ninety-nine years old, the LORD appeared to Abram and said to him, ... "I will give to you and to your descendants after you, the land of your sojournings, all the land of Canaan, for an everlasting possession...."* (Genesis 7:1,8)

> *"I am God Almighty; be fruitful and multiply; a nation and a company of nations shall come from you, and kings shall come forth from you. The land which I gave to Abraham and Isaac, I will give it to you, and I will give the land to your descendants after you."* (Genesis 35:11-12)

Also, Canaan was the promised **land**. It was an actual, physical, geographical landmass. Canaan was the land promised to the Israelites.

Although it took its name from an evil man and was occupied by the enemies of God, it was a place covenanted to God's chosen ones. Further, although Abraham had several sons, God's covenant concerning the land did not apply to Esau, the son of flesh, but only to Isaac, the son of promise, and to the heirs of Isaac's son, Jacob, who was renamed Israel (Genesis 32:28). Two passages from Genesis make this point clear:

> *But God said, "No, but Sarah your wife will bear you a son, and you shall call his name Isaac; and I will establish My covenant with him for an everlasting covenant for his descendants after him. As for Ishmael, I have heard you; behold, I will bless him, and will make him fruitful, and will multiply him exceedingly. He shall become the father of twelve princes, and I will make him a great nation.* **But My covenant I will establish with Isaac....**" [emphasis added] (Genesis 17:19-21)

> *And behold, the LORD stood above it and said, "I am the LORD, the God of your father Abraham and the God of Isaac; the land on which you lie, I will give it to you and to your descendants. Your descendants will also be like the dust of the earth, and you will spread out to the west and to the east and to the north and to the south; and in you and in your descendants shall all the families of the earth be blessed. Behold, I am with you, and will keep you wherever you go, and will bring you back to this land; for I will not leave you until I have done what I have promised you." Then Jacob awoke from his sleep and said, "Surely the LORD is in this place, and I did not know it."* (Genesis 28:13-16)

THE PROMISED LAND WAS....

As the promised land, Canaan was a land of newness. Living there brought a new way of life, from nomadic wanderers to settled farmers. Living there brought a new type of government, from judge or prophet to king. Living there brought a new way of serving God. Worship changed from the ritual of Moses' Tabernacle to the spontaneous joy of David's Tabernacle to the grandeur of Solomon's Temple.

Canaan was a permanent place. Here the Israelites could send down roots, for they were done with their desert wanderings. Here temporary shelters gave way to permanent dwellings, tents to homes. Here crops could be both planted and harvested since there was no need to be constantly on the move.

Canaan was a fruitful place. Here sand and dry wadis gave way to rich forests and flowing streams. Manna and quail were succeeded by milk and honey (Numbers 13:27). Grains, corn, and olives grew profusely, and a cluster of grapes required two men to carry it (Numbers 13:23). This richness not only provided food and shelter for people, but it blessed animals as well. Herds of cows, oxen, sheep, goats, and donkeys were cared for by nomads in mountains or valleys, meadows or plains.

Canaan was a land of fulfillment for both people and God. In Canaan, the men and women who had once been overcome became the overcomers; the defeated became the victorious. In Canaan, the Israelites received their inheritance, the land they were to conquer, possess, and occupy. In Canaan, the Israelites came into a short time of rest (Joshua 22:4).

Concerning the fulfillment of God, in Canaan, God's people were separated from the sin of Egypt and the self of the desert, which they had left behind. Here, God could communicate with His chosen ones, a people set aside to worship only Him.

BUILD AN ALTAR

Before the Israelites entered Canaan, Moses warned them concerning the importance of honoring the commands of God.

> *Then Moses and the elders of Israel charged the people, saying, "Keep all the commandments which I command you today. So it shall be on the day when you shall cross the Jordan to the land which the LORD your God gives you, that you shall set up for yourself large stones and coat them with lime and write on them all the words of this law, when you cross over, so that you may enter the land which the LORD your God gives you, a land flowing with milk and honey, as the LORD, the God of your fathers, promised you. So it shall be when you cross the Jordan, you shall set up on Mount Ebal, these stones ... Moreover, you shall build there an altar to the LORD your God, an altar of stones; you shall not wield an iron tool on them. You shall build the altar of the LORD your God of uncut stones, and you shall offer on it burnt offerings to the LORD your God; and you shall sacrifice peace offerings and eat there, and rejoice before the LORD your God. You shall write on the stones all the words of this law very distinctly."* (Deuteronomy 27:2-8)

As soon as the crossing was complete, the Israelites settled in a place called Gilgal, where some important events took place. First, as a reminder for the future generations, Joshua called for the building of a memorial. He had one man from each tribe take a stone out of the Jordan River, and he commanded that an altar be made from those stones (Joshua 4:8, 20-24). Then, going one step further, he commanded that stones from Canaan be put in the Jordan River to mark the place where the priests who had held the ark had been standing (Joshua 4:9). Thus, the Israelites' first acts in the promised land were to humble themselves before their God, to build altars, and to worship Him.

BE CIRCUMCISED

A second thing that happened to the Israelites at Gilgal was pain. When God had made His covenant with Abraham, the seal of that agreement was the circumcision of all males in Israel (Genesis 17:10-11). Throughout the long desert trek, the rite had not been kept. However, now the command came: *"Make for yourself flint knives and circumcise again the sons of Israel the second time"* (Joshua 5:2). So Joshua did as God commanded.

What a test of obedience and trust this was! Humanly speaking, circumcising grown men is a very painful process, one that requires a long and uncomfortable period of recovery. Militarily speaking, circumcision at that time must have seemed like the most foolhardy of acts. To have all but incapacitated the army of Israel just after invading the land teeming with enemies was to invite disaster. Yet the purpose of the test was to show God's sovereignty and care for His chosen ones. At this critical time, He supernaturally defended a helpless people. Responding to their obedience, God instilled such fear into the kings of the Ammonites and Canaanites that their hearts melted and they lost their no fighting spirit (Joshua 5:1). Instead of attacking the Israelites when they were weakest, they did nothing, thus proving the Israelites were the strongest.

CELEBRATE THE FEAST OF PASSOVER

A third occurrence at Gilgal was the first observance of Passover in the promised land. The Israelites passed through the Jordan River on the tenth day of the first month (Joshua 4:19). On the fourteenth day, they commemorated the breaking of Pharaoh's power and their exodus from Egypt (Joshua 5:10). The next day, they ate unleavened bread made from the produce of the land (Joshua 5:11). The day following that, the manna ceased; the Israelites were now responsible for their own food supply as it was provided in Canaan (Joshua 5:12).

ENGAGE IN WARFARE

Then, as a prelude to future conquest, God did a magnificent thing. Years earlier He had introduced Himself to Moses in a supernatural way, meeting him on the mountain, speaking to him from a burning bush, and introducing Himself as I AM WHO I AM, the LORD, the God of Abraham, the God of Isaac, and the God of Jacob (Exodus 3:1-15). To a people desperately needing to be loved and cared for, He, their LORD, would be a loving God, the compassionate fountain of life who was concerned for His downtrodden children. In an equally meaningful way, God now made Himself known to Moses' successor, Joshua. Realizing that the people of Israel were about to undergo a seven-year military campaign and that they would need a powerful, wise commander, He again introduced Himself, but this time He used a new name, one that would meet the present need.

> *Now it came about when Joshua was by Jericho, that he lifted up his eyes and looked, and behold, a man was standing opposite him with his sword drawn in his hand, and Joshua went to him and said to him, "Are you for us or for our adversaries?" He said, "No; rather I indeed come now as captain of the host of the LORD." And Joshua fell on his face to the earth, and bowed down, and said to him, "What has my lord to say to his servant?" The captain of the LORD'S host said to Joshua, "Remove your sandals from your feet, for the place where you are standing is holy." And Joshua did so.* (Joshua 5:13-15)

Immediately after this, the Israelites plunged into warfare to take the land promised to them by God. With some difficulty, they learned and submitted to God's will and ways. The first rule that they learned in their warfare was not to depend on their natural senses but on belief in God. Jericho was tightly shut; no one went out or in (Joshua 6:1). As such, it was considered impregnable. Yet, no matter how the Israelites viewed the situation, God saw it with a different eye and communicated His vision to His people. He said to Joshua, *"See, I have given Jericho into your hand...."* (Joshua 6:2).

As before in the matter of circumcision, when the fear of the LORD preceded and governed obedience, God worked miracles. In the most unlikely of battle plans, the priests and armed men walked around the city, accompanying the ark of the LORD. On the seventh day, when the priests blew the trumpets, the armed men shouted in response, and invincible Jericho literally fell to the army of the LORD (Joshua 6:3-21).

A second principle of warfare is interdependence, the awareness that one person's behavior affects the whole army. When the Israelites invaded Canaan, they entered the land of the Amorites. The Amorites were a rebellious people, and that rebellion rubbed off on the Israelites. God had placed the city of Jericho under a ban (Joshua 6:17-18). That meant that no once could take the spoils of war since everything and everyone in the city had been declared holy to the LORD and therefore belonged to God. The Israelites had been specifically warned that there was danger in violating the ban. Even so, one young man, Achan, disobeyed God's order. He took silver, gold, and clothing from Jericho and hid them in his tent. By so doing, he robbed God (Joshua 7:20-21).

As a result, when the army of Israel next approached the city of Ai to conquer and destroy it, they met with disaster. The Israelites lost the battle and thirty-six brave men (Joshua 7:4-5). Their only salvation was that their leader sought the LORD. After God revealed the problem of Achan's sin, and after godly discipline was carried out, order was restored. The price of rebellion was steep, as one man's actions tragically and adversely affected all.

Following this, the Israelites took Ai and then continued to Mount Ebal. There, in obedience to God's command, Joshua built an altar to the LORD (Deuteronomy 27:4), offered sacrifices, and wrote the law of Moses on the altar stones. Then, with all the Israelites present, he read God's Word with its blessings and curses. Everyone in the promised land, from elder to officer to judge to priest to Levite to soldier to woman to child heard the law of the land.

Next, the Israelites quickly crossed Canaan from east to west, driving a wedge between the northern and southern sections. Turning their attention first to the south, Joshua fought and defeated the confederacy of Amorite kings aided by supernatural forces, giant hailstones, and the sun standing still (Joshua 10:11-13).

> *Thus Joshua struck all the land, the hill country and the Negev and the lowland and the slopes and all their kings. He left no survivor, but he utterly destroyed all who breathed, just as the LORD, the God of Israel, had commanded ... Joshua captured all these kings and their lands at one time, because the LORD, the God of Israel, fought for Israel.* (Joshua 10:40,42).

After a respite in the camp of Gilgal, it was time to address the situation in the north. Here the enemies were the Canaanites, Amorites, Hittites, Perizzites, Jebusites, Hivites, and the Gergashites (Joshua 24:11). Once more, obedience brought victory.

> *Joshua captured all the cities of these kings, and all their kings, and he struck them with the edge of the sword, and utterly destroyed them; just as Moses the servant of the LORD had commanded. However, Israel did not burn any cities that stood on their mounds, except Hazor alone, which Joshua burned. All the spoil of these cities and the cattle, the sons of Israel took as their plunder; but they struck every man with the edge of the sword, until they had destroyed them. They left no one who breathed. Just as the LORD had commanded Moses his servant, so Moses commanded Joshua, and so Joshua did; he left nothing undone of all that the LORD had commanded Moses.* (Joshua 11:12-15)

Additionally, Joshua defeated the giants. He attacked those called the Anakim in the hill country of Israel and Judah, cut them off, and destroyed their cities until none were left in the land (Joshua 11:21). The result of all this conquest was not just victory but inheritance and rest (Joshua 11:23).

After doing all that the LORD had said to do, after all ungodly enemies had been defeated, Joshua oversaw the division of the promised land among the tribes of Israel. Excluding the tribes of Reuben, Gad, and the half tribe of Manasseh, which had chosen to dwell east of the Jordan River, and the tribe of Levi, which received God as its part, every son of every tribe was given a portion of land. Each one received his inheritance just as God had promised.

> *So the LORD gave Israel all the land which he had sworn to give to their fathers, and they possessed it and lived in it. And the LORD gave them rest on every side, according to all that He had sworn to their fathers, and no one of all their enemies stood before them; the LORD gave all their enemies into their hand.* (Joshua 21:43-44)

Shortly before Reuben, Gad, and Manasseh departed to their own land, the whole congregation assembled at a place called Shiloh and set up the tent of meeting (Joshua 18:1). For a long time, this was the religious center of the land.

KNOW GOD'S WORD

Looking back at the time of warfare and the conquering of Canaan, one key occurrence needs to be studied further. When the second battle of Ai had been fought and won, the Israelites made a second altar to God, offered sacrifices on it, and wrote the Law of Moses on its stones (Deuteronomy 27:4). Then, as every member of the Israelites, from the youngest to the oldest, stood before Mount Gerizim and Mount Ebal, Joshua blessed them and read the Law, with its blessings and curses, to them.

Joshua did this so everyone – all the men, women, children – would know both the covenant and the God of Israel. Since all had heard Joshua as he read the Law aloud and since all had learned of the blessings for those who honored it and the curses for those who did not, no one could later claim ignorance of the Law. They were without excuse if they violated God's covenant.

Joshua also read the Law to proclaim the authority of God over the land. Since the previous owners of the land worshipped pagan deities, these false gods had been in authority over the land. However, with the LORD fighting on behalf of the Israelites, these pagan peoples and deities were soon conquered and removed from the land. The Israelites took possession of the land, nullified the pagan laws, and declared the Law of God to be sovereign. Holy Law was now the law of the land.

Time passed with the Israelites occupying the land of Canaan. Then Joshua called all the Israelites together for his farewell address. Much as Moses had done before him, Joshua began by reviewing the Israelites' past. He then talked of their military success and of the division of the land. He exhorted his people to remain true to God and to do all that was written in the book of the law. He also warned them:

> "So take diligent heed to yourselves to love the LORD your God. For if you ever go back and cling to the rest of these nations, these which remain among you, and intermarry with them, so that you associate with them, and they with you, know with certainty that the LORD your God will not continue to drive these nations out from before you; but they shall be a snare and a trap to you, and a whip on your sides and thorns in your eyes, until you perish from off this good land which the LORD your God has given you." (Joshua 23:11-13)

Next, after exalting God as Savior, Lord, and Commander,

Joshua's now famous words rang out:

> "Now, therefore, fear the LORD and serve Him in sincerity and truth; and put away the gods which your fathers served beyond the River and in Egypt, and serve the LORD. If it is disagreeable in your sight to serve the LORD, choose for yourselves today whom you will serve; whether the gods which your fathers served which were beyond the River, or the gods of the Amorites in whose land you are living; but as for me and my house, we will serve the LORD." (Joshua 24:14-15)

Following the declaration of the Israelites to serve the LORD (Joshua 24:21), Joshua wrote their covenant in the book of the law of God (Joshua 24:26). He then dismissed the company to return to their homes, and then he died.

The Israelites' rest didn't last long. Problems soon arose. To even the most unstudied observer, these difficulties were a direct result of the people's inability or unwillingness to obey God. Time and again they had been commanded to follow God, take the land, possess it, and occupy it. They were to show no mercy on the heathen, the entrenched, sinful dwellers of the promised land. However, the tribes of Judah and Benjamin didn't drive out the Jebusites (Joshua 15:63; Judges 1:21), and the tribes of Ephraim and Manasaah didn't drive out the Canaanites (Joshua 16:10; 17:12). Neither did Zebulun, Asher, Naphtali, or Dan conquer the enemies in their lands (Judges 1:30-34). As a result of their disobedience, decline set in.

REJECT APOSTASY

Unfortunately, rebellion was not the sum of the Israelites' sins. The people ignored Joshua's warning and began to serve the Baals. Further, they intermingled with the peoples of the nations surrounding them, who they should have conquered and destroyed. Since they did not do right before God, His hand came heavily against them (Judges 2).

As their apostasy worsened, the LORD raised up a long series of adversaries and judges to deal with His people (e.g. Judges 3; 4; 11). In His mercy, whenever His children called out to Him in repentance, He would move, and, by the power of His hand, He would judge and destroy the foe and would save the Israelites from their affliction. However, no sooner were they saved than they once again returned to their evil ways.

Even the priesthood did not honor God (1 Samuel 2:12-17; 8:1-

3). In fact, the priesthood became so evil it was directly responsible for the loss of the Ark of the Covenant or the presence of God among His chosen people (1 Samuel 4). Two priests, Hophni and Phineas, took the ark onto the battlefield with no godly authorization to do so and lost it to the Israelites' archenemy, the Philistines. When this happened, Ichabod, which means the glory has departed from Israel, was written over God's chosen ones (1 Samuel 4:21-22).

Although the ark was eventually returned to the Israelites, the presence of God remained away. Even so, the Israelites, not yet finished with apostasy, committed another horrible sin. Chosen and separated by God, they had not remained a separate people. Called to be a testimony of His greatness, they had become a manifestation of their own evil. Not accepting the call to be different in the midst of an evil world, the Israelites desired to be like the other nations (1 Samuel 8:5). Specifically, they rejected the LORD as their leader and demanded a human king.

As a result of their own willfulness and rebellion, the Israelites lost the blessings of God. However God, wholly merciful, didn't turn His back on them. Instead, He gave them exactly what they asked for.

Saul, a descendant of a mighty man of valor (1 Samuel 9:1), was the people's choice for king. Since there was no taller or more handsome man in all of Israel (1 Samuel 9:2), he, by outward appearance, met the people's requirement for kingship. Yet Saul was also God's choice for king; he was the right man to teach the people a very hard lesson. Anointed into the office of king, he began to rule the LORD'S inheritance well. He engaged in battle with the Ammonites and defeated them (1 Samuel 11).

Then Saul's true nature began to show. His reign was referred to as a *"bloody house"* (2 Samuel 21:1). He reverted to evil, refusing to obey the command of the LORD (1 Samuel 13:13). He ruled in terror and madness, even sentencing his own son, Jonathan, to death for eating some honey (1 Samuel 14:43-44). He pursued the just and plunged the Israelites into even deeper depths of sin than they had already known.

As Saul led the Israelites into error, his own sins carried him far from God. Already king, he took an office that was not his: he tried to serve as priest (1 Samuel 13:8-12). Further, in defiance of the absolute command of God to destroy the Amalekites utterly, he instead spared the king and some sheep, oxen, and lambs (1 Samuel 15:1-9). When confronted with his evil, instead of repenting, he made excuses (1 Samuel 15:15), lied (1 Samuel 15:20), and blamed others for his own sin (1 Samuel 15:21).

The result of such evil was a loss of leadership. Samuel declared to Saul: *"For rebellion is as the sin of divination, and insubordination is as iniquity and idolatry. Because you have rejected the word of the LORD, He has also rejected you from being king"* (1 Samuel 15:23).

The ultimate truth was that Saul sought and feared people more than he desired or feared God. He was more interested in saving face with his people than in repenting of his sins and restoring his relationship with God. He revealed the truth of his own heart when, in spite of his sins, he asked Samuel to return with him and to honor him before the elders of the people. When Saul said, *"I have sinned; but please honor me now before the elders of my people and before Israel, and go back with me, that I may worship the LORD your God"* (1 Samuel 15:30). The two pronouns, say it all: "my" people and "your" God. The Lord was not Saul's God. The Israelites had a leader who did not know or honor the One who had raised him to be king.

In the midst of Saul's reign of terror, God raised up another king. He called from the sheepfold a young man named David to rule Israel, one who would cause His people to return to and walk under the banner of God.

After an early and victorious confrontation with a giant named Goliath, David began his preparation for kingship as a hunted fugitive. A target of Saul's jealous rages, he was forced to flee into the wilderness (1 Samuel 1:1-18). For years he encountered every kind of hardship while constantly running for his life (1 Samuel 20-30). Yet, even while undergoing such intense persecution, things began to happen.

First, David was not alone. A ragtag band of rejects, the dregs of society, began to gather around him in the desert (1 Samuel 22:2). This motley group shared all his hardships with him, staying faithful through every test and trial. Ultimately these men changed in the desert as David did, and they became the valiant warriors who made up the king's army.

Second, David married. One day, needing to make preparation for a feast, some of David's men approached a harsh but rich man who was aptly named Nabal, which means fool. He, true to his name, scorned David as king and refused him any provision. However, Nabal's wife, Abigail, was of a different persuasion. She knew her husband was wrong and that his stubborn folly was about to bring destruction on his house. She also knew she could neither agree with his decision nor allow his error. Sending gifts ahead of her, she went out to meet David and bowed before him. Although she personally had done no wrong in this situation, it was she who repented; she took responsibility for Nabal's sin on herself and asked David's forgiveness. As a result of her righteous behavior, when godly judgment resulted in the death of Nabal, David asked Abigail to be his wife (1 Samuel 25:2-42).

Third, David became king. In his downward spiral of wickedness, Saul committed the ultimate offense. Since he had forsaken God, God had forsaken Him. Therefore, he no longer heard from God (1 Samuel 28:6). Desperate for information concerning an upcoming battle, he sought it from a demonic source by consulting a medium in Endor (1 Samuel 28:7-19). The result of his evil was the immediate loss of his kingdom and his life. In the same battle he had inquired about, he died and his army was slaughtered by the Philistines (1 Samuel 31:1-6).

With the death of Saul, David became king. Having been anointed by Samuel years before, he was now appointed by God to rule, initially as king of Judah in Hebron (2 Samuel 2:4), and then, after a civil war between the house of David and the house of Saul, he became king of all Israel (2 Samuel 5:1-4).

WORSHIP GOD

As head of a united kingdom, David's premier act was to honor God. He and his men went to Jerusalem, fought and defeated the Jebusites, and made that city the capital of Israel. Not only was it the center of government, since David established his throne there, but it was the spiritual center as well.

Amidst great music and joy, sacrifice and celebration, David brought the Ark of the Covenant, which had not been sought after during the reign of Saul, to its new abiding place in the tabernacle in Jerusalem (2 Samuel 6:1-18). From Mount Zion, holy worship rose unto God day and night.

It is important to realize that although the ark moved to a new dwelling place, the Tabernacle of Moses, with its outer and inner court ministries, stayed where it was. It did not cease functioning. While the tradition and ritual of animal sacrifice ground on at Gibeon without the ark of the presence of God, the LORD was in Jerusalem enjoying a new order of worship.

The key to David's reign was obedience to God. He loved his Lord with all his heart and administered God's justice and righteousness to all people (2 Samuel 8:15). Although David enjoyed great military success (2 Samuel 5:6-10; 8:1-14), suffered in sin with Bathsheba (2

Samuel 11), was rejected in his compassion for Mephibosheth (2 Samuel 9), and endured the tragedy of his son Absalom trying to usurp his throne (2 Samuel 15-18), David never forgot or failed to return to his Lord.

With David's death, the quarrelling began. Although Solomon was meant to succeed David, Adonijah, another of David's sons, exalted himself and rose up to rule (1 Kings 1:5-53). Seeking to bully his way into the kingship by manipulation and intimidation, he was nevertheless denied the throne. While the people, again intrigued by the outward appearance of a handsome man (1 Kings 1:6), expected Adonijah to be king, the Lord appointed Solomon.

Like Saul, Solomon began well. He destroyed David's enemies and, having asked for and received wisdom from God, he ruled well. He amassed a fortune, the half of which could not be imagined or told. He built the house of God and brought the ark of the presence of the Lord to its permanent dwelling place on Mount Moriah. When the temple was dedicated during the Feast of Tabernacles the glory of the Lord filled the place and supernatural fire came down from heaven and consumed the burnt offerings and sacrifices (2 Chronicles 5:13-14; 7:1).

CELEBRATE THE FEAST OF TABERNACLES

This Feast of Succoth or Tabernacles at which Solomon's Temple was dedicated was the final part of the third annually required feast in Israel. Also known as the Feast of Ingathering, it is described in Scripture.

> *Also you shall observe the Feast of the Harvest of the first fruits of your labors from what you sow in the field; also the Feast of the Ingathering at the end of the year when you gather in the fruit of your labors from the field.* (Exodus 23:16)

> *On exactly the fifteenth day of the seventh month, when you have gathered in the crops of the land, you shall celebrate the feast of the LORD for seven days, with a rest on the first day and a rest on the eighth day. Now on the first day you shall take for yourselves the foliage of beautiful trees, palm branches and boughs of leafy trees and willows of the brook; and you shall rejoice before the LORD your God for seven days. You shall thus celebrate it as a feast to the LORD for seven days in the year. It shall be a perpetual statute throughout your generations; you shall celebrate it in the seventh month. You shall live in booths for seven days; all the native-born in Israel shall live in booths,*

> *so that your generations may know that I had the Israelites live in booths when I brought them out from the land of Egypt. I am the LORD your God.* (Leviticus 23:39-43)

The Feast of Tabernacles was to commemorate the Israelites' desert journey and to remind the people of the temporary tents and shelters which their ancestors had lived in for forty years. When the Israelites left Egypt, their first stopping place was at Succoth (Numbers 33:3-5). That name means booths or huts. During the feast, the Israelites were to make their own temporary shelters and to live in them in order to identify more fully with the hardships of their ancestors and to remember God's blessings.

This feast was also known as the Feast of Ingathering. Since it took place after the final harvest of corn, olives, grapes, and fruit, it has often been declared to be the basis of the Canadian and American Thanksgiving celebrations.

Rest

To properly appreciate this celebration, it is necessary to understand several of its themes. First, Tabernacles was a feast of rest. It began and ended with a holy convocation in which no laborious work was to be done. It was a time to unwind and to enjoy the end of both a busy sacred year and a labor-intensive agricultural season. Since the harvest was over at the time of the feast, the people were not to strive any more but were to relax and feel good about a job well done.

Unity

Tabernacles was also a feast of unity. All the people of Israel were to gather in Jerusalem as one and to celebrate together. They were to leave their individual homes, to become one community of God's people, and to enjoy communal fellowship.

Equality

In addition, Tabernacles was a feast of equality. It was a time in which social class and distinction broke down. At this gala, all were considered equal before God.

Joy

Tabernacles was also a feast of joy and celebration. To keep the observance, the people wandered through the streets of Jerusalem waving tree branches. The palm branch symbolized victory, the willow branch symbolized mourning turned to happiness, the olive branch symbolized peace, and the myrtle branch symbolized the joy of restoration – all perfect expressions of the greatness and mercy of God.

Prayer

Further, Tabernacles was a feast of prayer. Both the harvest and the feast preceded the early rainy season. While the people gave thanks for the provision just gathered, they also took time to ask God's abundant blessing on the rain that would nourish the next year's crops.

Sacrifice

Tabernacles was a feast of sacrifice as well. While all of the Israelites' holy days involved the sacrifice of animals, the Feast of Tabernacles topped them all. In decreasing quantities, for eight days, the ritualistic slaughter went on (Numbers 29), offering the Israelites' best unto God.

The Coming King

Finally, Tabernacles was a feast for the coming king. The hidden but ultimate meaning of this particular festivity was to look for and prepare for the coming of the king, the Messiah. *"Then it will come about that any who are left of all the nations that went against Jerusalem will go up from year to year to worship the King, the LORD of hosts, and to celebrate the Feast of Booths"* (Zechariah 14:16).

With all this in mind, the Feast of Tabernacles was the perfect time to celebrate the dedication of Solomon's Temple. At this time God's chosen people cheerfully gathered together, joyously offered prayer and worship, and eagerly wished for their king to come. It is no wonder that God's fire fell and His presence came to dwell in the temple.

MORE APOSTASY AND WARFARE LEAD TO CAPTIVITY

Yet in spite of this miracle, it wasn't long before Solomon slid into sin. For the first time in centuries, Egypt gained a foothold among the people of Israel when Solomon married Pharaoh's daughter (1 Kings 3:1). He then married other foreign wives who taught him to worship heathen gods (1 Kings 11:1-4). As the Israelites fell into deeper apostasy, the LORD raised up adversaries against Solomon. After forty years of rule, he died, and his son, Rehoboam, ruled in his place.

Rehoboam was a tyrant, and he put a hard yoke on the Israelites. His harsh policies led directly to the division of the country. Although he retained leadership of the southern kingdom, known as Judah (but which also included the tribe of Benjamin), the other ten tribes rebelled against the house of David and became the northern kingdom of Israel (1 Kings 12:1-24). From then on, Judah and Israel existed as separate kingdoms with separate kings. Though occasionally led by honorable rulers, for the most part their kings led the kingdoms into apostasy and eventual judgment.

For example, the northern kingdom was led by an evil man named Jeroboam. Under his leadership, God's religious order was completely profaned as he introduced a new priesthood; changed the dates of feasts; made two golden calves, which he declared to be the gods of Israel; and changed the place of worship from Jerusalem to Bethel and Dan (1 Kings 12:25-33).

The southern kingdom fared no better. Ahaz, king of Judah, profaned God's house. He brought a new altar into the house of the Lord, a copy of one he had seen in Damascus (2 Kings 16:10-14). To add to the depravity, he also moved the laver where the priests were to wash their hands and feet when they came near the altar to minister or to offer sacrifice (Exodus 30:17-21). With no true altar and no holy laver, the ritual of atonement was impossible to fulfill. As a result, the people could no longer approach holy God for atonement. Thus, Ahaz had removed the way to righteousness.

In another example of degeneration, Athaliah rose to power. She was the mother of Ahaziah, a king of Judah. When her son died, she had all the royal offspring of the house of David murdered, and then she assumed rulership over the land. However, God saved one heir, Joash, and for six years he was hidden in the house of the LORD (2 Kings 11:1-4). When Joash was old enough to be crowned king, Athaliah hypocritically screamed, *"Treason! Treason!"* (2 Kings 11:14).

In the midst of national turmoil and religious apostasy, wars were fought and prophets were ignored. The people forgot God had defeated their enemies and had driven off the giants (Deuteronomy 2:21). The people, whose well being depended on obedience to God's covenant, had repeatedly broken every one of His commands, and yet they still expected His blessings. They didn't believe that at some point God's mercy and compassion would have to be balanced by His justice and righteousness. When God's judgment finally fell, He lifted His protection from them, and they were soon conquered. The people of Israel were carried away to Assyria (2 Kings 17:5-6), and the people of Judah were led into captivity in Babylon (2 Chronicles 36:9-10; 36:20). The walls of Jerusalem were broken down, the LORD'S house was plundered and burned (2 Chronicles 36:19).

A long season of darkness settled over the promised land until ... a star shone over a manger in Bethlehem ... and *"The people who were sitting in darkness saw a great Light, and those who were sitting in the land and shadow of death, upon them a Light dawned"* (Matthew 4:16).

Chapter 20

THE PROMISED LAND:

EACH SAINT'S INTIMACY WITH JESUS

After crossing the Jordan River the Israelites entered the land of Canaan. So too, each saint, after dying to self, enters the promised land. For the Israelites, Canaan was an actual landmass, the place where they arrived at the end of a physical journey. It was and is an actual geographical territory in what is now known as the Middle East. However, to each saint, the promised land is not a natural state but a spiritual one, the place he (or she) comes to after a long spiritual journey.

To recall, all of the Israelites' journey involved actual places. Egypt, the Red Sea, the desert, the Jordan River, and Canaan were (and are) real lands or waters on which or through which the feet of God's chosen people trod. They were places which even today are marked with the pathways and ruins of ancient civilizations and are alive with its modern ones. In the parallel journey of each saint, the physical places have become spiritual places. To each saint Egypt was not a country but the world of sin; the Red Sea was not a large body of water but a place to identify with Christ in death, burial, and resurrection; the desert was not an actual wilderness but a barrenness of soul and spirit because of concentration on self; the Jordan River was not a boundary that forbade access to the promised land but an entry that allowed each saint, after death to flesh and self, into the presence of God.

Just so, on the saint's journey, Canaan is not a land mass or privileged real estate that is given to him (or her) by God but a spiritual place of fulfillment, freedom, and joy. While it is a place of spiritual warfare, it is also where each saint receives his inheritance and then his rest. It is a place of dedication and absolute submission to the worship of God. It is the earthly conclusion of a long journey that began in utter darkness but ends in His marvelous light.

THE PROMISED LAND IS....

As the Israelites discovered about their Canaan, for each saint the promised land is a place of newness. Old things have passed away. It is a place where each saint, while maintaining the fellowship God has placed him (or her) in, finally takes his eyes off his spouse, parent, child, neighbor, friend, church leader, job, or bank account and onto God as the true and only Source of life, wisdom, and grace. It is an area in which each child of God becomes totally dependent on his Lord for a newness of inspiration, instruction, and revelation. It is the land to which the body, which was crucified with Christ, and the mind (intellect, will, and emotions), which no longer glorifies self, yields to a new awareness of the presence, majesty, grandeur, power, loveliness, and wonder of God.

For each saint, the promised land is also a permanent place. As each saint progresses further and further away from Egypt and the desert, he (or she) is more and more able to see the evil and the depravity found there. Having had the power of sin broken by his Savior; having been separated from it by his Deliverer; and having been kept, tested, and strengthened in the desert by his Shepherd, a saint develops an overwhelming determination never to return to those places. He also has a desire to send down roots so deep in the promised land that no storm or gust of wind could ever tear him out of or away from the presence of God.

In addition to the gift of permanence in the promised land, each saint has a yearning within to abandon old tents and to destroy old huts that once served to shelter the saint and then to build the true abiding place of God. As awe of God grows in the magnificence of this new place, no crude hut will any longer suffice. As fear of God increases, no tattered tent can house the saint's most treasured inheritance, his (or her) Lord. Thus, he makes plans to build a permanent, glorious castle for the King.

For each saint, the promised land is a fruitful place as well. Even good seeds planted in the desert would have died from scorching sun and lack of water. There, saints would have watched in frustration as their fields had to be abandoned before they had come to harvest because the cloud of God moved on. However, in the promised land, there is no more failure and frustration. Seeds planted by the Spirit of God fall into good ground, die, and then burst forth in multiplied resurrection life. Instead of barrenness and lack of supply, they yield an abundant, fruitful harvest.

Further, for each saint, the promised land means fulfillment. Each heart is desperately hungry and thirsty for deeper relationship with the living God. While in the desert, many Christians had the experience of seeking God among those they believed to be or who were purported to be the body of Christ. All too often they ended up in the fellowship of flesh, following human leaders. If any dared to point out that the deceptive euphemism Sunday Morning Worship Service might more accurately be labeled Sunday Morning Self Service, he (or she) may have had to endure slander and persecution by "brothers and sisters" when he refused to continue in the fellowship of flesh. Not so in the promised land! There, the hungry and thirsty don't seek flesh but God. They are nourished by fresh loaves of the Bread of Life and full cups of Living Water. There they are in communion with holy God and find fellowship with holy people.

Yet there is more. For each saint, the promised land is a place of brokenness into the deeper things of God. It is where each child of God allows the final dregs of his (or her) humanness to be poured out so that he might be an empty vessel through which God can pour Himself out to others. It is where each saint finally realizes that God does not want the part but the whole, that He desires to possess his whole being and to have his whole heart. It is where the saint comes to understand that in order for this to happen, he must make changes within his heart. It is where the deep-seated sins a saint is often unaware of are revealed by the Holy Spirit. Then God asks him to decide if he, like those who followed Joshua, will fight until they are conquered by the power of God or if he, like those in the generations after Joshua, will allow them to remain in his heart, weakening him, ensnaring him, and drawing him away from wholehearted relationship with his Father. It is where the deep-seated sins a saint is aware of but is unable to overcome by himself are brought under conviction of the Holy Spirit. It is where each saint will cast self attempts at sanctification aside and submit to a position of brokenness, dependence, reliance, and confidence in God so that his inner enemies will be destroyed by the power of God's right arm. It is where a saint gives up the power of faith in himself and truly learns to love and trust his Lord and to know that his survival depends on faith in Him. It is where the final preparations are made for the saint's union with the heart of Christ.

BUILD AN ALTAR

After passage into the promised land, each saint has no time to lay down his (or her) arms. If anything, he becomes aware that living in Canaan requires even greater diligence and caution. In Egypt, each saint battled the world; in the desert he fought flesh and self; and in Canaan his enemy is the devil. In fact, the promised land is full of the enemies of God. Even giants have strongholds there. Collectively known as sin, all must be conquered and destroyed before a saint can receive his full inheritance and come into his rest.

Therefore, it is of utmost importance that every saint who has crossed into the promised land immediately stops all extraneous activity and builds an altar to God. The stones the Israelites placed in the Jordan River and built on its bank were to commemorate God's supernatural power in the caretaking and safety of His chosen people. So too, each saint must realize that he (or she) was enabled to enter Canaan only through the divine intervention of God. Each is called to express his reverence for God by building Him an altar of love; by thanking Him for His guidance, protection, and preservation as he journeyed from sin into the presence of God; and by placing himself in God's care. Each must build an altar as a testimony that God's unchangeable, absolute perfection has succeeded in altering him. He does so by offering his heart to God.

BE CIRCUMCISED

Immediately after offering his (or her) heart, each saint will be tested to see if he will leave it in God's care or will take it back. He will be asked to undergo circumcision.

The Israelites' circumcision was a cutting away of a foreskin of flesh. It was a sign of their covenant relationship with God (Romans 4:11). While saints are released from the obligation of undergoing a physical circumcision (Galatians 5:1-4), yet each must be circumcised in heart (Romans 2:25-29). This is a seal of righteousness.

Circumcision is that time when a saint voluntarily offers his (or her) heart to Jesus and allows Him to lay it open, examine it, clear out blockages, remove hardened tissues, cut away hurts, and cauterize wounds. It is only complete when he allows Jesus access to **every** area, and, no matter now old, no matter how deep or hidden, no matter how painful, he desires the scalpel in the hand of the Master Surgeon to do its work perfectly so the heart will be completely healed.

Yet, circumcision is even more. It is becoming painfully aware and having to admit that all upcoming experiences and victories cannot be lived or won as the result of a person's strength in flesh since he (or she) has just endured the aching, smarting, throbbing removal or stripping away of flesh by the hand of Christ (Colossians 2:11).

Circumcision is a vulnerable time, because each saint feels misery as a result of his (or her) surgery. This might include the ache of losing loved ones who refuse to cross the Jordan River or the distress of no longer allowing old wounds to be used as excuses for present behavior. Such may appear to be foolishness to the natural world or may seem like a perfect time for the saint's enemies to attack. However, though each saint is in a weakened condition, God supernaturally protects him and gives him time to grow and mend.

CELEBRATE THE FEAST OF PASSOVER

Just after entering the promised land, each saint must bring to mind his (or her) Passover. To the Israelites, Passover signified the power of Pharaoh was broken; to each Christian, Passover signified the power of sin was broken. Although Passover occurred in Egypt, it was celebrated, at least once, in the desert (Numbers 9:5). Further, to honor the fact that God did indeed bring every saint out to bring him in, Passover was to be celebrated in the promised land too. Each saint must earnestly remember the blood of Christ has covered and cleansed the doorposts of his heart and sin need no longer dictate his life. While Satan is a powerful enemy, his authority over every saint has been removed.

ENGAGE IN WARFARE

With these preliminaries over, each saint is quickly plunged into warfare. The battleground is the human heart. In general terms, while Egypt was the battle for the body and the desert the war zone for the mind, the promised land is where a person's heart or spirit must be conquered. The heart of each saint is, above all else, that which God desires most. Therefore, it is, above all else, that which the enemy will seek to keep from Him.

Since the heart is so important to promised-land existence, each saint must learn more about his (or her) heart. The heart is one of the most important organs of the body. Leviticus 17:11 says that the life is in the blood. Since the heart pumps blood to every part of the human body, if the heart stops beating, death follows.

The mind is also associated with the heart. The mind is

intelligence, will, and emotions; it is the soul or personality of a person. The Bible links the mind to the heart, declaring that the heart is the center of intellect, reasoning, and understanding (Matthew 9:4; 13:14-15; Mark 2:6). It also shows that the heart is the center of the human will (Colossians 3:15; 2 Corinthians 9:7). Finally, it shows that the heart it is the home of human emotion, such as joy (John 16:22), grief (John 14:1), gladness (Acts 2:26), and sorrow (Psalm 13:2).

That the heart is connected with both body and mind is irrefutable. However, this is not the whole story. God created humans as three-part beings. By His grace, a human being is not just body and mind (or outer and inner court); he (or she) is also spirit. A person's spirit is the innermost part of his being, his holy of holies, his innermost sanctuary, the center or heart of his being.

As body and mind have certain functions concerning the heart, so does a person's spirit. It is with the heart that a person believes unto righteousness (Romans 10:10). The heart is the home of a person's conscience (2 Samuel 24:10; Acts 2:37; 1 John 3:19-22), the place where God's law is written (Hebrews 8:10), and where his (or her) center of worship is located. In Jewish history, it was the innermost room of the tabernacle or temple that held the glorious presence of God. So it is with His human temples. God dwells in the innermost sanctuary or deep in the heart of every born-again Christian (1 Corinthians 3:16; Ephesians 3:17).

The Bible declares the heart can be good. With it, a saint loves God (Matthew 22:37), obeys (Romans 6:17), and rejoices (Acts 2:26). A regenerate heart is known to be enlightened (2 Corinthians 4:6), wise (Proverbs 10:8), steadfast (Psalm 57:7), pure (Matthew 5:8), or blameless (Psalm 101:2).

On the other hand, although people have a hard time admitting it, the Bible also declares the heart to be evil (Genesis 6:5). It is the place where people's fiercest, strongest, and most deeply entrenched enemies are gathered. Like the Israelites, who found wicked kings, evil kingdoms, and even frightful giants in Canaan, each saint finds his (or her) heart to be the seat of deep-rooted, hostile adversaries. The Bible states: *"The heart is more deceitful than all else and is desperately sick; who can understand it?"* (Jeremiah 17:9).

Once making that declaration, the Word describes specific enemy strongholds or sins that make a heart evil. In an abridged listing, the heart is the center of adultery (Matthew 5:28), doubt (Mark 11:23), fear (Psalm 27:3; Isaiah 35:4), hatred (Leviticus 19:17), lust (Romans

1:24), lack of repentance and stubbornness (Romans 2:5), rebellion (Jeremiah 5:23), pride (Proverbs 16:5; 21:4), arrogance (Jeremiah 49:16), idolatry (Psalm 44:20-21), and deceit (Psalm 32:2). Further, Matthew 15:19 declares the heart to be the dwelling place of evil thoughts, murders, fornications, thefts, false witness, and slander.

Lest it should be argued that these sins apply only to the unsaved or that the heart of the saved is perfect and without evil, each saint must learn from David. David, the man after God's own heart, was convicted of imperfection in his own. When he faced and acknowledged the giants of lust, adultery, and murder in his heart, he could only cry out to God to cleanse him and to create in him a clean heart (Psalm 51:10).

If a saint is honest with himself (or herself), the inescapable truth is that the heart of the unsaved is not holy and the heart of the saved is not perfect. While the heart or the spirit is regenerated or is being reborn from above at the time of salvation, the heart does not come to life in completely mature perfection. The apostle Paul reflects this when he writes *"Therefore we do not lose heart, but though our outer man is decaying, yet our inner man is being renewed day by day"* (2 Corinthians 4:16).

It is this, the presence of both good and evil in one heart that triggers the war within every saint. If he (or she) does not acknowledge this and does not let God deal with it, he becomes like a Pharisee, a hypocrite who is clean on the outside but dirty on the inside, a whitewashed tomb (Matthew 23:27-28). The truth is that the degree of purity or impurity in a saint's heart determines how closely he can walk to God in spirit.

One way to help each believer to grow closer to God is to test himself (or herself). Hebrews 4:12 declares the Word of God is a discerner of the thoughts and intents of the heart. If the heart of each saint is perfectly pure, God would not have left a means to test it. One of the reasons God has given His written Word is so that each saint has a plumb line against which he is to measure his thoughts, words, and actions. Another test is to compare the fruit of the saint's heart with the fruit that poured out of Jesus' heart. If it is not of the same quality and quantity, the saint's heart is less than perfect. To some degree, evil is present.

Can any Christian looking at this abbreviated list of inner sins honestly declare that none of them to any degree is found in him (or her)? Can any saint state without reservation that he is a completed, perfected temple? Can't each saint recall how it was only after the

Israelites struggled with and defeated the enemy entrenched in Canaan that they received their inheritance and entered their rest?

Some firmly believe that whenever a sinner becomes a saint, he (or she) is automatically freed of all sin, that as soon as the Spirit of God takes up residence in his heart, the enemy flees. However, this idea is not supported in Scripture. The Israelites had to fight long and hard to defeat their foes and to drive them from Canaan. So must each saint. The Israelites needed deliverance from Egypt, deliverance in the desert, and deliverance from enemies in the promised land. Just so, each saint who needed deliverance from the power of sin and deliverance from self also needs deliverance or separation from the enemies in his (or her) heart.

Enemies in the heart have already lost the battle against the power of sin to enslave the body and the power of self to govern. They have had to retreat from the front line of battle against the body and the middle ranks of warfare against the soul or mind. Some have fled, but others have fallen back and regrouped, concentrating themselves in the one place they yet have a stronghold: the heart.

The evil forces of sin are not gentlemen. Just because a sinner becomes a saint or their master loses another soul to **the** Master, does not mean they voluntarily desert or quit their positions. Rather, they flee inward, hide, dig in, and conceal themselves. Legally, because Jesus is Lord, they have no authority over the believer; positionally, because they have not been discovered, confessed, and gotten rid of, they are still deep in the human heart.

All of this can be likened to a situation in life. Those who rent out rooms, apartments, or buildings sometimes find themselves having difficulty with bad tenants. Whether because these problem people lead disorderly lives, destroy the building, harass other residents, let others in who have no right to be there, or don't pay their rent, their uncivil behavior disqualifies them from remaining as occupants of the dwellings. While positionally they occupy a place, legally their landlord is in charge. If they break their rental agreement, the owner of the building or property has every right to exercise his (or her) authority and to evict the undesirable tenants.

However, just because the owner is displeased with the ungodly tenants does not mean they will sweetly pack up and leave. Instead, some will choose to stay until forced to move. It is only when the owner commands them to leave, backed by legal documents and, if necessary, law enforcement officials, that the unwanted tenants are forced out or made to go. After the dwelling is empty, it can be cleansed, refurnished, and made ready for a new occupant.

Just so, if a saint's heart is occupied in even the smallest area by sin, he (or she) has an obligation to oust the undesirable. The Owner or Landlord of each saint's heart is God. In His authority and power, evil can be forced to go, and by the work of His Spirit, that saint's heart can be sanctified.

Like the unwanted tenants, the enemies in the heart bluff and deceive from their hiding places. Even though they are not the Owner of the saint, they try to control his (or her) life either by bursting out at the most awkward moments or by establishing a channel of behavior through which they can habitually manifest themselves. They exercise hollow, nonexistent authority, and if not confronted, they cause people to act after the manner of their names, such as lust, fear, and lies.

What shall a child of God say then? Is all hope lost? Is he (or she) forever bound or hindered by sin within? Is he helpless to see his situation ever changed? Is his promised-land existence to always fall short of all that God has for him? Shall he never be able to enter his rest?

By no means! Just as the true owner can evict the unwanted tenants, so the true Owner can evict the unwanted enemies in the hearts of the saints. Some of the best news in the good news is: *"We shall know by this that we are of the truth, and will assure our heart before Him in whatever our heart condemns us; for God is greater than our heart and knows all things"* (1 John 3:19-20). Victory is available for each saint, and that victory is in Christ.

First, Christ is the Judge. Since the hearts of men and women are evil and deceptive, no saint can judge his (or her) true state. However, each has a holy, impartial Judge. He and He alone searches the heart and knows all thoughts (1 Chronicles 28:9; Psalm 44:21). When any saint cries out, *"Search me, O God, and know my heart; try me and know my ... thoughts"* (Psalm 139:23), that is exactly what his Judge will do.

Yet, it does not stop there. As each Christian has met Jesus as Savior and as Lord, he (or she) is now ready to meet Him as Warrior. Each enters the promised land for a specific purpose: to worship God. For that to happen, God's enemies must be conquered – unmercifully destroyed – and the land they dwelt in must be possessed and occupied. To fight and succeed in such intensive supernatural warfare requires obedience to a supernatural leader. Joshua met the Captain of the Host (Joshua 5:13-14). Similarly, each saint meets Jesus, who is the Captain of the Host and the King of glory, as magnificently recorded in Psalm 24:7-10 and wondrously set to music in Handel's Messiah:

> *Lift up your heads, O gates, and be lifted up, O ancient doors, that the King of glory may come in! Who is the King of glory? The LORD strong and mighty, the LORD mighty in battle. Lift up your heads, O gates, and lift them up, O ancient doors, that the King of glory may come in! Who is this King of glory? The LORD of hosts, He is the King of glory.*

As the Lion from the tribe of Judah (Revelation 5:5), the LORD of Hosts will roar to shatter strongholds; His teeth will tear and devour enemies; His power will destroy adversaries.

The name LORD of Hosts implies that the Lord is Master over large numbers. One part of His host is the angelic army, which is ever ready to minister unto God and those who inherit salvation (Hebrews 1:14). Another part of His host is the army of the born again. Rather than comparing himself (or herself) to a grasshopper, each saint is a warrior under the banner of the captain of their salvation (Hebrews 2:10 NKJV).

As war for the heart is declared, every door and chamber of the heart is opened and a scouting party is sent in. If no enemy is present, that part of the heart is declared a royal chamber, a place where the Spirit of God is in residence. However, if sin is discovered there, the battle commences and continues until the last shred of enemy resistance is beaten back; the foe is conquered; and its former habitation is taken over, cleansed, and declared to be holy ground.

Sometimes, like the evil kings in Canaan, several enemies will form an unholy coalition, creating a stronghold of power within the heart that seems unbeatable. Be assured, saint, that no force and no numbers even begin to challenge the power and sovereignty of God. He will be faithful to lead His hosts in battle until each heart is systematically freed from internal enemy activity.

God is not just the Judge and the Warrior. In this battle for dominion, He is also the Sanctifier. He who delivers the heart makes it holy as well. When putting his (or her) confidence in the Lord, each believer must realize God is a God of deliverances (Psalm 68:20; 74:12). A saint experiences only one salvation and deliverance from the power of sin and Satan unto eternal life. However, once redeemed, a saint's need of God's cleansing power continues. Just so, redemption brings or admits God's authority into a saint's life or gives God permission to act on his behalf so that he may be sanctified and then continue to be separated from sin throughout the rest of his life.

Jesus is a saint's Sanctifier. To Him alone is granted permission to open every door and to clean the temple thoroughly. As a child of God yields more and more areas of his (or her) heart to His sanctifying power, he will become a fit dwelling place, a habitation of his King. As God scours the temple with the active knowledge and cooperation of the saint, that saint will be able to praise (Psalm 9:1) and love (Matthew 22:37) his God will his **whole** heart.

In his struggle to see his (or her) heart free from sin, each child of God will win some battles, like Jericho, and lose some, like the first attempt to defeat Ai. He may find his heart divided in preparation for the final campaigns. As each saint declares all-out war on ungodly foes, raises the banner of God, and fights with God in places and times of His choosing, victory will follow victory. Enemy after enemy will fall before the onslaught of Almighty God. Toeholds of enemy encroachment and strongholds of enemy power will be battered to pieces. In this war no mercy may be shown to the enemy and no bastion of evil may be left intact. All the heart must be free to worship God wholeheartedly.

Only when the LORD of Hosts declares the battle over, only when the enemies are defeated can each saint receive his (or her) inheritance. God will apportion to him both his land and his Lord. When all is done, each saint can enter his rest.

KNOW GOD'S WORD

As soon as the second battle of Ai was fought and won, the Israelites made another altar to God, offered sacrifices on it, and wrote the Law of Moses on its stones. While half the people stood before Mount Gerizim and the rest before Mount Ebal, Joshua blessed those gathered and read all the words of the Law, the blessings and the curses.

He did this for several reasons. First, Joshua did this so all of Israel – men, women, children, and even strangers in their midst – would know both the covenant and the God of Israel.

So too, each saint must set aside time, build an altar, and seek God. Each must reread, learn, and affirm the authority of the Word of God. Each must acknowledge that the Word of God is wholly true and that *"All Scripture is inspired by God and profitable for teaching, for reproof, for correction, for training in righteousness; that the man of God may be adequate, equipped for every good work"* (2 Timothy 3:16-17).

After familiarizing himself (or herself) with God's Word and learning of the blessings for those who honor His Word and the curses for those who do not, each saint should learn from the Israelites' experience and should know that he is without excuse if he chooses to violate God's covenant. Since each is personally responsible to read the Word, each is responsible to respond to it. Each must hear and heed it; each must live so his life is a living manifestation of that Word. Any who says he doesn't know the Word, who declares his ignorance of God's intent through His Word, who purposefully chooses the path of disobedience to the living Word is without excuse.

Joshua also read the Law of Moses to proclaim the authority of God over this once pagan land. The Israelites could not properly or powerfully take possession of Canaan without knowing, determining to honor, and then living by the declared Law of God. In proclaiming God's Law, the laws of the pagan nations were nullified, and the Law of God was declared to be sovereign. Holy Law was now the law of the land.

Similarly, by reading the Word of God each saint is proclaiming the authority of God over his (or her) life. No saint can exist without knowing God's laws and living by them. In the promised land, he must be governed by God's Word.

REJECT APOSTASY

Each child of God must follow the command of God and must continue to subdue the enemy. If he (or she) does not, rebellion and idolatry may lead to a falling away. If he is not careful, he may find himself in a cycle of apostasy – crying out and being delivered, only to return once more to apostasy.

If truly delinquent in his relationship with God, this saint may find himself (or herself) wanting to be like others. It seems beyond belief, but all too often the most saved, sanctified saint seems willing to compromise his set-apart position and to release the blessings of God and the treasures of heaven in order to be like those in the world.

In every community, some who call themselves saints live lives that are in no way different than those of the people in the world around them. Perhaps this lack of sanctification started when they began calling out for or were introduced to a "king." Not content to acknowledge that there is no King other than King Jesus, these saints wanted a human ruler, a man to play god. They then rejected the God who saved and delivered them and accepted the leadership of human dictatorship. Instead of letting worship and conscience, both parts of the heart or spirit, be a matter between themselves and God, they accepted a human mediator who eventually directed all attention to himself, "his" church, and "his" ministry. Thus, he successfully diverted the saint from worship of God to a person. That is apostasy.

Every Israelite was once under the slavery of Pharaoh, and each saint was once held in bondage by Satan. Since the Israelites also chose and then suffered under the dreadful leadership of a human king, Saul, it goes without saying that each saint will experience his (or her) Saul, an ungodly person who seeks unlawful, unholy authority and power by which to control the priesthood. This Saul is a leader in the counterfeit church system who wants to dictate all matters concerning the saint's home, friendships, job, involvement in earthly government, and relationship with God. He also demands the saint's full attention and financial support.

If any saint is truly seeking to discern the truth, God will expose these fanatics of flesh. Their leadership is marked by a return to enforced slavery within the religious system. Under their guidance, evil and terror break out. They persecute the just and crush any who threaten their self-erected thrones. Perhaps the most telling sign of evil is witchcraft, the manipulation, intimidation, domination, and control of all things.

Each saint who knows or has known this type of leader must fervently search for and cry out for a different type, one like David. Throughout Scripture, David, Israel's shepherd-king, is likened to Jesus, the Great Shepherd.

No saint needs a human dictator to command him (or her) in matters concerning home, friendships, job, human government, or relationship with God. Surely each needs council and prayer as he treads these highways and byways but not **control.**

About such matters, God's Word speaks clearly. For example, concerning marriages and especially those wives who are downtrodden in the home, Jesus' Word says: *"But the one who joins himself to the LORD is one spirit with Him"* (1 Corinthians 6:17). Through reconciliation by the blood of Christ, a Christian is one in spirit with God. Due to this, in a marriage in which both are children of God, no husband or wife is to interfere with the conscience, heart, or spirit of the other in matters relating to God. Even while acknowledging that the man is the head of the woman and that woman was created to be his helpmate (Genesis 2:18-22) in terms of their marriage, in terms of their standing in God's eyes they are spiritually equal (Galatians 3:28). Therefore, one must not attempt to dominate the other's spirit, make the other's decisions of conscience, or keep the other from obeying God.

Regarding each saint's relationship with God, the Bible states that only Jesus is or could ever be the mediator between God and mankind (1 Timothy 2:5). While godly leadership has a major role to play in the edification of the Church (Ephesians 4:11-16), each Christian is yet singly responsible for his (or her) own relationship with God. People and denomination cannot lead him to God and cannot open his heart to worship. Only Jesus can.

Concerning a saint's job, the Word is equally clear: *"Do not be bound together with unbelievers; for what partnership have righteousness and lawlessness, or what fellowship has light with darkness?"* (2 Corinthians 6:14). Christians should not be business partners or have other legal ties with nonbelievers. If a saint is not to be bound to unbelievers, even at work, with whom is he to be yoked? The words of Jesus give the answer. *"Take My yoke upon you and learn from Me, for I am gentle and humble in heart; and You will find rest for Your souls. For My yoke is easy and My burden is light"* (Matthew 11:29-30)

Finally, in regard to human government, Scripture says that each saint is to pray for those in authority over him (or her) so he can lead a tranquil life of godliness in dignity (1 Timothy 2:2). Further, although he is also to be subject to the governing authorities (Romans 13:1), this does not mean he should obey them blindly. Nowhere does the Word say a saint has to bow to the dictates of his pastor or priest, adhere to his political views, or vote for his preferred candidates. Nowhere does Scripture state a saint is to compromise himself to human authority that is evil. If a religious, business, or government leader commands a believer to do something that is directly against God's Word, then the saint should choose God over that person.

The only true leader or king that a saint can accept is the one who walks in the footsteps of God, bringing his (or her) company or nation and those he governs under the authority of God. If he is not giving away spiritual riches instead of accruing physical ones, serving instead of being served, willing to die for his people, walking in humbleness, and leading a life of unquestioned integrity, he is not a true king.

David and Jesus were and are true Kings. Their hearts of compassion were deep, flowing wells. Both had strength of leadership, hope where there was no hope, and a fervent desire to do only the will of God (John 6:38; Acts 13:22). Both led their master's flock (2 Samuel 5:2; John 10:11-16). David was the forerunner of godly kings, but today the only King any saint can accept is King Jesus.

Toward this King, each saint must make a commitment. Like the ragtag band which followed David, Jesus calls out to the wounded and hurt to join Him. No matter if a saint has been declared the dregs of worldly society or mockingly proclaimed the laughingstock of the religious system, Jesus, who was Himself rejected, accepts anyone who hurts as He once hurt. He seeks to encircle him (or her) with arms of love, strengthen him with His own strength, and give him a place as a soldier in the army of the Lord.

Jesus demands a second commitment too. As David did, Jesus is looking for a bride. Although each saint was once bound to Satan and although many saints were once ensnared in the false church system, both former masters can now be declared to be Nabals, or fools. When the saint's King comes seeking provision for a feast, like Abigail, each can send Him a gift, approach Him, humble himself (or herself), and repent. He must let the grace granted by the New Covenant speak for him. When he is finally rid of past entanglements, he can eagerly respond to the King's invitation to be His bride.

Jesus has long been the anointed King. Soon this anointment will become His appointment, the time He returns to the earth to rule. The grounds for His doing so were legally established two thousand years ago at Calvary, where Satan, the ruler of this world, was soundly and forever defeated. Until the dream becomes the reality and Jesus comes back, each saint, as a warrior, must possess and occupy even while he (or she) prepares himself to be a bride.

WORSHIP GOD

In addressing Jesus as King or in associating himself (or herself) with His reign, it is necessary for each saint to come into an awareness of the importance of participation in holy prayer and praise. Each must understand that one way of sustaining himself in the promised land is through worshipping the One who led him there.

Praise and worship is one of the most powerful weapons in spiritual warfare. Led by the Holy Spirit and offered unto God, it becomes the harmony of Holy Spirit and human spirit honoring the King. To glorify God in praise, each child of God must throw off the yoke of tradition and offer God his (or her) sacrifice of praise in the privacy of his prayer closet or on the busiest of streets, in solemn assembly or in unpracticed delight. As led by the Spirit of God in singing, clapping, waving, shouting, crying, leaping, dancing, bowing, or falling on his face before Him, with all of his heart he expresses through worship the love for God that burns in his now-freed heart.

For the Israelites in Canaan, praise and worship changed from the methodical ritual of Moses' Tabernacle to the joyous, spontaneous outpourings of love in David's. For each saint in the promised land, with no veil to separate him (or her) from the presence of God, he experiences unutterable joy in exalting God heart-to-Heart.

David's son, Solomon, began the final thousand years of Israel's history preceding the coming of Christ. He built Solomon's Temple and moved the ark of the presence into it. So too, in this new millennium, each saint must raise a temple for God, dedicate it to Him, and see His presence infill it. By so doing, he (or she) can enter into the spirit of the Feast of Tabernacles.

CELEBRATE THE FEAST OF TABERNACLES

For each Christian, Tabernacles is a Feast of Booths. It is an awesome reminder of the state of his (or her) heart before God purged and indwelt it. The believer's booths may have been the temporary, leaky shelters, such as bars, drug dens, or pornography shops that he inhabited before coming to Christ. Too, they may be the huts and hovels of counterfeit Christianity that he endured in the desert. In celebrating the Feast of Tabernacles, each saint can thank God that these booths are now abandoned and that he has a permanent home as long as he stays in the promised land.

For each Christian, Tabernacles is also a Feast of Harvest or of Ingathering. God has a plan for each saint, a field in which he (or she) is to work. To the Israelites, Tabernacles was a celebration that followed the final harvest. It was a time for the people to review the fruit of their labors. To the saint today, when he sees that souls have been saved and lives have been changed as a result of his obedience to God, that the gospel was carried to the world, or that the Church was edified by his ministry, he should offer thanks for God's bountiful goodness. To celebrate Tabernacles, instead of self-congratulations, a chorus of praise for a job well done should arise to the Lord of the Harvest.

Rest

To enjoy this feast completely, many aspects must be celebrated. First, each Christian must realize that Tabernacles is a time of rest. Spiritual rest is not inertia or passivity; it is trust in God. For any saint to be celebrating this holiday, he (or she) has been brought to the position of acknowledging his enemies are bigger than he is and far too numerous to handle alone. Since he has had to rely on the knowledge of God to identify them and the power of God to defeat them, he has had to come to a place of complete trust in God. That is holy rest.

For a saint, true rest can come when his (or her) conscience is liberated from the demands of accountability to other people. In Egypt or the world, God freed the body from the power of sin. In the desert, He freed the mind or the intellect, will, and emotions from self. In the promised land, God frees the conscience from the power of unholy accusation and judgment from either human sources or evil forces.

When any saint can stand in the midst of a crossfire in which former worldly friends are heckling him (or her) because he has "gone religious" and in which present brothers and sisters in Christ are accusing him of "falling away" because he will not walk in their path or under their control, he has come into rest. When a saint knows that no matter how things look he is truly in the will of God, he has come into rest. When accusations and judgments no longer sting, he has come into rest.

Rest comes when the saint discovers that he (or she) is not accountable to people but to God. If a saint can stand in the light of God's judgment and receive the witness of His approval, his conscience is clear. The opinions, slanders, judgments, and even curses of unholy men and women who continue to judge after the flesh do nothing but fall back on those who have done the judging (Matthew 7:2).

Unity

Tabernacles is also a time of unity. For a saint, unity does not mean being in harmony with the world (John 17:16) or becoming part of the false religious system that places tolerance, secular humanism, and cultural relevance above accord and union with true God. Rather, unity is oneness with God (1 Corinthians 6:17); it is sonship with God, the Father, marriage to God, the Son (Ephesians 5:23-32), and brotherhood with God, the Holy Spirit (1 Corinthians 6:19). Jesus is the Vine and each saint is a branch (John 15:5). In Him each saint lives and moves and has his being (Acts 17:28). Further, it is with Christ, not people, that each saint is biblically identified with crucifixion (Romans 6:6), burial (Romans 6:4), resurrection and new life (Ephesians 2:5), suffering and inheritance (Romans 8:17), and rulership (2 Timothy 2:12).

Unity with Christ involves all of each saint. It is a oneness in body with all parts submitted to God (Romans 10:3). It is a oneness of mind (1 Corinthians 2:16) in which each saint's intelligence becomes the knowledge, wisdom, counsel, and discernment of God. Further, his (or her) will becomes the will of God, and his emotions become an expression of divine feelings. Most of all, it is a oneness of spirit, of being so conformed to the likeness of God that each saint becomes a testimony in behavior as well as in word of the eternal Life that dwells within him. Without unity with Christ, a saint cannot have unity with other people.

Equality

In addition, Tabernacles is a time of equality. While God does give more responsibility to some saints, and while some saints may receive various rewards for righteous labors, He does not show partiality to them. All are equal in the eyes of the Lord. No saint is more loved than another; no saint is more saved than another. Salvation equalizes the body of Christ. Salvation is by faith, not by works. It is an expression of what God has done, not what people can do. Since God's demand for justice and His command that people be made right with Him is the same for everyone, each must accept God's free gift of salvation. When he (or she) does, each is justified and sanctified. God does not play favorites.

Joy

Tabernacles is a time of joy as well. Under the New Covenant, a saint has no restrictions as to where, when, or how to worship God. Led by the Holy Spirit, a saint is free to burst forth and celebrate Jesus.

Prayer

For each saint, Tabernacles is a time of prayer. A saint will someday come to the end of his (or her) earthly pilgrimage. Hopefully in the promised land rather than in the desert, he awaits either the coming of Christ or being called home. Yet maintaining a presence there or possessing and occupying the land is not easy. Knowing that those who endure to the end will be saved (Matthew 24:13), each saint needs, through prayer, to keep in close contact with God. No communion with God will last without ongoing prayer. Each saint is required to be in constant touch with God, and he may do so in a variety of ways, such as by reading the Word, singing, petitioning, interceding, praising, waiting, and listening.

Sacrifice

Further, Tabernacles is a feast of sacrifice. Each saint's portion in the promised land is a gift from God. The sad thing is that a saint does not always like God's choice for his (or her) inheritance. Therefore, it is a sacrifice for him to function where God has set him. Examples of this would be a wife moving to her husband's hometown, neither liking the area nor being accepted in it and yet knowing God has placed her there for a reason; a saint being assigned to a job he detests but every attempt to quit or be transferred is checked or forbidden by God; or growing up in a godless home which all instinct says to flee from but God says to stay.

God desires each saint to function where He has put him (or her). Who is better qualified to pray than someone whose roots go down deep, someone who will seek God for truth and then pray His will concerning the well-being of relatives, friends, neighbors, businesses, churches, schools, and hospitals? Another saint may be constantly on the move. Even if he is in a region only briefly, while he is there he should find out all he can about it and do all he's instructed by God to do concerning it. If nothing else, he can act as the vanguard and pray that God will raise up intercessors for that territory. Or, he can pray that the truth of the history (including religious roots), government, media, entertainment, businesses, and its leaders would be exposed and that the place would submit to the government of God. (Jeremiah 29:7). All this requires great sacrifice of personal desires, time, and finances. None of it should receive human reward. In addition, no matter how cruel the call to sacrifice, it is important to note that if a saint willfully leaves the place God set him in, he moves out of his personal promised land and out of the will of God for him.

The Coming King

Finally, Tabernacles is a feast for a King. For this world and all the nations and people in it, there is but one King: Jesus. *"And the LORD will be king over all the earth; in that day the LORD will be the only one, and His name the only one"* (Zechariah 14:9). Jesus is Savior,

Deliverer, and Lord. Jesus is also the soon and coming King. While on previous parts of his (or her) journey, each believer has met Him as Lamb and Lord, and soon each will meet Him as Lion and King. *"Now to the King eternal, immortal, invisible, the only God, be honor and glory forever and ever. Amen"* (1 Timothy 1:17).

Since the appearance of King Jesus is to be the highlight of promised-land existence, it is necessary that each saint heed the cautions not to cease vigilance, lay down arms, or relax his (or her) holy guard. A quick glance at Israel's history will remind him that apostasy was greatest in the promised land.

The Israelites endured Egypt, trudged through the desert, and then committed some of the worst sins against God in Canaan. Though kept, cared for, governed, and protected by God, though given inheritance and rest, when they became lax, they lost it all.

So too for each saint! If any should get to the point where he (or she) says, "I've got it made!" it's a sure sign he hasn't. Such a declaration is an open invitation for his heart to prove him wrong. It is one thing to have remained in Egypt for lack of vision. It is another thing to have prolonged a desert trek because of unbelief and rebellion. However, it is something else altogether to come into the presence of God, to have holy communion, to remain a while, and then to turn away and reject the presence of the living God. A fall from such dizzying heights can only bring disaster (Hebrews 6:6).

No Christian should duplicate the Israelites' apostasy. He (or she) must not co-mingle with the world or be induced by its slaves to honor its heathen gods. He need not be divided in his heart in which one part wants to commit idolatry, worship at new altars, keep unholy feasts, or profane the priesthood while the rest seeks to remain true to God, however tenuously. He need not have a fatal attraction to the ever-present Athaliahs, the self-raised usurpers who wish to remove and destroy the true King. He need not ignore the warnings of holy prophets or let the seeds of backsliding come to full fruit as wavering hearts are dominated by evil religious leaders.

Saint, take joy in the fact that Jesus' return is drawing ever closer. Soon and very soon, the light that shone over a dark Jewish village two thousand years ago will be succeeded by the appearance of the Light of the World, King Jesus. Flames of fire will burn in His eyes as an evidence of love for those who accepted Him and as a witness of His wrath against those who did not. As King of kings, His glory will shine, lighting the way for you, child of God, to come to Him.

Has not your spirit made this known to you? Has not your heart been informing you? Do you not know that even now day is breaking through and the bright and brilliant Morning Star is arising in your heart that He may bless you even to the end of your journey through the promised land?

Chapter 21

THE PROMISED LAND:

THE CHURCH'S COMMUNION WITH GOD AND WITH EACH OTHER

As the Israelites and as each saint finish their earthly pilgrimages in the promised land, so must the full assembly of saints, the Church, end its journey there too. For it to be in any other place would mean God's body is out of His will and His presence.

As God made and kept promises to the Israelites and to each saint concerning the promised land, so He has made them to His Church. He has promised it a place of its own. For the Church to enjoy the land given to it, it must learn more about that land. It must learn where it is, what it is, and what it is not.

THE PROMISED LAND IS NOT....

The Church's promised land is not a physical dwelling place. When the Israelites crossed the Jordan River, they found themselves in a specific area of land. However, when the Church crosses the Jordan River, it will not find itself possessing a particular piece of real estate or occupying special buildings; instead, it will be in the spiritual kingdom of God on earth.

Also, in spite of the teaching of the words in the deeply moving spiritual song, "Swing Low, Sweet Chariot," the promised land is not heaven. When the Israelites crossed the Jordan River, they did not invade celestial palaces or enter the throne room of God. Similarly, when the Church crosses the Jordan River, it will not find itself striding down heavenly hallways; rather, it will be in a spiritual place on earth, enjoying His heavenly presence.

Third, the promised land is not that place of victorious living after the Church's removal from the earth. When the Israelites crossed the Jordan River, they were not caught away by God to a new world. When the Church crosses the Jordan River, it will not be caught away to a new world; instead, it will be expected to live victoriously right here on earth as it prepares for and awaits the return of the King.

Fourth, the promised land is not a kingdom of this world. It is not a conglomerate of worldly systems that have been confronted, infiltrated, cleaned up, or conquered by people through various works of flesh and then grandly handed over to Jesus. When Jesus forcefully declared: *"My kingdom is not of this world"* (John 18:36), He forever renounced ungodly world systems.

THE PROMISED LAND IS....

If the Church's promised land is not actual land, heaven, a place of escape, or a kingdom of the world, it is, at least in part, the place where the kingdom of God exists in the world. When Jesus came to earth two thousand years ago, He declared the kingdom of God to be at hand (Mark 1:15). After His death and resurrection, He declared all authority in heaven and on earth had been given to Him (Matthew 28:18). His sacrifice and victory over death made His kingdom a reality rather than a promise.

Therefore, the promised land can, to some extent, be identified with that separate and unique kingdom where Jesus reigns supreme. From this consecrated stronghold on earth He can rule over His Church and can extend His Father's kingdom. In this place sin and self have been dethroned, and Jesus, the King of the kingdom, has been enthroned right here on earth.

The promised land is a place of newness (Isaiah 42). As opposed to the temporary sojourning in the desert, it is a place of permanence. For the Church, it is a place of great fruitfulness. When God birthed His new Church in Jerusalem two thousand years ago, He sent a mighty rushing wind upon those who were gathered in the upper room waiting on Him. These valiant few were filled with His Holy Spirit, and this infilling and empowerment by His Spirit was considered a down payment on the Church's inheritance (Ephesians 1:13-14). It was only a part of the fullness, an earnest, or a pledge of future payment in full for a later time when God would express His mighty power through His Church on the earth.

Further, the promised land is a place of fellowship and intimate communion. This communion takes place not only between one part of the body of Christ and another, but, more importantly, between the whole body and its living God.

The promised land is the place where the Church bows to its Savior, Lord, and King in utter admiration, awe, and reverence. It is the place where the Church has free, glorious, and continuous access to the presence of God. It is the place where the Church, because it has learned to fear God, is quick to offer Him worship in both word and deed.

The promised land is where wars are fought in the heart of the assembly of God; where the sacred is separated from the profane; where light allowed to shine in the darkness; and where righteousness is victorious over sin, transgression, and iniquity. It is where the corporate body sees its enemies destroyed and driven out by the power of God, and where His Holy Spirit is then asked to come in to possess and occupy the conquered territories.

The promised land is the place where the body of Christ has come into true submission to its Head. It is the place where the body of Christ desires to unite its heart with the heart of its God. It is the place of final preparation for the bride's marriage to the Lamb.

When the promised land truly becomes the place where all the Church's opposition to God ceases, it will be the place of fulfillment, inheritance, maturity, and victory in God. It will be a place of rest.

Having learned of the Church's promised land, it is wise to learn about the inhabitants of that land. This special place has been given to the chosen ones of God, those who have received His promises, who have persisted in their long, arduous journeys, who have determined to possess and occupy. It would be nice to think that this place is occupied by those totally free from the world, flesh, self, and the attacks of the devil. However, such is not the case. While the promised land is meant to be the home of the family of God, to some extent it is the dwelling place of the enemies of God, of warring tribes, and even of giants.

When God gave Canaan to the Israelites, it was occupied by a number of His enemies. It was the Israelites' job to obey God's directions, to destroy these foes, to release the land from bondage, and then to possess and occupy it. Just so, God has given the Church a spiritual place in which to dwell that is inhabited by many of His enemies. Under the direction of Jesus, the Captain of the Hosts, He has commanded His Church to conquer and destroy the entrenched enemy, to free the area, to take possession, and to remain in that place, not budging one inch, even if the enemy tries to retake it.

God places great value on people and land, on His chosen ones and the place He has prepared for them. In Scripture, they are often seen as inseparable. For instance, both were involved in the covenant God made with Abram. First, God declared He would show an obedient Abram a new land (Genesis 12:1), a land that was identified as Canaan (Genesis 12:5). Then God said He would give that land to Abram's descendants (Genesis 12:7). Later, God again approached Abram, changed his name to Abraham, and declared he would be a father of nations (Genesis 17:4). To solidify the perpetual relationship of the land and the people who were to dwell there, God decreed:

> "I will establish My covenant between Me and you and your descendants after you throughout their generations for an everlasting covenant, to be God to you and to your descendants after you. I will give to you and to your descendants after you, the land of your sojournings, all the land of Canaan, for an everlasting possession; and I will be their God." (Genesis 17:7-8)

Later, under the Law, God issued commands that prevented the separation of the land from its inhabitants. Land inherited by certain tribes or families was to remain in their possession permanently. If land was sold, it had to be sold within tribe or family (1 Kings 21:3; Leviticus 25:23); if land was leased, it returned to its original owner at the Jubilee year (Leviticus 25:10); if land was inherited, it could only pass to a son or certain other relatives (Numbers 27:8-11; Deuteronomy 21:16). The titles of land were not to be muddied or tampered with in Israel, and no land was to be given away or allowed to be lost to those outside the borders of Israel for any reason at any time.

Today, the Church must realize that God still highly prizes land and people. While one is a spiritual realm occupying ground in the earthly realm and the other is comprised of born-again members of that realm, to Him they are inseparable. Both are involved in God's New Covenant with Abraham's descendants of faith, the Church. Both are involved in God's desire that those He loves and leads find their place. He has appointed certain saints to particular spheres of influence or areas of ministry on this earth so that His land and His people stay together and work in harmony.

When the Israelites did as God said to do, He preceded them in battle, fought for and with them, and destroyed the enemy by His great power. After – and only after – this happened did they receive, possess, and occupy Canaan, the land promised to them hundreds of years earlier. So too with the Church. When the army of God comes to attention, has been properly trained, follows its Lord into battle, and allows Him to conquer and destroy the enemy, it will receive the land that has long been promised. It is only after the battle and the victory that the Church will receive its territory and come into its rest.

The Land

To better understand this inheritance that is so precious to God and to the Church, once again the physical situation in the Old Testament must be studied. For the Hebrews, Canaan, son of Ham and grandson of Noah, long ago settled in the land that became known as Canaan (Genesis 10:15-20). Later, God promised this land to Abraham and his descendants, so Canaan became the promised land (Genesis 12:5-7). Then God changed the name of Abraham's grandson from Jacob to Israel. Thus, when his descendants entered Canaan, it became eventually became known as the land of Israel. Its inhabitants took their identity and name from their ancestor and their land and became known as Israelites.

For the Church, Jesus was and is the Christ, God's anointed One. He is Savior, Lord, King, and Judge of all the earth. His people are not his physical descendants, because Jesus did not marry or have children. Instead, they are God's spiritual descendants (Romans 9:8). They are settling in His promised land and are known by Jesus' name; they are called Christians. As Christians occupy His promised land, they bring it into the physical world where they live. Throughout the world, Christians walk where He walked, do as He did, stay where He stayed, and say what He said. They do the works Jesus did in His power, time, and way. They occupy His place. It is their inheritance.

In addition, before Boaz and Ruth could marry, Boaz had to act as a redeemer, gaining back his intended bride's lost ground (Ruth 3-4). When he approached the judges at the city gate, it was his responsibility to redeem Ruth. However, first he had to redeem her land. Just so, the remnant of the Church is beginning to cross into its promised land. There, they will meet their Lord. With shining eyes and bursting hearts they will glean in His field and ask Him to cover them with His mantle (Ruth 3:9). Yet, before the Beloved and the bride can marry, there must be a redemption. The bride has land that has been lost or given into the wrong hands. Jesus must redeem it or bring it back. Once the land is free, then Christ and His Church can become one.

Rest

This gigantic work, the redemption of the land, precedes the Church's rest. The Israelites never did enter a permanent rest. They didn't rest in the desert because they were always on the move. After Joshua parceled out the land, they only had a short rest before rebellion drove them into restlessness. Later, David's reign brought them another temporary rest, but even he declared that there remained a rest for the children of God (Hebrews 4:7-9).

To this day, there yet remains a rest, however, this time it is for God's family in the promised land. Rebellion, unbelief, and disobedience kept the Israelites from their rest, and if allowed to, these ungodly issues will also prevent the Church from entering its rest. However, if the Church will put sin behind it, will walk in obedience, will refuse to harden its heart against its Beloved, will leave rebellion in the desert (Hebrews 3:8-11), and will seek His ways (Hebrews 3:10), its rest awaits (Hebrews 4:9).

Seeking the ways of God is crucial to obtaining rest. The Israelites were concerned with God's acts, but Moses was concerned with His ways (Psalm 103:7). Similarly, in its desert experience the Church was concerned with acts or works, finally allowing methodology to become its hallmark. Its activities became marked by tradition, the repetition of particular works, certain words, or special behavior patterns to achieve certain results. Too, as the Israelites followed a set ritual in service to God, the desert Church followed form rather than faith, such as "Proclaim this and be rich," "Repeat this prayer ten times and be healed," and "Use only this liturgy and follow this order of worship." Such actions are an insult to the God who offered His people His Spirit so such dullness and repetition would not be necessary.

However, in the promised land, rest comes when interest in form turns to understanding why God does what He does (Isaiah 55:8-9) and in allowing Him to do it. Rest is relationship rather than relentless activity. It is knowing that who God is is much more important than attempting to duplicate or manipulate what He does. It is the end of striving or competing with God and the beginning of a new understanding of true faith and trust in Him. In the promised land, the cry of the Church is: *"Make me know Your ways, O LORD; teach me Your paths. Lead me in Your truth and teach me, for You are the God of my salvation; for You I wait all the day"* (Psalm 25:4-5).

BUILD AN ALTAR

Upon entering Canaan, the Israelites were confronted with three obligations. They were asked to build an altar to God, to circumcise themselves, and to celebrate Passover. Just so, to please God, upon entering the promised land the Church must serve the Lord in these same ways.

Once the Church truly realizes the bond between land, inhabitant, and God, it shouldn't be necessary to urge the people of God to erect an altar of praise to the One who led them in and who must keep them in. They will do so out of pure joy. The stones the Israelites used to build an altar commemorated God's power in bringing a whole nation into the promised land. The stones each saint used to build an altar are now a reminder that the saints are *"living stones ... being built up a spiritual house, a holy priesthood, to offer up spiritual sacrifices acceptable to God through Jesus Christ"* (1 Peter 2:5 NKJV). The stones that the Church uses to build an altar are stones it has picked up along its journey to the promised land. They are the stones of thanksgiving, submission, and dedication to the Living God for bringing the Church to that place where the greater measure of the Holy Spirit poured out on it will allow it to fulfill His great commission (Matthew 28:18-20).

BE CIRCUMCISED

Quickly after entry into the promised land, the Church must allow circumcision. God has taken particular interest in the condition of the heart of His bride. Just as the ark of the covenant was placed in the heart or the innermost room of the tabernacle and the presence of God is present in each saint's innermost chamber, his (or her) heart or spirit, so the true dwelling place of God is in the heart of His body, His Church, His bride.

If the body of Christ is the dwelling place of God, it must be an appropriate one. All scars and wounds must be cut away by the Master Surgeon. Of utmost importance, the Church must allow itself to be purged of all unforgiveness. Any hurts from past persecutions must be completely removed and the area given time to heal so a root of bitterness will not keep it from victory in the trials that will shortly be upon it. This circumcision of heart will be accompanied by a time of pain and weakness, and yet, though seeming to be vulnerable, it will be a time of safety and protection for the true Church.

If the heart of each individual saint is fraught with good and evil, so is the heart of the sum of the saints, the Church. To the same degree that each saint found that his (or her) heart housed both good and evil, to the same measure that each child of God found he was not a perfectly whole, completely mature dwelling place, so also the Church must acknowledge that it is a house whose heart is divided. Along with righteousness, evil is in residence. Along with some wonderful strengths, such as the salvation and blessings of God, there are some awful weaknesses, such as fear, anger, rebellion, and unbelief.

Only by multiplying the individual, unrepented sin that remains in one saint by the millions of Christians who are guilty of exactly the same transgression can the depth of the problem of sin be revealed in the whole Church. Some of the sins that so affect the body of Christ are:

- stealing, or the cheating, fraud, or theft of money which was given by or extorted from the flock of God to do the work of the kingdom of God but which was then misused or misappropriated to build the kingdoms of men and women

- passivity, or sitting idly by while clergy and religious leaders engaged in the vilest of sins against God and against the flock they claimed to serve

- harlotry with any degree of allowance of or participation in drug cultures, drunkenness, and deviations from the Word and the intention of God in matters of sexual sins

- unbelief and its companions of murmuring, grumbling, complaining, disobedience, and rebellion

- anger, which escalates into rage, wrath, violence, and murder in thought as well as in deed

- pride, which is characterized by conceit, haughtiness, presumption, arrogance, sectarianism, and self-exaltation

- fear, which brings terror, panic, desertion of God, and lack of faith and love

- hypocrisy, or being false, phony, deceitful, pharisaic, pretentious, insincere, two-faced, double-minded, double-hearted, saying one thing and doing another, or appearing to be one thing while in truth being quite something else

- idolatry, or physically, mentally, or spiritually raising up, creating, fashioning, or forming false gods and worshipping them in the place of true God

If the heart of individual saints needs deliverance, so does that of the assembly of saints, the Church. No bride so divided could love her Lord with her whole heart; no body so blemished could serve its Lord with its whole heart.

If the Church's heart betrays it as the Israelites' did thousands of years ago, it will never enter its rest. The promised land is the place of rest. If the Church refuses to deal with the condition of its heart, it will never dwell in the promised land and will never be at rest. Its sins of heart will disqualify it.

Earlier, each saint had to learn, receive, and believe that God is a God of deliverances (plural) in order to be set free. Likewise, the Church must be released from its corporate oppression. God **is** a God of deliverances (present tense). God delivered before, and He delivers now. He delivered the one, and He delivers the many. Scripture declares God to be the same yesterday, today, and forever (Hebrews 13:8). God did deliver; He does deliver; and, as long as the need continues, He will deliver. He can and will free His Church from the snare of the fowler, if He is asked to.

As God is able to reclaim and change individual hearts, so He is able to cleanse the communal heart of His Church. As His Church seeks Him, agrees with Him in His revelation of the true condition of its heart, repents to Him, confesses its sin, and receives His forgiveness, it will be circumcised. Further, the areas which sin has occupied will be brought under submission to Him.

As land in the heart is redeemed by the loving touch of God, revival will come. Only as the heart of the Church is changed inwardly can it manifest the changes outwardly; only as it is cleansed can it become a bright light in a dark world.

CELEBRATE THE FEAST OF PASSOVER

In addition to building an altar and being circumcised, the Church must enjoy the spiritual Feast of Passover in the promised land. Only in so doing will come its restoration as the strong, powerful body which is entrusted and enabled to manifest the works of Christ on the earth.

The Word declares the whole Church has been purchased or redeemed by the blood of Christ (Acts 20:28). The Church must now learn that the blood of the Lamb is its first major weapon of warfare.

In acknowledging its redemption by the blood of the Lamb, the Church must drop the deceptive error that says it does not sin. If the Church had no sin it would not need to prepare itself for marriage by the removal of spot and wrinkle (Ephesians 5:27). If the bride was truly ready, her Groom would already have come for her.

Upon entering the promised land, the Church must understand that though Egypt and the desert are behind it, both were places of great sin. For the Israelites and for each saint, the brazen altar has always been the place of reconciliation with God; it is no less so for the whole body of Christ. The Church must continually pause there to ensure all is right with God. Any unrepented sin accumulated over the course of the journey must be placed under the blood of Jesus. Only through confession and forgiveness of sin can the Church remain in right relationship to God and, as a clean vessel, be enabled to do His works.

Even as the Church begins to cross over the Jordan River and to emerge in the promised land, it must pray to God that He would strengthen it so it will be able to pass the tests that will soon confront it. Having separated itself from the world with the exodus from Egypt and from the practice of human law and tradition with the departure from the desert, God still continues to weed out those in the counterfeit church system from those who are His true Church. While in the promised land, those who, through God, are successful in building His altar, submitting to circumcision, and celebrating reconciliation have passed His first tests. In all of this, the Lord has begun the process of restoration.

Restoration is renewal or restitution. It is returning to a former condition or bringing back the original state of something. It is to give back something lost or taken away, to put it back in the possession of its rightful owner. It is to bring something into existence again and to place it back in its former position. This does not necessarily mean a restructuring or a refurnishing of the old, but rather it is a replacement of another, newer one of the same kind.

Godly restoration involves not some but all of these concepts. As such, it encompasses the Church, the Lord, and the earth. For saints who are the Church, restoration means returning to a former condition. Once Adam and Eve walked with God. Their bodies, minds, and spirits were fully functional and in intimate communion with their Creator. However, when sin entered the world through their rebellion, their hearts or spirits (and thus all mankind's hearts or spirits) were cut off from the heart and Spirit of God. Through spiritual rebirth, each saint's deadened spirit was quickened or restored to communion with God. With his (or her) spirit regenerated, he became able to walk in His righteousness.

For the Lord, restoration is the return of something lost. It is His regaining possession of His lands and people. It is His receiving those things lost or taken away, and, as their rightful owner, once again assuming authority over them. It is His resuming fellowship and communion with those He so dearly loves with all His great heart of hearts.

For the earth, restoration means replacement. Due to the sins of humanity, of poor stewardship, and of the shedding of blood that has defiled it, the earth has been corrupted. Yet, in spite of this corruption, mankind has deified it. From millennia long past until today, people have worshipped this created object called Earth rather than revering the One who did the creating, Almighty and Holy God.

Without question, while early civilizations knew and admitted the existence of a supreme being, in searching for Him they fell into error and sin. They rebelled against the divinely ordained way of reconciliation with God and then substituted meaningless human ritual to accomplish this purpose. In so doing, they fell into idolatry. They began to honor the creation instead of the Creator.

The ancient roots of pagan religions have a common denominator. They worship the earth and honor the gods they believe to have power over the earth. To these, the earth is seen as a woman, Mother Earth, who is to be appeased by various rituals so she is willing to bless her people with the necessities of life. Usually accompanied by some form of fertility rite that often involves barbaric sacrifices or perverted sexual practices, these rituals were meant to keep Mother Earth's womb fertile to reproduce, repopulate, and replenish mankind's needs from her abundance.

Wherever such idolatrous things have occurred, God has been profaned, not honored. Also, where such things have happened, the earth has been corrupted, not honored. Since God will not be mocked (Galatians 6:7), He will not allow such pollution of His creation to go unjudged. If people refuse to heed God's command to seek first the kingdom of God and to trust that needful things, such as food and clothing, will come from Him (Matthew 6:25-33) rather than from the caprice of the ungodly, judgment is forthcoming.

Then, for the earth, restoration is not a restructuring of the old but a removal of, a remaking, and the introduction of a new earth of the same order. Although religious cults and those of New Age persuasion passionately deny it, God's answer to all earth worship will be the total destruction of the earth that has been so polluted and deified (Revelation 21:1). In fact, precisely because the earth has become a god, it will have to be destroyed.

Unbelieving men and women will be awestruck when Jesus appears from heaven in flaming fire (2 Thessalonians 1:7). They will stand by helplessly while the true God whom they deny destroys their false god, the earth, by fire (2 Peter 3:7). Then, after the first have passed away, a new heaven and earth will appear (Revelation 21:1-2). This will restore a heaven and earth of the same order as the old, yet a new one over which God will rule and reign forever.

For the Church, restoration is the end product of a process which begins with repenting, continues with returning to God, and goes on to being refreshed by God. Without repentance there can be no restoration. It is only **after** repentance and a return to God have taken place that times of refreshing in Him can occur. After the times of refreshing, Jesus will be released to come and restore all things. Concerning this, Acts 3:19-21 states:

> *Therefore repent and return, so that your sins may be wiped away, in order that times of refreshing may come from the presence of the Lord; and that He may send Jesus, the Christ appointed for you, whom heaven must receive until the period of restoration of all things about which God spoke by the mouth of His holy prophets from ancient time.*

The Church has long wanted to reverse the process and enjoy restoration without lowering itself to God's preliminary requirements. Yet, only as it submits to His order and repents will a purged, purified body be returned to its former condition. Then, and only then, will it be like its ancestor, the body that turned the world upside down (Acts 17:6 NKJV).

ENGAGE IN WARFARE

Even as godly restoration is going on, the Church will come to realize that for a short while at least, its future will involve heavy warfare. To succeed at such, the Church will need a leader, a commander of the army. First, the Church had to call out to its Redeemer. Then, it met its Master. Now, it must submit to its Commander-in-chief, LORD Sabaioth, the LORD of Hosts. His name is a second source of strength in promised-land warfare.

The LORD Sabaioth is the Redeemer (Isaiah 47:4); He is Husband and Maker (Isaiah 54:5). He is a great King (Jeremiah 46:18; Malachi 1:14), the God of Jacob (Psalm 46:7), and the God of Israel (Isaiah 48:2). He is the great and mighty God (Jeremiah 32:17-18) and the righteous Judge (Jeremiah 11:20). He is a sanctuary (Isaiah 8:13-14), the presence or the ark of God (2 Samuel 6:2).

In addition to these wonderful titles, LORD Sabaioth has some marvelous attributes. The LORD of Hosts is the One whom Isaiah describes as three times holy, the One whose glory covers the earth (Isaiah 6:3). He is so powerful that nothing is impossible to Him (Jeremiah 32:17-18). Further, He is omnipresent (Haggai 2:4-5) and a defender of His people (Zechariah 9:15). Therefore, as David (1 Samuel 17:45) and Hannah (1 Samuel 1:2, 11) discovered, He is the champion of impossible situations and hopeless causes, achieving great victories because He does not work by human might nor by fleshly power but by His Spirit (Zechariah 4:6).

Although from Samuel to Malachi, the books of the Old Covenant are full of the name LORD Sabaioth, the LORD of Hosts, He is not mentioned by that name in the New Testament. Who then is Redeemer, Lord, King, and God? Who is holy and powerful in the New Testament? None other than Jesus. The Church must honor and revere Jesus (John 5:23); the Church must be in awe of or fear Jesus (Acts 9:31; Ephesians 5:21). The Church must invoke the name of Jesus, LORD of Hosts, for help in its spiritual warfare (1 Corinthians 15:57). Only as it does so will the secret kingdoms of its heart be cleansed and the kingdom of this world become kingdom of the Lord and of His Christ (Revelation 11:15).

In many ways, spiritual warfare is similar to physical combat. First, any fighting group that is determined to ignore its leadership is headed for certain disaster. To win a war, an army must submit to the commands of its highest leaders. In like manner, the Church, as the army of God, must submit to its Head, Jesus. While some in the army of God may be green privates just out of basic training and others may be captains, colonels, or generals, **all** are under the higher authority of God. All must acknowledge Him as Leader and fall in behind Him. Further, just as privates, corporals, and sergeants must obey those in rank above them, so new or immature Christians should submit to the leadership of those more spiritually mature than them.

Second, like physical warfare, spiritual warfare demands

obedience. Soldiers are required to obey orders. The Church and its saints are warriors only if they are servants; their obedience is to submit to and carry out the will of God. The soldiers are not in charge of how the war is fought; the Lord is. God's army can triumph only as it receives and carries out the orders of the One who has already defeated the same enemies it is now facing.

Spiritual warfare is not a matter of personal preference. As the Israelites and as each saint had to learn, so now the Church must determine that being in God's army means following God's commands. The Israelites were not able to choose their enemies, and neither does the Church. The Israelites were not able to choose the means of defeating them, and neither does the Church. However, the Israelites were able to choose whether or not they would obey God's choices. Even if the orders seemed strange (Joshua 6:1-21; Judges 7), when they fought as commanded they won great victories; when they disobeyed, they met defeat.

So too with the army of God. If the Church obeys its Leader, it will see victory. If it rebels, it will lose the manifest presence of God. If it loses the presence of God, it will lose the power of God, and if it loses the power of God, it will be defeated. Like the Israelites, God has commanded the Church to possess and occupy the land that has been promised to it. For that to happen, it must call out to God and ask Him, either by a sovereign act or through His saved and sanctified army, to conquer and destroy the enemies who are entrenched there and to cast them away.

A third requirement of spiritual and of physical warfare is the need to accurately identify the enemy. The enemies of the Israelites were physical people who occupied the promised land and who tried to prevent God's people from entering it. In contrast, the enemies of the Church are spiritual. They are the minions of Satan who attack the bodies and souls of saints. While they are not people, they can sometimes manifest themselves through people. For the Israelites, those dwelling in Canaan were the Hittites, Girgashites, Amorites, Canaanites, Perizites, Hivites, and Jebusites. A loose translation of these names provides the Church with clues as to the identity of the foes deep within its promised land today: fear, restlessness, rebellion, greed or materialism, carelessness, wickedness, oppression, and depression. If the Church cannot discern these enemies, acknowledge their existence, and determine to fight them until they are defeated and driven off, it will never know the joys of place and peace in its promised land.

In addition to submitting to leadership, obeying orders, and identifying the enemy, the participants in spiritual warfare must familiarize themselves with the battlefield as their Hebrew counterparts did. Spiritual warfare is no hit-or-miss campaign. On the contrary, it requires sound strategy for victory. While different parts of the body of Christ can be engaged in different aspects of battle at any one time, there is one overall war. Since the point of spiritual warfare is to defeat God's enemies and to drive them out of areas they have illegally usurped and occupied, it should come as no surprise that the main battleground of such warfare is in the heart of the Church.

The heart of the bride of Christ must be a chamber of love, mercy, and compassion. Since Christ is enthroned there and since the foundation of His throne is righteousness and justice (Psalm 97:2), then righteousness and justice must be found there too. Additionally, the heart must have halls of holiness, chambers of honor, galleries of glory, rooms of reverence, apartments of beauty and majesty, and passageways of peace and joy.

Instead, the Church's heart is divided, and it must clear the battleground of the enemy troops gathered against it and trampling it into the ground. It must learn lessons from the battles of Jericho and Ai.

The Israelites gained victory at Jericho through obedience and trumpet blasts. Those enjoined in holy battle today must listen for the sound from God's trumpeters, those godly prophets who blast forth the sure word of God. The Church must stop listening and responding to the voices of people who mislead it and instead must listen and respond to the voice of God alone. His sheep know His voice (John 10:4). The sound of His word must precede and carry every battle, or it will end in disaster. The sound of His word will knock down walls and will destroy the enemies of God.

Concerning Ai, the army of God must learn that the sins of just one of its soldiers brings the judgment of God on all, that the actions of one errant, rebellious warrior affects the whole body (1 Corinthians 12:26). If one man, Achan, brought delay, defeat, and death to the Israelites, so today the behavior of one irresponsible saint can bring great harm to the whole body of Christ unless his (or her) sins are brought to light and godly discipline is measured out to him.

Also, on the battlefield, the Church must practice faith instead of fear. In clearing the land of enemy troops, it must believe that God said:

> "If you should say in your heart, 'These nations are greater than I; how can I dispossess them?' ... You shall not dread them, for

the LORD your God is in your midst, a great and awesome God. The LORD your God will clear away these nations before you little by little; you will not be able to put an end to them quickly, for the wild beasts would grow too numerous for you. But the LORD your God will deliver them before you, and will throw them into great confusion until they are destroyed. He will deliver their kings into your hand so that you will make their name perish from under heaven; no man will be able to stand before you until you have destroyed them." (Deuteronomy 7:17, 21-24)

God has a plan to free the heart of His Church and to defeat the enemy entrenched in the promised land. In His war campaign, He will drive a wedge between the rebellious kingdoms that divide the heart and pick them off, one by one. While some of these have been identified, such as fear, idolatry, and unbelief, another is often not recognized or accepted as a foe. One of the heart's most heinous enemies, that which divides it more than could ever be imagined, is denominationalism. Reminding the Church that a house or dwelling place of God divided against itself cannot stand (Matthew 12:25), God will bring His Church to its knees in repentance. He will make His word a living reality as judgment floods the house of God and as the barriers between groups of saints are knocked down. When denominationalism is conquered and brought under the authority of the LORD of Hosts, His remnant will possess and occupy a united heart.

While God is conquering the Church's internal enemies, He will also secure and protect the true Church while He destroys its external foes. When He is done purging, He will oversee the establishment of the resting place for His true Church. This resting place is neither a worldly, materialistic, humanistic kingdom such as the Israelites once sought nor the New Age, kingdom now, replacement theology, dominion theology, one-world religion that the false church system promotes. Rather, it is the spiritual home of the corporate body of Christ, the dwelling place of God, the sanctuary from which He sends out His saints to establish the kingdom of God on the earth and to prepare for His coming.

KNOW GOD'S WORD

Without weapons, no army could win a war. While guns, tanks, ships, jets, and missiles spit forth power in human conflict, the weapons of God are even more powerful. When employed in the way, place, and time of His choosing, they always bring victory. Already the Church's weapons of the blood of the Lamb and the name of the Lord have been discussed. Another of the Church's main weapons in warfare is the Word of God.

Victories at Jericho and Ai allowed the Israelites to penetrate further into Canaan. Similarly, victories there also allow the Church to plunge more deeply into its promised land. As it does so, it will come to Mount Ebal and Mount Gerizim. Here, as the Church reviews its covenant with God, as it meditates on the Law of the Lord, as it reads His Word and speaks that Word boldly forth, it will discover the unimaginable, immeasurable power of that Word.

When Joshua spoke forth the blessings and curses of God's Word and when the Israelites added their amens to them at Mount Ebal and Mount Gerizim, God was showing His people the clear-cut differences between the enemies who had occupied the land and the chosen ones to whom He had given it. It was a definitive listing of reasons why the heathen had been dispossessed and why God had conquered it and brought it under His authority (Deuteronomy 27-28).

In declaring the way His people were to live, God was also declaring against the way His enemies had lived. Since their behavior was found wanting, was judged, and was defeated, such evil was never to be permitted again. The Church needs to understand that those words are still in effect. God does not permit certain behavior in His land or His people. His Word clearly identifies His standard. If His people deviate from it, He will unleash His sword and bring down His judgments once again. If His Church says amen to His Word, it will be blessed; if it denies, ignores, or disobeys it, it will be riddled with problems.

When spoken in love, God's Word draws hearts toward Him. When spoken in mercy, God's Word comforts and soothes. When spoken in holy counsel, God's Word leads. When spoken in exhortation, God's Word builds, awakens, and excites. When spoken in battle, God's Word routs the enemy, sends terror into his heart, and defeats and destroys him. God's Word, the sword of the Lord, brings victory in warfare.

REJECT APOSTASY

What is keeping the Church from the full realization of its inheritance and rest? The answer is apostasy.

After the Israelites inherited the land of Canaan they fell away, and, in so doing, they lost the presence of God. Even after that presence was restored under David and the ark of the presence was installed in

Solomon's Temple, they fell away again. This apostasy was accompanied by civil war, alliances with unholy nations, and mockery of a religious system steeped in idolatry that celebrated false holidays on false altars through an unholy priesthood.

Things aren't so different today. Civil war has split the Church into multiple groups and denominations, each calling itself the true Church. Church government has corrupted itself by compromising with the world. The Church has witnessed a phenomenal rise in false gods, false altars, and false worship. Further, in many cases, a tainted priesthood is dishonoring rather than honoring God.

Sometimes, it is almost impossible to distinguish the Church from the world out of which it was called. At times, politics, rather than the passion of Christ, is preached from compromised pulpits, and social programs all but obscure spiritual ones. At other times, some churches may hypocritically involve themselves in the unholy plans of earth festivals or gushingly ally themselves with Hollywood stars who want to use those churches to promote their causes of feeding the world or fighting certain diseases, even while the churches brazenly refuse to care for their own. Some youth pastors take their lesson plans from popular, ungodly novels. The Church seems to have forgotten the warning given to the remnant of Judah: *"the LORD is with you when you are with Him. And if you seek Him, He will let you find Him; but if you forsake Him, He will forsake you"* (2 Chronicles 15:2).

As it did in Saul's time, the true army of God will emerge during the apostasy. The ragtag remnant, the dregs of religious and civil society, will gather round King David's successor, Jesus; join forces with Him; and follow Him. Small in number, they will be living proof that the way to God is a straight and narrow path, and there are few who find it (Matthew 7:14).

Similarly, the true bride will emerge from among the rejects. As Abigail, the true Church will prove to be a handmaiden willing to bow to her Lord. The bride will not be comprised of those who merely profess Christianity but of those who have truly come into relationship with the living God and who know He is holy, pure, and perfect in all His ways. She will be comprised of those who are determined that nothing – no person, no god, no cult, no divisions, no deceptions, and no human tradition – will keep her from intimate relationship with Him. She will be comprised of those who remain accountable to God and in fellowship with saints but who declare themselves to be neither subject to nor answerable to unholy leaders. She will be comprised of those who respect the anointing of God rather than those who fear people. She will be comprised of those to whom the declaration that the Lord is her Husband (Isaiah 54:5) means absolutely everything.

WORSHIP GOD

As the true Church grows in knowledge and awareness of its true God, it grows in knowledge and awareness of the need to worship its true God. Moses, King David, and King Solomon built tabernacles and a temple where their people could worship their God. Of these three structures for worship, David's was unique. It was unprecedented in the history of Israel. David's tabernacle was not a building; it was a tent. Rather than being enclosed so that only a few could enter, it had no walls, so all could approach God. It had no veil separating the people from the Ark of the Covenant, so the people could worship in the very presence of God. There were no animal sacrifices, only the spiritual sacrifices of praise and thanksgiving (1 Chronicles 16:4). There was no specified order of worship, so worshippers could sing (1 Chronicles 15:16; 15:22), play their instruments (1 Chronicles 23:5), dance (1 Chronicles 15:29), or rejoice (1 Chronicles 16:10) day and night in ways of their choosing as they adored their God.

This moment in history when David's tabernacle was the epicenter of worship was a foretaste or a prophetic unveiling of how worship in the true Church should be. Today, God is worshipped in a temple not made by human hands (Acts 7:48). This temple is the Church, the assembly of saints. The apostle Paul points this fact out to the believers in Corinth when he writes: *"Do you not know that you are the temple of God and that the Spirit of God dwells in you?"* (1 Corinthians 3:16). Today, God is to be worshipped in spirit (John 4:24), not in ritual. Here, in His holy temple built in a way of His choosing, the people of His choosing dedicate the temple to Him, ask Him to fill it with His Spirit, bow before Him, honor Him, praise Him, and worship Him.

CELEBRATE THE FEAST OF TABERNACLES

It is sad to say that a large part of the Church is not yet in the promised land. As a vanguard precedes the main body of an army, so more and more individual saints have been crossing the Jordan River ahead of the rest of the body of Christ. Yet, the Church, as a whole assembly of God, has not entered Canaan. Since this is true, the Church has not known the fullness or the joy of the spiritual celebration known as the Feast of Tabernacles.

In its future Feast of Tabernacles, the Church will celebrate the Feast of Booths. It will remember the buildings it once thought were the Church before it discovered that its saints were the Church. It will recall the church buildings or cathedrals that idolized men and women's creativity and witnessed to their limited concept of God. It will be reminded of the shelters that housed it and the locations it lived in before finally arriving at the heart and will of God. Joyful, it will someday realize that it need never again dwell in such hopeless, finite, temporary shelters.

The Feast of Tabernacles, also called the Feast of the Harvest, was to be celebrated after the final harvest had been brought in. This feast is particularly significant since, unlike Passover and Pentecost, it has not yet been realized or come to pass in the Church. God desires *"all people to be saved and to come to a knowledge of the truth"* (1 Timothy 2:4 NIV). Therefore, He has planned that lost souls from every nation will be brought into His kingdom. For the Church, God's harvest is the last call. It is the final worldwide reaping of souls out of the world and into the kingdom of God. When the harvest is complete, the world will be rocked by rejoicing as untold millions, now a part of His Church, join their brothers and sisters around the globe to celebrate their God, praising Him and thanking Him for His mercy, grace, power, and love.

In celebrating this feast, the true Church must be careful. God's Church has seen the duplication or the counterfeiting of His ordinances, offices, gifts, and fruit and has witnessed both His name being taken in vain and His blood being denigrated by an apostate, worldly church system. These same issues are now happening concerning His feasts.

While God's Church has been slow in finding and assuming its rightful place, while it has dawdled in the desert, the counterfeit church system has been active. It has assumed a false identity and has established a fake Feast of Tabernacles. In its nefarious way, it is commanding both the true Church and the world to celebrate.

Like Jeroboam, who changed the date of God's feast from the seventh to the eighth month (1 Kings 12:32-33), causing all who celebrated it to partake of a false festival, so today many who are in rebellion to God have changed His plan and order. They have inaugurated a counterfeit feast and are busily trying to pass it off as the real thing.

Church, be warned! The counterfeit Feast of Tabernacles resembles the holy one in many ways. However, while it looks good and sounds good, it is the spawn of sin and evil. Judge! Discern! Do not be deceived! God clearly commands His Church to celebrate **His** feast, so His body must partake only of the holy and true one. The false feast leads the true Church into the camp of New Age theology and into the domination of religious cults. It leads to antichrist and to perdition.

For safety's sake, the Church must study the true Feast of Tabernacles. It must compare and contrast it with the false festival into which the world and its dupe, the religious system, are leading the unwary. Only by the grace of God can the Church learn and discern which feast it will be a part of.

Rest

First, Tabernacles is a feast of rest. For His body, this does not mean a dropping of the guard or a plunging into passivity. Rather, it means the cessation of the restlessness that accompanies unbelief. Rest is the certainty of knowing that no matter the situation, God is able. It is the absolute trust in the safety and security that He offers. It is a time in which striving in flesh ceases, so great productivity and fruitfulness is gained in spirit. It is the enthronement of the presence of God in the innermost chamber of the temple of God and the removal of the staves or carrying poles, so God is no longer moved about. He is now permanently at home in the heart of His Church.

The Bible declares God worked for six days and rested on the seventh (Genesis 2:2). So must people. If work has continued for two thousand years from Adam to Abraham and two thousand years from Abraham to Jesus and two thousand years from Jesus' birth to His return, that is six thousand years or six days (2 Peter 3:8). It is time for the Church to celebrate the seventh period of one thousand years (or one day) in spiritual rest with God during the period known as the millennium.

The counterfeit of all of this is the "rest" of false peace promoted by the world and the false religious system. The world, which does not know Jesus as Savior, cannot know Him as Jehovah-shalom, the Lord who is peace. Since it has ignored and rejected the Prince of Peace, it does not and cannot have His peace. Therefore, the world cannot promote or give away that which it does not have – true peace.

Too, the false church system is full of false prophets who trumpet, *"'Peace, peace,' but there is no peace"* (Jeremiah 6:14). These false prophets are in rebellion against God. They declare God is a God of love but deny He is also a God of justice and righteousness. Since they do not teach that saints and sinners alike are accountable to God for sin, they do not accept the fact that judgment is coming. Through false words they seduce men and women into a false sense of security and irresponsibility. They then call out for people to be at peace with each other rather than guiding them to peace with God.

Unity

Next, Tabernacles is a feast of unity. Godly unity always centers around Jesus; each saint's eyes should be fixed on him (Hebrews 12:2). The common denominator of holy unity is not people with their denominations and cults. Instead, it is a bonding of those whose hearts are one with God. The root of holy unity is not agreement with human or satanic wisdom, customs, creeds, or traditions. Rather, it is an awareness of those who know each other in spirit and who recognize the presence of God in each other. True unity is oneness in spirit with God: *"There is one body and one Spirit, just as also you were called in one hope of your calling; one Lord, one faith, one baptism, one God and Father of all who is over all and through all and in all"* (Ephesians 4:4-6).

Too, there is one Son, one sacrifice, one Shepherd, one flock. There is one Head of one Church. When Jesus said He would build His Church, He used the singular form of the word Church. Therefore, there is only one Church, and it is of God, not of mankind.

As has been aptly said, unity is not conformity to uniformity. It is a meeting of kindred spirits (Philippians 2:20) whose goal is spiritual fellowship with God (Philippians 2:1-2). Therefore, for the true Church, unity is the oneness of the saved, called out, spirit-filled assembly of men and women who, after uniting in heart with God, find unity in fellowship with each other.

The world and the false church system have a different version of unity. In sin and error, the world teaches that unity means everyone is united under one civil government. At first propagandized and made to appear voluntary, this decision must ultimately be enforced by an army, such as in Nazi Germany. The concept of world peace and unity is gaining in popularity and one day will be enforced by a worldwide army. Further, in striving for false unity, the world advances the idea of entrapping all the earth's finances into one central financial headquarters or world bank. Another counterfeit face of worldly unity is the absolute necessity to harness and limit God under the yoke of one unholy, world religion. Instead of honoring the godly ordained body which is founded on the Rock, it demands the creation of a universal, unholy, manmade religion that is demonically inspired and that worships power, not God.

The world and the Church have been prepared for one world religion headed by one person as they have accepted the unscriptural organizations of leadership found in local assemblies and denominational hierarchies. Under the counterfeit church system, one-person dictatorships abound. One leader is often considered the god of a local Church, and he (or she) rules "his" Church with an iron hand. He has the final word in personal as well as religious matters and demands to be obeyed whether he is right or wrong. All opposition is shouted down or removed. He controls all church offices, chairmanships, and church boards and dictates in unholy ways the manifestations of the gifts and the expressions of the fruit of the Spirit.

Then, moving from local Church to denominational headquarters, there exists an ascending pyramid of authority with one man or woman on top. Although the headquarters may be organized into boards of directors or heads of departments, one person often rules those professing obedience to that particular brand of religion.

By such error at the local and denominational levels, the world has been prepared to accept the same pattern of control at the universal level. Thanks to the tradition of the false church system's order of government, the world is looking for religious unity from people rather than from God. It doesn't realize it is casting its future into the hands of a Saul rather than a David. Those who know no better, those who have been taught and who have grown accustomed to such error, and those who exercise no discernment will see the rise of a religious dictator who will promise unity and peace. Contrary to holy unity, he (or she) will introduce and promote a demonic deception of unity that, if followed, will allow mankind to be one with him and with each other even as it costs them unity with God.

Equality

The Feast of Tabernacles is also a feast of equality. For the Church, this means that through a born-again experience, all members of the body of Christ are equal with each other or are the same in the eyes of God. God shows no partiality within His body (Deuteronomy 10:17; Acts 10:34). To Him, each saint is a living stone who, when added to all the other stones, forms His Church. While the works of saints will yield lesser or greater rewards, the position of all saints is equal under God.

For the world, sinners are also equal in the eyes of God. God is not biased or unfair with them either; He judges all impartially. All who are in sin, all who have refused to ask Jesus to be their Savior, are condemned by God. The unsaved, equally lost, will spend eternity in the same place, the lake of fire (Revelation 20:15).

Again, the world and the counterfeit church system rebel against God's sovereignty in this matter. They refute godly equality and offer substitute, heretical theories of impartiality. They downplay the truth that people are equal with other people and instead give rise to the error that people are equal with God.

One way in which the world, especially those bound into New Age error, pervert the principle of equality is by reducing God to the level of paganism. Rather than acknowledging that God is the Creator, and therefore the Ruler, of all things, they make God the equal to that which is created.

In a lie known as pantheism, they declare that since God is in all things then God is all things. Therefore, everything is God. Further, they revert to heathenish motivations and methods of worship and declare that since God is the sun, trees, and animals, it is proper to worship them. However, the Bible is clear that God alone is to be worshipped:

> *You shall worship the Lord your God and serve Him only.* (Luke 4:8)

> *For the LORD is a great God, and a great King above all gods, in whose hand are the depths of the earth; the peaks of the mountains are His also. The sea is His, for it was He who made it; and His hands formed the dry land.* (Psalm 95:3-5)

These verses clearly show God's majesty as Creator and Ruler over the earth and declare the earth's need to worship Him rather than to accept worship. (See also Exodus 20:4-6; Deuteronomy 17:5; Psalm 46; Psalm 47; Psalm 114:7; Romans 1:25.)

A second corruption of holy equality which is espoused not only by the world but also by parts of the false church system is that people can evolve to become like God and then can be equal with God. They declare that people can become gods. However, the truth declares there is only one true God to whom all men and women are subject. The Bible is filled with instructions to mankind to give thanks, honor, and praise to God rather than to receive it themselves. For example:

> *He [God] is exalted above all the peoples.* (Psalm 99:2)
>
> *For we are the true circumcision, who worship in the Spirit of God and glory in Christ Jesus and put no confidence in the flesh* (Philippians 3:3)
>
> *All the peoples have seen His glory. Let all those be ashamed who serve graven images, who boast themselves of idols* (Psalm 97:7)

(See also Psalm 2; Revelation 22:9). Nowhere does the Word even imply that people are the equal of God.

Joy

The Feast of Tabernacles is a time of joy. It is a celebration of God in which old, former, traditional methods of praise and worship are replaced by spontaneity of worship in and by the Holy Spirit. It is the Church walking on higher heights and in deeper depths of worship, expressing itself in new ways full of joy in the Lord, and doing things decently and in order as led by the Holy Spirit of God.

No one knows God better than His own Spirit. No one knows the way He prefers to be worshipped at any given time or situation than His own Spirit. No one can better lead and instruct the Church in holy worship than the Holy Spirit. True worship is the Spirit of God leading the saints of God into fearful and holy expressions of joy that honor, glorify, and exalt Jesus. In turn, He, as the Church's High Priest, offers their sacrifices of praise unto God and reveals the Father to them (Matthew 11:27; Hebrews 13:15).

Yet here too is a counterfeit exercise of joy. Denominational churches which do not know God call their dead, traditional song services worship. Evangelical churches, which admit the presence but not the power of the Holy Spirit, refuse to be led past predetermined boundaries by Him. Even Pentecostal churches are now reverting to predetermined lists of songs diligently practiced for three hours on Thursday night and are calling that the spontaneity of the Holy Spirit on Sunday morning. Or, relying on the use of overhead projectors, expensive sound systems, and hype and splash, they make worship an intellectual or emotional experience instead of an exercise of spirit. All these counterfeits of worship bring death to the Church.

Or, in the opposite extreme, to prove that "the Holy Spirit has freedom to lead the show," anything goes. All too often praise and worship is accompanied by the pounding of fast-paced, overly loud music. When this happens, the response to praise is determined by the tone and tempo of the music rather than by divine direction. As the music plays, the congregation pours into the aisle to dance, jump, or move about in some way, all the while shouting or belting out the lyrics and acting as if they are at a rock concert rather than a worship service. If the music is slow and quiet, few know what to do, since a restless Church cannot quietly dwell in His presence. With no discernment being exercised, much of the Church is unaware as to which spirit is leading them or which god is being appealed to or honored. Whole bodies cross the threshold from divine to demonic and never even know it. While this may be a joy to Satan, it surely is not to the Lord God.

A second aspect of joy must be discussed. To the Church joy is not a fleeting, temporary reverie produced by pleasant feelings or surroundings. It is an internal rejoicing of spirit. Since it is given by God and is a result of relationship with God (Romans 14:17), the world doesn't have it.

While at first it may seem contradictory, for the Church suffering is a part of joy. God has affirmed this in His Word: *"Consider it all joy, my brethren, when you encounter various trials...."* (James 1:2). To do so produces endurance. Further, His Word says: *"And not only this, but we also exult in our tribulations...."* (Romans 5:3). To do so produces perseverance, character, and hope. It is only through trials that a saint can enter the kingdom of God (Acts 14:22), and only as he (or she) endures under trial that he will receive the crown of life (James 1:12).

In contrast to this, the world and the false church system do not let God reach them and teach them through suffering. They do not allow God to have His way in the areas of tests, trials, and tribulations. They do not allow growth through hardship.

The counterfeit theology of the counterfeit church produces a counterfeit joy. Deceivers, mocking the Word of God, tell all who begin to experience a test or a trial to think positively, to confess positively, and to name and claim their humanly determined need or heart's desire so they will suffer as little as possible. Instead of producing joy, these spurious religious rituals produce a desperate people which knows no joy, a people which cannot endure, a people which has no character, a people which cannot find its place in the kingdom of God, and a people which has been robbed of the treasures of hope and the crown of life.

Prayer

Another aspect of Tabernacles is that it is a feast of prayer. Even in the midst of celebration there can be no distraction from communion with God. In ancient Israel, one of the branches waved during the Feast of Tabernacles was that from the olive tree, and it symbolized the anointing of the Holy Spirit. Through prayer, the Church must seek the anointing of the Holy Spirit, the power and ability from God to do what He has asked it to do.

The anointing of God is absolutely crucial to the Church. David was anointed before he could be king (1 Samuel 16:13), and Old Testament priests were anointed before they could serve God (Exodus 28:41). If the kings and priests in the Church are to serve God today (Revelation 1:6), it can only be with His anointing. They must seek that in prayer.

As with all other aspects of the Feast of Tabernacles, a demonic counterfeit of prayer exists. The world would deny and ignore prayer altogether, instead aggrandizing people and their abilities. Meanwhile, the false church system would pray but to the wrong god. It may be seen doing and may be heard saying the right things, but since it doesn't know the Son or the Father, its petitions are heard by the wrong master.

Just as bad, the prayers offered by members of the religious organization are often critical, judgmental, and condemning in nature and can cause great harm to the body of Christ. In fact, they can be used to conjure up all kinds of devilish attacks against the true people of God. Satan is still bent on destroying the true Church and is not above answering the prayers of the unwise and undiscerning in his attempt to do so.

Sacrifice

For the Church, the Feast of Tabernacles is a celebration of sacrifice as well. God's Church must pattern itself after its Lord. It must suffer the things He suffered; it must endure the things He endured. In no way is this belittling or trying to imitate His sacrifice at the cross for the salvation of the world, but it is walking in His steps even when the path may lead to pain and suffering.

Jesus came to earth as a Suffering Servant (Isaiah 53; Philippians 2:5-7). The Son of Man suffered many things (Mark 8:31), and He had to die before rising again (Luke 24:46). So must His body. If it is to conform to His image, the Church must suffer too. Christ warned the Church to expect tribulation (John 16:33). It must face the fact that life is not one long joyride from here to eternity. Salvation in not a ticket to endless bliss here on this earth.

Christ suffered for the Church so it could be saved. He also suffered as an example to His disciples. To encourage them, the apostle Peter wrote to the saints who were scattered around the Roman Empire and who were suffering:

> *For you have been called for this purpose, since Christ also suffered for you, leaving you an example for you to follow in His steps.* (1 Peter 2:21)

> *Beloved, do not be surprised at the fiery ordeal among you, which comes upon you for your testing, as though some strange thing were happening to you; but to the degree that you share the sufferings of Christ, keep on rejoicing, so that also at the revelation of His glory, you may rejoice with exaltation.* (1 Peter 4:12-13)

Jesus Himself told His followers:

> *"Truly I say to you, there is no one who has left house or brothers or sisters or mother or father or children or farms, for My sake and for the gospel's sake, but that he will receive a hundred times as much now in the present age, houses and brothers and sisters and mothers and children and farms, along with persecutions; and in the age to come, eternal life."* (Mark 10:29-30)

In spite of these words of warning concerning sacrifice, the world and the counterfeit religious system dispute or refute the need of it. To sacrifice is to deny self of something earnestly wanted to gain a holy end. The world and the counterfeit church system have no intention of denying themselves anything. They are out for all they can get. Further, they do not intend to offer the things they gained to God but instead intend to expend them all on themselves.

The world even goes so far as to declare that if God is a loving God, He has no right to allow suffering. Even if it is in His will, is a part of His plan, or will result in maturity or in the salvation of a lost soul, He has no right to ordain or permit suffering.

The false church system, while not so outwardly rebellious, has its own views of suffering. Those in it who do not know God or His Son are usually those who do not recognize the existence of a demonic world led by Satan. Therefore, they can only explain suffering as bad luck or the breaks of life or just what the suffering one "deserved." Their only response when someone is hurting is to "discuss" the situation publically and perhaps send a note or a sympathy card. Then they consider their duty done.

Yet some others have an even worse attitude toward suffering. Some are greedy and will sacrifice nothing so they may be, at least materially speaking, prosperous at all costs. Some are the immature who have never learned that sacrifice means to give rather than take or to bless rather than be blessed. Therefore, they are always clamoring for more, not for less. Some are the ignorant who disagree that an anointing of God could be lost through sin and therefore deny that any harsh but necessary discipline might be of God. In their zeal to be free of suffering, they declare the corrective work of God to be of the devil.

All of these handle their denials of the need for sacrifice in similar ways. They contradict the intention of the will of God by calling on the power of unholy gods to get them out of the very situation through which He is trying to reach them. Or, mimicking those who falsely profess joy, they whisk trial and tribulation away by works of flesh, positive thinking, and positive confession. Or, they simply end the trial by prematurely proclaiming it to be over. In all this ungodly activity, they never stop to realize that, in depriving themselves of a sacrifice, they have nothing to lay on the altar before God.

The Coming King

Finally, Tabernacles is the Feast of the King. To cross the promised land, God introduced His Church to the LORD of Hosts. Who is the LORD of Hosts? He is the King of glory (Psalm 24:10)!

The true Church has long been looking for its King. In the Old Covenant, it was only after the high priest passed through the veil into the Holy of Holies that he could see the glory of God. Just so, when the Church passes through the veil or crosses the Jordan
River to possess and occupy the promised land, it has every right to expect to see its King.

To counteract this wondrous meeting, the world and the counterfeit church system offer a counterfeit king. Already seen as Saul, the ungodly king who usurped priestly or religious duties, this counterfeit king's true identity is the antichrist. Even now the spirit of antichrist is rising. All over the world, the ungodly are waiting for the appearance of their leader.

World, be on guard! Church, be warned! The antichrist is coming. In appearance, attitude, and behavior, the antichrist will mimic Jesus Christ. However, in no way will he be Jesus Christ. His intention is to beguile everyone into error. As Saul plunged the Israelites into witchcraft, so the spirit of antichrist is doing the same to the world now. As Saul brought apostasy to the Israelites, so the spirit of antichrist is doing the same in the Church now.

In appearance, the antichrist will be like Jesus. Isaiah 53:2 says that Jesus was not a comely man and that He had no beauty or desirable form. Even so, He attracted people. However he presents himself, the antichrist will be favorably looked on by blind and undiscerning men and women. His empty promises, his charisma, and his background will make him seem like a savior. He will be welcomed by masses of people.

In attitude, at first the antichrist may try to imitate Jesus in His grace and goodness. Yet all too soon his true nature will become apparent. As Samuel once warned the Israelites what Saul would be like, the Church is now warned about the unholy one:

> *This will be the procedure of the king who will reign over you: he will take your sons and place them for himself in his chariots and among his horsemen and they will run before his chariots. He will appoint for himself commanders of thousands and of fifties, and some to do his plowing and to reap his harvest and to make his weapons of war and equipment for his chariots. He will also take your daughters for perfumers and cooks and bakers. He will take the best of your fields and your vineyards and your olive groves and give them to his servants. He will take a tenth of your seed and of your vineyards and give to his officers and to his servants. He will also take your male servants and your female servants and your best young men and your donkeys and use them for his work. He will take a tenth of your flocks, and you yourselves will become his servants. Then you will cry out in that day because of your king whom you have chosen for yourselves, but the LORD will not answer you in that day.* (1 Samuel 8:11-18)

In behavior, although the antichrist may try to mimic Christ in leadership and power, his true goal is to usurp religious authority around the world. To Israel and the Jewish faith, he may present himself as a world hero who promises to bring peace, to restore the temple in

Jerusalem, and to reinstitute animal sacrifice. To the western world, he may promise to unite the hodgepodge of churches and denominations into "one faith;" may produce spurious signs, wonders, and miracles; and may seek governorship and control of the Church. However, once the religious system is under his rule, he will not allow holy worship of God; instead, he will demand to be worshipped as God. He will declare himself to the religious head not of one people but of the whole world. The final result of his domination will be to subject the world to total slavery. Any who allow him to have his way or who accept him as lord and god will be back in the slime pits of Egypt.

Long ago the Jews looked for the promised Messiah. They wanted a militant king, one who would break the oppression of Roman rule. Instead they were sent a Suffering Servant who broke the oppression of spiritual rather than physical bondage. Since he didn't meet their demands to restore an earthly kingdom, the Jews rejected Jesus.

So now the Church has been promised that the King is coming (Revelation 22:12-13). As before, different ideas are developing as to what He will be like. While the true Church delights to submit to His authority, desires the earth to be purged of evil, and seeks the overthrow of spiritual bondage in order to freely worship true God, the false church system, by raising itself to a position of rulership and dominance, demands to be the authority, wants the restoration of the present polluted heavens and earth, and intends to impose religious legalism on all to divert worship from God.

The Church is at a crossroads. Once again, it must choose. Egypt was intended to lead sinners to their Savior. The desert was designed to introduce saints to their Lord. The promised land was prepared to bring saints to their King. The Church's King is Christ. The world's and the counterfeit church system's king is the antichrist.

God's body has been called upon to celebrate His feasts. However, it can only so worship Him in spirit and truth (John 4:23). Jesus, the Lamb of God, was slain for the sins of the world on the very day that the sacrificial lambs were slaughtered for the atonement of sins according to the ritual of the Old Testament Feast of Passover. Fifty days later the Holy Spirit descended on God's Church at the very time that the streets of Jerusalem were filled with those celebrating the Feast of Pentecost. If God has so ordained that the Church's true Passover occurred on the actual day of the Jewish Passover and the Church's true Pentecost occurred on the very day of the Jewish Pentecost, it is likely that the Church's true Tabernacles will occur on the very days of the

Jewish Feast of Tabernacles in a time and a year of God's choice.

Someday in the not-too-distant future, God's trumpet will sound, calling His Church to attention and asking it to remember and prepare. He will then lead His body through a day of mourning and atonement for sin. Finally, He will bring His own into victory, triumph, and rest from their enemies. He will bring them into joy and celebration even as they look for and long for the return of their King, the Lord Jesus Christ, the One who will usher in the millennial age. This is the Church's true feast of Tabernacles.

The time to choose is now. God has no other plan. He has no other day or dispensation that provides a chance to change, to mature, or to prepare. This is it! The end times are here! The Church is witnessing the last days and hours, the winding down of earthly affairs.

One of the Israelites' worst insults to God was to demand a human king. Have we learned from that tragedy, or are we still, for lack of discernment and love, ready to reject our true King in favor of the temporal, earthly pleasures of the antichrist? As we prepare to celebrate Tabernacles in the promised land, who will be our King?

Long years ago, when Absalom tried to usurp David's throne and David went into exile, those near the situation were forced to declare which leader they would follow. Before the exiled king returned, many had to declare whom they would serve (2 Samuel 15:13-37).

This is now the position of the Church. Its Leader is in exile only for a short while. Before His triumphant return, every man and woman will have to declare whether they accept or reject Him, will serve or abuse Him, are with Him or against Him.

For the Church in the promised land, the earthly journey is over. However, make no mistake, the King will return....

> *For the Lord Himself will descend from heaven with a shout, with the voice of the archangel and with the trumpet of God, and the dead in Christ will rise first. Then we who are alive and remain will be caught up together with them in the clouds to meet the Lord in the air, and so we shall always be with the Lord.* (1 Thessalonians 4:16-17)

So be it.

Amen and amen.

EGYPT

Abraham's Covenant
Passover
Outer Court
Enemy: Pharaoh
Slavery/Oppression/Bondage
Dead Works
Enforced Labor
Stationary/Going Nowhere

Poverty
Old Adamic Nature
Rejection
Leeks and Garlic
Death
Courtship
Lamb
Savior/Deliverer
Freedom
Salvation
Egypt

DESERT

Moses' Covenant
Pentecost
Inner Court
Enemy: Self
Immature Freedom
Works of Flesh
Busy-ness
Wandering in Circles

Earnest/Down Payment
Fleshly/Soulish Nature
Acceptance
Manna and Quail
Burial
Betrothal
Lord
Master
Carnality
Sanctification
Mount Sinai

PROMISED LAND

The New Covenant
Tabernacles
Holy of Holies
Enemy: Satan
Maturity
God Works
Rest
Advancing the Kingdom of God
Fullness of Inheritance
Spirit Beings
Unity With God
Milk and Honey
Resurrection
Wedding Feast
Lion
King
Obedience
Glorification
Mount Zion

PART VIII:

JOURNEY'S END

PART VIII

JOURNEY'S END

CHAPTER 22

JOURNEY'S END:

THE CITY OF GOD

As yet the journey is not complete. Those who are in the promised land must continue marching until they reach their final home.

Few people start out on a journey without a firm, settled destination in mind. Just so, the Israelites, each saint, and the Church, all those who have traveled from Egypt to Canaan, must know where they are going. As each had a beginning to their passage, so each has an end.

In the world, many men and women are active people who always seem to be on the move, going somewhere. They determine a destination and go there. Yet some, while engaged in an almost eternal round of activity, seem to be milling about, going nowhere. Do they truly know where they are going? Are they are clear about their final destination?

Too, in the world, when people go places, they know when they arrive at their predetermined destinations and why they are there. For example, a man may go to a doctor's office for a check up, a woman may go to a coffee shop to buy a hot drink, and a child may go to school to participate in educational, recreational, and social activities. Yet, those who do not know where they are going cannot know when (or if) they have arrived or what they are doing there.

The Israelites, each saint, and the Church should know their final destination, the place that is journey's end for them. Since they are required to travel beyond the promised land, they should be aware of where, what, or who is the end of their earthly pilgrimage. They should know when they will arrive and why they are going there.

Furthermore, each saint should now have at least the beginning of an understanding that the Israelites' journey from Egypt to Canaan was much more than just an historical event or an instructive glimpse into the past. It is, in fact, a prophetic journey that reveals the past, present, and future for each saint and for the Church.

The Israelites' journey is the means by which those faithful to God can see the plight and place of the Israelites in the natural course of events and can understand some of the upsets it has caused and endured in the spiritual. It is the way in which each saint and the true Church can begin to realize and respond to all the needs, whether physical or spiritual, of the people of Israel to whom they owe so much. It is that by which a single saint and the sum of the saints can measure and compare their own journeys, seeing them as if in a mirror.

Though thus far the journeys of the Israelites, each saint, and the Church have been presented as three parallel pilgrimages, we have come to the point where the journeys merge, where the lives of all involved touch, and where, in an overall perspective, the three can be seen as one.

JOURNEY'S END FOR THE ISRAELITES

The nation of Israel now physically occupies the land of Canaan. However, even the most unlearned student of the times would have to declare that the unstable, inflammatory situation that now exists between this land and people and the rest of the world is not the end of the story. While God did intend that His people should occupy this land, He never meant it to be their final stopping place or the end of their journey. The Israelites must yet march on to their journey's end.

The Word declares the LORD is the God of Israel (2 Kings 19:20), the Holy One of Israel (2 Kings 19:22), and the God of Abraham, Isaac, and Jacob (Exodus 3:15). He called Israel His firstborn son (Exodus 4:22). He declared Israel to be holy to the LORD, the first of His harvest (Jeremiah 2:3), and the tribe of His inheritance (Jeremiah 10:16). Even in the secularism, socialism, and sin that mark present-day Israel, God will never renounce all of that or to turn away from His land and people.

James 1:17 declares God to be unchanging. What He was He is now and ever will be. Therefore, He is still Israel's God. He claims the land and people for His own, and He is still fully concerned with their wellbeing. He is still interested in fashioning Jerusalem to be the center of His kingly reign.

> *For the LORD has chosen Zion; He has desired it for His habitation. "This is My resting place forever; here I will dwell, for I have desired it. I will abundantly bless her provision; I will satisfy her needy with bread. Her priests also I will clothe with salvation, and her godly ones will sing aloud for joy. There I will cause the horn of David to spring forth; I have prepared a lamp for Mine anointed. His enemies I will clothe with shame, but upon himself his crown shall shine."* (Psalm 132:13-18)

For the Israelites, journey's end is in sight, but the road there is rough. When the Israelites were held in Egypt, they were mocked, scorned, hated, abused, and enslaved. God rescued them from Pharaoh, and their enemies met disaster by the power of His might.

Later, when Jesus came, the Israelites rejected Him. After doing so, they fell on hard times. No other nation has ever been called on or been able to endure the brutality, devastation, and carnage that the world and the Church have inflicted on God's chosen ones. However, as God rescued the Israelites from one nation before, He will redeem them from the whole world now. As the enemies of Israel, who are also the enemies of God, were destroyed before, so their present enemies will meet with disaster now.

Yet, despite the integrity of His intent and His Word, clouds are gathering over the promised land. Not believing in the God of Israel, the nations are gathering against His land and people. It would not be a surprise to see a combined army of Arab nations, united by hatred and the false strength of large numbers, try once more to do what their forefathers determined to do. It would not be a surprise to see them rebel against the authority of God who sovereignly gave the land of Canaan to the descendants of Abraham as their eternal possession. Further, intent upon the total extermination of the Jewish race, it would not be a surprise to see them declare war in an effort to defeat and destroy all Jews and to possess and occupy the covenanted land.

Whether or not this speculation comes to pass, the Bible speaks of two future wars, one in which the armies of the north, perhaps a confederation of Russia and its allies, attack Israel (Ezekiel 38:15-16) and the other a final global war in which a united, worldwide army of the enemies of God gather against His children in a confrontation known as Armageddon (Revelation 16:14-16).

As they approach journey's end, the Israelites are blessed in the knowledge that the Word also refers to their unchangeable God as the Hope of Israel, its Savior in times of distress (Jeremiah 14:8). Few things will be of more importance or comfort to them than confidence in this name in the fast-approaching times of troubles, the days of tribulation.

In the midst of such turmoil and destruction, the Israelites will suffer horribly, becoming but a remnant that finally acknowledges God. In the midst of their troubles, they will at last truly realize that they can have faith in no person, including self, but only in Him. As they see Him again and again deliver them from giants, as they suffer through tragedy and disaster, they will accept and admit that no hope of salvation exists but in Jesus Christ, His Son.

In a miraculous move of faith, they will call out for Jesus their Savior to save them from their sins as well as to save them from their enemies. Finally understanding that who their God is is much more important than what He can do for them, they will mourn for Him whom they have pierced and cry out to Him whom they rejected.

In response, He who first came for sin will return for salvation. Hearing the voice of His children, God will act. *"According to their deeds, so He will repay, wrath to His adversaries, recompense to His enemies ... A Redeemer will come to Zion, and to those who turn from transgression in Jacob...."* (Isaiah 59:18-20).

Thus, by the power of God, the remnant of the Israelites will be saved. Journey's end for these chosen ones is God. He will bless them with fellowship, safety, and security, and their Messiah, Jesus, will encircle them with arms of love even as He saves them.

Without question, the times of the Gentiles are almost fulfilled; the iniquity of the nations is nearing completion. Too, the times of the Israelites' restoration – as seen in events such as the *aliyah*, the immigration of the Jews from the diaspora back to Israel – is near. If ever a nation needed to call out to God, if ever a people needed to proclaim, *"Blessed is the One who comes in the name of the LORD!"* (Psalm 118:26), that nation is Israel and that time is now.

JOURNEY'S END FOR EACH SAINT

If the Israelites have rebelled against God and have repeatedly tried to thwart His judgment concerning their journey's end, so too have many saints. As a result, they are in confusion, knowing neither their final destination nor their reason for going there.

One reason a saint may not be able to identify his (or her) eternal home or to understand his purpose in being there is that he is miserably confused. First, he has never been taught that life exists for him beyond the confines of a building or a denomination or that he has a goal beyond the next communal service. Second, he has never broken out of his own passivity to investigate the matter for himself.

Yet, as he (or she) rests and waits for God in the promised land, each saint comes to realize that he is a reflection of Abraham, his ancestor in faith. Abraham obeyed God by going to a place he would receive as an inheritance, but at the same time he didn't know where he was actually going (Hebrews 11:8). Further, even while Abraham lived in the promised land, he knew his journey was not finished (Hebrews 11:9), and so he looked for a further destination, the city of God (Hebrews 11:10).

Likewise, each saint comes to know that the hope of Abraham has also always been the promise and hope of every believer. Like many who have gone before, he (or she) can only acknowledge that he is but an alien and stranger (1 Peter 2:11), an exile on this earth (Hebrews 11:13). His journey will end only when he finds that place of his own (Hebrews 11:14), that better, heavenly country and the city that God has prepared for him (Hebrews 11:16). There, he will dwell in the mansion that Christ has prepared for him (John 14:2).

As each saint pushes on toward journey's end, he (or she) truly comes to the understanding that only God can judge his heart (Jeremiah 11:20; Hebrews 4:12). Only He knows where that saint is in his travels and how far he has to go. Only He knows whether that saint is truly resting in the promised land or whether he never really left Egypt and is just pretending he did.

Though each saint knows his (or her) final pathway will not be easy, he is assured that Jesus is his Redeemer and therefore his Owner. He understands that through God's Holy Spirit, Christ's power and presence are maintained within him. He realizes it is not by his own strength but through Christ's power that his enemies are conquered, his battles are won, and his heart is cleansed. He knows it is not through his own faithfulness or determination of will but through Christ's presence that enables him to obey God's commands and to endure to the end (Matthew 24:13).

The one who is willing to push on to his (or her) final destination is the saint, king, or priest who knows that the condition of his heart has been forever changed, who realizes that the LORD has written His law in his heart (Jeremiah 31:33), who acknowledges the holy fear that keeps him true (Jeremiah 32:40), who has been cleansed from iniquity and idols, who has been given a new heart and a new Spirit which enables him to walk in God's statutes and to obey His judgments (Ezekiel 36:25-27). Further, he loves to have it so. He is delighted when he learns that his final destination is union with God; is oneness in relationship with Abba, Father; is inseparable, eternal communion with Jesus, who is Savior and Deliverer, Lord and King; is fellowship with the Holy Spirit.

Whether through physical death or Jesus coming to take him (or her) to that heavenly place, he will know the moment he arrives and will know that his reason for being there is to love, praise, and worship his God. When face to face with the God of all glory, he will no longer be limited by physical, mental, and spiritual imperfections so he can bow in submission and then join the everlasting choirs of heaven as they forever declare the worthiness and majesty of their God.

JOURNEY'S END FOR THE CHURCH

As the Israelites were brought out of Egypt to worship God, so the true Church has been called and separated from the world to have the freedom to join her God and to worship Him in spirit and in truth (John 4:23). It does so as the bride of Christ (Revelation 19:7; 21:2; 21:9; 22:17).

According to *Smith's Bible Dictionary*,[7] earthly marriage is an allegory or an allusion to the spiritual relationship between God and his people. Further, as described in *A Christian Love Story*,[8] a traditional Hebrew wedding gives clues about the forthcoming marriage of the Son of God to His Church. Its symbolism declares the method and the meaning of the Lamb's union with His bride.

In earlier days in Israel, since a bride was essentially bought, marriage between a young man and woman was arranged. After the parents of the bride and her groom had come to an agreement, the terms were confirmed by oaths, and then presents were given to the bride.

For his part, after the bride's price was settled, the groom

---

[7] Smith, William. *Smith's Bible Dictionary*. Riverside Book and Bible House. 3rd Printing. pp. 382-384.

[8] Levitt, Zola. *A Christian Love Story*. Zola Levitt Ministries, Inc. 1978. pp. 3-7.

returned to his father's house. There, he prepared a place for her, a bridal chamber, where the couple would spend their honeymoon shut off from the world. The construction of this bridal chamber could take up to a year, and the father of the groom was the judge as to when it was completed.

For her part, the bride waited. From the time of her espousal until her groom came for her, she was considered to be married legally and was regarded as the groom's wife. Undefiled, with oil lamp ready in case he came at night (Matthew 25:1-12) and ready to go whenever her groom appeared for her, she anticipated, prepared for, and longed for her coming union with her beloved.

The marriage ceremony was the removal of the bride from her father's house to that of the groom or of his father. Here, with many invited to share their happiness, the couple celebrated with much feasting and festivity for seven days. Then the groom conducted his bride to their bridal chamber so that their union might be complete.

Nothing could be a more descriptive revelation of the coming marriage of the Lamb of God with His bride, of the union of Christ with His Church. The true bride has been bought for a price, and her espoused Husband has overwhelmed her with treasures, such as salvation, righteousness, sanctification, His presence, and His Spirit. Her Groom has gone to prepare a place for her (John 14:2-3). The Father decides as to when the preparations are complete and when His Son will return for His bride (Mark 13:32).

The true Church is betrothed to Jesus, the Son and the Lamb of God. Therefore, it is necessary that she exercise great care to submit to no other, to keep from relationship with any other, and to keep herself pure and holy for her one Beloved.

When He does come and take her back to His Father's house, the marriage supper of the Lamb will be a time of great festivity, celebration, and joy. Then Jesus will lead His bride into their bridal chamber to consummate their marriage, to enjoy full union in spirit, mind, and body.

Even now, the true bride is resting, ever more filled with longing and love and awaiting the moment when all is ready and the Father releases the Son to come for her. She is actively taking part in the removal of spot and wrinkle, and she is allowing the cleansing of all vestiges of self-indulgence and individualism so that she, the true assembly of saints, can be claimed by Her Beloved. Rather than clothing herself in the tattered rags of a harlot, she is adorning herself in lovely, white wedding finery; is robed; is veiled; is perfumed; and is bejeweled as a pure bride. She is contemplating the One known as Husband and is waiting to be taken away.

Let there be no mistake! It cost Jesus everything to come into His glory (See Isaiah 53.). He humbly offered Himself, He suffered and died on a cross, and He was buried before rising to glory and finding His journey's end seated in heaven at His Father's right hand. So must the Church be willing to do if she is to share eternity with Him.

For the Church, journey's end is with her God, eternally at home in heaven with Him. Bowing before her Savior and Deliverer in thanksgiving and awe, kneeling before her Lord in faithfulness and obedience, on her face before her King vowing love and devotion, her journey's end is to be in His presence. She will spend eternity arm in arm and heart to heart with her Bridegroom, knowing Him, loving Him, and worshipping Him.

God has always desired a marriage between His Son and His people, those believing Jews and Gentiles who have received salvation through the blood of the Lamb and who have become His Church. He longs for the time that the Lamb and the bride are one in union and communion, both with Christ and in Christ. As Paul explains, *"For I am jealous for you with a godly jealousy; for I betrothed you to one husband, so that to Christ I might present you as a pure virgin"* (2 Corinthians 11:2).

All who have undertaken this journey, whether Israelite, saint, or the assembly of God, are not going to a place but to a Person. Their destination is the heart of their Creator, their Beloved, their Husband. He is God the Father, Abba; He is God the Son, Savior, Deliverer, Lord, and King; and He is God the Holy Spirit, Comforter, Keeper, Helper, and Guide. Therefore, for the Israelites, each saint, and the Church, if their march doesn't end in the arms of the Lord, then it has been a journey for nothing. If it doesn't end in the heart of God, then it has been time and effort wasted.

All the journeys are pilgrimages to God made possible by the first and second comings of Jesus, His Son. In the near future, when the Israelites, each saint, and the Church undertake the final steps of their journeys, their parallel paths will merge, since all are going the same place and all are seeking the same Person. If all the journeys end in union with God, the lives of those involved in the journeys must necessarily touch. When the Israelites' Messiah comes to save them, when each saint's Lord comes to raise him (or her), when the Church's Groom comes to lead His bride to her new, eternal home, the journeys, begun at different times in different places for seemingly different reasons will merge – and end.

All of God's own will be safe in His arms and in His heart. Journey's end is eternal union and communion with God. It is loving Him and being loved by Him.

At the prospect of such everlasting bliss, can each Israelite now cry out, *"Hosanna to the Son of David; Blessed is He who comes in the name of the LORD"* (Matthew 21:9)!? Can each saint now cry out, *"Come quickly, Lord Jesus"* (Revelation 22:20)!? Can the Spirit and the bride say *"Come"* (Revelation 22:17)!?

Come!

AUTHOR'S PAGE

Susan Pryor lives in beautiful western New York State near family and friends. Early in her Christian walk, the Lord impressed the Scripture *"But we will devote ourselves to prayer and to the ministry of the word"* (Acts 6:4) into her spirit. Later, indicating one of the specific ways she was to engage in the ministry of the word, He told her to write a book. After completing the first one, several more followed, each in a small way exposing her concern that the true Church must come back to its roots in Jesus Christ and must understand that its primary reason for being is to worship God.

Other books by Susan Pryor:

Jesus is Lord

The Five-Fold Ministry: True or False

70x7

Jehovah-Jesus

Available through Amazon or Kindle

My deepest gratitude to my daughter, Megan Tasdeler, for her skill, patience, and persistence in editing this book and to my son-in-law, Aydin, for designing the cover and doing amazing technical things to publish this book and to make it a reality.

www.ingramcontent.com/pod-product-compliance
Lightning Source LLC
Chambersburg PA
CBHW071959150426
43194CB00008B/933